THE PRINCIPLE OF SUBSIDIARITY AND ITS ENFORCEMENT IN THE EU LEGAL ORDER

In this book, Katarzyna Granat analyses and evaluates Europe's experience with the Early Warning System (EWS) which allows national parliaments to review draft legislative acts of the European Union for their compatibility with the subsidiarity principle. The EWS was introduced in response to the perceived 'democratic deficit' of the EU and its 'creeping' competences, and represented one of the landmark reforms of the Lisbon Treaty. The purpose of this book is to present and critically analyse the functioning of the new mechanism of subsidiarity review and the role that national parliaments have played within this system.

Compared to the existing leading publications on the Europeanisation of national parliaments and contributions on the EU principle of subsidiarity, this book offers—for the first time—a profound legal analysis of the procedure enriched by a comprehensive empirical analysis of the activities of national parliaments. It is directed at scholars of EU law and policy, European and national officials, and legal practitioners working in and with the national legislatures.

Volume 3 in the series Parliamentary Democracy in Europe

Parliamentary Democracy in Europe

The European Union is founded on the idea of 'representative democracy'. Its citizens are directly represented in the European Parliament, but Union democracy is equally based on indirect forms of representation especially through the European Council and the Council—two Union institutions whose members will be democratically accountable to their national parliaments. The good functioning of the Union democracy assumes, therefore, the good functioning of the democratic institutions of each Member State.

What is the role and relationship between the European and the national parliaments in the democratic functioning of the Union? Do they exercise distinct or complementary functions? Has the European Parliament adopted a structure similar to national parliaments; and how do national parliaments assume their 'European' functions? These questions have gained particular relevance in recent years. Not only has the Lisbon Treaty conferred new functions upon national parliaments, especially concerning the scrutiny on the compliance with the subsidiarity principle (the so called 'Early Warning System'), the coordination of fiscal and economic policies at the European level has led to significant restrictions of national parliamentary powers.

The new Hart Series on 'Parliamentary Democracy in Europe', encompassing both monographs and edited collections, aims to answer some of these questions. The series offers new insights into rules and conventions shaping parliaments and parliamentary democracy in Europe. Its aim is to provide a better understanding of the role parliaments are playing in European constitutional law and its idea of 'representative democracy'.

Series Editors

Nicola Lupo
Robert Schütze

Interparliamentary Cooperation in the Composite European Constitution
Edited by Nicola Lupo and Cristina Fasone

The Italian Parliament in the European Union
Edited by Nicola Lupo and Giovanni Piccirilli

The Principle of Subsidiarity and its Enforcement in the EU Legal Order: The Role of National Parliaments in the Early Warning System
Katarzyna Granat

The Principle of Subsidiarity and its Enforcement in the EU Legal Order

The Role of National Parliaments in the Early Warning System

Katarzyna Granat

•HART•
OXFORD • LONDON • NEW YORK • NEW DELHI • SYDNEY

HART PUBLISHING

Bloomsbury Publishing Plc

Kemp House, Chawley Park, Cumnor Hill, Oxford, OX2 9PH, UK

HART PUBLISHING, the Hart/Stag logo, BLOOMSBURY and the Diana logo are trademarks of Bloomsbury Publishing Plc

First published in Great Britain 2018

A catalogue record for this book is available from the British Library.

Library of Congress Cataloging-in-Publication data

Names: Granat, Katarzyna, author.

Title: The principle of subsidiarity and its enforcement in the EU legal order : the role of national parliaments in the early warning system / Katarzyna Granat.

Description: Oxford [UK] ; Portland, Oregon : Hart Publishing, 2018. | Series: Parliamentary democracy in Europe ; volume 3 | Includes bibliographical references and index.

Identifiers: LCCN 2017057336 (print) | LCCN 2017057593 (ebook) | ISBN 9781509908684 (Epub) | ISBN 9781509908677 (hardback : alk. paper)

Subjects: LCSH: Subsidiarity—European Union countries. | Federal government—European Union countries. | Central-local government relations—European Union countries. | Exclusive and concurrent legislative powers—European Union countries. | Jurisdiction—European Union countries.

Classification: LCC KJE5080 (ebook) | LCC KJE5080 .G73 2018 (print) | DDC 341.242/24—dc23

LC record available at https://lccn.loc.gov/2017057336

ISBN: HB: 978-1-50990-867-7
ePDF: 978-1-50990-869-1
ePub: 978-1-50990-868-4

Typeset by Compuscript Ltd, Shannon

Acknowledgements

This book is a revised and updated version of the PhD thesis that I defended in December 2014 at the European University Institute. I would like to thank my supervisor Bruno de Witte for his support during the process of writing the thesis, as well as for his advice and kindness. I started this work under the supervision of Miguel Maduro whom I would like to thank for his guidance and counsel during the earlier stages of the writing process. My thanks are also due to Loïc Azoulai, Damian Chalmers and Thomas Christiansen who were part of the PhD defence panel and provided invaluable criticism and numerous suggestions for improving the book. Finally, I wish to thank Robert Schütze and Nicola Lupo for accepting this book for their series 'Parliamentary Democracy in Europe' and offering their insights on the manuscript. I was able to improve and finalise the manuscript thanks to my Marie Curie fellowship at Durham Law School under EU grant agreement No 267209.

Beyond the fruitful time that I have spent in Florence, I have also benefited from a number of research stays elsewhere. I am grateful to Damian Chalmers and Jan Komárek for hosting and advising me at the London School of Economics, and to Armin von Bogdandy for welcoming me to the Max Planck Institute in Heidelberg. I wish to thank Judge Marek Safjan and the members of his Cabinet at the Court of Justice of the European Union for involving me fully in the life of the Court. I am thankful to the director of the NYU Jean Monnet Center, Gráinne de Búrca, and to my colleagues at Durham Law School who provided a supportive environment to work on the manuscript.

This book has benefited considerably from innumerable discussions with scholars, experts and colleagues who have offered comments, criticism and suggestions. Particular thanks are due to Rainer Arnold, Katrin Auel, Ciarán Burke, Ian Cooper, Maria Anna Corvaglia, Marise Cremona, Adrienne Héritier, Federico Fabbrini, Pietro Faraguna, Cristina Fasone, Diane Fromage, Peter Lindseth, Giuseppe Martinico, François-Xavier Millet, and Takis Tridimas, as well as civil servants of the national parliaments who patiently responded to my enquiries.

I wish to thank especially my EUI friends—Rebecca, Boris, Maciej, Niels, Tiago, Lucila, Berenika, Stephen, Dina, and Leonardo—for our wonderful time in Florence and beyond. And I would not be able to accomplish this book without the support and love of my husband Jan-Peter Siedlarek, my parents and siblings.

This book is dedicated to my little boy, Jonathan.

Katarzyna Granat
October 2017

Table of Contents

Introduction

THIS BOOK CRITICALLY reviews and evaluates the European Union's (EU) experience with the principle of subsidiarity and its policing by national parliaments under the Early Warning System (EWS). A landmark reform launched with the Lisbon Treaty (2009), the EWS was seen as an answer to the EU's democratic deficit and 'competence creep' and an attempt to strengthen perceived federal and democratic safeguards within the EU.[1] This book presents an analysis of the principle of subsidiarity through the lens of the EWS and the role that the newly empowered national parliaments have played within in the EU on the basis of this system.

The Treaty on the European Union (TEU) enshrines the principle of subsidiarity that governs the exercise of competence, and was first introduced in the Maastricht Treaty (1993). The subsidiarity principle requires that

> the Union shall act only if and in so far as the objectives of the proposed action cannot be sufficiently achieved by the Member States either at central level or at regional and local level, but can rather, by reason of the scale or effects of the proposed action, be better achieved at Union level.[2]

Under the EWS, national parliaments, as arguably the most democratically legitimated national institutions, can assess any draft legislative proposal submitted by the Commission for its compatibility with the subsidiarity principle and can issue a reasoned opinion to indicate a violation. The Lisbon Treaty thereby offered a new avenue for the policing of the subsidiarity principle, complementing its judicial enforcement by the Court of Justice of the European Union (the Court/CJEU).

The main questions this book addresses are rooted in the practice of the subsidiarity review mechanism as observed thus far, especially, but not limited to, the three 'yellow cards' that national parliaments had triggered by the end of 2016. How is the subsidiarity principle understood under the Lisbon Treaty? What is the role of national parliaments in its policing? Why do national parliaments participate in the EWS, and why do they go beyond the narrow role granted by Protocol No 2? And what does this say about the purpose of the EWS? Finally, how does the EWS contribute to limiting and reversing the 'competence creep' and improving the EU's democratic credentials?

These questions are posed within the framework provided by a series of recent and ongoing challenges to the project of European integration that have taken place since the entry into force of the Lisbon Treaty. Those challenges include first and foremost the eurozone debt crisis, which began in 2009 on the heels of the global financial crisis, and which peaked in 2011 and 2012 with profound consequences for EU economies and political systems. The crisis arguably fuelled the rise of populist movements often sceptical or openly hostile to the

[1] R Schütze, *From Dual to Cooperative Federalism: The Changing Structure of European Law* (Oxford University Press, 2009) 257.

[2] Art 5(3) TEU.

European Project in many Member States including France (Front National) and Germany, where the right-wing party, Alternative für Deutschland (AfD), entered Parliament as the third largest party after the 2017 federal elections. In addition, the foundations of the EU as a community of liberal values and the rule of law have been challenged from within, in particular by governments in Poland and Hungary. Finally, on 23 June 2016 the United Kingdom (UK) in a referendum voted to leave the Union. On 29 March 2017, the UK government triggered the EU withdrawal procedure under Article 50 TEU, thereby putting a stop to decades of deeper integration and EU expansion. Keeping in mind the problems currently faced by the EU, this book will hence discuss how can we 'live with subsidiarity' without undermining the EU's 'capability to function'.[3]

The key finding of the book is that national parliaments in their active participation in the EWS exercise a broad scrutiny of the subsidiarity principle, which generally includes a check on the competence of the EU to act, the proportionality of the proposal and its political merits. This approach goes significantly beyond the narrow subsidiarity question as to which level of government is best placed to act. The analysis in this book suggests that this approach presents an attempt by the national parliaments to leverage the new tool granted to them by the Lisbon Treaty to increase their influence in the EU legislative procedure across the board.

I. EXISTING SCHOLARSHIP ON THE SUBSIDIARITY PRINCIPLE AND NATIONAL PARLIAMENTS

The book draws upon two streams of research by legal scholars and political scientists. The first is the literature concerning the subsidiarity principle. Since the Maastricht Treaty, scholars extensively contributed to the understanding of subsidiarity and the procedures aiming at making it more operative introduced in subsequent treaties. In particular, Antonio Estella provided a legal and political critique of the subsidiarity principle, 10 years after the entry into force of the Maastricht Treaty, focusing on the role of the Court in its interpretation and application.[4] One of his key arguments was that the subsidiarity principle failed as a counter-majoritarian instrument binding the EU's legislation, because of the Court's concerns about its own legitimacy and its own integration agenda. Specifically, subsidiarity—a principle that could endanger further EU integration—demanded from the Court scrutiny that was political rather than legal in character, and as such, the principle was largely left ignored. The entry into force of the Lisbon Treaty that brought to the forefront the subsidiarity principle has resulted in a number of new studies of the subsidiarity principle, often offering a comparative or global perspective.[5]

The second body of literature that this study builds upon is formed by research on the involvement of national parliaments in EU affairs. Academic interest in national parliaments

[3] P Pescatore, 'Mit der Subsidiarität leben' in O Due, M Lutter and J Schwarze (eds), *Festschrift für Ulrich Everling* (Baden-Baden, Nomos, 1995) 1080 (own translation).

[4] A Estella de Noriega, *The EU Principle of Subsidiarity and its Critique* (Oxford, Oxford University Press, 2002).

[5] See M Evans and A Zimmermann, *Global Perspectives on Subsidiarity*, vol 37 (Dordrecht, Springer, 2014); M Jachtenfuchs and N Krisch, 'Subsidiarity in Global Governance' (2016) 79 *Law and Contemporary Problems* 1.

dates back to well before the Lisbon Treaty.[6] The seminal edited volume of Maurer and Wessels studied the institutional and procedural developments in national parliaments as a response to the challenges of EU integration.[7] They established a 'considerable' change in the legal and institutional aspects over time: the creation of EU affairs committees (EACs); the establishment of the procedure of 'mandating' in some Member States; and an early involvement of parliaments in the scrutiny of EU documents. Yet, they also highlighted the only 'modest' impact of national parliaments on the real life patterns of access to information and influence, scoring below what the EU Treaties and national provisions offered.[8] The analysis of real patterns of behaviour of national parliaments led Maurer and Wessels to define four models of parliamentary involvement: first, strong policymakers and 'national players'; second, 'potential' or latent 'national players'; third, 'modest policymaking legislatures'; and fourth, 'slow adapting parliaments'.[9] O'Brennan and Raunio confirmed these results in another volume on the topic. In their view, 'national parliaments have proven that they are capable of institutional adaptation and learning', and hence they 'should no longer be simply labelled as losers or victims of integration'.[10] A subsequent volume edited by Tans, Zoethout and Peters sought to identify common elements in the ways in which national parliaments are involved in the EU decision-making process.[11] The findings point to a set of shared values: adherence to democratic principles; adherence to the principle of ministerial accountability; a leading role for EACs; and mutual dependence in the executive–legislative relationship. However, practical problems in investing national parliaments as sources of input legitimacy led the authors to suggest other avenues for parliamentary participation, for example, direct accountability of EU institutions to parliaments or the possibility to bring actions before the Court.[12] The Lisbon Treaty reforms strengthened the role of national parliaments in the EU and prompted multiple enquiries into how national parliaments make use of their new powers. Most prominently, the *Palgrave Handbook of National Parliaments and the European Union*, based on a comparative study of all 28 Member State parliaments, proposed five ideal types of parliamentary involvement: 'policy shaper'; 'government watchdog'; 'public forum'; 'EU expert'; and 'European player'.[13] Nevertheless, most

[6] P Norton (ed), *National Parliaments and the European Union (London, Frank Cass 1996)*; A Cygan, *National Parliaments in an Integrated Europe: An Anglo-German Perspective* (The Hague, Kluwer Law International, 2001); P Kiiver, *The National Parliaments in the European Union: A Critical View on EU Constitution-Building*, vol 50 (The Hague, Kluwer Law International, 2006); P Kiiver (ed), *National and Regional Parliaments in the European Constitutional Order* (Groningen, Europa Law Publishing, 2006).

[7] A Maurer and W Wessels, 'Major Findings' in A Maurer and W Wessels (eds), *National Parliaments on their Ways to Europe: Losers or Latecomers?* (Baden-Baden, Nomos, 2001).

[8] A Maurer and W Wessels, 'National Parliaments after Amsterdam: From Slow Adapters to National Players' in A Maurer and W Wessels (eds), *National Parliaments on their Ways to Europe: Losers or Latecomers?* (Baden-Baden, Nomos, 2001) 435.

[9] ibid 461–62.

[10] J O'Brennan and T Raunio, 'Introduction: deparliamentarization and European integration' in J O'Brennan and T Raunio (eds), *National Parliaments within the Enlarged European Union: from 'victims' of integration to competitive actors?* (London, Routledge, 2007) 16.

[11] O Tans, 'Introduction: National Parliaments and the European Union: In Search of Common Ground' in O Tans, CM Zoethout and J Peters (eds), *National Parliaments and European Democracy: A Bottom-up Approach to European Constitutionalism* (Groningen, Europa Law Publishing, 2007) 4.

[12] O Tans, 'Conclusion: National Parliaments and the European Union: Coping with the Limits of Democracy' in O Tans, CM Zoethout and J Peters (eds), *National Parliaments and European Democracy: A Bottom-up Approach to European Constitutionalism* (Groningen, Europa Law Publishing, 2007) 247.

[13] C Hefftler et al (eds), *The Palgrave Handbook of National Parliaments and the European Union* (Basingstoke, Palgrave Macmillan, 2015).

national parliaments act as 'government watchdogs' showing that EU scrutiny is focused on the national level.[14]

In the particular area of the EWS, Philipp Kiiver enquired into the procedure and the content of the reasoned opinions issued within the COSAC pilot project between 2004 and 2011, identifying different approaches in parliaments towards the EWS.[15] Kiiver's research brought out two issues. First, the EWS can be seen as an 'imperfect' accountability mechanism: the Commission must justify its measure, but this justification covers the proposal only at an initial stage and the only sanction available is indirect, through opposition in the Council.[16] The accountability within the EWS according to Kiiver is also at least partially a legal one—national parliaments often bring forward legal arguments, normally typical of courts rather than parliaments—which in turn means parliaments are willing to look for new ways to enforce accountability.[17] The motive of accountability through the involvement of national parliaments is also discussed in Adam Cygan's monograph. According to the latter, 'national parliaments have a duty to pursue accountability', which is required for achieving greater EU legitimacy.[18] The EWS arguably does not present an adequate answer, because it does not provide sufficient output legitimacy.[19]

Kiiver's second point builds upon the fact that arguments from national parliaments often have a legal character, although they are likely inherently politically motivated. Kiiver's idea of national parliaments as a Council of States is based upon the role of the French Conseil d'Etat, which is consulted by the government before a bill is sent to the Parliament.[20] Kiiver sees a possibility that a coalition of active chambers, most likely the upper chambers, which are more independent from national executives, will develop and assess the lawfulness and justifications of EU drafts in an advisory rather than a co-legislative manner.[21] In addition to granting national parliaments a formal role in the EU legislative process, the EWS has also been seen elsewhere as a forum of representation connecting citizens with the EU, and as a forum for deliberation of substance of EU policies thereby constituting a 'virtual third chamber' in addition to the two EU legislators, the European Parliament (EP) and the Council.[22]

Other studies of the EWS have shown that the EWS has made national parliaments more aware of their European function[23] and overall mobilised them in EU affairs.[24] National

[14] C Neuhold and J Smith, 'Conclusion: From "Latecomers" to "Policy Shapers"?—The Role of National Parliaments in the "Post-Lisbon" Union' in C Hefftler et al (eds), *The Palgrave Handbook of National Parliaments and the European Union* (Basingstoke, Palgrave Macmillan, 2015) 675 and 684.

[15] P Kiiver, *The Early Warning System for the Principle of Subsidiarity: Constitutional Theory and Empirical Reality* (London, Routledge, 2012) 77 and 136.

[16] ibid 103.

[17] A Cygan, *Accountability, Parliamentarism and Transparency in the EU* (Cheltenham, Edward Elgar Publishing, 2013) 125.

[18] ibid 7–9.

[19] ibid 214.

[20] Kiiver, *The Early Warning System for the Principle of Subsidiarity* (n 15) 127.

[21] ibid 133.

[22] I Cooper, 'A "Virtual Third Chamber" for the European Union? National Parliaments after the Treaty of Lisbon' (2012) 35 *West European Politics* 441.

[23] A Jonsson Cornell and M Goldoni, *National and Regional Parliaments in the EU-Legislative Procedure Post-Lisbon: The Impact of the Early Warning Mechanism* (Oxford, Hart Publishing, 2017) 353.

[24] D Fromage, *Les parlements dans l'Union Européenne après le Traité de Lisbonne: la participation des parlements allemands, britanniques, espagnols, français et italiens* (Paris, L'Harmattan, 2015) 415.

parliaments remained generally resilient despite such obstacles for their powers as the eurozone crisis.[25] Nonetheless, the EWS is perceived as failing to generate the expected democratisation of the EU.[26] The practice of the EWS arguably did not enhance the democratic character of the EU legislative process,[27] and further reforms are necessary to make the views of national parliaments 'constitutionally relevant'.[28]

Against the background of the existing literature on the topic, this monograph contributes to the studies on the role of national parliaments in EU affairs, and explores the functioning of the EWS in a number of new ways. The focus of the book is exclusively on the EWS, which demands a careful analysis of the principle of subsidiarity and its scrutiny, taking into account the first six years of practice of the EWS. The book considers novel aspects of the procedure that have not been studied yet, such as, for example, the relationship between the Member State governments and their national parliaments under the EWS and the scrutiny of delegations to the Commission by national parliaments. In addition, the book encompasses 'classic' aspects of the EWS such as the historic development of the subsidiarity principle and the adjustment of national provisions for the operation of its scrutiny. The combination of both perspectives makes the book a particularly focused and comprehensive study of the principle of subsidiarity and its enforcement within the newly introduced EWS.

II. RESEARCH APPROACH

This book studies the role of national parliaments in the policing of the subsidiarity principle primarily from a legal point of view, but also takes into account the political context of the mechanism. This concerns, in the first place, the design and the role of the subsidiarity review process. Going beyond existing studies on the subsidiarity principle and national parliaments, the book conducts an empirical analysis of all the reasoned opinions issued by national parliaments between the introduction of the EWS in 2009 and the end of 2016.[29]

The methodological approach of the book is novel within the field. The book explores in depth three specific case studies of the EWS on the types of concerns that parliaments bring out in their reasoned opinions. Those case studies present instances where participation by national parliaments was particularly active and offer a thorough examination of key issues linked to the application of the subsidiarity principle: (i) the connection between the scrutiny of the principle of conferral and the principle of subsidiarity; (ii) the unexpected use of the EWS to scrutinise delegations to adopt a delegated or implementing act; and (iii) the application of the principle of subsidiarity to EU fundamental rights proposals. The choice of case studies does not try to be representative of all the possible ways national parliaments can act within the EWS but is instead driven by the following considerations. The first case

25 D Jančić, 'EU Law's Grand Scheme on National Parliaments: Perpetual Missing Link or a Solution for Democratic Legitimacy?' in D Jančić (ed), *National Parliaments after the Lisbon Treaty and the Euro Crisis: Resilience or Resignation?* (Oxford, Oxford University Press, 2017) 299.

26 ibid 308.

27 Cornell and Goldoni (n 23) 353.

28 Jančić (n 25) 302.

29 Note that some of the Commission proposals with the reference COM(2016) were issued in 2017. Those proposals and the reasoned opinions concerning them have also been taken account of in this book.

study on competence review was chosen due to its predictability: the principle of conferral and the principle of subsidiarity are close neighbours, and the existence of a competence to act is a pertinent legal and political issue in the EU legislative process. The second case study, instead, shows a rather unexpected use of the EWS to scrutinise draft legislative acts with the delegations to the Commission to adopt delegated or implementing acts. Finally, the third case study was selected to show how the EWS interacts with a very relevant EU law issue, fundamental rights protection, which does not involve any of the externalities that are often at stake in other Commission proposals, for example in the field of the internal market.

In exploring diverse groups of national parliaments, the book adopts what might be termed an accordion approach. Depending on the purpose of each chapter, the scope of the legislatures subject to analysis might stretch or squeeze much in the manner of an accordion, varying between broad sweeps and narrowly focused sections. In particular, chapter four provides a comprehensive overview of the measures adopted in the national parliaments of *all* Member States to enable the subsidiarity review process, and categorises them into groups. The idea is to present a complete catalogue of the different designs of ex ante subsidiarity scrutiny. Chapter five examines the impact of the Lisbon Treaty on executive–legislative relations; parliamentary majority–opposition relations; and the representation of the regional interests. This demands an analysis of a narrow sample of Member States selected according to a number of relevant features such as federal and centralised structure of the Member State; majoritarian (Westminster model) and consensus models of executive–legislative relations; and elected and unelected chambers within the bicameral structure of parliaments. The limited number of national systems aims to represent the main archetypical political systems, while not claiming that all the possibilities are exhaustively explored. The following chapters, which focus on the principle of conferral; delegated and implementing acts; and fundamental rights, respectively, have a two-tiered structure. To establish the role of national parliaments in these fields it is necessary to first 'stretch the accordion' by giving an overview of the concerns of national parliaments expressed in their reasoned opinions, and then to 'squeeze' it by focusing narrowly on the three specific case studies of Commission proposals.

III. STRUCTURE

This book is divided into two main parts. The first part concentrates on the notion of subsidiarity; the design of the EWS; and its implementation at the European and national level. The second part focuses on the content of the reasoned opinions issued by national parliaments. Three case studies tackle concerns of national parliaments with regard to the principle of conferral; delegations to adopt a delegated or implementing act; and fundamental rights.

To discuss the role of national parliaments in the EWS, it is first necessary to delve in detail into the notion of the subsidiarity principle. Accordingly, chapter one examines the origin and the characteristics of the subsidiarity principle in the EU Treaties. This chapter also discusses the reasons behind the introduction of the EWS: the EU's 'competence creep' and its democratic deficit. Chapter two reviews the growing role of national parliaments in the EU and their investment with the scrutiny of the subsidiarity principle by the

Lisbon Treaty. The basic rules of the operation of the EWS; the 'Barroso initiative', the other main avenue for national parliaments' involvement; and the possibilities of interparliamentary cooperation are discussed here. Chapter three then focuses on the scope of the EWS. Based on a textual, structural and functional interpretation of the Treaties, this chapter presents a set of arguments supporting a narrowly tailored subsidiarity scrutiny. In this regard, the three 'yellow cards' triggered so far by national parliaments are assessed to draw conclusions on the possible consequences for the EWS. Chapter four deals with the mechanisms adopted by Member States at the national level to conduct subsidiarity scrutiny and, based on the involvement of relevant committees, indicates three possible procedures: centralised, decentralised and mixed, combining both of the former. Having established the applicable procedures and their impact on the number of reasoned opinions issued, chapter five analyses in detail the content of reasoned opinions of parliaments in the UK, Germany, Poland and Belgium. The aim is to show how the subsidiarity review impacts upon the executive–legislative relationship; the rapport between the majority and opposition in EU affairs; and whether it gives any voice to regional interests. The detailed analysis of the parliamentary debates also enables drawing some conclusions on the motivation of national parliaments to participate in the EWS.

The second part of this book investigates the application of the EWS in three different areas: (i) competence; (ii) delegated and implementing acts; and (iii) fundamental rights. First, chapter six assesses the scrutiny of the principle of conferral under the EWS. To this end, this chapter offers a case study of the Commission proposal on the right to strike. Second, chapter seven analyses the scrutiny of delegations of powers to the Commission to adopt delegated and implementing acts under the EWS. The case study of the Commission proposal for a Tobacco Products Directive illustrates this activity of the national parliaments. Third, chapter eight considers the scrutiny of fundamental rights proposals under the EWS. The case study of the Commission proposal concerning the share of women on company boards tackles the question how the subsidiarity principle interacts with the protection of fundamental rights in the EU.

The conclusion draws upon the analysis in the previous chapters of this book and assesses whether national parliaments, through their reasoned opinions, help to diminish the 'democratic deficit' and the 'competence creep' in the EU. In this light, the chapter also discusses some recent suggestions for reform of the EWS.

1

The Subsidiarity Principle in the EU Treaties

I. INTRODUCTION

THE PRINCIPLE OF subsidiarity raises 'fundamental questions about the appropriate locus of political and legal authority within a complex and multiple-layered polity'.[1] Specifically, subsidiarity addresses the issue of the *exercise* of competences in areas shared by Member States and the European Union.[2] The purpose of the subsidiarity principle is 'to arbitrate the tension between integration and proximity in all matters dealt with by the Union and its Member States'.[3] As a 'constitutional safeguard of federalism', subsidiarity aims at restraining the exercise of powers allocated to the EU.[4] In other words, subsidiarity decides whether, in a specific case in which the EU already has a competence, the EU should act or whether the action should be taken at the national level.[5]

This chapter offers an in-depth analysis of the 'deliciously vague' subsidiarity principle.[6] Section II describes the origin of the subsidiarity principle and its roots in German Basic Law. Section III discusses subsidiarity in Switzerland and the United States (US) as a principle connected to organisation of federal systems. Section IV then moves to the development of the subsidiarity principle within the EU legal order, first introduced by the Maastricht Treaty. This section elaborates on the guidelines that were established over time and the more recent focus on the procedural aspect of the principle. At this point, the relationship between the subsidiarity principle and the two other principles of Article 5(3) of the Treaty on the European Union (TEU) are elaborated on. Section V then deals with the enforcement of the subsidiarity principle by the Court of Justice of the European Union (CJEU). Specifically, the limits and the recent trends in the CJEU's case law are discussed together with the new 'subsidiarity action' introduced by the Lisbon Treaty. The final section, section VI, provides the context for the establishment of the Early Warning System (EWS): the problem of broadening of EU competence and the insufficient democratic legitimacy of EU policies.

[1] G de Búrca, 'Reappraising Subsidiarity's Significance after Amsterdam' (1999) Harvard Jean Monnet Working Paper Series 7/99, 43.

[2] AG Toth, 'Is Subsidiarity Justiciable?' (1994) 19 *European Law Review* 268, 269.

[3] K Lenaerts, 'The Principle of Subsidiarity and the Environment in the European Union: Keeping the Balance of Federalism' (1993) 17 *Fordham International Law Journal* 846, 848.

[4] R Schütze, *From Dual to Cooperative Federalism: The Changing Structure of European Law* (Oxford, Oxford University Press, 2009) 247.

[5] AG Toth, 'The Principle of Subsidiarity in the Maastricht Treaty' (1992) 29 *Common Market Law Review* 1079, 1082.

[6] JHH Weiler, 'The Reformation of European Constitutionalism' (1997) 35 *Journal of Common Market Studies* 97, 127.

II. CHARACTERISTICS OF THE SUBSIDIARITY PRINCIPLE

A. Origin of the Subsidiarity Principle

Many scholars see the roots of the modern notion of subsidiarity in Pope Pius XI's encyclical *Quadragesimo Anno* (1931).[7] In the encyclical, the Pope offers a principle of social order which at its core can be read as an expression of the principle of subsidiarity:

> Just as it is gravely wrong to take from individuals what they can accomplish by their own initiative and industry and give it to the community, so also it is an injustice and at the same time a grave evil and disturbance of right order to assign to a greater and higher association what lesser and subordinate organizations can do. For every social activity ought of its very nature to furnish help to the members of the body social, and never destroy and absorb them.[8]

Here we already find a preference for allocating responsibilities to the lower levels of organisation as long as these have the capability to exercise them effectively. This foreshadows the elements of subsidiarity in its modern use in the EU.

Having said that, there are also important differences between the European and the Catholic versions of subsidiarity. First, the former is narrower because it concerns democratic public bodies, while the latter deals with much broader collective entities and society as a whole.[9] Second, the EU subsidiarity principle can be viewed independently from the Catholic understanding. Even without *Quadragesimo Anno*, Europe might have arrived at a similar idea. Thus, one can think of the EU subsidiarity principle as deriving from alternative political positions and not just from Catholic ideology.[10]

Other roots of the subsidiarity idea can be traced back to two German traditions on the structure of the state: federalism and liberalism.[11] The German federalist notion of the state focuses on the relationships between its different components and the functions they fulfil. Isensee finds in this tradition (eg, in the work of Althusius, von Humboldt, and Hegel) hints of the idea of subsidiarity, without arguing for a direct expression of subsidiarity in this work.[12] More direct evidence for the presence of subsidiarity ideas as an organising principle can be found in the liberalist theory of the state. In the liberalist tradition, the state is legitimate only to the extent that it is organised according to the subsidiarity principle.[13] Nevertheless, the liberalist perspective arguably knows only the individual and the state and, as such, does not speak to intermediary levels of organisation.[14]

[7] See, eg, J Isensee, *Subsidiaritätsprinzip und Verfassungsrecht: eine Studie über das Regulativ des Verhältnisses von Staat und Gesellschaft* (Berlin, Duncker & Humblot, 2001) 18ff. DZ Cass, 'The Word that Saves Maastricht? The Principle of Subsidiarity and the Division of Powers within the European Community' (1992) 29 *Common Market Law Review* 1107, 1110.

[8] *Quadragesimo Anno* point 79, English translation available at: w2.vatican.va/content/pius-xi/en/encyclicals/documents/hf_p-xi_enc_19310515_quadragesimo-anno.html.

[9] NW Barber, 'The Limited Modesty of Subsidiarity' (2005) 11 *European Law Journal* 308, 310.

[10] ibid. See also Isensee (n 7) 71.

[11] Isensee (n 7) 35.

[12] ibid 37.

[13] ibid 45.

[14] ibid 46.

B. Subsidiarity in the German Basic Law

The German Basic Law does not explicitly refer to subsidiarity as a principle. However, there is a strong case that the spirit of the principle entered the German Constitution from the country's scholastic tradition and from there led to the inclusion of subsidiarity in EU law.

At the time of the creation of the Basic Law in 1949, the political and legal environment was receptive to the notion of subsidiarity. Indeed, a reference to the principle of subsidiarity was included in the draft Constitution prepared by the Constitutional Convention at Herrenchiemsee in 1948, even though this reference was ultimately dropped.[15] There are several reasons for the removal. First, the religious heritage of the concept may have worried the drafters.[16] Second, some of the drafters may have been satisfied that Article 1 of the draft included a sufficient commitment against an overreaching state and thus believed that a further reference to subsidiarity was unnecessary at the time.[17]

Likewise, the final text of the Basic Law approved in 1949 did not formally include the subsidiarity principle.[18] However, this lack may be explained by the fact that the Basic Law was expected to be of a provisional nature, and thus the drafters may have steered clear of nascent legal concepts.[19] Overall, it can be argued that the forces behind the Basic Law sought to establish an order based on an ethical individualism that is also found in the subsidiarity principle, purposefully distancing the new German state from the collectivist state of the recent past.[20]

Finally, the inherently federal structure of the German state under the new Basic Law strongly reflected the ideal of subsidiarity.[21] The component Länder of the new federal state had an interest in limiting the powers of the federal level and were able to imprint this view on the Constitution through their close involvement in its creation and approval.[22]

Beyond indications that the drafters of the Basic Law may have been concerned with the notion of subsidiarity, there are also indications in the text of the Constitution itself that support the case that the German Basic Law carried the subsidiarity principle from its religious roots towards modern times.[23] Most fundamentally, the federal structure of the German state is explicitly build up from below. Article 30 of the Basic Law concerning the sovereignty of the Länder assigns all state powers to the Länder unless specifically provided for otherwise in the Basic Law. In addition, there is a positive limited enumeration of powers at the federal level (Article 73 of the Basic Law) and a list of conditions that determine whether the Länder or the federal state should act in a given area (Article 72 of the Basic Law).

15 ibid 143.
16 ibid.
17 ibid.
18 ibid 145.
19 ibid.
20 ibid 146.
21 ibid 147.
22 ibid.
23 ibid 223ff.

Initially, Article 72 of the Basic Law was drafted very broadly, requiring only that a law met certain conditions relating to 'the uniformity of living conditions beyond the territory of any Land' for the federal level to act. However, on judicial review, this notion was found to be non-justiciable, because any given law could readily be drafted to meet this requirement.[24] In its modern version, in force since 1994, Article 72(2) of the Basic Law states that in the field of concurrent legislative competences, the Federation should act 'if and to the extent that the establishment of equivalent living conditions throughout the federal territory or the maintenance of legal or economic unity renders federal regulation necessary in the national interest'. The newly added necessity clause requires the federal level to demonstrate a specific need to act for each new law. This amended provision echoes the subsidiarity principle and can be regarded as its first incorporation into constitutional law.[25] Under the new version of Article 72 of the Basic Law, the federal level has primacy in the exercise of competence shared with the Länder when the conditions of Article 72(2) of the Basic Law are fulfilled and the federal level decides to act. In that case, a matter is beyond the influence of the Länder.[26] However, Article 72(2) of the Basic Law sets out the specific conditions that the federal government is required to meet for it to take action.[27] In addition, the Länder remain a valid alternative to the federal level if they can achieve the relevant objectives themselves, individually or acting jointly.[28] These two aspects of the German Basic Law are both reminiscent of counterparts in the implementation of the subsidiarity principle in EU law. First, once the EU decides to act and meets the conditions to act under the subsidiarity principle, then the Member States can no longer regulate on their own. Second, there is no explicit requirement for the EU to act whenever the national level cannot achieve the objective sufficiently and where the objective would be better achieved at the EU level.

There are certain limits to the expression of subsidiarity in Article 72(2) of the Basic Law. First, the Basic Law addresses only the division of powers between the federal and the state, ignoring, for example, municipalities and civic organisations.[29] In contrast, the regional and local levels are explicitly recognised in the Lisbon Treaty as valid levels on which to exercise competences, highlighting the multilayered nature of the national level itself.[30] Second, Article 72(4) of the Basic Law does not automatically return competences to the Länder if and when the conditions of Article 72(2) of the Basic Law are no longer fulfilled, but leaves this to the discretion of the federal level.[31] This discretion is not included in the EU subsidiarity provisions.

Article 72(2) of the Basic Law demands a dual test reviewing whether there is a case for federal legislation in addition to whether the legislation goes beyond what is necessary to achieve the objectives set in that provision.[32] The Basic Law foresees a judicial safeguard

[24] ibid 230.
[25] ibid 358.
[26] ibid 359
[27] ibid.
[28] ibid 360.
[29] ibid.
[30] de Búrca, 'Reappraising Subsidiarity's Significance after Amsterdam' (n 1) 16.
[31] Isensee (n 7) 360.
[32] G Taylor, 'Germany: The subsidiarity principle' (2006) 4 *International Journal of Constitutional Law* 115, 120.

of the subsidiarity principle in the form of review by the Federal Constitutional Court on the application of the Bundesrat or a Land.[33] In contrast, there is no political safeguard of subsidiarity. An initiative to give the Bundesrat the role of a parliamentary watchdog of the subsidiarity principle did not gain the necessary support.[34]

There is by now a significant body of jurisprudence produced by the Federal Constitutional Court on the enforcement of the subsidiarity principle. Nonetheless, the Court's interpretation of the tests involved in Article 72(2) of the Basic Law remains unclear, echoing some of the issues with the CJEU's jurisprudence on subsidiarity. For example, no precise meaning has been given by the Court to the terms 'equal living conditions' or 'national interest'.[35] Nonetheless, there are several cases in which the Court has found federal legislation incompatible with the subsidiarity principle, for example, in the 'Junior Professors' case.[36] These decisions led to an amendment of Article 72(2) of the Basic Law in 2006 that restricted its applicability to a limited number of areas of concurrent competence,[37] such as, for example, the residence of foreign nationals, public welfare, the law relating to economic matters (mining, industry, trade, commerce etc), and regulation of educational training or state liability.

It is notable that after German law had served as inspiration for the EU's inclusion of subsidiarity in the Maastricht Treaty, the subsidiarity principle found its way back from EU law into German law. Specifically, according to Article 23 of the Basic Law adopted in 1992, Germany participates in the development of an EU 'that is committed to democratic, social and federal principles, to the rule of law, and to the principle of subsidiarity, and that guarantees a level of protection of basic rights essentially comparable to that afforded by this Basic Law'. Germany is thus re-importing the subsidiarity principle to the German constitutional system.[38]

Article 23 of the Basic Law enumerates the subsidiarity principle and presents an important tie between German law and EU law. It regulates the way Germany acts within the EU, for example, requiring the representatives of Germany in the EU to adhere to the subsidiarity principle in both the division and the exercise of competences at the EU level.[39] In addition, it commits Germany to an EU based on subsidiarity, re-emphasising the importance of the principle for German constitutional law.[40] The inclusion of subsidiarity in the EU Treaties directs new attention to Germany's own commitment to subsidiarity in the organisation of the German federal state.[41]

[33] Art 93(2a) of the Basic Law. This judicial safeguard did not exist before 1994 since both the German scholarship and the Federal Constitutional Court perceived Art 72(2) of the Basic Law as expressing a political decision of the federal legislator to legislate. See M Rau, 'Subsidiarity and Judicial Review in German Federalism: The decision of the Federal Constitutional Court in the *Geriatric Nursing Act* Case' (2003) 4 *German Law Journal* 223, 227.

[34] Deutscher Bundestag, Bericht der Gemeinsamen Verfassungskommission, Drucksache 12/6000, 05.11.93, 33.

[35] Rau (n 33) 233.

[36] G Taylor, 'Germany: A slow death for subsidiarity?' (2009) 7 *International Journal of Constitutional Law* 139, 143.

[37] ibid 146.

[38] Isensee (n 7) 334.

[39] ibid 371.

[40] ibid.

[41] ibid 334.

III. SUBSIDIARITY IN OTHER LEGAL SYSTEMS

Subsidiarity as an explicit constitutional principle has been ascribed a marginal role in federal constitutions.[42] It is not explicitly written into the Australian, Brazilian, Canadian and US Constitutions.[43] This has been explained by the existence of other means to deal with the question of which level of government does what, such as the enumeration of powers.[44] For example, in Canada the Constitution Act of 1867 provides a distribution of legislative competences between the federal and provincial governments, which includes a list of areas of exclusive jurisdiction of the federal legislature and a list of areas of exclusive jurisdiction of provincial legislators, in addition to areas of joint jurisdiction.[45] Nonetheless, the Canadian federal legislature can also legislate in areas not explicitly listed 'for the peace, order and good government of Canada' which can lead to excessive centralisation of power.[46] The principle of subsidiarity is as such not enshrined in the text of the Constitution Act.[47] Yet, as observed by one commentator, subsidiarity has been implicitly present in the case law of the Supreme Court of Canada, most visibly in a national concern doctrine and a provincial inability test.[48] More recently subsidiarity was directly invoked by the Supreme Court of Canada as a constitutional principle linked to the balance of power of the two levels of government.[49] The Canadian subsidiarity differs from the EU approach in various ways. Subsidiarity in Canada can apply in areas where the federal legislature has no explicit competence at all, while in the EU subsidiarity only applies in areas of shared competence. In Canada, subsidiarity works only upwards, meaning that it does not allow the transfer from the federal down to the provincial level; finally, the Canadian federal legislature is not obliged to proof the inability to act of the provinces.

The following sections analyse the understanding of subsidiarity in the US and Switzerland, their enforcement and safeguards. Some comparisons are drawn with the approach to subsidiarity in the EU.

[42] M Jachtenfuchs and N Krisch, 'Subsidiarity in Global Governance' (2016) 79 *Law and Contemporary Problems* 1, 10. For a comparative law perspective on subsidiarity see also W Vandenbruwaene, 'The Judicial Enforcement of Subsidiarity. The comparative quest for an appropriate standard' in P Popelier, A Mazmanyan and W Vandenbruwaene (eds), *The Role of Constitutional Courts in Multilevel Governance* (Antwerp, Intersentia, 2013).

[43] Jachtenfuchs and Krisch (n 42).

[44] ibid.

[45] ss 91–95 of the Canadian Constitution Act.

[46] s 91 of the Canadian Constitution Act.

[47] E Brouillet and B Ryder, 'Key Doctrines in Canadian Legal Federalism' in P Oliver, P Macklem and N Des Rosiers (eds), *The Oxford Handbook of the Canadian Constitution* (Oxford, Oxford University Press, 2017) 425.

[48] E Brouillet, 'Canadian Federalism and the Principle of Subsidiarity: Should We Open Pandora's Box?' (2011) 54 *The Supreme Court Law Review: Osgoode's Annual Constitutional Cases Conference* 601, 618. See also A Follesdal and V Muñiz Fraticelli, 'The Principle of Subsidiarity as a Constitutional Principle in the EU and Canada' (2015) 10 *Les ateliers de l'éthique/The Ethics Forum* 89.

[49] Brouillet (n 48) 626–31.

A. Subsidiarity in Switzerland

In Switzerland, subsidiarity is explicitly enshrined in the country's Constitution. The cantons exercise all powers of government except for those that are vested in the federation by the Constitution.[50] The Swiss Constitution foresees that '[t]he principle of subsidiarity must be observed in the allocation and performance of state tasks'.[51] The principle of subsidiarity, together with the principle of municipal autonomy, underscores the importance of subnational government in Switzerland.[52]

While no safeguard procedure similar to the EWS has been introduced in Switzerland, other mechanisms are in force that might be seen as political safeguards of federalism.[53] For example, representatives of the cantons directly make up the Council of States, the Upper House of the Swiss Federal Assembly.[54] In addition, the Swiss Federal Constitution requires a referendum for constitutional amendments, for the accession of Switzerland to international organisations, and for emergency federal acts that do not have a constitutional basis and that are valid for more than one year. Such a referendum requires a double majority of votes of both 'the People and cantons' adding another layer of protection to the power of the lower unit of government.[55] Furthermore, the cantons can directly petition for legislation and also block federal legislation if at least eight cantons support the effort. For example, in 2003, 11 cantons successfully triggered this mechanism against a proposed tax reform that reduced the tax revenues of cantons.[56] Finally, while the Swiss Constitution does not provide for judicial review of the constitutionality of federal laws, such laws can be challenged in a referendum if at least 50,000 citizen petition for it.[57]

B. Subsidiarity in the US

Contrary to the Swiss Constitution, the subsidiarity principle is not explicitly mentioned in the Constitution of the United States. Nonetheless, it can be argued that subsidiarity is 'the key theoretical concept underlying a general theory of federalism' and thereby a key part of the American experiment in the form of the federal power principle.[58] The 'Virginia Plan'

[50] Arts 3 and 42 of the Swiss Constitution.

[51] ibid, Art 5a.

[52] A Ladner, 'Switzerland: Subsidiarity, Power-Sharing, and Direct Democracy' in F Hendriks, A Lidström and J Loughlin (eds), *The Oxford Handbook of Local and Regional Democracy in Europe* (Oxford, Oxford University Press, 2011) 201.

[53] On the interparliamentary cooperation in Switzerland see K Granat, 'National Parliaments as Political Safeguards of Federalism: Interparliamentary Cooperation in the EU, US and Switzerland' in D Jančić (ed), *National Parliaments after the Lisbon Treaty and the Euro Crisis: Resilience or Resignation?* (Oxford, Oxford University Press, 2017) 273.

[54] Art 150 of the Swiss Constitution.

[55] Art 140(1) of the Swiss Constitution. The 'double majority' means the majority of the voters and the majority of 12 out of 23 votes (there are 26 cantons, but six of them count as half-cantons and have half a vote).

[56] W Linder and I Steffen, 'Swiss Confederation' in K Le Roy and C Saunders (eds), *Legislative, Executive, and Judicial Governance in Federal Countries* (Montreal, McGill-Queen's University Press, 2006) 308.

[57] Art 141 of the Swiss Constitution.

[58] D Halberstam, 'Federalism: Theory, Policy, Law' in M Rosenfeld and A Sajó (eds), *The Oxford Handbook of Comparative Constitutional Law* (Oxford, Oxford University Press, 2012) 585.

drafted by Madison and put forward during the Constitutional Convention of 1787 framed the powers of the national government as 'to legislate in all cases to which the separate States are incompetent, or in which the harmony of the United States may be interrupted by the exercise of individual Legislation'.[59] This phrasing recalls the notion of lower-level insufficiency that underlies the application of the subsidiarity principle in the EU today. Despite this prominent inclusion in the early deliberations on the Constitution, the subsidiarity principle did not enter the final draft. It was instead replaced with the explicit enumeration of federal powers in Article I, section 8.

Despite its formal omission in the wording of the Constitution, there is an active debate surrounding whether and to what extent the subsidiarity principle operates in the US federal system. Bermann makes a powerful case for the view that subsidiarity is not being respected in the US as a procedural or jurisdictional principle. One part of his case rests on the extent to which Congress is 'limited in any significant way out of respect for the states' capacity to accomplish the federal government's general objectives' in a field that falls within Congress's remit.[60] Here, it is concluded that while there are areas where Congress may leave for example the implementation of regulations to the states ('cooperative federalism'), overall it has not developed structured adherence to the subsidiarity principle in practice.[61] If the US Congress does not appear to apply the principle of subsidiarity in its legislative process, there may be space for the Supreme Court to enforce it. However, here it is underlined that the Court has 'denied itself a role in enforcing subsidiarity' despite possibly having the tools to do so under the Interstate Commerce Clause.[62]

In place of subsidiarity, the US system is seen to rely on the political process to protect the rights and interests of the states and lower levels of government. An influential view by Wechsler sees sufficient political safeguards in place in the US to protect the states' interests.[63] These consist of the following main elements. First, a 'burden of persuasion on those urging national action'.[64] Second, the states' involvement in the federal government itself through elections of representatives in electoral districts formed within the states[65] and the Electoral College's role in selecting the president.[66] Third, the structure of the Senate which awards each state two senators arguably amplifies their power.[67] Finally, due to the Electoral College Wechsler also sees the US President as necessarily 'responsive to local values that have large support within the states'.[68] The extent of these safeguards and

[59] M Farrand (ed), *The Records of the Federal Convention of 1787* (New Haven, CT, Yale University Press, 1911) 20.

[60] GA Bermann, 'Taking Subsidiarity Seriously: Federalism in the European Community and the United States' (1994) 94 *Columbia Law Review* 331, 404.

[61] ibid 416.

[62] ibid 417.

[63] H Wechsler, 'The Political Safeguards of Federalism: The Role of the States in the Composition and Selection of the National Government' (1954) 54 *Columbia Law Review* 543, 559. See a contrasting view claiming that judicial review is necessary to maintain and reinforce the political safeguards of federalism in LA Baker, 'Putting the Safeguards Back into the Political Safeguards of Federalism' (2001) 46 *Villanova Law Review* 951.

[64] Wechsler (n 63) 545.

[65] Art I, s 2 of the US Constitution and Clause 1 of the 17th Amendment to the US Constitution.

[66] Art II, s 1 of the US Constitution.

[67] Wechsler (n 63) 547.

[68] ibid 558.

their ability to constrain the federal government has been challenged but Wechsler's main argument found its way into the Supreme Court's decision in the *Garcia v San Antonio Metropolitan Transit Authority* case.[69]

In addition to the structural safeguards described by Wechsler, legal and political scholarship has identified additional political safeguards of federalism in the role and incentives of political parties[70] and in the importance of state-level implementation of federal laws. The latter is illustrated in the extent to which the Affordable Care Act of 2010 was implemented to various degrees by the states allowing them to 'limit or shape the federalization of government functions'.[71] Finally, there are 'informal political safeguards of federalism' through which states can influence federal policy,[72] including for example through interparliamentary cooperation among the state legislatures.[73] Overall, it is notable that 'federal law [is] the exception and not the rule … many areas of law remain mostly at the state level, even after 220 years of American federalism'.[74]

In contrast to Bermann and others who see no application of subsidiarity in the US and focus on political safeguards of states' rights, other scholars perceive the subsidiarity principle as an organising principle that plays an active role in the US. These scholars argue that the US system has been infused with subsidiarity considerations from the beginning, and the case law of the US Supreme Court on Congress's enumerated powers—the dormant Commerce Clause; intergovernmental immunities; pre-emption; federal jurisdiction—suggest there is judicial enforcement of subsidiarity.[75] For example, they point to new vigour in restraining the federal government since the 1990s, embodied in the *United States v Lopez* case in which the US Supreme Court struck down the federal Gun Free School Zones Act but allowed similar laws at state level, as well as some newer case law, such as the *National Federation of Independent Businesses v Sebelius* case, where the majority of the Justices found that the individual mandate requiring that uninsured individuals buy health insurance was not a proper exercise of Congress's powers under the Commerce Clause. Together these cases indicate that the US Supreme Court can offer a safeguard for states through the Commerce Clause and the Necessary and Proper Clause under the Jones & Laughlin Steel doctrine that finds that Congress can act on intrastate activities only if these '*substantially* burdened interstate commerce'.[76] It is however worth noting that these arguments tend to

[69] *Garcia v San Antonio Metropolitan Transit Authority*, 469 US 528 (1985). See fn 11 of the judgment. However, the dissenting opinion of Justice Powell, joined by Chief Justice Rehnquist and Justice O'Connor, noted that Wechsler's view of sufficient political safeguards did not reflect the current state of affairs.

[70] LD Kramer, 'Putting the Politics Back into the Political Safeguards of Federalism' (2000) 100 *Columbia Law Review* 215, 278ff. See also J Bednar, *The Robust Federation: Principles of Design* (New York, Cambridge University Press, 2009) 116. On political parties as political safeguards, see also S Jenkins and DD Roscoe, 'Parties as the Political Safeguards of Federalism: The Impact of Local Political Party Activity on National Elections' (2014) 44 *Publius: The Journal of Federalism* 519, 537.

[71] AR Gluck, 'Federalism from Federal Statutes: Health Reform, Medicaid, and the Old-Fashioned Federalists' Gamble' (2013) 81 *Fordham Law Review* 1749, 1768.

[72] JD Nugent, 'The Informal Political Safeguards of Federalism' (Midwest Political Science Association, Chicago, 27–30 April 2000) 6. This notion is further elaborated in JD Nugent, *Safeguarding Federalism: How States Protect their Interests in National Policymaking* (Norman, OK, University of Oklahoma Press, 2012) 54ff.

[73] Granat, 'National Parliaments as Political Safeguards of Federalism (n 53) 269.

[74] SG Calabresi and LD Bickford, 'Federalism and Subsidiarity: Perspectives from US Constitutional Law' (2014) 55 *Nomos LV* 123, 138.

[75] ibid 158.

[76] ibid 149.

deal with questions of allocations of powers and how subsidiarity may guide such decisions. In the EU context, the application of the subsidiarity principle is restricted to such areas that fall in the arena of shared competences and thus focuses primarily on the exercise of powers.[77]

IV. SUBSIDIARITY IN THE EU TREATIES

A. Historical Development

The Treaty of Rome of 1957 contained the first traces of the subsidiarity principle.[78] Some of its provisions, especially Articles 100 and 235 EEC, concern the distribution and exercise of competences between the Community and the Member States and explore possible approaches and criteria that are reminiscent of the later subsidiarity principle such as conditions setting out necessity for the EU to act.[79] Moreover, directives issued under Article 189 EEC incorporated some aspects of subsidiarity: the Community level established the binding objective leaving to the Member States the choice of form and methods for their implementation.[80] These provisions are marginal, however, and cannot really be seen as evidence of the subsidiarity principle in the Rome Treaty.[81]

In 1984, an early draft proposal for an EU treaty (the 'Spinelli draft') adopted by the European Parliament (EP) included a concept of the subsidiarity principle. Specifically, in cases of concurrent competence, the EU was to 'carry out those tasks which may be undertaken more effectively in common than by the Member States acting separately, in particular those whose execution requires action by the Union because their dimension or effects extend beyond national frontiers'.[82]

The idea of subsidiarity was first introduced in the Treaty text by the Single European Act of 1987, where it concerned Community action in the area of environmental policy and limited Community action in that field to cases in which the objectives of the policy can be better achieved at the Community level than at the level of individual Member States.[83] However, the application of subsidiarity in the field of environmental policy has been questioned since this area especially demanded action at the EU or international level.[84]

A number of reasons spoke in favour of the introduction of the subsidiarity principle in the EU. First, subsidiarity was seen as a response to the lack of a clear division of different

[77] VC Jackson, 'Subsidiarity, the Judicial Role, and the Warren Court's Contribution to the Revival of State Government' (2014) 55 *Nomos LV* 190, 192.

[78] Lenaerts, 'The Principle of Subsidiarity and the Environment in the European Union' (n 3) 852. See also Communication of the Commission to the Council and the European Parliament on the principle of subsidiarity, 27.10.1992, SEC(92)1990.

[79] C Calliess, *Subsidiaritäts-und Solidaritätsprinzip in der Europäischen Union* (Baden-Baden, Nomos, 1996) 31–35.

[80] ibid.

[81] ibid.

[82] Art 12(2) of the Draft Treaty establishing the European Union [1984] OJ C 77/33.

[83] Art 130r(4) EEC.

[84] Toth, 'The Principle of Subsidiarity in the Maastricht Treaty' (n 5) 1092.

types of competence in the treaties.[85] The second reason built upon the first: in the uneasy cases of deciding upon the limits of EU powers, subsidiarity was perceived as a complementary criterion of 'better' achieving the objective.[86] Third, the aim of subsidiarity was to prevent 'excessive centralisation' occurring through treaty amendments, jurisprudence and harmonisation.[87] Finally, subsidiarity was supposed to boost 'pluralism and the diversity of national values'.[88]

The Maastricht Treaty, in Article 3b EC,[89] first provided the fully-fledged formulation of the subsidiarity principle:

> In areas which do not fall within its exclusive competence, the Community shall take action, in accordance with the principle of subsidiarity, only if and in so far as the objectives of the proposed action cannot be sufficiently achieved by the Member States and can therefore, by reason of the scale or effects of the proposed action, be better achieved by the Community.

Subsidiarity became a general principle applicable to all policy areas of the Treaty outside the exclusive competence of the Community.[90] In addition, the Maastricht Treaty articulated a democratic angle of the subsidiarity principle, by referring in the preamble and Article A TEU to taking decisions 'as closely as possible to the citizen'.[91]

The principle of subsidiarity was greeted as 'an important, if undervalued' part of the relation between Community and Member States and a form of division of power between them.[92] However, at the same time it was seen as a step back, weakening the Community and slowing down European integration.[93] Although it was said that even without subsidiarity, 'one could [also] have lived quite happily and in peace in the European home', subsidiarity remained a constitutional principle of EU law.[94]

The Maastricht formulation of the subsidiarity principle became the basis for its wording in the ill-fated Constitutional Treaty and of today's subsidiarity in the Lisbon Treaty.[95] The current Article 5(3) TEU reads as follows:

> Under the principle of subsidiarity, in areas which do not fall within its exclusive competence, the Union shall act only if and in so far as the objectives of the proposed action cannot be sufficiently achieved by the Member States, *either at central level or at regional and local level, but can rather,* by reason of the scale or effects of the proposed action, be better achieved at Union level (emphasis added).

[85] P Craig, 'Subsidiarity: A Political and Legal Analysis' (2012) 50 *Journal of Common Market Studies* 72.
[86] ibid 73.
[87] ibid.
[88] ibid.
[89] Later renumbered as Art 5(2) EC by the Amsterdam Treaty.
[90] G de Búrca, 'The Principle of Subsidiarity and the Court of Justice as an Institutional Actor' (1998) 36 *Journal of Common Market Studies* 217, 218.
[91] ibid 219.
[92] Cass (n 7) 1134.
[93] Toth, 'The Principle of Subsidiarity in the Maastricht Treaty' (n 5) 1105.
[94] P Pescatore, 'Mit der Subsidiarität leben' in O Due, M Lutter and J Schwarze (eds), *Festschrift für Ulrich Everling* (Baden-Baden, Nomos, 1995) 1094.
[95] Art I-11(3) of the Constitutional Treaty. See NW Barber, 'Subsidiarity in the Draft Constitution' (2002) 11 *European Public Law* 197.

There is also a new subparagraph:

> The institutions of the Union shall apply the principle of subsidiarity as laid down in the Protocol on the application of the principles of subsidiarity and proportionality. National Parliaments ensure compliance with the principle of subsidiarity in accordance with the procedure set out in that Protocol.

This new paragraph and the difference it makes for the application of the subsidiarity principle for EU institutions is discussed separately in chapter two. Besides this addition of the EWS into the text of Article 5(3) TEU, two differences between the Maastricht and the Lisbon subsidiarity are visible: a substantive one and a textual one. In terms of substance, the new subsidiarity formula has an added value because of its reference to the sufficiency of national action at 'central level or at regional and local level'. The Maastricht wording of the subsidiarity principle, by mentioning only the Community and Member State levels '[did] not reflect the philosophy of allowing smaller units to define or achieve their own ends'.[96] Regarding the textual change, the subsidiarity principle in the Maastricht Treaty combined the two parts of the subsidiarity test: first, that the objectives of the proposed action cannot be sufficiently achieved by the Member States, and second, that they can therefore be better achieved by the Community. The Maastricht Treaty used the linking phrase 'and can therefore', whereas its Lisbon Treaty version uses the formula 'but can rather'. How should this change thus be read? It has been suggested that 'and can therefore' in the Maastricht version implied that the negative criterion acted as an independent criterion of equal importance relative to the positive one.[97] The Lisbon version 'but can rather' seems to imply a stronger causal connection between the two. Yet, as they are different tests, it is unclear how the 'but' can be read in any way other than 'and'. The Edinburgh Declaration and the Amsterdam Protocol, discussed below, both state that Community action has to satisfy both limbs of the subsidiarity principle.[98]

B. Concepts of Subsidiarity

Conceptually, one can distinguish between material and procedural subsidiarity.[99] The latter concerns a number of procedural conditions that EU action needs to implement in order to be seen as compatible with the subsidiarity principle.[100] The material dimension of subsidiarity can be verified from two angles inherent in the wording of Article 5(3) TEU: the national insufficiency test and the comparative efficiency test.[101] Under the first test, the EU can act only when the proposed action cannot be sufficiently achieved at the national level. This concerns the inadequacy of means at a Member State's disposal for achieving

[96] de Búrca, 'Reappraising Subsidiarity's Significance after Amsterdam' (n 1) 19.
[97] In German '*und daher*'. Calliess (n 79) 97.
[98] Edinburgh Declaration (n 115) 18 and Art 5 of the Amsterdam Protocol (n 121).
[99] A Estella de Noriega, *The EU Principle of Subsidiarity and its Critique* (Oxford, Oxford University Press, 2002) 105.
[100] ibid. See further section IV of this chapter.
[101] Schütze (n 4) 250.

the objectives of the proposed action.[102] The second test demands that the EU shall act if the objectives of the proposed action can rather 'by reason of the scale or effects of the proposed action, be better achieved at Union level'. In other words, the EU should not act 'unless it could *better* achieve the objectives of the proposed action'.[103]

The tests have been labelled in various ways. One way of describing the components of material subsidiarity is as 'negative' and 'positive' criteria.[104] The 'negative criterion' concerns the insufficiency of Member State action, whereas the 'positive criterion', to be checked only if the first is confirmed, implies a comparative cost–benefit analysis at the different levels of government (including the 'null option' of EU inaction).[105] Other reading of Article 5(3) TEU indicates that insufficiency of national action refers to the 'Member State's sense of self-government, and what it believes it can do itself. This goes to wider issues than legal effectiveness such as how far a measure forms part of a wider valued tradition'.[106] The second test inherent in the subsidiarity principle is a 'federal' one: 'whether one central measure would be more effective than twenty-eight different ones'.[107]

The national insufficiency test asks whether an objective can be achieved sufficiently by the Member States. The question here is whether passing the test requires all, some, or only a single Member State to be in a position to achieve the objective and whether this includes Member States' operating jointly or only acting individually. One interpretation concludes that it needs to be checked whether the objective of the measure can be achieved through the unilateral action of a single, multiple, or all the Member States' acting independently.[108] Arguably smaller Member States may lack financial or other resources to achieve the objective sufficiently, and in such cases, limits on the autonomy of larger Member States in order to achieve an objective at the EU level could then be justified.[109] A different reading proposes that the EU can act if one or more Member States do not have adequate means.[110] In practice, the first interpretation appears to be consistent with the second one for many EU proposals. For example, the objective of the proposal on the strengthening of certain aspects of the presumption of innocence and of the right to be present at trial in criminal proceedings states as its objective 'common minimum rules for certain aspects of the right to presumption of innocence'.[111] If a single Member State was unable to adopt these standards, the overall objective would be violated, and thus the proposal would pass the national insufficiency test.

[102] K Lenaerts, 'Subsidiarity and Community Competence in the Field of Education' (1994) 1 *Columbia Journal of European Law* 1, 22. According to the Commission this test, which it labels the 'comparative efficiency test' includes also lack of financial means. See Communication of the Commission to the Council and the European Parliament on the principle of subsidiarity, 27.10.1992, SEC(92)1990, 10.

[103] Schütze (n 4) 250.

[104] Calliess (n 79) 94.

[105] ibid 103.

[106] D Chalmers, G Davies and G Monti, *European Union Law: Cases and Materials* (Cambridge, Cambridge University Press, 2014) 395.

[107] ibid.

[108] Calliess (n 79) 99.

[109] D Edward, 'Subsidiarity as a Legal Concept' in P Cardonnel, A Rosas and N Wahl (eds), *Constitutionalising the EU Judicial System: Essays in Honour of Pernilla Lindh* (Oxford, Hart Publishing, 2012) 100.

[110] Lenaerts, 'Subsidiarity and Community Competence in the Field of Education' (n 102) 22.

[111] 'Proposal for a Directive on the strengthening of certain aspects of the presumption of innocence and of the right to be present at trial in criminal proceedings' COM(2013) 821 final.

Another question is if the subsidiarity principle bars the EU from acting when Member States could achieve the objective by acting in a form of an intergovernmental cooperation. The textual interpretation of the Maastricht Treaty permitted the conclusion that the EU should not act in such a case; however such an approach would not boost the process of EU integration.[112] The Treaty of Lisbon abolished the three-pillar structure in favour of creating the EU, yet the intergovernmental method is maintained for the Common Foreign and Security Policy and in the area of police and judicial cooperation in criminal matters in which Member States still possess significant powers. Enhanced cooperation can be undertaken only as 'a last resort, when it has established that the objectives of such cooperation cannot be attained within a reasonable period by the Union as a whole'.[113] Therefore, to answer the initial question of whether the EU should not act when Member States could proceed in a form that is binding only for a limited group of them, it seems that this is only a further possibility in cases allowed by the Treaty in which Member States could not agree in the Council.[114]

C. Guidelines for the Application of the Subsidiarity Principle

Although the two tests inherent in the subsidiarity principle have not changed since the Maastricht Treaty, over time, EU institutions adopted a number of recommendations for the application of this principle. In December 1992, the European Council meeting in Edinburgh prepared guidelines for the implementation of the subsidiarity principle 'to increase transparency and openness in the decision-making process of the Community'.[115] Those guidelines were laid down in the 'Overall Approach' annexed to the European Council's conclusions. Subsidiarity is labelled here as a 'dynamic concept' working both ways: to expand and restrict (or discontinue) Community action depending on the circumstances.[116] The Overall Approach provided that when addressing the subsidiarity question, 'should the Community act?', the Community action has to fulfil at least one of the following conditions. First, 'the issue under consideration has transnational aspects which cannot be satisfactorily regulated by Member States'.[117] Second, 'actions by Member States alone or lack of Community action would conflict with the requirements of the Treaty ... or would otherwise significantly damage Member States' interests'. At this point, the Overall Approach gives some examples of treaty requirements that could be at stake: the need to correct distortion of competition, avoidance of disguised restrictions on trade, and strengthening of economic and social cohesion. The third guideline conditioned compliance with subsidiarity on the 'clear benefits [of Community action] by reason of its scale or effects compared with action at the level of Member States'.[118] Moreover, harmonisation of

[112] Toth, 'The Principle of Subsidiarity in the Maastricht Treaty' (n 5) 1099.
[113] Art 20(2) TEU.
[114] See ch 3.
[115] European Council in Edinburgh, 11–12 December 1992, Conclusions of the Presidency (Edinburgh Declaration) 2.
[116] Conclusions of the Presidency, Overall Approach to the Application by the Council of the Subsidiarity Principle and Article 3b TEU, Annex 1 to Part A (Overall Approach) 16.
[117] ibid 19.
[118] ibid.

national laws was compliant with subsidiarity only when harmonisation was necessary to achieve a treaty objective. A common position of the Member States in relations with third countries (countries outside the EU) as such could not justify a Community action. Finally, the Overall Approach provided that the subsidiarity reasoning had to be 'substantiated by qualitative or, wherever possible, quantitative indicators'.[119]

As a compromise between Germany and the United Kingdom (UK) (both supporters of accommodating subsidiarity in the treaties) on the one hand, and France together with some southern Member States (in favour of mentioning the subsidiarity principle only in the preamble) on the other, Protocol No 30 'on the application of the principles of subsidiarity and proportionality' was added to the Amsterdam Treaty.[120] The Amsterdam Protocol borrowed the idea of subsidiarity as a 'dynamic concept' from the Edinburgh Conclusions and restated that compliance with subsidiarity must be demonstrated by 'qualitative or, wherever possible, quantitative indicators'.[121] In comparison, however, the 'Overall Approach' distinguished quite clearly among the three legal concepts within Article 3b EC: principles of attribution of power, subsidiarity, and proportionality. For example, it placed the provisions on the form of action (choosing directives over regulations and framework directives over detailed measures) and on the consideration of financial and administrative burdens in the legislative process under the proportionality principle ('nature and extent of Community action').[122] The Amsterdam Protocol repeated that same recommendation, however, without a direct connection either to the subsidiarity or proportionality principle. In this way, the protocol created a link between the two principles.[123] This linkage, or, rather, confusion of the two principles is visible in the practice of the EWS, in which some national parliaments see the choice of a regulation over a directive as a subsidiarity violation.

The Amsterdam Protocol also provided guidelines on the subsidiarity principle, repeating almost exactly those enshrined in the Overall Approach:

— The issue under consideration has transnational aspects which cannot be satisfactorily regulated by action by Member States.
— Actions by Member States alone or lack of Community action would conflict with the requirements of the Treaty (such as the need to correct distortion of competition or avoid disguised restrictions on trade or strengthen economic and social cohesion) or would otherwise significantly damage Member States' interests.
— Action at the Community level would produce clear benefits by reason of its scale or effects compared with action at the level of the Member States.[124]

Yet, the Amsterdam Protocol did not indicate if the conditions for Community action had to be fulfilled cumulatively or if fulfilment of one of them, for example, the transnational

[119] ibid.

[120] M Heilbronner, 'Die Justiziabilität des Subsidiaritätsprinzips im Lichte der Subsidiaritätsprotokolle' in I Pernice (ed), *Der Vertrag von Lissabon: Reform der EU ohne Verfassung?; Kolloquium zum 10 Geburtstag des WHI* (Baden-Baden, Nomos, 2008) 138.

[121] Paras 3 and 4 of the Protocol on the application of the principles of subsidiarity and proportionality (Amsterdam Protocol).

[122] Overall Approach (n 116) 20–21.

[123] de Búrca, 'Reappraising Subsidiarity's Significance after Amsterdam' (n 1) 32.

[124] Para 5 of the Amsterdam Protocol (n 121).

character of the action, suffices for the Community to act.[125] In contrast, the Overall Approach used an 'and/or' connector between the guidelines, implying that fulfilment of one of the guidelines allows the Community to go forward with its proposal. The Amsterdam Protocol is therefore often seen as a mere extract of the central principles established in the Edinburgh Overall Approach;[126] the guidelines 'largely restate the broad political questions in open-ended terms, and do not provide strong legal criteria to answer them'.[127] However, no new criteria were established in the following years, either by the protocols to the Lisbon Treaty or in the Interinstitutional Agreement on Better Law-Making (2016).[128] It is the Amsterdam criteria to which the Commission[129] and national parliaments still refer.[130]

D. Procedural Subsidiarity

Article 296(2) of the Treaty on the Functioning of the European Union (TFEU) prescribes that EU legal acts have to state the reasons on which they are founded and refer to respective proposals, initiatives, recommendations, requests, or opinions as demanded by the Treaties. In this respect, the CJEU's case law maintains that the statement of reasons for an EU measure must show 'clearly and unequivocally the reasoning of the author of the measure in question' allowing concerned persons to learn the reasons for the measure and to enable the Court to review the measure, but it is not required for that statement to go into every relevant point of fact and law.[131] Whether the obligation to provide a statement of reasons has been satisfied, this 'must be assessed with reference not only to the wording of the measure but also to its context and the whole body of legal rules governing the matter in question'.[132] Where a legislative act is reviewed for its compliance with the subsidiarity principle, the statement of reasons must make clear that the questions relevant to this principle were sufficiently considered.[133] The purpose of the procedural subsidiarity is thus to ensure that EU institutions undertake a 'process' to make sure that the material subsidiarity is implemented.[134]

The Edinburgh Overall Approach indicated that the compliance of a Community action with the subsidiarity principle had to be substantiated by 'qualitative or, wherever possible quantitative indicators'.[135] The Commission proposed that it will consult

[125] See Estella de Noriega (n 99) 107–14.

[126] Calliess (n 79) 66.

[127] de Búrca, 'Reappraising Subsidiarity's Significance after Amsterdam' (n 1) 26.

[128] Interinstitutional Agreement between the European Parliament, the Council of the European Union and the European Commission on Better Law-Making [2016] OJ L123 (Interinstitutional Agreement of 2016) 1–14.

[129] 'Report from the Commission on Subsidiarity and Proportionality, 18th Report on Better Lawmaking covering the year 2010' COM(2011) 344 final, 2.

[130] See, eg, House of Commons, 'Reasoned opinion on the Draft Directive of the European Parliament and of the Council on improving the gender balance among non-executive directors of companies listed on stock exchanges and related measures' COM(2012) 614.

[131] Case C-62/14 *Gauweiler and Others*, EU:C:2015:400, para 70 and the case law cited there.

[132] ibid.

[133] Opinion of Advocate General Kokott of 23.12.2015 in Case C-358/14 *Poland v Parliament and Council*, EU:C:2015:848, para 174.

[134] Estella de Noriega (n 99) 105.

[135] Overall Approach (n 116) 19.

at the pre-legislative stage on whether the proposal is compatible with the subsidiarity principle.[136] A recital of the proposal's preamble would refer to the compatibility with the principle of subsidiarity, and the explanatory memorandum will provide more detail in this respect, when necessary.[137] The Commission should also prepare an annual report on the observance of Article 3b EC in its activities to be debated in the EP. Indeed, the Commission drafted its first report on the subsidiarity principle in 1994, later replaced by broader reports on 'Better Lawmaking'.[138]

The Interinstitutional Agreement between the EP, the Council and the Commission obliged the Commission to show in the proposal's explanatory memorandum that the principle of subsidiarity was complied with, and the EP and the Council should complement the amendments of Commission proposals by a justification if such proposals contain a 'more extensive or intensive' Community action.[139] The institutions obliged themselves, following their internal procedures, to check proposals continuously for subsidiarity violations. The agreement also provided that the EP will hold a public debate on the Commission's annual subsidiarity report in the presence of the Commission and the Council.

Despite the attempt to bring more clarity to the application of the subsidiarity principle, the Edinburgh Guidelines and the Interinstitutional Agreement were perceived as 'vague and only indicative'.[140] Nonetheless, they represented an effort to make subsidiarity 'operational'.[141]

The Amsterdam Protocol maintained all the obligations for the Commission when proposing legislation: wide consultations before proposing legislation; inclusion of subsidiarity justification in its proposals, where necessary in an explanatory memorandum; and minimisation of any financial or administrative burden for the Community and Member State authorities on different levels making it proportional to the objective to be achieved.[142] The Commission should also submit its annual report on Article 3b EC.[143]

Article 5(3) TEU directs that EU institutions 'apply the principle of subsidiarity' as foreseen in Protocol No 2 that establishes the conditions for the application of the subsidiarity principle. Protocol No 2 merely repeats the obligations for draft legislative acts set already in the Amsterdam Protocol, namely, that before proposing legislation the Commission should conduct wide consultations.[144] The legislative proposals require a justification on the subsidiarity compliance, including a statement on its financial impact and, in cases of directives, implications for national (and regional) rules.[145] Moreover, legislative proposals should demonstrate with 'qualitative and, wherever possible, quantitative indicators' that the proposal's objective can be better achieved at the EU level.[146] Finally, legislative drafts

[136] ibid 22.
[137] ibid.
[138] de Búrca, 'Reappraising Subsidiarity's Significance after Amsterdam' (n 1) 33.
[139] Interinstitutional declaration on democracy, transparency and subsidiarity, Bull. EC 10-1993, 119.
[140] I Pernice, 'Framework Revisited: Constitutional, Federal and Subsidiarity Issues' (1995) 2 *Columbia Journal of European Law* 403, 408.
[141] C Timmermans, 'Subsidiarity and Transparency' (1999) 22 *Fordham International Law Journal* 106, 108.
[142] Para 9 of the Amsterdam Protocol (n 121).
[143] ibid.
[144] Art 2 of Protocol No 2.
[145] ibid, Art 5.
[146] ibid. The Edinburgh Declaration (n 115) 19 made it an obligation to provide indicators for both the national insufficiency test as well as the comparative efficiency test. Protocol No 2 followed however para 4 of the Amsterdam Protocol (n 121) which demands such indicators only with regard to the latter test.

should consider the need to minimise any financial or administrative burden for the EU, national entities, and citizens. It should be commensurate with the sought objective.

Over the years, a number of ways to justify the compatibility of Commission proposals with the principle of subsidiarity have been established: in the road maps or inception impact assessments prepared for major initiatives; in the impact assessments; in explanatory memoranda; and in recitals of the proposal's preamble.[147] The road maps and inception impact assessments (road maps for initiatives subject to an impact assessment) that describe the problem and the objectives of the EU action contain an initial justification with regard to the subsidiarity principle.[148]

The explanatory memorandum accompanying a Commission proposal aims to explain it to other institutions and the public and is required for all legislative and non-legislative proposals for adoption by the Council or by the EP and the Council.[149] Protocol No 2 does not refer to, as did the Amsterdam Protocol, justification of compliance of a proposal with the subsidiarity principle in explanatory memoranda 'whenever necessary'.[150] However, the Interinstitutional Agreement on Better Law-Making requires a subsidiarity justification for each Commission legislative proposal.[151]

The subsidiarity justification in explanatory memoranda was often seen as superficial, simply reiterating that the proposal complies with the subsidiarity principle.[152] In 2015, under the 'Better Regulation' agenda, the Commission obliged itself to improve explanatory memoranda accompanying each of its proposals.[153] With regard to the subsidiarity principle, an explanatory memorandum should 'explain the Union dimension of the problem' and conduct both a 'necessity test' and 'effectiveness test'.[154]

Impact assessments, introduced in 2003, have been seen as a tool to assess compliance of EU legislation with the subsidiarity principle.[155] The Commission is obliged to provide impact assessments for its legislative and non-legislative proposals, delegated acts and implemented measures that are likely to have significant economic, environmental, or social effects.[156] Impact assessments deal with 'the existence, scale and consequences of a problem and the question whether or not Union action is needed'.[157] They discuss,

[147] See 'Report from the Commission on Subsidiarity and Proportionality' COM(2012) 373 final, 3 and 'Report from the Commission on Subsidiarity and Proportionality' COM(2016) 469 final, 2.

[148] Commission Staff Working Document, 'Better Regulation Guidelines accompanying the document Communication from the Commission to the European Parliament, the Council, the European economic and social Committee and the Committee of the Regions' SWD(2015) 111, 7 (Better Regulation Guidelines).

[149] ibid 37.

[150] Para 9 of the Amsterdam Protocol (n 121).

[151] Art 25 of the Interinstitutional Agreement of 2016 (n 128).

[152] D Wyatt, 'Is the European Union an Organisation of Limited Powers?' in A Arnull et al (eds), *A Constitutional Order of States? Essays in EU Law in Honour of Alan Dashwood* (Oxford, Hart Publishing, 2011) 18.

[153] Communication from the Commission to the European Parliament, the Council, the European Economic and Social Committee and the Committee of the Regions, 'Better regulation for better results—An EU agenda', COM(2015) 215, 5.

[154] Better Regulation Guidelines (n 148) 38.

[155] 'Communication from the Commission on Impact Assessment' COM(2002) 276, 14. Note that Art 12 of the Interinstitutional Agreement of 2016 (n 128) does not explicitly demand such a section but uses a more convoluted statement when discussing impact assessments: 'The principles of subsidiarity and proportionality should be fully respected, as should fundamental rights'.

[156] Art 13 of the Interinstitutional Agreement of 2016 (n 128).

[157] ibid, Art 12.

using qualitative and quantitative indicators, broader issues such as short-term and long-term costs of EU action and its economic, environmental and social impact.[158] Impact assessments should also include where possible an assessment of lack of EU action ('cost of non-Europe') and the effect on competitiveness and the administrative burdens in such cases.[159]

The Commission's 'Better Regulation' guidelines provide that an impact assessment should verify whether the EU action at stake is compatible with subsidiarity by studying whether the issue has transnational aspects that Member States cannot adequately address and whether, comparatively, EU-level action would generate greater benefits because of its scale or effectiveness.[160] The guidelines indicate that subsidiarity evaluation will likely take place a number of times and that the rationale of the impact assessment process is to check whether proceeding with EU action 'would make sense'.[161] The subsidiarity assessment should provide 'concrete arguments, specific to the issues being analysed and substantiated with qualitative, and where possible, quantitative evidence'.[162] Impact assessments are drafted in English, with an executive summary prepared in all official EU languages.[163] The EP insists, however, that the principle of multilingualism should apply to impact assessments relating to vital aspects of public and political opinion.[164]

The Commission also prepared a 'toolbox' compiling information and guidance for EU policymakers on various stages of policy initiatives, including carrying out an impact assessment.[165] Specifically, when assessing subsidiarity, policymakers should perform a 'necessity/relevance test' and an 'EU added value test'.[166] The former should show the 'Union relevance' of the initiative at stake by taking into consideration the geographical scope, number of businesses or actors involved in the Member States, and the 'level of economic damage' and establish whether a significant cross-border problem is at stake. The latter test considers advantages and disadvantages from EU action in comparison to those resulting from regional or national action by public or private entities.[167]

Finally, the Regulatory Scrutiny Board, an independent group of Commission officials and outside experts, checks the quality of all impact assessments. The board issues recommendations relating to subsidiarity and added value justification of proposals among a number of aspects of draft impact assessments.[168]

158 ibid.

159 ibid.

160 Better Regulation Guidelines (n 148) 21.

161 ibid.

162 ibid.

163 ibid 16.

164 European Parliament resolution of 4 February 2014 on EU Regulatory Fitness and Subsidiarity and Proportionality—19th report on Better Lawmaking covering the year 2011, P7_TA(2014)0061, point 42–50.

165 European Commission, Better Regulation 'Toolbox', available at: ec.europa.eu/info/better-regulation-toolbox_en.

166 ibid 23.

167 ibid. The Better Regulation Guidelines give more detail on 'EU added value' test. The examples of added value include coordination gains, improved legal certainty, greater effectiveness or complementarity. Yet, as those are hard to prove in quantitative terms, an added value test is frequently limited to qualitative indicators and ultimately a political judgment. See Better Regulation Guidelines (n 148) 60.

168 See European Commission, Regulatory Scrutiny Board, Annual Report 2016, 15.

Impact assessments have contributed to 'taking subsidiarity seriously' by the Commission.[169] The increased use of the impact assessments in the pre-legislative phase has been seen as a 'move towards proceduralization' in the subsidiarity monitoring.[170]

E. The Relationship Between the Principles of Article 5 TEU

Beyond subsidiarity, Article 5 TEU encompasses the principles of conferral and proportionality. Broadly speaking, the principle of conferral governs the limits of Union competences, while subsidiarity and proportionality govern the use of those competences.[171] Specifically, the principle of conferral allows the EU to act only within the limits of competences conferred upon it by the Member States in the Treaties to achieve their objectives.[172] The principle of proportionality demands that EU action does not exceed what is necessary to achieve the Treaties' objectives and should be applied in line with Protocol No 2.[173] The EU legal scholarship dealt especially with the understanding of the relationship with other principles of Article 5 TEU, a situation which has an impact on the issues that should be tested under Protocol No 2.[174]

The principle of conferral can be seen as a 'pre-question' demanded by a systematic interpretation of Article 5 TEU, a reason why competence and subsidiarity cannot be separated.[175] The question of whether the EU has a non-exclusive competence to regulate a matter is seen by some as a 'responsibility criterion', the first step in the application of the subsidiarity principle.[176] A contrary view posits that the Amsterdam Protocol provided for 'tangible contours' to the concept of subsidiarity, allowing for its legal application as 'a benchmark for the exercise of nonexclusive Community competences in specific cases', in addition to the Lisbon Treaty's 'emphasis on the task of separation of competences'.[177] In this context, subsidiarity cannot settle the question of competence, even though the question might be related to the more general idea of subsidiarity.[178]

[169] Craig, 'Subsidiarity' (n 85) 77.

[170] X Groussot and S Bogojević, 'Subsidiarity as a Procedural Safeguard of Federalism' in L Azoulai (ed), *The Question of Competence in the European Union* (Oxford, Oxford University Press, 2014) 235. While Groussot and Bogojević acknowledge that a number of reasoned opinions criticised insufficient justification of Commission proposals (at 240), they separate the EWS from impact assessments as two different 'competence-based tools'. However, in fact the reasoned opinions often refer to the insufficient explanatory memoranda which may make the differentiation between the two tests not that clear-cut. Moreover, the significance of impact assessments for Groussot and Bogojević seems to lie more in the judicial review of EU measures (at 243).

[171] Art 5(1) TEU.

[172] Art 5(2) TEU.

[173] Art 5(4) TEU.

[174] See P Kiiver, *The Early Warning System for the Principle of Subsidiarity: Constitutional Theory and Empirical Reality* (London, Routledge, 2012) 98–100; C Ritzer, M Ruttloff and K Linhart, 'How to Sharpen a Dull Sword—The Principle of Subsidiarity and its Control' (2006) 7 *German Law Journal* 733, 737.

[175] Calliess (n 79) 64.

[176] A Cygan, *Accountability, Parliamentarism and Transparency in the EU* (Cheltenham, Edward Elgar Publishing, 2013) 133. Cygan puts forward a three-step test of the subsidiarity principle: 'responsibility criterion', 'necessity requirement' and 'efficiency criterion'.

[177] T von Danwitz, 'Subsidiaritätskontrolle in der Europäischen Union' in K Hansmann, K-P Dolde, S Paetow and E Schmidt-Assmann (eds), *Verfassung-Umwelt-Wirtschaft Festschrift für Dieter Sellner zum 75 Geburtstag* (München, CH Beck, 2010) 40.

[178] ibid 41.

Similarly, there are a number of views regarding the relationship between subsidiarity and proportionality. According to the one viewpoint, there is a clear difference between the questions asked by subsidiarity and proportionality. The latter asks whether the action at stake is necessary to achieve the objective and whether it goes further than what is necessary to achieve that objective, while the former question concerns the issue of which level should take a given action.[179] Moreover, proportionality does not manifest subsidiarity because the Court applies proportionality throughout the treaty provisions, while subsidiarity concerns only those areas that do not fall into EU-exclusive competence.[180] An opposite view talks about a 'close relationship'[181] or even 'cannibalization' of subsidiarity by the proportionality principle by tying the 'who' and 'how' questions together.[182] Arguably the subsidiarity principle expressed in Article 5(3) TEU contains elements of the proportionality principle such as adequacy, necessity and proportionality *sensu stricto*.[183] Adequacy is expressed by the phrase 'by reason of the scale or effects of the proposed action, be better achieved at Union level', whereas the 'if' and 'in so far as' in the subsidiarity formula enshrined necessity and proportionality *sensu stricto*, respectively.[184] A similar view maintains that subsidiarity takes into consideration elements of proportionality—the necessity of action at the EU level—'without exhausting the content of the proportionality principle'.[185]

A more complex understanding of the middle position is provided by Lenaerts, who maintains that subsidiarity can be understood both in *sensu stricto* (the 'if' question) and *lato sensu* (the 'in so far as' question) terms.[186] Subsidiarity *lato sensu* does involve a proportionality assessment which, according to Lenaerts, implies that two expressions of the proportionality principle are at stake in Article 3b EC, current Article 5(3) TEU.[187] The use of 'and in so far as' with regard to EU action, both in the first version of the subsidiarity formula of the Maastricht Treaty and in its current Lisbon version, 'indicates the permissible *extent* of such action' and 'makes it difficult to distinguish sharply between subsidiarity and proportionality'.[188] Yet, while the proportionality test involved in subsidiarity questions concerns only shared competences, the proportionality principle in general refers to all types of competence. In addition, the proportionality aspect involved in subsidiarity protects specifically the sovereignty of Member States, whereas the general proportionality principle applies to values protected under EU law.[189]

[179] Edward (n 109) 100.

[180] Toth, 'The Principle of Subsidiarity in the Maastricht Treaty' (n 5) 1083.

[181] T Blanke, 'The Principle of Subsidiarity in the Lisbon Treaty' in N Bruun, K Lörcher and I Schömann (eds), *The Lisbon Treaty and Social Europe* (Oxford, Hart Publishing, 2012) 253.

[182] Groussot and Bogojević (n 170) 237.

[183] J Ziller, 'Le principe de subsidiarité' in J-B Auby and J Dutheil de la Rochèr (eds), *Traité de droit administratif européen* (Bruxelles, Bruylant, 2014) 529.

[184] ibid.

[185] J-V Louis, 'Quelques remarques sur l'avenir du contrôle du principe de subsidiarité' in A De Walsche and L Levi (eds), *Mélanges en hommage à Georges Vandersanden: promenades au sein du droit européen* (Bruxelles, Bruylant, 2008) 291 (own translation).

[186] Lenaerts, 'The Principle of Subsidiarity and the Environment in the European Union' (n 3) 875.

[187] ibid 883.

[188] Lenaerts, 'Subsidiarity and Community Competence in the Field of Education' (n 102) 3, 25. Lenaerts argues that Art 3b contains in fact two expressions of the proportionality principle.

[189] Lenaerts, 'The Principle of Subsidiarity and the Environment in the European Union' (n 3) 884.

Against the overview of possible stances on the mutual relationship between principles expressed by the legal scholarship, Schütze's understanding of Article 5 TEU presents a systematised approach to all three principles. In his approach, the conferral question is a 'general "whether" of Union action' that is answered by the policy area as a whole.[190] In other words, the competence question asks whether the EU can generally act in any given area. In contrast, the focus of subsidiarity is on a specific act at stake. Furthermore, Schütze ties together subsidiarity's 'whether' question and proportionality's 'how' question, arguing that together they imply that subsidiarity has to be understood as '*federal* proportionality'.[191] Similar to Lenaerts, cited above, Schütze maintains that the distinction between these principles lies in the issues that they protect: the private rights of an individual in cases of proportionality and the 'collective autonomy' of a group under subsidiarity.[192] Proportionality should then be restricted to safeguarding private rights against excessive public interference.[193] Hence, the relevant content of Article 5 TEU can be summarised as follows:

> [T]he enumeration principle will tell us whether the Community *can* act within a policy field. The subsidiarity principle would examine whether a European law *disproportionately restricts national autonomy*; and the principle of proportionality would, finally, tell us whether a European law *unnecessarily interfered with liberal values*.[194]

V. SUBSIDIARITY IN THE COURT OF JUSTICE

A. The Limits of CJEU Jurisprudence on the Subsidiarity Principle

Subsidiarity is clearly legally binding, and it remains under the judicial control of the CJEU.[195] After the introduction of subsidiarity into the Maastricht Treaty, scholars expected an overflow of litigation on the new principle.[196] But already it was expected that the Court would not conduct a subsidiarity check 'any further than is absolutely necessary for ensuring and respecting the Rule of Law'.[197] After Maastricht, only a handful of subsidiarity challenges were brought before the Court, and this trend has continued under the expanded subsidiarity regime following the Lisbon Treaty.[198] Overall, in its jurisprudence

[190] Schütze (n 4) 263.
[191] ibid.
[192] ibid.
[193] ibid 264.
[194] ibid.
[195] T Schilling, 'A New Dimension of Subsidiarity: Subsidiarity as a Rule and a Principle' (1995) 14 *Yearbook of European Law* 203, 212.
[196] Toth, 'The Principle of Subsidiarity in the Maastricht Treaty' (n 5) 1101.
[197] N Emiliou, 'Subsidiarity: An Effective Barrier Against "the Enterprises of Ambition"?' (1992) 17 *European Law Review* 383, 405.
[198] Craig, 'Subsidiarity' (n 85) 80. The most significant cases include Case C-84/94 *United Kingdom v Council*, ECLI:EU:C:1996:431 (Working Time Directive); and Case C-233/94 *Germany v Parliament and Council*, ECLI:EU:C:1997:231 (Deposit-Guarantee Schemes). See Estella de Noriega (n 99) 137–76. The cases that concern the subsidiarity principle brought before the entry into force of the Lisbon Treaty but decided after its entry into force include: Case C-176/09 *Luxembourg v Parliament and Council*, ECLI:EU:C:2011:290; Case C-539/09 *Commission v Germany*, ECLI:EU:C:2011:733, para 85; and the Opinion of Advocate General Trstenjak *in Commission v Germany*, ECLI:EU:C:2011:345, paras 81–85.

the Court has limited its scrutiny of the reasoning of the Commission on subsidiarity matters and indeed in no case to date has the Court found a violation of subsidiarity.

The first reason for the Court's restraint lies in subsidiarity being 'political in nature'.[199] As a result, its enforcement must arguably remain within the purview of political institutions, and this limits the ability of the Court to apply a high level of legal scrutiny.[200] Others have argued that subsidiarity is both a legal and a political principle.[201] For example, Schütze talks about the political and the judicial nature of subsidiarity, with only the latter concerning its 'substantiation' before the Court.[202] The Court itself in the Tobacco Products Directive litigation clearly distinguished that the initial, political review of subsidiarity is in the hands of national parliaments, while the Court has to decide whether the EU legislature 'was entitled to consider, on the basis of a detailed statement, that the objective of the proposed action cannot be better achieved at EU level'.[203]

A second, related reason for the limited judicial scrutiny lies in the character of the subsidiarity principle as a 'catch-all formula of good government and common sense, rather than a well-defined political or philosophical principle', and without 'clear legal content'.[204] The 'bipolar ethos' inherent in the subsidiarity principle, specifically the preservation of national autonomy and comparative efficiency of centralisation, explains the adherence of the Court to the separation of powers: the Court has tried to avoid 'substituting its own judgment for that of the institutions, in assessing a choice which was ultimately perceived as political'.[205]

A third possible explanation is the political agenda of the Court guided by the 'idea of integration', which may be endangered by the 'anti-integration' character of the subsidiarity principle, directed specifically against the growth of EU competences.[206] Finally, if Member States adopted a legislative act via qualitative majority voting, the adoption decision implied that there were enough Member States that thought a given EU action fulfilled the subsidiarity test, rendering judicial review superfluous.[207] Some commentators now urge the Court to insist 'more sternly on transparency and reason-giving in support of legislative choices made'[208] and to give up on the manifest-error doctrine by adopting a 'doctrinal framework' for subsidiarity and proportionality.[209]

[199] T Tridimas, 'The Rule of Reason and its Relation to Proportionality and Subsidiarity' in A Schrauwen (ed), *Rule of Reason: Rethinking Another Classic of European Legal Doctrine* (Groningen, Europa Law Publishing, 2005) 120.

[200] J Peters, 'National Parliaments and Subsidiarity: Think Twice' (2005) 1 *European Constitutional Law Review* 68, 70.

[201] de Búrca, 'Reappraising Subsidiarity's Significance after Amsterdam' (n 1) 3.

[202] Schütze (n 4) 257.

[203] Case C-358/14 *Poland v Parliament and Council*, ECLI:EU:C:2016:323, paras 112 and 114.

[204] Estella de Noriega (n 99) 96, 139.

[205] A Biondi, 'Subsidiarity in the Courtroom' in A Biondi, P Eeckhout and S Ripley (eds), *EU Law After Lisbon* (Oxford, Oxford University Press, 2012) 220.

[206] Estella de Noriega (n 99) 7.

[207] Craig, 'Subsidiarity' (n 85) 81.

[208] S Weatherill, 'The Limits of Legislative Harmonization Ten Years after Tobacco Advertising: How the Court's Case Law has Become a Drafting Guide' (2011) 12 *German Law Journal* 827, 859.

[209] M Kumm, 'Constitutionalising Subsidiarity in Integrated Markets: The Case of Tobacco Regulation in the European Union' (2006) 12 *European Law Journal* 503. Such an 'S&P Framework' consists of the following three prongs: 'federal intervention has to further legitimate purposes, has to be necessary in the sense of being narrowly tailored to achieve that purpose, and has to be proportionate with regard to costs or disadvantages relating to the loss of Member States' regulatory autonomy'.

Overall, the common view is that the CJEU did not become an effective guardian of subsidiarity.[210] Its vague pronunciations of subsidiarity compliance provided drafting instructions for EU institutions, and in consequence made it harder for the Court to annul such a legislative act over subsidiarity issues in the future.[211]

The broadening of EU competences and the extension of majoritarian decision-making in the Lisbon Treaty arguably put the Court under much stricter public scrutiny.[212] In consequence, the Court is expected to increase its control over the exercise of competences by the EU and advance a counter-majoritarian approach when reviewing EU legislation.[213] The fact that the CJEU has never declared an EU act as violating subsidiarity should not have a deterrent effect on bringing cases before the Court.[214]

B. Post-Lisbon Subsidiarity Case Law

Since the entry into force of the Lisbon Treaty, the Court has considered subsidiarity only in a small number of CJEU cases.[215] The few available judgments point to two trends in the Court's analysis of subsidiarity: (i) the significance of the cross-border nature of a proposal in justifying EU action; and (ii) the need to substantiate compliance with the subsidiarity principle through evidence and, in particular, the use of impact assessments for the analysis of the subsidiarity question. These trends emphasise two aspects of subsidiarity in the Treaties, as discussed previously.

The first aspect in the subsidiarity case law is the cross-border test in instances concerning the internal market, for which an almost automatic prejudice for EU action appears to apply. The Amsterdam Protocol indicated this test as a guideline to justify action at the EU level: the issue at stake has transnational aspects that cannot be regulated satisfactorily at the national level.[216] According to Advocate General (AG) Maduro in the *Vodafone* case, action should be taken at the EU level whenever the EU has 'a special interest in protecting and promoting economic activities of a cross-border character' and 'the national democratic process is likely to fail to protect cross-border activities'.[217] That was

[210] G Martinico, 'Dating Cinderella: On subsidiarity as a political safeguard of federalism in the European Union' (2011) 17 *European Public Law* 649, 655. For a view that the CJEU applied subsidiarity, but under a different heading of review see T Horsley, 'Subsidiarity and the European Court of Justice: Missing Pieces in the Subsidiarity Jigsaw?' (2012) 50 *Journal of Common Market Studies* 267, 270.

[211] Weatherill, 'The Limits of Legislative Harmonization' (n 208).

[212] M Poiares Maduro and L Azoulai, 'Introduction' in M Poiares Maduro and L Azoulai (eds), *The Past and Future of EU Law: The Classics of EU Law Revisited on the 50th Anniversary of the Treaty of Rome* (Oxford, Hart Publishing, 2010) XIX.

[213] ibid.

[214] Ziller (n 183) 533.

[215] According to a search on curia.europa.eu, when inserting 'Art 5(3) TEU' in the field 'references to case law and legislation' six cases were brought before the Court after the entry into force of the Lisbon Treaty: C-547-14 *Philipp Morris Brands and Others*, ECLI:EU:C:2016:325; C-477/14 *Pillbox 38*, ECLI:EU:C:2016:324; C-358/14 *Poland v Parliament and Council*, ECLI:EU:C:2016:323; C-276/14 *Gmina Wrocław*, ECLI:EU:C:2015:635; C-508/13 *Estonia v Parliament and Council*, ECLI:EU:C:2015:403; C-507/13 *United Kingdom v Parliament and Council*, ECLI:EU:C:2014:2481 (action of annulment withdrawn by the UK).

[216] Art 5 of the Amsterdam Protocol (n 121).

[217] Case C-58/08 Opinion of AG Poiares Maduro in *Vodafone and Others*, ECLI:EU:C:2009:596, para 34.

the case with the roaming retail prices in the *Vodafone* litigation. Generally speaking, the EU should take action in cases in which there is a transnational dimension of an issue that national process may fail to regulate and that will, in turn, increase the added value of EU legislative intervention.[218] In its decision, the Court did not repeat this argument, but simply referred to the regulation's objective 'to contribute to the smooth functioning of the internal market'.[219]

The case law concerning the Tobacco Products Directive highlights issues arising with subsidiarity scrutiny when the objective of an EU act concerns the functioning of the internal market based on Article 114 TFEU.[220] The new directive was challenged in the CJEU in three different proceedings on a number of grounds including compliance with the subsidiarity principle of various aspects of the directive. Specifically, it was contested whether the prohibition of menthol cigarettes[221] and the new rules on e-cigarettes were compatible with the subsidiarity principle.[222] AG Kokott,[223] conducting the subsidiarity review of the directive, analysed both the substance of the EU measure and the statement of reasons.[224] With regard to the substance of the directive, the AG focused mainly on the cross-border dimension of the problem arguing that it is impossible to address at national level.[225] The AG's opinion specified that since the aim of Article 114 TFEU is to eliminate obstacles to cross-border trade, 'as a rule' Member States cannot sufficiently achieve this objective.[226] Poland tried to counter this argument by arguing that the issue of menthol-flavoured tobacco does not have a cross-border dimension because of diverse consumption patterns and economic structures among the Member States and the fact that the biggest markets in this respect (Poland, Slovakia and Finland) can provide for 'health-related action' at the national level.[227] The AG disagreed with this reasoning and pointed out that the objective of the directive is to remove obstacles for the trade of tobacco products while simultaneously ensuring a high level of health protection, and this can be done only when all characterising

[218] The cross-border character of an activity implying a need for an EU-level regulation is not always obvious. For example, AG Maduro in the *Vodafone* case differentiates between the justification for the harmonisation of the wholesale and retail roaming prices. Whereas few could dispute that the wholesale roaming price had a cross-border character, it was argued by some that the retail prices could have been regulated at the national level once the wholesale prices were harmonised. However, as AG Maduro explained, EU-level regulation of the retail prices was needed, as the retail roaming prices were just a small part of domestic communications, and the national regulators might have failed to protect this cross-border activity.

[219] C-58/08 *Vodaphone and Others*, ECLI:EU:C:2010:32, para 76.

[220] Directive 2014/40/EU of the European Parliament and of the Council of 3 April 2014 on the approximation of the laws, regulations and administrative provisions of the Member States concerning the manufacture, presentation and sale of tobacco and related products and repealing Directive 2001/37/EC [2014] OJ L127/1.

[221] C-547/14 *Philip Morris Brands and Others*, ECLI:EU:C:2016:325 and C-358/14 *Poland v Parliament and Council*, ECLI:EU:C:2016:323.

[222] C-477/14 *Pillbox 38*, ECLI:EU:C:2016:324.

[223] The AG provided the most extensive opinion on subsidiarity in the *Poland v Parliament and Council* case, referring to that opinion in the other proceedings. Opinion of AG Kokott in Case C-358/14 *Poland v Parliament and Council*, ECLI:EU:C:2015:848. According to the AG, the *Philip Morris Brands and Others* and *Pillbox 38* cases concern subsidiarity 'only briefly' (see ECLI:EU:C:2015:853, para 273 and ECLI:EU:C:2015:854, para 159 respectively).

[224] Opinion of AG Kokott in Case C-358/14 *Poland v Parliament and Council*, ECLI:EU:C:2015:848, para 140.

[225] ibid, paras 151–53.

[226] ibid, para 154.

[227] ibid, para 155.

flavours are prohibited.[228] Moreover, the AG argued that differences in consumption patterns across the Member States do not matter as such. The core of the problem is whether there is or will be cross-border trade in this area and whether the obstacles can be 'efficiently' removed by Member States on their own.[229] The AG concluded that there exists a 'lively' cross-border trade in the tobacco market, with differences between Member States on the rules of characterising flavours, and therefore the EU did not commit a manifest error in the assessment of the facts in its appraisal of the question of subsidiarity.[230]

The Court did not follow by discussing the details of cross-border trade, but, instead, focused on the objectives of the directive. It assessed that even if one of the objectives of the directive, ensuring a high level of protection of human health, could be better achieved at the national level, the other objective, improvement of the functioning of the internal market for tobacco, would be shattered if tobacco with characterising flavours was permitted in some Member States and forbidden in others.[231] The 'interdependence' of those objectives makes the EU level better placed to achieve them.[232] Moreover, in the view of the Court, the subsidiarity principle does not aim to set limits on EU action on the basis of the situation in a specific Member State assessed individually, but, instead, simply demands that the action can be better achieved at the EU level in view of the objectives of the Treaties.[233] The Court rejected Poland's argument that since menthol cigarettes are consumed predominantly in only three Member States, the objective of protection of human health could be better achieved at the national level. That argument was rejected because, in fact, menthol cigarettes had a market share greater than the EU-wide market share in at least eight additional Member States.[234]

The second aspect of the Court's subsidiarity case law is the relatively recent focus on the duty to justify EU action with specific evidence, in particular, the reference to impact assessments in that question. This is in contrast to earlier judgments, when the Court's review of the procedural aspects of subsidiarity often required not more than a mention of the reasons for the Community to act in the preamble of the proposal.[235] The *Vodafone* case concerning roaming charges is seen as the beginning of this trend[236] and is the first case in which the Court referred to the impact assessment to support the review of the proportionality principle,[237] following up on the similar application of that impact assessment by AG Maduro.[238] The AG underlined that the intent of the EU legislator is not enough to show compliance of the act with the subsidiarity principle, but that it instead should be required to compare the benefits of EU action with the possible problems and the costs of national action.[239]

228 ibid, para 157.
229 ibid, para 158.
230 ibid, para 160.
231 ibid, para 117.
232 ibid, para 118.
233 ibid, para 119.
234 ibid, para 120.
235 Estella de Noriega (n 99) 157.
236 Groussot and Bogojevic (n 170) 246.
237 C-58/08 *Vodafone and Others*, ECLI:EU:C:2010:32, para 55.
238 Case C-58/08 Opinion of AG Poiares Maduro in *Vodafone and Others*, ECLI:EU:C:2009:596, para 39.
239 ibid, para 30.

In the subsequent *Luxembourg airports* case, the Court again referred to the impact assessment showing that the Commission pondered a number of options with regard to the airport charges that were at stake.[240] Moreover, in both the *Luxembourg airports* and the *Vodafone* cases, the Court referred to the guidelines established by the Amsterdam Protocol when deciding on the compatibility of the regulation at stake with the subsidiarity principle.[241] However, it is notable that the Court did not demand that each of the provisions of the directive have a separate subsidiarity justification.[242]

Finally, before the Tobacco Products Directive case, there remained cases in which the Court appeared to be more lenient. For example, in the VAT case, the Court was once more satisfied with a mere recital in the preamble of the directive, stating that its objective of harmonisation of VAT systems of the Member States can be better achieved at the EU level.[243]

The Tobacco Products Directive litigation finally provided a more elaborate enquiry into procedural subsidiarity, again referencing the evidence in the impact assessment. The preamble of the directive in that case contained the classic subsidiarity justification,[244] but the impact assessment provided an explicit subsidiarity justification covering one page.[245] In it, the Commission points out how the different national approaches to tobacco limit the functioning of the internal market and argues that the directive would produce 'clear benefits'. These drew on the more detailed analysis and comparison of the effects of doing nothing and pursuing different options.

AG Kokott assessed the procedural subsidiarity angle since Poland claimed that the Commission's directive lacks sufficient subsidiarity justification, more specifically that only one recital of the directive's preamble deals with subsidiarity.[246] The AG confirmed that the directive only reproduces the text of Article 5(3) TEU.[247] Despite this 'empty formula' used by the EU legislator, the AG found that other recitals in the preamble, even though they do not directly reference subsidiarity, but, rather, justify the use of Article 114 TFEU, are nonetheless relevant to the subsidiarity question because of the overlap in the reasoning applicable to internal market and subsidiarity provisions.[248] Moreover, the AG underlined that the explanatory memorandum in the Commission proposal and the impact assessment discussed the insufficiency of national rules and the added value of EU action and that both were available to EU institutions and national parliaments in the legislative procedure.[249]

[240] C-176/09 *Luxembourg v Parliament and Council*, ECLI:EU:C:2011:290, para 65.

[241] C-58/08 *Vodafone and Others*, ECLI:EU:C:2010:32, para 72; C-176/09 *Luxembourg v Parliament and Council*, ECLI:EU:C:2011:290, para 76.

[242] C-508/13 *Estonia v Parliament and Council*, ECLI:EU:C:2015:403, para 53.

[243] C-276/14, *Gmina Wrocław*, ECLI:EU:C:2015:635, para 41.

[244] Recital 60 of the preamble of Directive 2014/40/EU.

[245] Commission Staff Working Document, 'Impact Assessment Impact accompanying the Proposal for a Directive of the European Parliament and of the Council on the approximation of the laws, regulations and administrative provisions of the Member States concerning the manufacture, presentation and sale of tobacco and related products' SWD(2012) 452, Part 1, 46. The subsidiarity justification in the explanatory memorandum was a shorter version of that justification in the impact assessment.

[246] Opinion of AG Kokott in Case C-358/14 *Poland v Parliament and Council*, EU:C:2015:848, para 175.

[247] ibid, para 177.

[248] ibid, para 180.

[249] ibid, paras 182–85.

The AG advised the EU legislature to avoid 'empty formulas' and substantiate the preamble with regard to the subsidiarity principle in future legislative acts, but she did not find a violation of the procedural aspect of the subsidiarity principle.[250]

Moreover, when assessing the 'added value' of EU action,[251] the AG pointed out that although it might be an 'automatic' case with regard to Article 114 TFEU legislation, it still demanded a quantitative and qualitative test.[252] The AG established that the market at stake has a 'substantial trade volume and affects the lives of millions of Union citizens every day' ('quantitative test') and that the issue at stake is 'beyond national boundaries', confirming a common European interest ('qualitative test').[253] Again, the AG found no manifest error of assessment in the Commission's reasoning and argued that the directive therefore also passed the positive aspect of the subsidiarity test.[254]

The Court decision focused less on the details of the quantitative and qualitative test, but instead highlighted the availability of information in the Commission documents. It conducted its assessment 'not only by reference to the wording of the contested act, but also by reference to its context and the circumstances of the individual case': both the proposal and the impact assessment have provided 'sufficient information' pointing out 'clearly and unequivocally' the benefits of EU action.[255] Moreover, since Poland participated in the legislative procedure, it cannot raise an argument that it did not know the reasoning behind the measures intended by the EU legislature.[256] In addition, when assessing the proportionality of the prohibition of mentholated tobacco, the Court considered another aspect of Article 5 of Protocol No 2 that sets the procedural requirements for EU acts, namely, the need to take into account that any burden upon the economic operators should be minimised and commensurate with the sought objective. The lost jobs and revenue due to the prohibition were mitigated, in the view of the Court, by giving the industry and consumers until 2020 to adapt and by showing in the impact assessment that the ban will decrease the number of smokers.[257]

In summary, the recent judgments of the CJEU indicate that compliance with the subsidiarity principle may derive almost automatically from the cross-border nature of a proposal at hand, for example, to achieve the objective of internal market integration. However, in making this case, as with other arguments, the Commission will likely be expected to go beyond the empty formulas found in recitals of previous legislation and provide specific evidence such as the cost–benefit analysis found in supporting impact assessments in order to satisfy the procedural requirements of the subsidiarity principle. As such, the subsidiarity jurisprudence of the Court did not change substantially since its early pronouncements on the issue. It remains to be seen whether the Court will sharpen its enquiry into the procedural aspect of subsidiarity.[258]

[250] ibid, para 188.
[251] ibid, para 162.
[252] ibid, paras 164–65.
[253] ibid, para 167.
[254] ibid, para 168. At this point the AG referred to the preamble of the Act.
[255] C-358/14 *Poland v Parliament and Council*, ECLI:EU:C:2016:323, paras 122–23.
[256] ibid, para 125.
[257] ibid, paras 100–01.
[258] J Öberg, 'Subsidiarity as a Limit to the Exercise of EU Competences' [2016] *Yearbook of European Law* 1.

C. Subsidiarity Action

Finally, a new source of subsidiarity focus in the Court might be connected to the subsidiarity requests coming from national parliaments, according to Article 8 of Protocol No 2.[259] The Court is competent

> in actions on ground of infringement of the principle of subsidiarity by a legislative act, brought in accordance with the rules laid down in Article 263 [TFEU] by Member States, or notified by them in accordance with their legal order on behalf of their national Parliament or a chamber thereof.

However, Article 8 of Protocol No 2 did not grant national parliaments independent standing before the CJEU, as a category, national parliaments can be seen as 'indirect semi-privileged applicants'.[260] Since the ex post subsidiarity review procedure has not yet been applied, it is difficult to predict whether and how it will be enforced. The question remains whether national parliaments should have gained an independent standing before the Court. In favour of giving national parliaments independent standing before the Court are 'the periodic failings of national executives to reflect the concerns of national Parliaments in Council negotiations'.[261] In fact, an argument could be made that, already, the national design of the rules on subsidiarity action sometimes allows national parliaments a lot of independence in the subsidiarity action.[262] The involvement of national parliaments in the subsidiarity action may thus create a chance for some new subsidiarity case law.

VI. REASONS FOR INTRODUCTION OF THE EWS

The EWS was seen as a way of satisfying both federal and democratic safeguards within the EU.[263] National parliaments could act as a safeguard on EU institutions in checking if such institutions comply with the subsidiarity principle, and at the same time they could provide democratic input.

A. 'Competence Creep'

The decision to grant national parliaments the power to control the subsidiarity principle was connected with the EU Member States' dissatisfaction with the Court's case law on subsidiarity and seen as a palliative against 'competence creep'.[264] The phenomenon of

[259] Biondi (n 205) 223.

[260] K Granat, 'Institutional design of the Member States for the ex post subisidiarity scrutiny' in M Cartabia, N Lupo and A Simoncini (eds), *Democracy and Subsidiarity in the EU: National Parliaments, Regions and Civil Society in the Decision-Making Process* (Bologna, Il Mulino, 2013) 432.

[261] S Weatherill, 'Better Competence Monitoring' (2005) 30 *European Law Review* 23, 40. Because Weatherill's point was raised at the time of the Constitutional Treaty, the action, in Weatherill's view, was to cover matters already signalled in the ex ante reasoned opinion procedure.

[262] Granat, 'Institutional design of the Member States for the ex post subisidiarity scrutiny' (n 260) 446ff.

[263] Schütze (n 4) 258.

[264] S Weatherill, 'Competence Creep and Competence Control' (2004) 23 *Yearbook of European Law* 1, 6.

'competence creep', the situation in which the scope of action taken by the EU has tended to 'creep' outwards beyond that foreseen by the Treaty was in particular connected to the broad framing of the current Articles 114 TFEU and 352 TFEU.[265] In consequence, a clearer delimitation of EU competence became part of the agenda after the Treaty of Nice.[266] The Laeken Declaration on the Future of the European Union urged a 'better division and definition of competence in the European Union'.[267]

B. 'Democratic Deficit'

The other reason for involving national parliaments directly was the perception that '[d]emocracy was not part of the original DNA of European Integration'[268] and that the 'democracy issue' of the EU is that EU institutions suffer from a legitimacy crisis.[269] The EU's democratic deficit is to be understood in the light of 'input' and 'output' legitimacy that are two 'legitimizing beliefs' for the exercise of governing authority.[270] Input-oriented legitimacy means that 'political choices are legitimate if and because they reflect the "will of the people"—that is, if they can be derived from the authentic preferences of the members of a community'.[271] Under output-oriented legitimacy, 'political choices are legitimate if and because they effectively promote the common welfare of the constituency in question'.[272] Viewed from this perspective, the transfer of competence from the national level to the EU level within the process of European integration raised the question of the legitimisation of EU authorities and laws and about the EU's input and output legitimacy.

The transfer of power expresses the idea that competences that used to be exercised at the national level have 'disappeared'.[273] While at the Member State level, the law is enacted by democratically elected parliaments, the European level is perceived by EU citizens as not having the same democratic legitimacy. With the transfer of power, however, the legislative process at the EU level has strengthened the position of governments 'by making the statal

[265] S Weatherill, 'Using National Parliaments to Improve Scrutiny of the Limits of EU Action' (2003) 28 *European Law Review* 909, 910.

[266] P Craig, *EU Administrative Law* (Oxford, Oxford University Press, 2012) 369.

[267] Laeken Declaration on the future of the European Union, Annex I to Presidency Conclusions (Laeken, 14–15 December 2001) 21–22.

[268] JHH Weiler, 'In the Face of Crisis: Input Legitimacy, Output Legitimacy and the Political Messianism of European Integration' (2012) 34 *Journal of European Integration* 825, 837.

[269] JHH Weiler, 'The Transformation of Europe' (1991) 100 *Yale Law Journal* 2403, 2472.

[270] FW Scharpf, *Governing in Europe: Effective and Democratic?* (Oxford, Oxford University Press, 1999) 6. Weiler adds a third pillar of democratic legitimacy, narrative (entity, myth, dream, political Messianism): in the EU the 'justification for action and its mobilizing force derive not from process, as in classical democracy, or from result and success, but from the ideal pursued'. See Weiler, 'In the Face of Crisis' (n 268) 832.

[271] Scharpf (n 270) 6.

[272] ibid.

[273] LFM Besselink, 'National Parliaments in the EU's Composite Constitution: A Plea for a Shift in Paradigm' in P Kiiver (ed), *National and Regional Parliaments in the European Constitutional Order* (Groningen, Europa Law Publishing, 2006) 119. Besselink points also to the use of 'transfer' instead of more neutral 'attribution' or 'conferral' of competence.

executive branch the ultimate legislator in the Community'.[274] In addition, the scrutiny of governmental decisions at EU level remains a national process, one aimed at holding into account national actors.[275] This creates an input legitimacy deficit. A parallel transfer of democratic legitimacy has not accompanied the transfer of competences; the EU level has not received more legitimacy. National parliaments 'appear[ed] as the net losers in the new institutional equilibrium resulting from EC membership'.[276] Two attempts have been made to solve the EU's 'democratic issue'; the first centred on the EP, the second on national parliaments.

The first of the attempts has been to increase the role of the directly elected EP in the legislative process. Indeed, the EP 'emerged as a winner in the Lisbon Treaty' as a result of the extension of the ordinary legislative procedure, whereby decisions are taken jointly by the EP and the Council, and the conferral of more control over the appointment of the President of the EU Commission.[277] Those claiming the second-order character of EP elections (a well-known claim of Reif and Schmitt is that EP elections have the character of a protest vote against governments in power and that the electoral turnout is lower each time) might also have softened their views after the 2014 EP elections.[278] The elections' outcomes[279] show that 'traditional left–right and pro-anti-European integration counter-balanced the traditional determination to punish national governments', proving some politicisation of these elections.[280]

The second attempt to strengthen the EU's democratic legitimacy was the reinforcement of the role of the national parliaments within the European legislative process. This approach was grounded in the diagnosis of a 'democratic disconnect' of the EU supranational institutions, limiting the EU's legitimacy. Contrary to the idea of the 'democratic deficit', which applies to the EU institutions per se, the 'disconnect' arises from the assertion that it is the national level that ultimately carries legitimacy for cultural and historical reasons, and without more involvement of national parliaments, the EU remains disconnected from this source of legitimacy.[281] As a consequence, democratisation efforts should focus on the linkages between EU institutions' producing norms and the democratically legitimised national level that oversees and controls them, in contrast to a 'democratic deficit'

[274] Weiler, 'The Transformation of Europe' (n 269) 2430.

[275] Besselink (n 273) 119.

[276] B de Witte, 'Community Law and National Constitutional Values' (1991) 18 *Legal Issues of European Integration* 1, 8.

[277] P Craig, *The Lisbon Treaty: Law, Politics, and Treaty Reform* (Oxford, Oxford University Press, 2010) 72.

[278] K Reif and H Schmitt, 'Nine Second-order National Elections—A Conceptual Framework for the Analysis of European Election Results' (1980) 8 *European Journal of Political Research* 3. *cf* A Follesdal and S Hix, 'Why there is a Democratic Deficit in the EU: A Response to Majone and Moravcsik' (2006) 44 *Journal of Common Market Studies* 533, 536.

[279] The 2014 turnout was 43.09% in comparison to 43% in 2009, hence it did not improve, but also did not fall. See further: www.results-elections2014.eu/en/turnout.html.

[280] See A Trechsel, 'The Nationalization and Europeanization of European Elections, 30 June 2014', available at: www.eui.eu/DepartmentsAndCentres/RobertSchumanCentre/Opinions/3006Trechsel. For a more critical view see JHH Weiler, 'Fateful Elections? Investing in the Future of Europe' (2014) 12 *International Journal of Constitutional Law* 273.

[281] P Lindseth, 'Delegation is Dead, Long Live Delegation: Managing the Democratic Disconnect in the European Market-Polity' in C Joerges and R Dehousse (eds), *Good Governance in Europe's Integrated Market* (Oxford, Oxford University Press, 2002) 151.

perspective that concentrates solely on the democratisation of EU institutions, independent from the national level.[282]

The core element in the process of reconnecting the EU with national parliaments was the EWS, and this avenue of reform, and not the changes in the position of the EP, will be the focus of this book. Declaration No 23, annexed to the Nice Treaty, first invited national parliaments to participate in the debate on the future of the EU. Next, the European Council, meeting in Laeken on 15 December 2001, adopted a Declaration on the Future of the European Union that pointed towards a new role for national parliaments.[283] Specifically, under the heading of 'better division and definition of competence in the European Union', the Declaration asked the question 'how is the principle of subsidiarity to be applied here?', also making sure that a new division of competences would not cause a 'creeping expansion of the competence of the Union' or encroach upon the exclusive competences of Member States or regions.[284] In the section on democracy, transparency and efficiency in the EU, the Declaration posed questions about the role of national parliaments, namely, whether they should be represented in a new institution and whether they should concentrate on the question of division of competences between the EU and the Member States. As an example of this function, the Declaration put forward an idea of a preliminary check concerning compliance with the subsidiarity principle.[285] To answer these and other questions, the European Council decided to convene the Convention on the Future of Europe.[286]

C. Alternative Proposals

The Convention set to deal with both the issue of 'competence creep' and the issue of the 'democratic deficit'. Following the indications of the Laeken Declaration, the Convention established two separate working groups, one dedicated to the subsidiarity principle (Working Group I) and one to the role of national parliaments (Working Group IV).

Working Group I discussed a number of institutional ideas for the protection of the subsidiarity principle. The 'political monitoring' possibilities studied by Working Group I included the creation of 'a Mr (or Ms) "subsidiarity" to assist each member of the European Council and the European Parliament, with verifying and giving a timely opinion on the compliance of proposals the principle of subsidiarity'.[287] At a later stage, a position of a 'Mr (or Ms) subsidiarity' within the Commission, or of a Vice-President of the Commission, ensuring the compliance of proposals with subsidiarity, was discussed.[288] In this case, it was decided, however, that every commissioner should be responsible for compliance with the subsidiarity principle in the areas under his or her competence, in addition to

[282] ibid.

[283] Laeken Declaration (n 267). For the critical appraisal of the post-Laeken reforms, see G Davies, 'The Post-Laeken Division of Competences' (2003) 28 *European Law Review* 686, 695.

[284] Laeken Declaration (n 267) 22.

[285] ibid 23.

[286] ibid 24.

[287] European Convention, Mandate of the Working Group on the principle of subsidiarity of 30.05.2002, CONV 71/02, 4.

[288] European Convention, Summary of the Meeting of 17.06.2002, CONV 106/02, 2.

the Commission's own competence to decide on its internal organisation.[289] Another option was the creation of an ad hoc institution consisting of national parliamentary representatives, a proposal which, however, at later stages of the debates, was perceived rather negatively.[290] The creation of an ad hoc body was ruled out as too cumbersome for the decision-making process.[291]

The 'legal monitoring' options included the creation of an ad hoc 'subsidiarity chamber' within the CJEU.[292] However, Working Group I concluded that the Court could take such an organisational measure itself.[293] Moreover, Working Group I also pondered establishing an ex ante judicial mechanism, between the adoption of the EU legislative act and its entry into force, inspired by provisions of the Member States for monitoring the constitutionality of laws.[294] In fact, the vision of creating a Constitutional Council for the Community as an equivalent to the French Conseil constitutionnel had been proposed much earlier. Such a constitutional council 'would have jurisdiction only over issues of competences (including subsidiarity) and would decide cases submitted to it after a law was adopted, but before coming into force'.[295] Their project put forward that any Community institution, Member State, or the majority of the EP could bring such an action. The Constitutional Council would consist of the President of the CJEU and members of Member States' constitutional courts. However, Working Group I abandoned the idea of a constitutional council, as in the view of the group, the introduction of a judicial review during the legislative phase would lead to the loss of the political nature of the subsidiarity review.[296] In addition, granting such powers was perceived as problematic, as the CJEU would control subsidiarity at a different stage from conferral or proportionality principles.[297]

None of the ideas above has been given a 'green light'. Both working groups concluded that national parliaments should be granted a competence to review the subsidiarity principle.[298] Working Group I offered three guidelines on the control of the subsidiarity principle. First, EU institutions should reinforce their scrutiny of the subsidiarity principle during the drafting and examination of proposals. Second, an 'early warning system', with a role for national parliaments, should be created. Third, an opportunity for ex-post referral to the CJEU on subsidiarity issues should be provided.[299] It was thus proposed, in agreement with Working Group IV, that national parliaments would be involved in the EU legislative procedure 'for the first time in the history of European construction' through a process of monitoring of the subsidiarity principle.[300] While putting all national parliaments on

[289] European Convention, Conclusions of Working Group I on the Principle of Subsidiarity, CONV 286/02, 5.

[290] European Convention, Summary of the Joint Meeting of 22.07.2002, CONV 210/02, 2.

[291] Conclusions of Working Group I on the Principle of Subsidiarity, CONV 286/02, 2.

[292] Mandate of the Working Group on the principle of subsidiarity, CONV 71/02, 5.

[293] Conclusions of Working Group I on the Principle of Subsidiarity, CONV 286/02, 8.

[294] ibid 9.

[295] JHH Weiler, UR Haltern and FC Mayer, 'European Democracy and its Critique' (1995) 18 *West European Politics* 4, 38.

[296] Conclusions of Working Group I on the Principle of Subsidiarity, CONV 286/02, 9.

[297] ibid. For criticism of the idea of subsidiarity monitoring between the moments of adoption and entry into force (in the manner of the French Conseil constitutionnel), see the opinion of AG Jacobs given to Working Group I: European Convention, Summary of the Meeting on 25.06.2002, CONV 156/02, 3–4.

[298] European Convention, Summary of the joint meeting on 22.07.2002, CONV 210/02, 1.

[299] Conclusions of Working Group I on the Principle of Subsidiarity, CONV 286/02, 3.

[300] ibid 5.

an 'equal footing', the system did not make the procedure more cumbersome and did not create any new bureaucracy.[301] Both the EWS and the possibility of bringing a subsidiarity action before the Court were seen as a 'process-based approach' in contrast to the creation of a new institution.[302] The enhanced involvement of national parliaments was seen as a way to strengthen the EU's democratic legitimacy and 'bring it closer to the citizens'.[303]

The EWS was finally introduced by the Lisbon Treaty after the failure of the Constitutional Treaty. The subsidiarity review places itself between the national level and the EU level, allowing national parliaments to contribute to the EU constitutional order, not confining their role to the national level, as in the case of scrutiny of the government in EU affairs, but broadening it to the EU arena. In this sense, the subsidiarity review also avoids identifying the democratic deficit in only one institution (eg, the Council) and transferring the decision-making to an alternative institution (eg, the EP). In contrast, improving only the national level as a point of reference could have been perceived as unsatisfactory, because the democratic deficit may also affect the Member States themselves (eg, as they often also do not fulfil the 'democratic and constitutional ideals of full representation and participation').[304]

For its purpose as a democratic safeguard, the subsidiarity review provides for an interaction between national parliaments and EU institutions, predominantly the Commission. The legislative act created in this process captures the involvement of the national and European polity. To tackle the 'competence creep' within the EU, the EWS offers checks on any tendency of the EU to take shared competences away from the Member States.

VII. CONCLUSION

This chapter set out to offer an analysis of the subsidiarity principle. This principle was provided already in the papal encyclical and in German federalism and liberalism. As a constitutional principle, subsidiarity was found first in German Basic Law. The study of subsidiarity in Switzerland and the US, as the question central to the organisation of federal systems, has shown that the degree to which other systems rely on that principle varies significantly. Nonetheless, subsidiarity was then taken as a role model by the EU legal order, first in the Maastricht Treaty and then in the Lisbon Treaty. The guidelines for the application of the subsidiarity principle established in the 'Overall Approach' and in the Amsterdam Protocol attempted to provide tangible contours to the 'national insufficiency' and the 'comparative efficiency' tests. In fact, they provide assistance in the enforcement of that principle for EU institutions and national parliaments alike. The most promising have, however, been the impact assessments and other tools of procedural subsidiarity. They offer help in avoiding the 'empty formulas' in the justification of compliance of EU legislative proposals and adopted acts with the subsidiarity principle. This chapter

[301] ibid 6.

[302] European Convention, Final Report of Working Group IV on the role of national parliaments, CONV 353/02, 11.

[303] ibid 2.

[304] M Poiares Maduro, 'Europe and the constitution: what if this is as good as it gets?' in JHH Weiler and M Wind (eds), *European Constitutionalism Beyond the State* (Cambridge, Cambridge University Press, 2003) 84.

has also discussed the relationship between this principle and the principles of conferral and proportionality. The structure of Article 5(3) TEU analysed here is important for the boundaries of the review of the subsidiarity principle by the national parliaments, discussed in detail in chapter three. Yet, before the focus of this book became national parliaments, this chapter offered a recap of the flaws in the subsidiarity case law of the Court already established in the relevant literature. Additionally, this chapter pointed out some new tendencies in the jurisprudence of the Court such as the focus on the cross-border elements of EU action and the reference to impact assessments. The 'subsidiarity action' enshrined in Protocol No 2 might offer a new source of subsidiarity case law in future. Nonetheless, as such, the subsidiarity jurisprudence of the Court, which is so often criticised for not taking subsidiarity seriously, did not seem to have changed substantially. This aspect, together with the problem of broadening the EU competence and the insufficient democratic legitimacy of the EU actions, in light of the lack of another suitable mechanism to answer to those critical points, led to the establishment of the EWS, to be discussed in detail in the next chapter.

2

The Involvement of National Parliaments and the EWS

I. INTRODUCTION

FIRST THE FAILED Constitutional Treaty and then the Lisbon Treaty granted national parliaments several new functions, above all elevating the national parliaments to the position of 'subsidiarity watchdogs'.[1] Protocol No 2 annexed to the Treaty on the European Union (TEU) and the Treaty on the Functioning of the European Union (TFEU) enshrines the Early Warning System (EWS), in which national parliaments may issue reasoned opinions concerning the compatibility of a Commission proposal with the principle of subsidiarity.

The question posed here sets the background for the forthcoming chapters: how is the EWS regulated in the Treaties? This chapter aims to discuss this question starting from an analysis of the treaty changes that granted national parliaments a position in European integration. In this respect, section II explores the relevant provisions of the Treaty of Maastricht, the Treaty of Amsterdam, the Constitutional Treaty, and the Treaty of Lisbon. In section III, this chapter discusses the design of the EWS reflecting first on the role assigned to national parliaments under this procedure and then reflects on the part of the EU legislature (the European Parliament (EP) and the Council) and of the Committee of the Regions in the subsidiarity scrutiny. At this point, the chapter then discusses the up-to-date application of the mechanism by national parliaments, taking into account the period from the entry into force of the Lisbon Treaty (1 December 2009) until the end of 2016. Because the EWS is not the only tool available to national parliaments to comment on draft EU acts, section IV explores the 'Barroso initiative'. Finally, section V aims to show that national parliaments do not operate in a vacuum. There are a number of ways they can exchange their views on subsidiarity and also establish broader interparliamentary cooperation.

II. THE GROWING ROLE OF NATIONAL PARLIAMENTS IN THE EU TREATIES

A. The Maastricht Treaty

The Maastricht Treaty was the first to offer formal recognition of national parliaments within primary law. The preceding national-level reforms[2] had gained attention at the

[1] I Cooper, 'The Watchdogs of Subsidiarity: National Parliaments and the Logic of Arguing in the EU' (2006) 44 *Journal of Common Market Studies* 281.

[2] See ch 4.

EU level, and this attention culminated in the inclusion of the first provisions concerning national parliaments in the Maastricht Treaty declarations: Declaration No 13 'on the role of national parliaments in the European Union' and Declaration No 14 'on the conference of the parliaments'.

Specifically, Declaration No 13 encouraged national parliaments to be more involved in the activities of the EU. To fulfil this aim, the declaration suggested an increased information exchange between the national parliaments and the EP. In addition, national governments were to ensure that their parliaments receive Commission draft legislative proposals in 'good time for information or possible examination'. Moreover, Declaration No 13 called upon national parliaments and the EP to arrange regular meetings between the parliamentarians interested in the same issues. Finally, Declaration No 14 encouraged members of the EP and of national parliaments to meet as the Conference of the Parliaments (*Assises*), consisting of members of the EP and members of national parliaments.

The Treaty of Maastricht was thus the first step towards including the national parliaments in the EU context. However, the innovations on their own were not of great legal importance, as the declarations did not have a binding character.

B. The Treaty of Amsterdam

Protocol 'on the role of national parliaments in the European Union' to the Amsterdam Treaty had similar aspirations as the Maastricht declarations. It aimed to encourage 'greater involvement' of national legislatures in EU affairs. In comparison to the Maastricht declarations, the Amsterdam Protocol on the Role of National Parliaments in the European Union declared as its aim the enhancement of the ability of national parliaments to share their views on EU matters of interest. First, to this end, Commission proposals were to be 'made available in good time' so that the governments can forward them to their parliaments.[3] Second, the Commission was to share with national parliaments a broader range of documents. The protocol added that all Commission consultation documents (green and white papers and communications) had to be forwarded 'promptly' to the national parliaments.[4] This obligation was incumbent upon the Commission.[5] The protocol further established a minimum period of six weeks between the point at which a legislative proposal is made available in all languages and the point at which it is placed on the Council agenda to be adopted, in order to grant national parliaments time to discuss it.[6] The second part of the protocol concerned the Conference of European Affairs Committees (COSAC).[7]

In the context of the subsidiarity review presented in the following sections, it is worth underlining that the second protocol, the Protocol 'on the application of the principles of subsidiarity and proportionality', did not mention the role of national parliaments at all.

[3] Para 2 of the Amsterdam Protocol on the Role of National Parliaments in the European Union.

[4] ibid, para 1.

[5] J O'Brennan and T Raunio, 'Introduction: deparliamentarization and European integration' in J O'Brennan and T Raunio (eds), *National Parliaments within the Enlarged European Union: from 'victims' of integration to competitive actors?* (London, Routledge, 2007) 13.

[6] Para 3 of the Amsterdam Protocol on the Role of National Parliaments in the European Union.

[7] See section V of this chapter.

National parliaments were not yet seen as partners, fit to discuss subsidiarity issues with EU institutions. However, in the provisions on COSAC, interestingly, we read that this institution was invited to approach the EP, the Council and the Commission on the legislative activities of the EU in relation to the application of the principle of subsidiarity.[8]

C. The Constitutional Treaty

The Constitutional Treaty was the first attempt to go beyond protocols and to prescribe a role for national parliaments in the Treaty itself.[9] First, the Treaty recognised the role of national parliaments via the principle of representative democracy. Within the decision-making process in the European Council and the Council, governments are themselves democratically accountable either to their national parliaments or to their citizens.[10] Second, the Treaty also provided for information rights for national parliaments, namely with regard to the flexibility clause,[11] participation in the evaluation mechanisms of EU policies and political monitoring of Europol and the evaluation of Eurojust's activities,[12] and in the ordinary[13] and the simplified revision procedures.[14] Finally, national parliaments were to be notified about incoming EU membership applications.[15]

The Constitutional Treaty also contained two protocols relevant to national parliaments: Protocol No 1 on the Role of National Parliaments in the European Union and Protocol No 2. Since their content is almost entirely the same as in the relevant Lisbon Treaty protocols, they are discussed in the following section.

D. The Treaty of Lisbon

Due to the collapse of the Treaty Establishing a Constitution for Europe, it was the Lisbon Treaty that finally introduced national parliaments into the Treaty as a 'new player in the institutional balance'.[16]

Whereas the Constitutional Treaty acknowledged the intermediary role of national parliaments in the principle of representative democracy, the Treaty of Lisbon lifted their position in the institutional framework of the EU itself. Article 12 TEU recognises national parliaments' active contribution to the good functioning of the EU.[17] This provision

[8] Para 6 of the Amsterdam Protocol on the Role of National Parliaments in the European Union.

[9] This might have a symbolic character because the parliaments were included in the Amsterdam Protocol and hence in the Treaty. In a formal sense, protocols have the same legal value as the treaties to which they are attached. See K Lenaerts and P Van Nuffel, *Constitutional Law of the European Union* (London, Sweet & Maxwell, 2011) 823.

[10] Art I-46(2) of the Treaty establishing a Constitution for Europe (Constitutional Treaty).

[11] ibid, Art I-18.

[12] ibid, Art I-42(2).

[13] ibid, Art IV-443(2).

[14] ibid, Art IV-444(3).

[15] ibid, Art I-58(2).

[16] Y Devuyst, 'The European Union's Institutional Balance after the Treaty of Lisbon: Community Method and Democratic Deficit Reassessed' (2007) 39 *Georgetown Journal of International Law* 247, 314.

[17] This provision was not foreseen in the Constitutional Treaty, and thus, for example, the obligation to forward legislative and non-legislative documents directly to national parliaments was foreseen only in Protocol No 1 to the Constitutional Treaty, in contrast to Art 12 TEU, which contains all the main functions of national parliaments.

enumerates the key functions of national parliaments. At the beginning, it refers to the rights of national parliaments indicated in Protocols No 1 and No 2: the right to receive all EU draft legislative acts directly from the EU institutions and the scrutiny of the subsidiarity principle.[18] Next, with regard to the Area of Freedom, Security and Justice, national parliaments gained information rights concerning the content and results of the evaluation of the implementation of EU policies in that area by Member States' authorities. In addition, national parliaments together with the EP may evaluate Eurojust's and Europol's activities.[19] Article 12 TEU mentions, moreover, the function of national parliaments in the revision procedure of the Treaties.[20] Finally, national parliaments are notified of applications for accession to the EU[21] and take part in the interparliamentary cooperation between national parliaments and the EP.[22] Outside Article 12 TEU, other important functions of national parliaments are included in Article 71 TFEU (information on the proceedings of the Council's standing committee on the operational cooperation on internal security), Article 81(3) TFEU (notification of planned applications of the special *passerelle* in the area of family law) and Article 352(2) TFEU (flexibility clause).

Protocols No 1 and No 2 contain detailed provisions concerning national parliaments. Specifically, Protocol No 1 'on the Role of National Parliaments in the EU' provides that the Commission keeps national parliaments abreast of its agenda: it directly forwards to national legislators, contemporaneously as to the EP and the Council, a number of non-legislative acts, such as the green and white papers and communications, its annual legislative programme, or any other instrument of legislative planning or policy.[23] Further, Protocol No 1 obliges the Commission and the EP to forward draft legislative initiatives directly to national parliaments at the same time as these are forwarded to the other institutions. Similarly, the Council forwards legislative drafts originating from a group of Member States, the Court of Justice, the European Central Bank, or the European Investment Bank.[24] In Article 3, Protocol No 1 foresees the subsidiarity review mechanism, the details of which are elaborated in Protocol No 2. Protocol No 1 also imposes an eight-week period between the submission of a translated draft legislative act to national parliaments and its being placed on the Council's agenda for the Council's adoption or for adoption of a position under a legislative procedure.[25] During this time, EU institutions cannot reach an agreement on the legislative proposal at stake. An exception to the eight-week period may occur in urgent, duly justified cases, but even then, in contrast to the Amsterdam Protocol, the Council may adopt such a proposal only 10 days after it was placed on the Council's agenda. Other information rights for national parliaments concern the agendas for, and the outcomes of, meetings of the Council (including its minutes),[26] the initiatives of the European Council on the planned *passerelles* (change from the unanimity to qualified majority in the

[18] Art 12(a) and (b) TEU.
[19] ibid, Art 12(c).
[20] ibid, Art 12(d).
[21] ibid, Art 12(e).
[22] ibid, Art 12(f).
[23] Art 1 of Protocol No 1 on the Role of National Parliaments in the European Union (Protocol No 1).
[24] ibid, Art 2.
[25] ibid, Art 4.
[26] ibid, Art 5.

Council or change from special to ordinary legislative procedure)[27] and the annual report of the Court of Auditors.[28] Finally, Protocol No 1 provides for interparliamentary cooperation, which is elaborated upon in section V of this chapter.[29]

At this juncture, the competences of national parliaments under Protocol No 2 are omitted and discussed in the following part on the subsidiarity review.

III. THE DESIGN OF THE EWS

A. The Competences of National Parliaments Under Protocol No 2

The second subparagraph of Article 5(3) TEU states that

> [t]he institutions of the Union shall apply the principle of subsidiarity as laid down in the Protocol on the application of the principles of subsidiarity and proportionality. National Parliaments ensure compliance with the principle of subsidiarity in accordance with the procedure set out in that Protocol.

The EWS procedure to which Article 5(3) TEU refers is established in Protocol No 2, and its design is the following.

On the basis of Articles 4 and 5 of Protocol No 2, the Commission, the EP and the Council shall forward draft legislative acts to national parliaments providing a justification regarding the principle of subsidiarity and proportionality for each proposal, including a detailed statement to enable the appraisal of compliance with these principles. Article 3 of Protocol No 2 provides that for the purposes of Protocol No 2, draft legislative acts are understood as proposals from the Commission, initiatives from a group of Member States, initiatives from the EP, requests from the Court of Justice, recommendations from the European Central Bank, and requests from the European Investment Bank for the adoption of a legislative act.

Article 6 of Protocol No 2 grants national parliaments eight weeks from the date of transmission of a draft legislative act to submit a reasoned opinion to the presidents of the EP, the Council and the Commission explaining why the draft is not in compliance with the principle of subsidiarity. The institution from which the draft originates should 'take account' of the reasoned opinions received. If, however, the number of reasoned opinions exceeds certain thresholds, Article 7 of Protocol No 2 foresees that one of two special procedures will be triggered.[30]

First, in the procedure labelled as the 'yellow card',[31] if the reasoned opinions issued by national parliaments are equal to at least one-third of all the votes allocated to national parliaments, the draft must be reviewed.[32] For the proposals in the area of freedom, security

[27] ibid, Art 6.

[28] ibid, Art 7.

[29] ibid, Arts 9 and 10.

[30] Reasoned opinions count as votes. Protocol No 2 assigns two votes for each national parliament: in Member States with a bicameral parliament, each of the two chambers shall have one vote.

[31] The notion of a 'yellow card' comes from football jargon. See J-V Louis, 'The Lisbon Treaty: The Irish "No": National Parliaments and the Principle of Subsidiarity–Legal Options and Practical Limits' (2008) 4 *European Constitutional Law Review* 429, 438. In football, the referee sanctions with a 'yellow card' a player of one team who has fouled a player of another team.

[32] In the EU of 28 Member States (56 votes in total) the necessary vote threshold is 19 votes.

and justice, the respective threshold is one-quarter of the votes of national parliaments.[33] Subsequently, the initiating institution may decide to maintain, amend, or withdraw the draft, giving reasons for its decision.[34]

Second, in the procedure commonly referred to as the 'orange card',[35] if the reasoned opinions against a proposal within the ordinary legislative procedure represent at least the simple majority of votes assigned to national parliaments, the Commission must review the draft legislative act.[36] Accordingly, the Commission may decide to maintain, amend, or withdraw the draft. If it decides to maintain the draft, the Commission should provide a reasoned opinion on the compliance of the draft with the subsidiarity principle.[37] This reasoned opinion of the Commission, together with the reasoned opinions of the national parliaments, is forwarded to the EU legislator (namely, the Council and the EP), which has the final word. The EU legislator should consider these opinions, and if a majority of 55 per cent of the votes in the Council or a majority of the votes cast in the EP is of the opinion that the proposal is contrary to the principle of subsidiarity, the legislative procedure is halted.

To operationalise the subsidiarity review, the Commission itself proposed several arrangements that 'ensure the smooth operation of the mechanism'.[38] Accordingly, the Commission gave national parliaments the possibility of deciding on the language in which they wish to receive legal drafts. This also means that the Commission sends proposals at different times, depending on when the translation is ready. To standardise the different moments of receipt, the Commission arranged to send a *lettre de saisine* (transmission letter) after the final language translation, a procedure which sets an identical deadline for all the national parliaments to submit a reasoned opinion.[39] In practice, it means that some parliaments have more time than others to study the legislative proposals. Moreover, the Commission obliged itself not to count August within the eight-week deadline, as it is the usual parliamentary recess month. With regard to the scope of reasoned opinions, the Commission urged national parliaments to distinguish in their opinions between the indications of subsidiarity violations and other critical comments on the draft legislative acts. This differentiation is necessary, in the view of the Commission, as 'the subsidiarity review will be applied alongside the political dialogue'.[40] Further, on the counting of national parliaments' submissions, the Commission committed itself to count all the different aspects of subsidiarity violations expressed in the reasoned opinions of national parliaments towards the thresholds of Protocol No 2. If the threshold is met within eight weeks, the Commission will issue an assessment of the criticised proposal. Most interestingly, the Commission

[33] The necessary vote threshold is at least 14 votes.

[34] Art 7(2) of Protocol No 2.

[35] The 'orange card', which was not mentioned in the Constitutional Treaty but agreed to in the Brussels European Council of June 2007, owes its name to the Dutch origin of this complementary mechanism. Louis (n 31) 438.

[36] Twenty-nine votes are needed to trigger the 'orange card'.

[37] Art 7(3) of Protocol No 2.

[38] Letter from President Barroso and Vice-President Wallström of 1 December 2009: Practical arrangements for the operation of the subsidiarity control mechanism under Protocol No 2 of the Treaty of Lisbon.

[39] On time frame, see P Kiiver, *The Early Warning System for the Principle of Subsidiarity: Constitutional Theory and Empirical Reality* (London, Routledge, 2012) 34–40.

[40] Letter from President Barroso and Vice-President Wallström (n 38) 4. On the political dialogue see section IV of this chapter.

expressed a commitment to reply to national parliaments' opinions that did not meet the threshold or that arrived after the deadline. This approach clearly goes beyond the wording of Article 7(1) of Protocol No 2, which prescribes that the Commission (or other institution from which the draft originates) 'shall *take account* of the reasoned opinions issued by national parliaments or by a chamber of a national parliament' (emphasis added). The commitment to reply to opinions that did not meet the threshold or that arrived after the deadline effectively implies a reply to every reasoned opinion of a national parliament.

Finally, the Commission highlighted that it will not submit modified proposals for another assessment of their compatibility with the subsidiarity principle.

Some critical points raised in the scholarship concern the effects of the procedure. At the stage when parliaments are supposed to send reasoned opinions, the Commission has already decided upon the compatibility of its proposals with subsidiarity.[41] Moreover, national parliaments may always direct complaints to the initiator of EU legislation, even without the EWS, as, if they are willing to do so, EU institutions can always take into account the arguments raised by national parliaments.[42] Finally, the fact that national parliaments could not stop the legislative act from being adopted, a 'red card', is seen as a major weakness.[43]

Other criticised issues concern the procedural aspects of the EWS. For example, national parliaments may assess the subsidiarity of legislative acts only. This is considered as limiting the effectiveness and function of the EWS.[44]

The essential procedural challenge is, however, the eight-week deadline to submit a reasoned opinion, as seen by scholars[45] and, more importantly, by national parliaments themselves. Replying to one of the COSAC's questionnaires, some parliaments suggested a 12-week period instead, or a compromise solution could be a 10-week period in the case of legislative proposals that bear significant economic or social importance and require more in-depth analysis.[46] In the view of national parliaments, a prolonged deadline would significantly slow down the EU legislative procedure (given its usual duration), but would also enable a thorough subsidiarity scrutiny, improvement in the quality of the reasoned opinions, and the possibility to examine more proposals, and it would facilitate interparliamentary cooperation.[47] Moreover, national parliaments suggested that some periods such as mid-December to New Year's Day, a recess in EU institutions, or a recess in national parliaments should be excluded from the eight-week deadline.[48]

[41] B Schima, 'Die Subsidiaritatskontrolle durch die nationalen Parlamente nach dem vertrag von Lissabon' (2013) 68 *Zeitschrift für öffentliches Recht* 373.

[42] See P Kiiver, 'European Treaty Reform and the National Parliaments: Towards a New Assessment of Parliament-Friendly Treaty Provisions' in J Wouters, L Verhey and P Kiiver (eds), *European Constitutionalism beyond Lisbon* (Antwerp, Intersentia, 2009) 141.

[43] I Cooper, 'A "Virtual Third Chamber' for the European Union? National Parliaments after the Treaty of Lisbon' (2012) 35 *West European Politics* 441, 450.

[44] X Groussot and S Bogojević, 'Subsidiarity as a Procedural Safeguard of Federalism' in L Azoulai (ed), *The Question of Competence in the European Union* (Oxford, Oxford University Press, 2014) 238.

[45] See, eg, Damian Chalmers' evidence to the House of Lords. European Union Committee, *10th Report of Session 2007–08, 'The Treaty of Lisbon: an impact assessment', Volume I: Report* (HL 62-I) 243; Cooper, 'A "Virtual Third Chamber" for the European Union? (n 43) 449.

[46] COSAC, 19th Bi-annual Report on EU Practices and Procedures (May 2013) 28.

[47] ibid.

[48] COSAC, 24th Bi-annual Report on EU Practices and Procedures (4 November 2015) 22–23.

B. The Subsidiarity Review from the Perspective of EU Institutions

In order to give a full overview of the design of the subsidiarity review, the role played by EU institutions also needs to be explored.

i. The European Parliament

The EP comes into play in the subsidiarity review mechanism if the national parliaments trigger an 'orange card'. In this case, the EP should reflect on whether the proposal raises subsidiarity issues by taking 'particular account of' the reasoned opinions of national parliaments and the reasoned opinion of the Commission.[49] If the EP, by the majority of its votes cast before the end of first reading, finds that the proposal is not compatible with the principle of subsidiarity, the process will result in a rejection of the legislative proposal.[50] If the majority of the votes are cast under the 'orange card', this does not make it easier for the EP to dismiss a Commission proposal, as the same majority (a simple majority) is needed in the first reading during the ordinary legislative procedure in order to adopt its position (Article 294(3) TFEU).[51] However, the phrase used in Article 7 of Protocol No 2 'before concluding the first reading' seems to mean that the vote on the compatibility of the proposal will take place separately, or at least before, the EP votes on the first reading.

Moreover, the possibility of stopping the analysis of the draft legislative act offered by Protocol No 2 may help the EP dismiss before the end of the first reading Commission legislative drafts that are unwanted for reasons other than subsidiarity. However, this outcome will depend upon how the EP formulates its objections against the act and if it reaches beyond the strict assessment of subsidiarity. Furthermore, for the Parliament, 'it is not the veto that is important, but the shadow of the veto' helping to state its preferences before other institutions more clearly.[52]

The internal procedures concerning reasoned opinions are the following. The reasoned opinions that national parliaments send to the President of the EP are referred to the committee responsible for the subject matter and forwarded for information to the committee responsible for respect of the principle of subsidiarity, the Committee on Legal Affairs.[53] The Committee on Legal Affairs appoints a 'standing rapporteur' for a six-month period to monitor the reasoned opinions received and to bring up the issues from those opinions in the committee debate or make recommendations to other committees in question.[54] If the reasoned opinions of national parliaments meet the 'yellow card' threshold, the EP has to wait for the decision of the sponsor of the criticised proposal.[55] In the case of an 'orange

[49] Art 7(3)(a) of Protocol No 2.

[50] ibid, Art 7(3)(b).

[51] Against see G Barrett, '"The King is Dead, Long Live the King": The Recasting by the Treaty of Lisbon of the Provisions of the Constitutional Treaty Concerning National Parliaments' (2008) 33 *European Law Review* 66, 81.

[52] J Ziller, 'French Reactions to the Treaty Establishing a Constitution for Europe: from Constitutional Welcome to Popular Rejection' in A Albi and J Ziller (eds), *European Constitution and National Constitutions: Ratification and Beyond* (The Hague, Kluwer Law International, 2007) 106.

[53] Rule 42(4) of EP Rules of Procedure. It is worth noting that the EP, as the only EU institution, translates all reasoned opinions from national parliaments into other EU languages. See at: www.europarl.europa.eu/relnatparl/en/about/subsidiarity.html.

[54] 'Report from the Commission on subsidiarity and proportionality' COM(2015) 315 final, 6.

[55] Rule 42(5) of EP Rules of Procedure.

card', the relevant subject matter committee, after pondering the reasoned opinions of the national parliaments and of the Commission and hearing the views of the Committee on Legal Affairs, may advise the EP to reject the proposal on the grounds of a subsidiarity violation or recommend amendments to the EP with respect to the principle of subsidiarity.[56] The Committee on Legal Affairs issues an opinion on the recommendation that is then annexed to the recommendation.[57] Next, the EP debates and votes on the recommendation.[58] The legislative procedure is closed if the EP approves the recommendation to reject the proposal by the majority of the votes cast. If the EP does not reject the proposal, the legislative procedure continues, taking on board any of the approved EP recommendations.

The parliamentary questions for written answers present another avenue for MEPs to intervene where national parliaments signalled a subsidiarity violation but did not manage to trigger an 'orange card'.[59] Whereas in some cases MEPs asked the Commission about the review of the subsidiarity principle, especially its outcomes and assessment in general terms,[60] some questions concerned specific proposals for which a national parliament issued a reasoned opinion.[61] For example, a French MEP underlined that with regard to the Commission proposal on roadworthiness tests, the French Parliament has issued a reasoned opinion outlining a violation of the subsidiarity principle and drafted a report on the lack of adequate subsidiarity justifications in the Commission's proposals.[62] The French MEP thus asked the Commission if it would take into account the concerns of the French Sénat.[63] In its reply, the Commission highlighted that the compatibility of proposals with the subsidiarity principle is an 'important subject, which is always thoroughly considered when proposing legislative initiatives' and relied on its Policy Orientations on Road Safety 2011–2020 and impact assessment to justify its proposal.[64]

The EP in the form of an own-motion report issues replies to the Commission's annual reports on subsidiarity and proportionality.[65] The EP's reports take note of the participation

[56] ibid, Rule 42(6).

[57] ibid.

[58] ibid.

[59] Rule 130 of EP Rules of Procedure.

[60] See, eg, question of MEP RJ Atondo of 29.09.2010, E-7782/2010, OJ C 243 E, 20.08.2011; question of MEP J Steinruck of 04.01.2011, E-011171/2010, OJ C 279 E, 23.09.2011; question of MEP J Ferreira of 22.02.2012, E-002099/2012, OJ C 110 E, 17.04.2013; question of MEP M Theurer of 30.05.2013, E-006119-13, OJ C 46 E, 18.02.2014; question of MEP C Davies of 20.01.2014, E-000459-14, OJ C 284, 26.08.2014.

[61] See, eg, question of MEP D Vlasto of 13.10.2011 on the respect for the subsidiarity principle as regards VAT on equestrian activities (concerns reasoned opinion of the French Senate), E-009190/2011, and the Commission reply of 28.11.2011, both in OJ C 154 E, 31.05.2012; question of MEPs L Fontana and M Salvini of 19.02.2013 on the violation of the subsidiarity and proportionality by the proposal for a directive on tobacco products (concerns reasoned opinion of the Italian Senate), E-001742-13, and the Commission reply of 04.04.2013, both in OJ C 371 E, 18.12.2013; question of MEP P van der Kammen of 23.09.2013 on the Commission proposal on the maritime spatial planning and integrated coastal management (concerns reasoned opinions of the parliaments of Poland, Sweden, Germany, Ireland, Romania, Belgium, Finland, Lithuania and the Netherlands), E-010797-13, and the Commission reply of 25.11.2013, both in OJ C206, 02.07.2014; question of MEP A Zijlstra of 06.02.2014 on the EPPO proposal (14 reasoned opinions), E-001249-14, and the Commission reply of 29.04.2014, both in OJ C 305, 09.09.2014.

[62] Question of MEP R Dati of 30.10.2012 on the Commission proposal for roadworthiness tests, E-009914-12, OJ C 310 E, 25.10.2013.

[63] ibid.

[64] Commission reply of 21.01.2013, E-009914/2012.

[65] Rules 52 and 132 of the EP Rules of Procedure.

in the EWS by national parliaments and state the problems encountered by the legislatures, urging the Commission to improve the subsidiarity justification of its proposals.[66] The EP has also expressed disappointment at the Commission's response in cases in which a 'yellow card' was triggered, pressing the Commission to reach out to individual national parliaments and explain its decision directly before the relevant parliamentary committees.[67] The EP also suggested that some aspects of the EWS, for example, the applicable thresholds to trigger the 'cards' or the extension of the deadline to submit a reasoned opinion, could be addressed in a possible future treaty revision.[68] Finally, the EP stressed the importance of interparliamentary cooperation to enhance the role of national parliaments in the EU legislative process.[69]

Protocol No 2 foresees also that the EP forwards its legislative act proposals and their amended drafts to national parliaments.[70] In practice, the EP's proposed reform of EU electoral law based on Article 223 TFEU has received a number of reasoned opinions.[71]

ii. The Council

From the perspective of the EWS, the most prominent of the Council's roles is in the 'orange card'. The legislative procedure stops if a majority of 55 per cent of the members of the Council is of the opinion that the proposal violates the subsidiarity principle.[72] In principle, since 1 November 2014, the Council acts by a qualified majority defined by 55 per cent of the members of the Council (but not less than 15 members) and representing Member States comprising at least 65 per cent of the population of the EU, while the blocking minority must include at least four Council members.[73] The 'orange card' procedure drops the representation requirement, which seems to strengthen the parliaments from less-populated Member States.[74] The reason behind this might be that the orange card demands at least a majority of the votes of the national parliaments, and given that the Council members would probably follow their parliaments—obviously depending on national systems—it should not be made harder for the Council to state subsidiarity violation.[75]

Other functions of the Council vis-a-vis national parliaments include forwarding to national parliaments draft legislative acts and their amended drafts originating from a group of Member States, the Court of Justice, the European Central Bank, or the European

[66] European Parliament, Resolution of 13 September 2012 on the 18th report on Better legislation—Application of the principles of subsidiarity and proportionality (2010), OJ C 353 E, 03.12.2013, 117, points 6–10 and 16.

[67] European Parliament, Resolution of 12 April 2016 on the Annual reports 2012–2013 on subsidiarity and proportionality, P8_TA(2016)0103, point 19.

[68] European Parliament, Report on the Annual Report 2014 on subsidiarity and proportionality, 29.03.2017, points 12 and 15.

[69] ibid, points 18–20.

[70] Art 4 of Protocol No 2.

[71] European Parliament, Resolution of 11 November 2015 on the reform of the electoral law of the European Union, PE/2015/2035. Six reasoned opinions were issued.

[72] Art 7(3)(b) of Protocol No 2.

[73] Art 16(3) and (4) TEU. Since 1 April 2017, Member States can no longer request the application of qualified majority as defined under the rules in the Nice Treaty. See Art 16(5) TEU.

[74] C Bickenbach, 'Das Subsidiaritätsprinzip in Art 5 EUV und seine Kontrolle' [2013] *Zeitschrift Europarecht* 523, 532.

[75] See, however, ch 5, on the difference in subsidiarity assessment between government and its parliament.

Investment Bank.[76] If a national parliament issues an opinion on any of those proposals, the president of the Council forwards it to the institution concerned or, in the case of proposals from a group of Member States, to the governments of the Member States.[77]

Finally, during the legislative procedure, the Council's Committee of Permanent Representatives (COREPER) reviews the EU's policies and actions and checks if the principles of legality, subsidiarity, proportionality, and providing reasons for acts are observed.[78]

iii. The Committee of the Regions

One of the novelties in the text of Article 5(3) TEU is that it distinguishes between the different levels of Member State action—central, regional and local—in comparison to the previous formulation of this provision, one which referred the Member States in general terms. Moreover, Article 6(1) of Protocol No 2 provides that in the EWS, national parliaments may consult, where appropriate, regional parliaments with legislative powers. Further, Article 8 of Protocol No 2 provides for the role of the Committee of the Regions in the subsidiarity review. Finally, the Committee of the Regions has a 'semi-privileged' standing against legislative acts in cases where the TFEU provides for consultation with the Committee.[79]

These regions-friendly provisions, first foreseen in the Constitutional Treaty, did not lead to establishing a formal institutional monitoring role for subnational actors.[80] In addition, the role of the Committee of the Regions is limited: it lacks legislative powers and consists of a mixture of members representing both politically 'strong' and 'weak' regions, undermining its political and representative function.[81] In direct connection to the EWS, the Committee of the Regions lacks the possibility of raising a 'yellow card' or 'orange card'. Still, the Committee of the Regions contributes to the subsidiarity monitoring of EU legislative proposals. It issues opinions on draft legislative acts with an assessment of the compliance with the principles of subsidiarity and proportionality.[82] In 2013, on the basis of the European Commission Work Programme, the Committee of the Regions published

[76] Art 4 of Protocol No 2.

[77] ibid, Art 6.

[78] Art 19(1)(a) Rules of Procedure of the Council.

[79] S Weatherill, 'Finding a Role for the Regions in Checking the EU's Competence' in S Weatherill and U Bernitz (eds), *The Role of Regions and Sub-National Actors in Europe* (Oxford, Hart Publishing, 2005) 151.

[80] ibid 150.

[81] A Cygan, 'Regional Governance, Subsidiarity and Accountability within the EU's Multi-Level Polity' (2013) 19 *European Public Law* 161, 167. See also D Fromage, 'Regional Parliaments and the Early Warning System: An Assessment and Some Suggestions for Reform' in A Jonsson Cornell and M Goldoni (eds), *National and Regional Parliaments in the EU-Legislative Procedure Post-Lisbon: The Impact of the Early Warning Mechanism* (Oxford, Hart Publishing, 2017) 130; G Vara Arribas and A-L Högenauer, 'Legislative Regions after Lisbon: A New Role for Regional Assemblies?' in C Hefftler et al (eds), *The Palgrave Handbook on National Parliaments and the European Union* (Basingstoke, Palgrave Macmillan, 2015) 145.

[82] Rule 55 of Committee of the Regions Rules of Procedure [2014] OJ L65/41. In practice, the CoR adopted 64 opinions in 2010 (Subsidiarity Annual Report 2010 at 6); 62 opinions in 2011 (Subsidiarity Annual Report at 14); 71 opinions in 2012 (Subsidiarity Annual Report 2012 at 8); 72 opinions in 2013 (Subsidiarity Annual Report 2013 at 9); 57 opinions in 2014 (Subsidiarity Annual Report 2014 at 9); 46 opinions in 2015 (Subsidiarity Annual Report 2015 at 6). All reports are available at: portal.cor.europa.eu/subsidiarity/Publications/Pages/Publicationsandstudies-.aspx> (accessed 7 October 2017).

its first Subsidiarity Work Programme, which selects legislative proposals with potential subsidiarity issues ('priority initiatives').[83] The selected proposals fulfil criteria such as political interest for local and regional authorities, raising concern for the competences of those authorities and a potential subsidiarity question.[84] The Committee of the Regions continued choosing such draft legislative acts, usually four or five per year, in the following years.[85]

Moreover, by 2007, the Committee of the Regions had begun operating a Subsidiarity Monitoring Network (SMN), an internet platform for the exchange of information between local and regional authorities within the EU and the EU institutions concerning documents and legislative and political proposals from the Commission.[86] Network partners (parliaments and governments of regions with legislative powers; local and regional authorities without legislative powers; local government associations; some national parliaments; and the national delegations to the Committee of the Regions)[87] may submit their subsidiarity and proportionality assessments of EU legislative proposals in 'open consultations'. These consultations concern all political or legislative documents that are the subject of a Committee of the Regions opinion.[88] Another venue is 'targeted consultations', for which the Committee of the Regions' rapporteur on a specific EU act invites the network partners to comment on subsidiarity and proportionality.[89] In 2012, the SMN launched a sub-network, REGPEX.[90] This network has a more exclusive character compared with the SMN as it provides a database for only those governments and parliaments of regions that have legislative powers.[91] The REGPEX partners submit opinions on EU draft legislative acts and exchange information with their counterparts.[92] The REGPEX contributions on a specific legislative proposal submitted within the eight-week deadline are translated, summarised and sent to the Commission.[93]

C. The Application of the EWS

The Commission's annual reports on the application of Article 5 TEU[94] are an unfailing source of data on the increase in the number of reasoned opinions; the spread of reasoned opinions; and the most and least active parliaments in the EWS. Those issues will be analysed in turn.

[83] Subsidiarity Work Programme for 2013, 1.

[84] ibid.

[85] See Subsidiarity Work Programmes for 2014, 2015 and 2016 available at: portal.cor.europa.eu/subsidiarity/activities/Pages/default.aspx.

[86] See: portal.cor.europa.eu/subsidiarity/thesmn/Pages/default.aspx.

[87] One hundred and fifty-five partners as of 1 May 2017: portal.cor.europa.eu/subsidiarity/thesmn/Pages/The-SMN-Partners.aspx.

[88] See: portal.cor.europa.eu/subsidiarity/Activities/Pages/Openconsultations.aspx.

[89] See: portal.cor.europa.eu/subsidiarity/activities/Pages/Targetedconsultations.aspx.

[90] Committee of the Regions, Subsidiarity Annual Report 2012, 5. See at: portal.cor.europa.eu/subsidiarity/regpex/pages/default.aspx.

[91] Seventy-seven partners as of 1 May 2017. See at: portal.cor.europa.eu/subsidiarity/regpex/Pages/partners.aspx.

[92] Committee of the Regions, Subsidiarity Annual Report 2012, 5–6.

[93] Committee of the Regions, Subsidiarity Annual Report 2015, 10.

[94] Art 9 of Protocol No 2.

The first conclusion that can be drawn from the Commission reports is that the number of reasoned opinions is increasing every year. While the beginnings were quite modest—in 2010, national parliaments issued 34 reasoned opinions[95]—in the following years, the numbers increased. In 2011, the national parliaments issued 64 reasoned opinions;[96] in 2012, 70;[97] and in 2013, 88.[98] The Commission noted a decrease in the number of reasoned opinions to 21 in 2014, justified by the decrease in the number of the legislative proposals in the last year of its office.[99] The number of received reasoned opinions fell to eight in 2015.[100] This number can be explained by a low number of legislative proposals.[101] In 2016, after two critical years, the EWS saw some revival, and 65 reasoned opinions were issued.[102] This sets the total number of reasoned opinions received by the Commission by 31 December 2016 at 350.[103] The 'yellow card' threshold was reached on three occasions thus far: in 2012, concerning the Commission proposal on the right to strike; in 2013, concerning the Commission proposal on the establishment of the European Public Prosecutor's Office; and in 2016, on the proposed amendments to the directive on the posting of workers in the framework of the provision of services.[104]

Second, the reports also show that the reasoned opinions spread unequally vis-a-vis Commission proposals; many Commission proposals receive a single reasoned opinion. However, each year there was a group of proposals that received a significant number of opinions, though not enough to trigger a 'yellow card'. For example, the most commented on proposals in 2010[105] were the Seasonal Workers Directive,[106] the Deposit Guarantee Schemes Directive,[107] and the provisions on food distribution to the most deprived

[95] 'Report from the Commission on subsidiarity and proportionality' COM(2011) 344 final, 4. The Commission generously included four reasoned opinions that arrived after the deadline or were not adopted by the chambers in accordance with their internal rules. Only for the 2012 data did the Commission state that the total number of reasoned opinions does not include those that transgressed the eight-week deadline or did not clearly state a subsidiarity breach. See Annex 1 to COM(2011) 345 and Annex 1 to COM(2013) 566.

[96] Report from the Commission on subsidiarity and proportionality, COM(2012) 373 final, 4.

[97] 'Report from the Commission on subsidiarity and proportionality' COM(2013) 566 final, 3.

[98] 'Report from the Commission on subsidiarity and proportionality' COM(2014) 506 final, 4.

[99] COM(2015) 315 final, 4.

[100] 'Report from the Commission on subsidiarity and proportionality' COM(2016) 469 final, 7.

[101] 'Communication from the Commission to the European Parliament, the European Council and the Council, Better Regulation: Delivering better results for a stronger Union' COM(2016) 615 final, 2.

[102] Annex 1 to the Report from the Commission, 'Annual Report 2016 on Subsidiarity and Proportionality' COM(2017) 600, 10.

[103] Additionally, based on data available on IPEX 29 reasoned opinions were issued in 2017 on Commission proposals with document number COM(2016).

[104] See F Fabbrini and K Granat, 'Yellow card, but no foul: The role of the national parliaments under the subsidiarity protocol and the Commission proposal for an EU regulation on the right to strike' (2013) 50 *Common Market Law Review* 115; I Wieczorek, 'The EPPO Draft Regulation Passes the First Subsidiarity Test: An Analysis and Interpretation of the European Commission's Hasty Approach to National Parliaments' Subsidiarity Arguments' (2015) 16 *German Law Journal* 1247; D Fromage, 'The Second Yellow Card on the EPPO Proposal: An Encouraging Development for Member State Parliaments?' (2016) 35 *Yearbook of European Law* 5; N Lupo, 'Il terzo "cartellino giallo" e i multiformi usi dell'early warning system' [2016] *Quaderni Constituzionali* 571; D Fromage and V Kreilinger, 'National Parliaments' Third Yellow Card and the Struggle over the Revision of the Posted Workers Directive' (2017) 10 *European Journal of Legal Studies* 125. See also ch 3.

[105] COM(2011) 344 final, 11.

[106] 'Proposal for a Directive of the European Parliament and of the Council on the conditions of entry and residence of third-country nationals for the purposes of seasonal employment' COM(2010) 379 final.

[107] 'Proposal for a Directive of the European Parliament and of the Council on Deposit Guarantee Schemes' COM(2010) 368 final.

persons in the Union.[108] In 2011, national parliaments issued the greatest number of reasoned opinions (nine) with regard to the proposals for the Common Consolidated Corporate Tax Base (CCCTB),[109] the temporary reintroduction of border control at internal borders in exceptional circumstances[110] (six reasoned opinions), and the Common European Sales Law[111] (five reasoned opinions).[112] In 2012, five reasoned opinions were issued on the Commission proposal[113] on the Fund for Aid to the Most Deprived.[114] In 2013, the draft directive establishing a framework for maritime spatial planning and integrated coastal management received nine reasoned opinions;[115] while the new Tobacco Products Directive[116] and the draft regulation on market access to port services and financial transparency[117] triggered seven each.[118] In 2014, the revision of waste legislation[119] and the proposed directive on the EU legal framework for customs infringement and sanctions[120] received the highest number at three reasoned opinions each.[121] Five reasoned opinions were offered in 2015 on the proposal for a relocation mechanism[122] in the context of the refugee crisis.[123] Finally, in 2016[124] national parliaments issued eight reasoned opinions to the Commission proposals

[108] 'Amended proposal for a Regulation of the European Parliament and the Council amending Council Regulations (EC) No 1290/2005 and (EC) No 1234/2007, as regards distribution of food products to the most deprived persons in the Union' COM(2010) 486 final.

[109] 'Proposal for a Council Directive on a Common Consolidated Corporate Tax Base (CCCTB)' COM(2011) 121 final.

[110] 'Proposal for a Regulation of the European Parliament and the Council amending Regulation (EC) No 562/2006 in order to provide for common rules on the temporary reintroduction of border control at internal borders in exceptional circumstances' COM(2011) 560 final.

[111] 'Proposal for a Regulation of the European Parliament and the Council on a Common European Sales Law' COM(2011) 635 final.

[112] Report From the Commission, 'Annual Report 2011 on Relations between the European Commission and National Parliaments' COM(2012) 375 final.

[113] 'Proposal for a Regulation of the European Parliament and the Council on the Fund for European Aid to the Most Deprived' COM(2012) 617 final.

[114] COM(2013) 566 final.

[115] 'Proposal for a Directive of the European Parliament and of the Council establishing a framework for maritime spatial planning and integrated coastal management' COM(2013) 133 final.

[116] 'Proposal for a Directive of the European Parliament and of the Council on the approximation of the laws, regulations and administrative provisions of the Member States concerning the manufacture, presentation and sale of tobacco and related products' COM(2012) 788 final.

[117] 'Proposal for a Regulation of the European Parliament and the Council establishing a framework on market access to port services and financial transparency of ports' COM(2013) 296 final.

[118] COM(2014) 506.

[119] 'Proposal for a Directive of the European Parliament and of the Council amending Directives 2008/98/EC on waste, 94/62/EC on packaging and packaging waste, 1999/31/EC on the landfill of waste, 2000/53/EC on end-of-life vehicles, 2006/66/EC on batteries and accumulators and waste batteries and accumulators, and 2012/19/EU on waste electrical and electronic equipment' COM(2014) 397 final.

[120] 'Proposal for a Directive of the European Parliament and of the Council on the Union legal framework for customs infringements and sanctions' COM(2013) 884 final.

[121] COM(2015) 315 final.

[122] 'Annex to the Regulation of the European Parliament and of the Council establishing a crisis relocation mechanism and amending Regulation (EU) No 604/2013 of the European Parliament and of the Council of 26 June 2013 establishing the criteria and mechanisms for determining the Member State responsible for examining an application for international protection lodged in one of the Member States by a third country national or a stateless person' COM(2015) 450 final.

[123] Annex to COM(2016) 469.

[124] Annex 1 to COM(2017) 600.

regarding corporate taxation[125] and mechanisms for an allocation of applicants claiming international protection in the EU.[126]

Third, the most active parliament throughout 2010–16 was the Swedish Riksdag, which issued a total of 57 reasoned opinions in six years, with a record 20 reasoned opinions in 2012. Other particularly active legislatures included the Polish (27), the British (25), the Dutch (26) and the French parliaments (23). The Austrian Parliament also issued a high number of reasoned opinions with 22; however, it was always the Bundesrats that dominated in the EWS, with 19 reasoned opinions.

These data show that national parliaments are active participants in the EWS. The three 'yellow cards' that have been triggered might have come as a surprise since some believed that the 'yellow card' and 'orange card' may never be triggered.[127] National parliaments have not yet managed to show an 'orange card' for any of the Commission proposals, confirming, indeed, that the high vote threshold poses a significant obstacle to its use.[128]

IV. THE 'BARROSO INITIATIVE'

The EWS is not the only procedure that national parliaments may use to offer their input into EU acts. The Commission headed by José Manuel Barroso gave priority to relations with national parliaments in EU policymaking. In February 2005, the Commission adopted a new approach to the relations with national parliaments.[129] The objectives included, inter alia, visiting national parliaments and drafting an annual report on relations with national parliaments.[130] Furthermore, following on from the European Council declaration on 'the ratification of the Treaty establishing a Constitution for Europe' of 18 June 2005 calling for a 'reflection period' after the failed French and Dutch referenda on the Constitutional Treaty, the Commission proposed 'Plan D' (for democracy, dialogue and debate), in order 'to stimulate a wider debate between the European Union's democratic institutions and citizens'.[131] In 2006, the Commission presented a developed 'Plan D'—a 'Citizens' Agenda'.[132]

[125] 'Proposal for a Council Directive on a Common Consolidated Corporate Tax Base (CCCTB)' COM(2016) 683 final; Proposal for a Council Directive on a Common Corporate Tax Base' COM(2016) 685 final.

[126] 'Proposal for a Regulation of the European Parliament and of the Council establishing the criteria and mechanisms for determining the Member State responsible for examining an application for international protection lodged in one of the Member States by a third-country national or a stateless person (recast)' COM(2016) 270 final.

[127] Kiiver, The Early Warning System for the Principle of Subsidiarity (n 39) 133.

[128] PL Lindseth, *Power and Legitimacy: Reconciling Europe and the Nation-State* (Oxford, Oxford University Press, 2010) 241.

[129] Vice-Commissioner Wallström presented to the Commission College 10 objectives on relations with national parliaments. See Report from the Commission, 'Annual Report 2005 on the Relations with National Parliaments' SEC(2006) 350 final.

[130] ibid 4. On the outcome of these visits see the first report published on the relations with national parliaments: Report from the Commission, 'Annual Report 2006 on the relations between the Commission and the national parliaments, Memo to the Members of the IRG, SP (2007) 2202/4, Brussels, available at: ec.europa.eu/dgs/secretariat_general/relations/relations_other/npo/docs/sp(2006)2202.pdf.

[131] 'Communication from the Commission to the Council, the European Parliament, the European Economic and Social Committee and the Committee of the Regions. The Commission's contribution to the period of reflection and beyond: Plan-D for Democracy, Dialogue and Debate' COM(2005) 494 final, 2.

[132] 'Communication from the Commission to the European Council. A Citizens' Agenda. Delivering Results for Europe' COM(2006) 211 final, 2–3.

The Citizens' Agenda foresaw a commitment to the respect of the subsidiarity principle, a situation which meant that the Commission will work with Member States and their national parliaments.[133] Specifically, the document anticipated a closer involvement of national parliaments in developing and implementing EU policy. The increased participation of national legislatures was, in the view of the Commission, a step to 'make European policies more attuned to diverse circumstances and more effectively implemented'.[134] At the time, the Commission was obliged to 'promptly' forward consultation documents to national parliaments, whereas the forwarded legislative proposals of national governments were to be 'made available in good time'.[135] To enhance the policymaking process, the Commission committed itself to forward all new legislative proposals and consultation papers directly to national parliaments, along with an invitation to react. This initiative is named the 'Barroso initiative' after the President of the Commission at the time and is often also referred to as 'political dialogue'.[136] The Barroso initiative can be defined as 'a broad political dialogue between the Commission and the national parliaments of the Member States on all aspects of the former's political agenda'.[137]

The participation of national parliaments in the political dialogue differs from that in the EWS. Taking into account the same time period as that utilised in the case of the EWS (2010–16), the number of opinions the Commission received is significantly higher. The number of received opinions was the following: 387 in 2010,[138] 558 in 2011,[139] 593 in 2012,[140] 553 in 2013,[141] 485 in 2014,[142] 342 in 2015[143] and 555 in 2016.[144] Those much larger numbers relative to the number of reasoned opinions have been explained by the fact that the Barroso initiative offers a 'safety net' for national parliaments: an always open channel to communicate with the Commission on issues that did not meet the eight-week deadline or cannot be presented as subsidiarity violations.[145]

The most active parliament in the Barroso initiative has been the Portuguese Parliament, even at the point where the number of opinions dropped to below 100.[146] The success of this legislature has been explained as a consequence of a new parliamentary procedure in 2006,

[133] ibid 8.

[134] ibid 9.

[135] Paras 1 and 2 of Amsterdam Protocol on the Role of National Parliaments in the European Union.

[136] See, however, that Jančić traces the 'Barroso initiative' to 2001 and the White Paper on EU governance: D Jančić, 'The Barroso Initiative: Window Dressing or Democracy Boost?' (2012) 8 *Utrecht Law Review* 78, 79.

[137] ibid 80.

[138] Report From the Commission, 'Annual Report 2010 on Relations between the European Commission and National Parliaments' COM(2011) 345 final, 6.

[139] COM(2012) 375 final, 5.

[140] Report From the Commission, 'Annual Report 2012 on Relations between the European Commission and National Parliaments' COM(2013) 565 final, 4.

[141] Report From the Commission, 'Annual Report 2013 on Relations between the European Commission and National Parliaments' COM(2014) 507 final, 5.

[142] Annex 1 to 'Annual Report 2014 on Relations between the European Commission and National Parliaments' COM(2015) 316 final, 3.

[143] Annex 1 to 'Annual Report 2015 on Relations between the European Commission and National Parliaments' COM(2016) 471 final, 3.

[144] Annex 1 to 'Annual Report 2016 on Relations between the European Commission and National Parliaments' COM(2017) 601 final, 3.

[145] D Jančić, 'The Game of Cards: National Parliaments in the EU and the Future of the Early Warning Mechanism and the Political Dialogue' (2015) 52 *Common Market Law Review* 939, 949.

[146] 2010: 106 opinions; 2011: 183 opinions; 2012: 226 opinions; 2013: 191 opinions; 2014: 118 opinions; 2015: 55 opinions; 2016: 57 opinions within the political dialogue, excluding the reasoned opinions.

allowing the chamber to pass written opinions on EU issues that touched upon its exclusive legislative competence and to give them a practical dimension by forwarding them to the Commission within the newly established political dialogue.[147] Other consistently active participants of the political dialogue include the Italian Senato della Reppublica, the Czech Senát, the Romanian Camera Deputaţilor, the German Bundesrat, the Italian Camera dei Deputati, and the Swedish Riksdag.[148] On the other side of the spectrum were the Estonian Riigikogu, the Slovenian Državni svet, and the Državni zbor, all of which often showed no activity at all.

There are five main differences between the Barroso initiative and the EWS: the type of acts under scrutiny; the time frame; the addressees of opinions; the scope of the review; and the fact there is a positive or negative assessment. First, the opinions issued within the political dialogue are not limited to EU draft legislative acts, but also apply to non-legislative documents: consultation documents (green and white papers, communications, or annual legislative programmes) can be commented on by national parliaments.[149] Second, whereas Protocol No 2 rigidly sets the eight-week deadline for reasoned opinions, the Barroso initiative can be triggered at any time during the legislative process. Third, concerning the addressees of opinions, while Protocol No 2 stipulates that the reasoned opinion is forwarded to the Commission and the EU legislator, the Barroso initiative is much more limited, as it operates only between national parliaments and the Commission.[150] Fourth, regarding the scope of the review, the Barroso initiative opinions may assess any political or legal aspect of Commission proposals,[151] in contrast to the subsidiarity-focused EWS.[152] Finally, Article 6 of Protocol No 2 provides that a reasoned opinion should focus on why the draft legislative proposal is not compatible with the subsidiarity principle. Regarding the Barroso initiative, the assessment of an act can be both negative and positive, stating that no violation of the subsidiarity principle is at stake. In addition to these differences, while the EWS is anchored in Protocol No 2, the Barroso initiative has an informal character and could be abolished by the Commission at any time.[153]

The opinions of national parliaments within the political dialogue receive responses from the Commission, in the same way as reasoned opinions in cases where no 'yellow card' or 'orange card' has been triggered. This is a consequence of the responsibility that the Commission undertook when the Lisbon Treaty was entering into force.[154] Moreover, at that point, the Commission asked national parliaments to 'distinguish in their opinions as far as possible between subsidiarity aspects and comments on the substance of the proposal,

[147] Jančić, 'The Barroso Initiative' (n 136) 89.

[148] While the position of these parliaments differs in the ranking each year, they remain in the top positions in the 2010–16 Commission reports. See, however, that the Romanian Camera Deputaţilor issued 0 opinions in 2010, but 40 in 2011.

[149] See, eg, opinions of the German Bundesrat, the Romanian Camera Deputaţilor and the Swedish Riksdag to the Commission White Paper 'Agenda for Adequate, Safe and Sustainable Pensions' COM(2012) 55 available at: www.ipex.eu/IPEXL-WEB/dossier/document/COM20120055.do#dossier-COM20120055; or the opinion of the Swedish Rikdagen on the Commission Work Programme for 2014, COM(2013)739, available at: www.ipex.eu/IPEXL-WEB/dossier/document/COM20130739.do.

[150] Kiiver, The Early Warning System for the Principle of Subsidiarity (n 39) 23.

[151] Jančić, 'The Barroso Initiative' (n 136) 80–81.

[152] See ch 3.

[153] Jančić, 'The Barroso Initiative' (n 136) 83.

[154] Letter from President Barroso and Vice-President Wallström (n 38) 5.

and to be as clear as possible as regards their assessment on a proposal's compliance with the principle of subsidiarity'.[155] In fact, national parliaments do not send two separate opinions on Commission proposals.[156] In truth, as will be shown in this book at several points, reasoned opinions also contain comments on different aspects of the proposals, not on subsidiarity exclusively. When no appropriate threshold has been reached, the Commission will reply to national parliaments' reasoned opinions in the political dialogue in any case. Because the Commission 'invited' national parliaments to differentiate between subsidiarity and non-subsidiarity arguments, the Commission must have assumed that opinions invoking very diverse arguments would arrive. In this way, the Commission has given national parliaments a 'free hand' in designing their opinions. Yet, the Commission also created a condition, stipulating that the received opinions would undergo a 'political assessment' on the part of the Commission.[157] Hence, if a parliament proceeds with a broad scrutiny of an EU legislative proposal, it should be aware of the 'political assessment' conducted by the Commission after the deadline passes.

Turning to the question, 'does the Barroso initiative have a visible impact at the EU level?' the Commission itself reports that '[a]s regards the improvement of policy formulation, it is true that it might not always be easy to measure the concrete impact of national Parliaments' opinions on a given final legislative act'.[158] Yet, in the early years of the political dialogue in a few cases, an influence on the EU legislative process was observed.[159] Looking at more recent data, the reactions to the proposal for the European Citizens' Initiative show that the political dialogue provided the EU legislators with an option that was retained in the final text.[160] In this case, the minimum number of Member States from which signatories of the Citizens' Initiative must come was lowered, and the one-year period for collecting signatures was established, reflecting the views expressed in the political dialogue.[161] This example, which in fact focuses on the substance of the proposal, proves that political dialogue presents a valuable alternative for addressing non-subsidiarity issues in the EWS.

[155] ibid 4.

[156] Jančić, 'The Barroso Initiative: Window Dressing or Democracy Boost' (n 136) 83. Yet, see an exception in the case of the Romanian Camera Deputaţilor which issued both a reasoned opinion and an opinion within the political dialogue on the 'Commission proposal for a Regulation of the European Parliament and of the Council on measures to reduce the cost of deploying high-speed communications networks' COM(2013) 147. In the reasoned opinion of 29.05.2013, the chamber claims subsidiarity violation due to the choice of legal form, insufficiency of impact analysis and consultations on the proposal, and lack of convincing economic added value of the proposal. The opinion within the political dialogue of 29.05.2013, though also questioning the legal form and insufficient impact assessment, goes into its substance and criticises among other things the definitions used in the proposal; lack of reference to the owners of plots of land for whom the regulation implies significant costs; and the lack of consideration of particularities of the rural areas, for which Romania and other Member States such as Finland have a special interest.

[157] 'After the deadline has expired, the Commission will provide a political assessment of the files for which the threshold has been reached and confirm the triggering of the subsidiarity control mechanism'. See Letter from Barroso and Wallström on Practical Arrangements (n 38) 5.

[158] Report from the Commission, 'Annual Report 2009 on Relations between the European Commission and National Parliaments' COM(2010) 291, final 9.

[159] Jančić, 'The Barroso Initiative' (n 136) 85.

[160] 'Proposal for a Regulation of the European Parliament and the Council on the citizens' initiative' COM(2010) 119 final.

[161] COM(2011) 345 final, 7.

V. THE EWS IN INTERPARLIAMENTARY COOPERATION

The EWS does not operate in a vacuum. It must be viewed against the background of interparliamentary cooperation in general.[162] The Maastricht Treaty Declaration No 13 'on the role of national parliaments in the European Union' called for greater involvement of national parliaments in EU affairs, especially through the exchange of information and regular meetings between national parliaments and the EP. Declaration No 14 'on the Conference of the Parliaments' proposed that the EP and the national parliaments should meet as a Conference of the Parliaments (or in the form of *Assises*)[163] as a consultative body on the 'main features of the European Union'. The presidents of the Council and of the Commission were to report on the state of the EU to the parliamentary conference.

In general terms, the cooperation within the 'multilevel parliamentary field' encompassing national and supranational parliamentary institutions participating in the EU decision-making process is visibly growing.[164] The existing networks can be divided according to bilateral–multilateral and formal–informal lines.[165] For the subsidiarity scrutiny, the most important are the multilateral ones, including formal networks such as the EU Speaker's Conference and COSAC, and informal networks of the Brussels national parliamentary representatives (NPRs).

A. The Conference of Speakers of European Union Parliaments

The oldest type of cooperation is the Conference of Speakers of European Union Parliaments, which can be dated as far as 1963.[166] The aim of the Conference is 'safeguarding and promoting the role of parliaments and carrying out common work in support of the interparliamentary activities'.[167] It meets annually and involves the speakers of parliaments of EU Member States and the EP's president. The composition of the Conference, although offering a prestigious position in the arena of interparliamentary conferences, puts a number of constraints on the functioning of the conference stemming from the constitutional systems of the speakers involved in terms of function and independence.[168]

[162] See D Fromage, 'Increasing Inter-Parliamentary Cooperation in the European Union: Current Trends and Challenges' (2016) 22 *European Public Law* 749.

[163] The first and only meeting of the *Assises* was held just before the Maastricht IGC in November 1990 with the aim to discuss the future development of the communities.

[164] B Crum and JE Fossum, 'Practices of Interparliamentary Coordination in International Politics: the European Union and Beyond' in B Crum and JE Fossum (eds), *Practices of Interparliamentary Coordination in International Politics* (Colchester, ECPR Press, 2013) 5–9.

[165] A Buzogány, 'Learning from the Best? Interparliamentary Networks and the Parliamentary Scrutiny of EU Decision-Making' in B Crum and JE Fossum (eds), *Practices of Interparliamentary Coordination in International Politics* (Colchester, ECPR Press, 2013).

[166] See 'The History of the EU Speakers Conference', available at: www.ipex.eu/IPEXL-WEB/euspeakers/getspeakers.do.

[167] Art 2 of the Stockholm Guidelines for the Conference of Speakers of the EU, available at: www.ipex.eu/IPEXL-WEB/euspeakers/getspeakers.do.

[168] C Fasone, 'Ruling the (Dis-)Order of Interparliamentary Cooperation? The EU Speakers' Conference' in N Lupo and C Fasone (eds), *Interparliamentary Cooperation in the Composite European Constitution* (Oxford, Hart Publishing, 2016) 271–74.

In 2008, the conference approved guidelines on interparliamentary cooperation that provide for the following aims: the promotion of the exchange of information and best practices between national parliaments and the EP; the safeguarding of the effective exercise of the subsidiarity and proportionality control; and the advancement of the cooperation with parliaments outside the EU.[169] In 2012, the Conference of Speakers established a new Inter-Parliamentary Conference for the Common Foreign and Security Policy and the Common Security and Defence Policy (CFSP/CSDP Conference);[170] in 2013, the Interparliamentary Conference on Article 13 of the Treaty on Stability, Coordination and Governance offering a forum to discuss budgetary policies;[171] and in 2017, the Joint Parliamentary Scrutiny Group for Europol (JSPG).[172]

Besides the aims defined in Protocol No 1, the EU speakers' conference promotes research activities with regard to tools of interparliamentary cooperation such as the Inter-Parliamentary EU information eXchange, or IPEX, which is an information platform and includes a database accessible on the IPEX website. IPEX was created on the basis of recommendations and agreements concluded by the Conference of Speakers of EU Parliaments in Rome (2000)[173] and The Hague (2004).[174] The IPEX website was launched in 2006 and amended in 2011.[175] The added value of IPEX was the distribution of legislative acts from the Commission to the IPEX database,[176] acts which, until the Lisbon Treaty, were formally available to national parliaments only via their governments. IPEX also allowed for the exchange of information about interparliamentary meetings and related news.

IPEX enables the exchange of information between national parliaments and the EP concerning different issues related to the EU, especially giving an overview of the reasoned opinions issued by national parliaments and other aspects of the subsidiarity review procedure. IPEX hosts the websites of the conferences of national parliaments: the Conference of Speakers of EU Parliaments, the CFSP/CSDP Conference, and the 'Article 13' conference.

IPEX has a board, which consists of the members representing national parliaments that have recently hosted, do host, or will next host the Conference of Speakers of EU Parliaments.[177] Other representatives of parliaments that intend to contribute to the

[169] The Lisbon Guidelines for interparliamentary cooperation in the EU, point I objectives, available at: www.ipex.eu/IPEXL-WEB/euspeakers/getspeakers.do.

[170] A Herranz-Surrallés, 'The EU's Multilevel Parliamentary (Battle)Field: Inter-Parliamentary Cooperation and Conflict in Foreign and Security Policy' (2014) 37 *West European Politics* 957; J Wouters and K Raube, 'The Interparliamentary Conference on Common Foreign and Security Policy: A Quest for Democratic Accountability in EU Security Governance' in N Lupo and C Fasone (eds), *Interparliamentary Cooperation in the Composite European Constitution* (Oxford, Hart Publishing, 2016).

[171] I Cooper, 'The politicization of interparliamentary relations in the EU: Constructing and contesting the "Article 13 Conference" on economic governance' (2016) 14 *Comparative European Politics* 196.

[172] V Kreilinger, 'A Watchdog over Europe's Policemen: The New Joint Interparliamentary Scrutiny Group for Europol' (2017) Jacques Delors Institute Working Paper 197, 1.

[173] See the Presidency Conclusions, available at: www.ipex.eu/IPEXL-WEB/euspeakers/getspeakers.do?id=082dbcc5319ee5f60131ae42612204a0.

[174] See the Presidency Conclusions and Guidelines, available at: www.ipex.eu/IPEXL-WEB/euspeakers/getspeakers.do?id=082dbcc5319ee5f60131ae26c80b043c.

[175] V Knutelská, 'Cooperation among National Parliaments: An Effective Contribution to EU legitimation?' in B Crum and JE Fossum (eds), *Practices of Interparliamentary Coordination in International Politics* (Colchester, ECPR Press, 2013) 41.

[176] The Commission obliged itself to 'transmit directly all new proposals and consultation papers' at the launch of the 'Barroso initiative' in 2006. See COM(2006) 211 final, 9.

[177] Art 4 of IPEX Guidelines as approved by the meeting of the Secretaries General, Rome, 13.03.2015.

conference and the representatives of the EP are also included on the board. Each national parliament may nominate up to two national IPEX correspondents, who fulfil such tasks as arranging the information concerning their parliaments on the website, keeping the materials on the scrutiny procedures up to date, and translating the text of key issues into English or French.[178]

Whereas some parliaments see IPEX as 'an excellent source of information about others' opinions', the functioning of IPEX is problematic.[179] The UK House of Lords has highlighted problems with translations of the documents uploaded by national parliaments and has advised that the IPEX board could introduce some technological solution, for example, 'automated translations'.[180] Some delay between the proceedings in national parliaments and the information on the website is visible.[181] Improving IPEX could be achieved via the timely electronic publication of reasoned opinions, including English translations, and by introducing certain 'warnings' (eg, by email) in cases in which a significant number of opinions have been issued. Some parliaments already provide 'courtesy translations' of their reasoned opinions.[182]

B. COSAC

The Conference of Parliamentary Committees for Union Affairs (COSAC) was established in 1989 on the initiative of the President of the French Assemblée nationale.[183] The idea was to provide a palliative to the perceived disconnection of national parliaments from EU affairs after the introduction of direct elections to the EP in 1979.[184] COSAC was first acknowledged in the Amsterdam Protocol on 'the role of national parliaments in the European Union' that elaborated on the Conference (now the Conference of Parliamentary Committees for Union Affairs of Parliaments of the European Union—COSAC), granting it specific functions.[185] First, COSAC's contributions on legislative acts and other initiatives in the area of freedom, security and justice with a direct impact on the rights and freedoms of individuals should inform the EP, the Council and the Commission. Second, COSAC was competent to alert these institutions to its own contributions concerning the 'legislative activities of the Union', in particular regarding the subsidiarity principle; the area of

[178] Art 8 of IPEX Guidelines.

[179] Edmund Wittbrodt, Chairman of the European Affairs Committee, Senat, Poland—Written evidence, 313, available at: www.parliament.uk/documents/lords-committees/eu-select/Role%20of%20national%20parliaments/national-parliaments-evidence.pdf.

[180] House of Lords, European Union Committee, *9th Report of Session 2013–14, The Role of National Parliaments in the European Union* (HL 151) point 141. On this issue see also Ian Cooper's evidence attached to the House of Lords report, 58.

[181] Knutelská (n 175) 42.

[182] ibid 43.

[183] Preamble to Rules of Procedure of the Conference of Parliamentary Committees for Union Affairs of Parliaments of the European Union [2011] OJ 229/1.

[184] History of COSAC at: www.cosac.eu/documents/.

[185] See criticism of this protocol with regard to the role of COSAC in A Maurer, 'National Parliaments in the European Architecture: From Latecomers' Adaptation Towards Permanent Institutional Change?' in A Maurer and W Wessels (eds), *National Parliaments on their Ways to Europe Losers or Latecomers?* (Baden-Baden, Nomos, 2001) 63–64.

freedom, security, and justice; and fundamental rights. However, the positions of COSAC did not have a binding force on national parliaments and were not prejudicial to their positions. Under the Lisbon Treaty, Article 9 of Protocol No 1 directly mentions the inter-parliamentary cooperation to be determined together by the EP and national parliaments. Article 10 of Protocol No 1 states that COSAC is competent to submit contributions to the EP, the Council and the Commission.[186]

COSAC's aim is to encourage the exchange of information and best practices between national parliaments and the EP, including their special committees. COSAC meets twice a year, during each Council presidency.[187] Each parliament can decide on its delegation, which may include up to six members, both from national parliaments and the EP.[188] As stated in the Lisbon Treaty, and repeated in the Rules of Procedure, COSAC contributions are not binding for national parliaments.[189] They should be adopted by consensus, and if this is not possible, by a three-quarters qualified majority, in which each delegation has two votes.[190] COSAC can also adopt conclusions.[191] The contributions that give COSAC the most visibility in the political terms often become a bone of contention between the delegations depending on each one's view of COSAC: as only a forum for exchange of practices or as a contribution to pressing political issues.[192]

From the EWS perspective, COSAC played an important role as an institution coordinating the first subsidiarity tests prior to the entry into force of the Lisbon Treaty.[193] This gave national parliaments the possibility of exchanging information and cooperating in actual Commission proposals. The first of these tests took place in 2005.[194] Moreover, since 2004, the COSAC Secretariat has produced bi-annual reports on 'Developments in European Union. Procedures and Practices Relevant to Parliamentary Scrutiny'.[195] They are, in fact, positively assessed by national parliaments as a 'useful tool in exchanging best practices amongst Parliaments/Chambers'.[196] The reports also dealt with and gave an overview of the adjustments introduced by Member States regarding the EWS and provided the first evaluations of the functioning of the subsidiarity mechanism.[197]

[186] Yet, the acronym of COSAC is not used.

[187] s 2.1 of the COSAC Rules of Procedure.

[188] ibid, s 3.1.

[189] ibid, s 1.3.

[190] ibid, s 7.5.

[191] ibid, s 10.

[192] B Dias Pinheiro, 'The Role of COSAC in the Changing Environment of National Parliaments in the EU: An Identity Crisis?' in N Lupo and C Fasone (eds), *Interparliamentary Cooperation in the Composite European Constitution* (Oxford, Hart Publishing, 2016) 308.

[193] For an overview of these tests, see: D Jančić, 'Representative Democracy Across Levels? National Parliaments and EU Constitutionalism' (2012) 8 *Croatian Yearbook of European Law and Policy* 227, 246; and Kiiver, *The Early Warning System for the Principle of Subsidiarity* (n 39) 76–91 who based his findings on these tests.

[194] See history of COSAC, available at: www.cosac.eu/documents/, 24. See the assessment of these tests in Kiiver, *The Early Warning System for the Principle of Subsidiarity* (n 39) 91–101 and Cygan, 'Regional Governance, Subsidiarity and Accountability within the EU's Multi-Level Polity' (n 81) 175.

[195] Available at: www.cosac.eu/documents/bi-annual-reports-of-cosac.

[196] See COSAC, 21st Bi-annual Report (June 2014) 11.

[197] See: COSAC, 13th Bi-annual Report (May 2010); 18th Bi-annual Report (September 2012); 19th Bi-annual Report (May 2013); 20th Bi-annual Report (October 2013); 24th Bi-annual Report (November 2015); 26th Bi-annual Report (October 2016).

The future role of COSAC is currently under discussion.[198] This discussion takes place in the light of the establishment and enhancement of other foras of cooperation, including possible ways of communicating between COSAC and these new conferences.[199] Other questions concern the organisation of COSAC's discussions, the quality of the debates or the adoption of contributions.[200]

C. National Parliaments' Representatives in Brussels

National parliaments have established NPRs based in Brussels to represent them at the EU level. NPRs are often described as 'key players' in interparliamentary coordination and exchange with EU institutions.[201]

NPRs were already present in Brussels before the entry into force of the Lisbon Treaty. In 1991, the Danish Folketing was the first Parliament to establish its representative in Brussels.[202] As of August 2017, all national parliaments, except for the Slovenian Državni svet, send their representatives.[203] The titles of the NPRs vary: most of them are 'the (Permanent) Representatives/Officers to the European Union', whereas others are styled as '(Permanent) Representatives to the European Parliament' or '(Permanent) Representatives to the EU institutions'.[204]

Whereas it can be said that NPRs 'mostly facilitate informal, day-to-day cooperation',[205] following functions of the NPRs can be distinguished.[206] First, their role is to provide a link between the EU and the national level and thus inform national members of the Parliament about EU issues. The NPRs may report on EU developments and political issues on a regular weekly basis or ad hoc on urgent matters or such matters that are interesting only to a limited number of MPs.[207] Second, NPRs play a representational function by building relationships between members of parliaments and EU institutions.[208] These may, for example, include organising visits of national MPs to the EP, liaising with the national MEPs, or participating in interparliamentary conferences.[209] Third, NPRs create links between national parliaments by updating each other regarding national positions.[210] This last function of

[198] See especially COSAC 21st Bi-annual Report. See also the points regarding COSAC in the EP Constitutional Affairs Committee discussion of on the EP report on the relations between European Parliament and national parliaments (A7-0255/2014) on 17.03.2014.

[199] Dias Pinheiro (n 192) 307–08. See also C Fryda, 'The Role of the COSAC Secretariat within the Evolving Landscape of Interparliamentary Cooperation: Challenges for the Future' in N Lupo and C Fasone (eds), *Interparliamentary Cooperation in the Composite European Constitution* (Oxford, Hart Publishing, 2016) 316.

[200] Dias Pinheiro (n 192) 307.

[201] A-L Högenauer and C Neuhold, 'National Parliaments after Lisbon: Administrations on the Rise?' (2015) 38 *West European Politics* 335, 346.

[202] COSAC, 11th Bi-annual Report, 23.

[203] See at: www.epgencms.europarl.europa.eu/cmsdata/upload/08738a29-ca92-48ce-ab96-3d5aa27bf600/NP_REPS_IPEX_+_COSAC_19.05.17.pdf.

[204] COSAC 11th Bi-annual Report, 25.

[205] Knutelská (n 175) 38.

[206] Högenauer and Neuhold (n 201) 342.

[207] COSAC, 11th Bi-annual Report, 28.

[208] Högenauer and Neuhold (n 201) 347.

[209] COSAC 11th Biannual Report, 26.

[210] Högenauer and Neuhold (n 201) 346.

the NPRs played a role in the triggering of the first 'yellow card', as they kept national parliaments constantly updated about the state of play.[211] The NPRs meet during the so-called 'Monday morning meetings', which were established in practice and are not regulated formally. Attendance is not obligatory unless requested by the representatives' Member States. In addition, invited representatives of the EP, Commission, or Council, who usually leave the meeting after the issue at stake is discussed, can attend the meetings.

D. Best Practices of Interparliamentary Cooperation in the EWS

The COSAC reports, which are based on questionnaires completed by national parliaments, highlight best practices in interparliamentary cooperation. Looking at interparliamentary cooperation from the perspective of reaching 'yellow card' and 'orange card' thresholds, the most used tool is a simple email exchange between parliaments, with an early notice of adopted reasoned opinions, followed by the use of the IPEX platform and the receiving and forwarding of information to national parliamentary representatives in Brussels.[212] In these cases, usually around half of the parliamentary chambers responding to COSAC's questionnaire replied that the information was helpful in drafting their own reasoned opinions. Other mechanisms of interparliamentary cooperation included passing or receiving information from the governmental representative; letters from chairpersons of committees or their members in other parliaments; discussions on the margin of COSAC meetings; and interactions at EP interparliamentary meetings or within the debates between parliamentary committees.[213] Although commentators place hope in COSAC to show more leadership within the EWS,[214] some parliaments expressly rejected the possibility that COSAC would coordinate subsidiarity checks as 'in contradiction to the conferral of relevant responsibilities to individual parliaments, which are exercised in accordance with Parliaments' own procedures and powers'.[215]

VI. CONCLUSION

The aim of this chapter was to show the increasing involvement of national parliaments as reflected in the Treaties. The Maastricht Treaty's declarations and the Amsterdam Protocol on the Role of National Parliaments encouraged national parliaments to become involved in EU affairs. The rather modest functions ascribed to national parliaments by those treaties evolved first in the Constitutional Treaty and were repeated and even strengthened by adding the 'orange card' procedure in the Lisbon Treaty. To date, the EWS offered national parliaments the strongest competence: the opportunity to check EU draft legislative proposals for their compatibility with the subsidiarity principle. The design of the procedure

[211] I Cooper, 'A yellow card for the striker: national parliaments and the defeat of EU legislation on the right to strike' (2015) 22 *Journal of European Public Policy* 1406, 1413.

[212] COSAC, 19th Bi-annual Report, 28–29.

[213] ibid 29.

[214] A Cygan, 'COSAC: Birth, Evolution, Failures and Perspectives' in N Lupo and C Fasone (eds), *Interparliamentary Cooperation in the Composite European Constitution* (Oxford, Hart Publishing, 2016) 217.

[215] COSAC, 21st Bi-annual Report, 21.

has been perceived as not ideal, and some critical issues concern the types of acts under review and the time available for review. The EU legislature comes into play in the EWS under the 'orange card' procedure, and compared with the ordinary legislative procedure, this process does not make it any harder for the EP to reject the Commission proposal at stake, while it facilitates such a rejection by the Council, whose vote omits the representation requirement. The involvement of the Committee of the Regions, particularly its SMN, enables regional parliaments to have a say on the subsidiarity issues and, in consequence, contributes to the EWS. The chapter also presented the latest data on the application of the EWS and the Barroso initiative, proving that both procedures are successfully and steadily used by national parliaments, although the participation varies across the chambers, with some showing more intense involvement than others. Finally, the blossoming interparliamentary cooperation, although currently also to some extent in search of internal reforms, has contributed to the formation of best practices and suggested improvements to the EWS. Having established the growing role of national parliaments at the EU level and especially the particularities of the design of the EWS, the following chapter will take a closer look at the scope of the EWS.

3

The Scope and Application of the EWS

I. INTRODUCTION

PROTOCOL NO 2 indicates that reasoned opinion should state why 'the draft in question does not comply with the principle of subsidiarity'.[1] However, to focus reasoned opinions on subsidiarity was not expected to be an easy exercise for national parliaments.[2] In practice, the process has indeed escaped the formal, tightly drafted bounds of the protocol.[3] Moreover, although it was hardly imagined that national parliaments would ever trigger a 'yellow card' with respect to an EU draft legislative act,[4] national parliaments have triggered three yellow cards so far: one each on the right to strike proposal (2012),[5] on the European Public Prosecutor's Office (EPPO) proposal (2013),[6] and on the revised Posted Workers Directive (2016).[7] This chapter deals with the scope of reasoned opinions under Protocol No 2, focusing mostly, but not exclusively, on those yellow cards, to establish how the subsidiarity principle is understood in the practice of the Early Warning System (EWS).

Accordingly, section II presents a set of textual, structural and functional arguments in favour of a narrowly tailored EWS. Section III discusses, in turn, the proposals, reasoned opinions and Commission replies for each of those cases. Specifically, the chapter shows that national parliaments draft reasoned opinions in a broad way that also encompasses an assessment of a proposal's legal basis, proportionality and merits. This section offers its own assessment of the proposals' compliance with the subsidiarity principle. Section IV discusses the consequences of the yellow cards for both the future of the EWS and the future of the proposals at stake. Section V then offers a number of broader observations on how national parliaments understand the subsidiarity principle.

[1] Art 6 of Protocol No 2.

[2] P Craig, *The Lisbon Treaty: Law, Politics, and Treaty Reform* (Oxford, Oxford University Press, 2010) 49.

[3] S Weatherill, 'Better Competence Monitoring' (2005) 30 *European Law Review* 23, 39.

[4] P Kiiver, *The Early Warning System for the Principle of Subsidiarity: Constitutional Theory and Empirical Reality* (London, Routledge, 2012) 133. See also the oral evidence given by Simon Hix in the House of Commons European Scrutiny Committee. House of Commons, European Scrutiny Committee, *Thirty-third Report of Session 2007–08, Subsidiarity, National Parliaments and the Lisbon Treaty, Oral evidence Q 50–52* (HC 563).

[5] 'Proposal for a Council Regulation on the exercise of the right to take collective action within the context of the freedom of establishment and the freedom to provide services' COM(2012) 130 final.

[6] 'Proposal for a Council Regulation on the establishment of the European Public Prosecutor's Office' COM(2013) 534 final.

[7] 'Proposal for a Directive of the European Parliament and of the Council amending Directive 96/71/EC of the European Parliament and of the Council of 16 December 1996 concerning the posting of workers in the framework of the provision of services' COM(2016) 128 final.

II. SCOPE OF THE REASONED OPINIONS UNDER PROTOCOL NO 2

What elements should national parliaments assess in their subsidiarity review? Is the EWS only concerned with the strict question as to whether a legislative act should be adopted at the EU level or the national level?[8] Or, rather, should national parliaments also consider the appropriateness of the legal basis of EU draft legislative acts, their proportionality and their substance? Is subsidiarity review a mask for a much simpler and more political question, namely, 'do we want this law or not?'[9] Arguably, subsidiarity assessment cannot be meaningfully separated from the political questions surrounding the issue at stake: the EWS encourages national parliaments to disguise their political concerns in subsidiarity arguments.[10] Parliamentary committees have advanced different answers concerning what a subsidiarity test encompasses, ranging from a strict test of subsidiarity violations to a broader check of Article 5 of the Treaty on the European Union (TEU).[11]

However, the question about the scope of subsidiarity review, although normative in nature, can be answered through a textual, structural and functional interpretation of the Treaties. What follows from this interpretation is an argument in favour of a narrow subsidiarity review that leaves aside the assessment of the legal basis, proportionality and merits of EU legal acts.

First, a textual interpretation of Protocol No 2 clearly shows that national parliaments may review the compliance of proposals solely with regard to their compliance with the principle of subsidiarity. While the preamble and title of Protocol No 2 refer to establishing the conditions for the application of the principles of subsidiarity and proportionality, the EWS, anchored in Article 7 of Protocol No 2, refers exclusively to the principle of subsidiarity. Specifically, Article 1 of Protocol No 2 provides that '[e]ach institution shall ensure constant respect for the principles of *subsidiarity* and *proportionality*' (emphasis added), while Article 6 of Protocol No 2 states that a national parliament shall specify 'why it considers that the draft in question does not comply with the principle of *subsidiarity*' (emphasis added). In turn, the Commission should answer to national parliaments by explaining 'why it considers that the proposal complies with the principle of *subsidiarity*' (emphasis added).[12] In consequence, a textual interpretation of Protocol No 2 indicates that national parliaments were granted a competence solely to review the compatibility of draft legislative

[8] For a study of the question of the scope of the reasoned opinions based on a pre-Lisbon COSAC exercise see Kiiver (n 4) 136–39. Depending on the approach of parliaments to subsidiarity scrutiny, they were divided into four groups: 'literalists', pseudo co-legislators', 'pre-emptors' and 'absentees'.

[9] G Davies, 'The Post-Laeken Division of Competences' (2003) 28 *European Law Review* 686, 695–96. See also J Peters, 'National Parliaments and Subsidiarity: Think Twice' (2005) 1 *European Constitutional Law Review* 68, 71.

[10] A von Bogdandy and J Bast, 'The Federal Order of Competences' in A von Bogdandy and J Bast (ed), *Principles of European Constitutional Law* (Oxford, Hart Publishing, 2010) 303–04.

[11] See, eg, for the German Bundestag 8. Sitzung des Unterausschusses Europarecht, Öffentliches Expertengespräch Prüfung des unionsrechtlichen Subsidiaritätsprinzips im Unterausschuss Europarecht des Rechtsausschusses des Deutschen Bundestages am 16 Juni 2010. Compare here opinions of Christian Calliess, favouring of a broad review of Art 5 TEU, and Franz Mayer, favouring a narrower review. In practice, the Bundestag adopted a broad approach for the assessment of the subsidiarity principle. See German Bundestag, Reasoned opinion of 09.03.2017 on COM(2016) 821. See also the UK House of Commons discussion on the principle of subsidiarity, UK House of Commons European Scrutiny Committee, *Subsidiarity, National Parliaments and the Lisbon Treaty, Thirty-third Report of Session 2007–08*, published on 21 October 2008, Oral Evidence taken before the European Scrutiny Committee. (See witness evidence by Alan Dashwood and Simon Hix).

[12] Art 7(3) of Protocol No 2.

acts with subsidiarity and not to assess whether they are proportional, whether their legal basis is correct, or whether their political merits are sound.

Second, a structural argument backs the view that the function of national parliaments under Protocol No 2 should be restricted to the control of the subsidiarity principle. The Lisbon Treaty did not grant national parliaments the position of a third legislative chamber in the EU structure, next to the EP and the Council. Indeed, while during the post-Nice period a number of propositions regarding an independent role for national parliaments were discussed, these were discarded, both for national and EU-related reasons.[13] From the national-level perspective, it was perceived that because of the increasing prominence of European affairs, the involvement of national parliaments at the EU level would affect the relationships between national executives and their parliaments, thereby 'erod[ing] traditional patterns of policy making in our polities'.[14] From the EU-level perspective, the proposal of granting a co-legislative role to national parliaments was rejected because it would have added another level of decision-making, complicating even further the already complex EU law-making system.[15] Specifically, the treaty framers rejected the idea of a 'red card'[16] allowing national parliaments to veto EU legislation.[17] This rejection reflects the intent to grant national parliaments only a narrow position in the EU legislative process rather than a much more involved role.[18] Working Group I on the Principle of Subsidiarity proposed a tailored EWS, without mentioning in its report a scrutiny of the aspects of proposals other than subsidiarity.[19] In fact, it was explained during the European Convention that the new mechanisms for subsidiarity scrutiny 'should not make decision-making within the institutions more cumbersome or lengthier, nor block it'.[20] Indeed, the structure of the Treaties demonstrates a substantial 'scepticism of the virtues of deeper direct involvement by national Parliaments in transnational law making'.[21] The works of the Convention could thus be seen as a historical argument elucidating the structural interpretation of the EWS and speaking in favour of a strict subsidiarity assessment.[22] Since Protocol No 2 to the

[13] See ch 1 and an overview in A Maurer and W Wessels, 'Major Findings' in A Maurer and W Wessels (eds), *National Parliaments on their Ways to Europe: Losers or Latecomers?* (Baden-Baden, Nomos, 2001) 23.

[14] ibid 22.

[15] R Uerpmann-Wittzack and A Edenharter, 'Subsidiaritätsklage als parlamentarisches Minderheitsrecht?' (2009) 44 *Europarecht* 313; R Schütze, *From Dual to Cooperative Federalism: The Changing Structure of European Law* (Oxford, Oxford University Press, 2009) 261.

[16] The 'red card' would have taken place if the national parliaments reached the two-thirds threshold of votes. See contribution by Gisela Stuart, member of the Convention 'The Early Warning Mechanism-putting it into practice' CONV 540/03, 6.02.2003, 3.

[17] P Birkinshaw, 'A Constitution for the European Union? A Letter from Home' (2004) 10 *European Public Law* 57, 73.

[18] NW Barber, 'Subsidiarity in the Draft Constitution' (2002) 11 *European Public Law* 197, 204.

[19] 'Conclusions of Working Group I on the Principle of Subsidiarity' CONV 286/02, 5.

[20] CONV 286/02, 2. For analysis of the discussions of the role of national parliaments in the Convention on the Future of Europe, see A Groen and T Christiansen, 'National Parliaments in the European Union: Conceptual Choices in the EU's Constitutional Debate' in C Hefftler et al (eds), *The Palgrave Handbook on National Parliaments and the European Union* (Basingstoke, Palgrave Macmillan, 2015).

[21] S Weatherill, 'Using National Parliaments to Improve Scrutiny of the Limits of EU Action' (2003) 28 *European Law Review* 909, 912.

[22] For the European Convention's discussion on this matter, see F Mayer, *Stellungnahme zum öffentlichen Expertengespräch Prüfung des unionsrechtlichen Subsidiaritätsprinzips im Unterausschuss Europarecht des Rechtsausschusses des Deutschen Bundestages am 16. Juni 2010* (2010) 17, available at: webarchiv.bundestag.de/archive/2010/0625/bundestag/ausschuesse17/a06/ua_europarecht/anhoerungen/01_Subsidiaritaet/02_Stellungnahmen/Stellungnahme_Mayer.pdf.

Lisbon Treaty embraced the EWS without major changes to the respective Protocol of the Constitutional Treaty, the position of the original drafters about a limited role for national parliaments with a narrowly defined EWS seems a reliable basis for interpretation of the scope of the EWS.

Third, a functional interpretation, based upon a comparative institutional analysis, provides a guide in favour of a restrictive understanding of the role of national parliaments under Protocol No 2.[23] According to this approach, specific functions should be allocated among alternative institutions on the basis of their relative capacity to carry out the task. This approach does not exclude a situation in which a number of institutions fulfil one task.[24] National parliaments seem better suited than EU institutions for controlling the subsidiarity of a legislative proposal.[25] In contrast, other institutions that are participating in the EU law-making process are more apt than national parliaments to evaluate the content of a legislative draft, its proportionality, or whether it has the correct legal basis.

To start with, it seems unquestionable that EU legislative institutions can assess the merits of a legislative proposal better than the national parliaments. The EU political process, by involving multiple institutions (the Commission, the Council and, usually, the EP) guarantees a more comprehensive consideration of all the interests involved. In contrast, national parliaments, because of their local points of view, may reveal a 'minoritarian bias', unable to consider the broader problems at stake.[26] The reasoned opinion of the Maltese Kamra tad-Deputati on the European Single Market for electronic communications illustrates this point well.[27] Arguing under the EWS against the Commission proposal, this chamber raised its concerns about the principle of subsidiarity, as '[f]or various reasons, such as the size of the country, its geographical legislation and the level of competition based on infrastructure, the Maltese market is different from markets in other Member States, and thus may require different measures'.[28] In sum, leaving the discussion on the merits of the Commission's proposal to the EU legislator avoids the drafting of reasoned opinions focusing on the local situation in a Member State instead of looking for the level that can better exercise treaty objectives.

[23] For an introduction to comparative institutional analysis, see NK Komesar, *Imperfect Alternatives: Choosing Institutions in Law, Economics, and Public Policy* (Chicago, IL, University of Chicago Press, 1994). Komesar compares institutions (market, courts and the political process) to choose which one among them is better able to decide on a specific social goal. This book applies Komesar's analytical framework to decide which institution—the national political process, the EU political process or the EU adjudicative process—can comparatively better scrutinise legal and political aspects of EU legislative proposals.

[24] eg, as is argued below, the correctness of legal basis is safeguarded ex ante by the Council and the EP and ex post by the CJEU.

[25] See the discussion in ch 1 on the dissatisfaction with the Court's subsidiarity case law.

[26] Komesar (n 23) approaches the political process through a two-force model of majoritarian and minoritarian influences. The former tends to produce public policies that are less narrow than those resulting from the latter. The over-representation of one of the forces results in a majoritarian or minoritarian bias that has a serious impact on the outcomes of the political process.

[27] 'Proposal for a Regulation of the European Parliament and the Council laying down measures concerning the European single market for electronic communications and to achieve a Connected Continent, and amending Directives 2002/20/EC, 2002/21/EC and 2002/22/EC and Regulations (EC) No 1211/2009 and (EU) No 531/2012' COM (2013) 627 final.

[28] Maltese Kamra tad-Deputati, Reasoned opinion of 7.11.2013 on COM(2013) 627, point 2.

Likewise, EU institutions seem more apt than national parliaments at protecting compliance of legislative acts with the proportionality principle.[29] A proportionality assessment involves an assessment of the necessity of a measure, its adequacy to achieve a desired goal, and its conciliation with competing interests (the 'least restrictive means' test).[30] Identifying and balancing these interests ascribes them some values.[31] Since the EU political process allows for the voicing of multiple interests (including the interests of the Member States, as represented by their ministers in the Council), it seems that the proportionality oversight can be better conducted via interaction between the various EU institutions rather than via individual evaluation by each national parliament. In addition, because the judicial process is characterised as an independent institution, the Court is fitter to conduct value assessments involved in the proportionality test without a single national bias.[32]

Finally, the functional interpretation shows that EU institutions are better equipped than national parliaments to review the legal basis of a legislative measure. The legal-basis question asks whether the EU has the powers that it seeks to exercise.[33] The Court of Justice of the European Union (CJEU)—the final interpreter of the EU Treaties, with an explicit function of reviewing the legality of EU legislative acts—seems to have the technical expertise concerning EU law that is needed to review whether the EU has the power to act within a specific area.[34] The argument that national parliaments should scrutinise the principle of conferral under the subsidiarity review just because the Court has not provided a sufficient safeguard in this respect can be rejected, since in a number of significant decisions the Court decided on vertical competences and not always in favour of the EU action, as was the case in the tobacco advertising judgment.[35] In order to avoid single-institutionalism and provide for an ex ante check on the legal basis, alongside the Court, the EP and the Council often provide expertise in this respect. This power has been granted to them directly by the respective rules of procedure, a situation which also contrasts with the lack of such a function in Protocol No 2, as presented by the textual argument.[36]

Assigning only a limited role to national parliaments by focusing their own review on subsidiarity only has been criticised from the start as 'virtually unenforceable, and

[29] For an opposite view, see C Calliess, 'Subsidiaritätskontrolle durch Bundestag, Bundesrat und Landesparlamente, § 23' in W Kluth and G Krings (eds), *Gesetzgebung—Rechtsetzung durch Parlamente und Verwaltungen sowie ihre gerichtliche Kontrolle* (Heidelberg, CF Müller, 2013) 580. Calliess argues that the 'not always clean' division between subsidiarity and proportionality in the jurisprudence of the Court speaks in favour of the inclusion of a proportionality check within the EWS.

[30] A Stone Sweet and J Mathews, 'Proportionality Balancing and Global Constitutionalism' (2008) 47 *Columbia Journal of Transnational Law* 72.

[31] P Craig, *EU Administrative Law* (Oxford, Oxford University Press, 2012) 592.

[32] Komesar indicates three distinctive aspects of the adjudicative process: competence (ability to assess complex cases); scale (ability to review cases); and independence (ability to be make even-handed decisions). Komesar (n 23) 123.

[33] K Lenaerts, 'The Principle of Subsidiarity and the Environment in the European Union: Keeping the Balance of Federalism' (1993) 17 *Fordham International Law Journal* 846, 866.

[34] See Art 263 TFEU.

[35] A von Bogdandy and J Bast, 'The European Union's Vertical Order of Competences: The Current Law and Proposals for its Reform' (2002) 39 *Common Market Law Review* 227, 257.

[36] See Rule 39 of the European Parliament Rules of Procedure (2017) and Art 19(1) Rules of Procedure of the Council (2016).

depend[ing] for its effectiveness on the restraint of the national parliaments'.[37] More recently, after the EWS came into force, such a version of narrowly tailored subsidiarity has been criticised as 'rather idealistic'[38] and as a missed opportunity 'to politicise the dialogue between the Commission and national parliaments'.[39] It has been argued that subsidiarity is more significant as a political principle, and national parliaments, which are political institutions, should be granted a possibility to interpret subsidiarity in a way they find appropriate.[40] Some scholars propose a 'political interpretation of the subsidiarity review' as a 'commitment to enhance representative democracy' in line with Article 10 TEU and propose giving national parliaments a role similar to that of constitutional courts, namely as 'protectors of constitutional essentials' in accordance with Article 4(2) TEU. One position argues that reducing subsidiarity to a 'technical exercise of competence review … betrays, by institutional design, a pro-European centripetal prejudice'.[41] According to this view, the EWS is 'an invitation to national parliaments and to their EACs in particular, to investigate, judge, influence and censure the legislative proposals of the Commission'.[42] In the same vein, elsewhere it is proposed that the EWS should be refocused on the principle of conferral and on the substance of proposals.[43]

The practice shows that in the case of the first yellow card, the withdrawal of the proposal in which the Commission did not find convincing subsidiarity arguments caused a misunderstanding within the national parliaments about their role in the EU legislative process. This was also confirmed by the major discontent of some national parliaments to the fact that the Commission did not withdraw the EPPO proposal. Although Protocol No 2 provides that the Commission may withdraw its proposal in the case of a yellow card, doing so could reasonably be expected in a case where the Commission itself is persuaded by the subsidiarity arguments expressed in a reasoned opinion. The outcome of the first yellow card was thus closer to a red card, and in the second and third yellow cards, national parliaments expected a 'red card' effect again. The possibility of allowing a red card procedure would have been 'an enormous concession to the supposed wisdom of national Parliaments at the expense of efficient problem solving initiated by the Commission and carried forward by the Council and European Parliament'.[44]

Another question concerns the subsidiarity scrutiny where there are not enough opinions for a yellow card. Why not allow a broad review? First, doing so would mean marrying the role already played by the 'Barroso initiative', which has also had some effect on EU policymaking as was shown in the previous chapter. Second, the number of opinions sent within the political dialogue outnumbers those within the EWS. Hence, it means that allowing broadly drafted reasoned opinions would also have probably increased their

[37] Barber (n 18) 203.

[38] W Gagatek, 'Polityczne i prawne znaczenie zasady pomocniczości w UE (po 20 latach od wejścia w życie Traktatu z Maastricht)' [2013] *Europejski Przegląd Sądowy* 31, 38.

[39] M Goldoni, 'The Early Warning System and the Monti II Regulation: The Case for a Political Interpretation' (2014) 10 *European Constitutional Law Review* 90, 101.

[40] Gagatek (n 38) 38.

[41] Goldoni (n 39) 102.

[42] ibid 106.

[43] D Jančić, 'The Game of Cards: National Parliaments in the EU and the Future of the Early Warning Mechanism and the Political Dialogue' (2015) 52 *Common Market Law Review* 939, 952–61.

[44] S Weatherill, 'Competence Creep and Competence Control' (2004) 23 *Yearbook of European Law* 1, 44.

total number. For the Commission, to review these opinions within a reasonable time and highlight subsidiarity arguments would have involved certain concessions concerning the speed and efficiency of the legislative procedure. Currently, some national parliaments draft broad reasoned opinions, but it could be assumed that, with a general concession in this regard, the number of reasoned opinions would grow. In consequence of 'excessive and unfocused' use of the subsidiarity review, then, the expected effect of the EWS to raise more subsidiarity awareness among EU institutions would be 'significantly weaken[ed]'.[45] This fact speaks against the 'intermediate' view (one that is between narrow and broad scrutiny) that national parliaments should not be stopped from commenting on all sorts of issues, in the framework of their EWS reasoned opinions, but that their formal reasoned opinions (or rather, the conclusions of their opinions) should be restricted to subsidiarity issues.

III. COMPARISON OF THE FIRST THREE 'YELLOW CARDS'

Against the framework presented above, the first three 'yellow cards' will be analysed to shed some light on the scope of the EWS in practice. Two of the yellow cards concerned cross-border issues in labour relations. The first yellow card triggered in May 2012 concerned the Monti II proposal on the exercise of the fundamental right to take collective action within the context of the freedom of establishment and the freedom to provide services. Twelve national parliaments issued reasoned opinions representing 19 votes out of 54 votes.[46] In May 2016, national parliaments questioned the proposed revision of the Posted Workers Directive that aimed to increase the protection of posted workers by, among other issues, making mandatory the application of any rules on remuneration set by law or universally applicable collective agreements in the host Member State to posted workers in all economic sectors. The revision attracted reasoned opinions from 14 national parliaments, representing 22 out of 56 votes. In contrast, the remaining yellow card triggered in October 2013 concerned the draft Council regulation 'on the establishment of the European Public Prosecutor's Office'. Fourteen national parliaments sent reasoned opinions, representing 18 out of 56 votes. In that case, the necessary number of opinions to trigger a yellow card was one-quarter (14 out of 56) as the draft legislative act was submitted on the basis of Article 76 TFEU in the area of freedom, security, and justice.

In none of the three cases did the number of reasoned opinions exceed the necessary threshold by a large amount. That fact, together with the observation that so far only three yellow cards and no 'orange cards' have been triggered, underlines the observation that these procedures are subject to relatively high hurdles and that a successful trigger suggests exceptional interest amongst national parliaments.

As regards individual parliaments, no national parliament submitted a reasoned opinion in all three of the yellow card procedures. The French Sénat, Latvian Saeima, Maltese

[45] Deutscher Bundestag, Protokoll der 8. Sitzung des Rechtsausschusses-Unterausschuss Europarecht, 'Öffentliches Expertengespräch zu dem Thema: "Prüfung des unionsrechtlichen Subisidiaritätsprinzips"', 16.06.2010, see expert testimony of Franz Mayer, 12 (own translation).

[46] Croatia joined in 2013, hence at the time the total of votes was 54.

Kamra tad-Deputati, Polish Sejm, Dutch Tweede Kamer, UK House of Commons, Romanian Camera Deputaţilor, Czech Senát, Hungarian Országgyűlés, Danish Folketing and Swedish Riksdag participated in at least two of the yellow cards. By contrast, the Austrian Bundestag and Bundesrat, German Bundestag and Bundesrat, Italian Camera dei Deputati and Senato della Repubblica, Hellenic Vouli ton Ellinon, Spanish Cortes Generales, Belgian Chambre des représentants and French Assemblée nationale did not participate in any of the yellow cards. It does, therefore, not appear to be case that the procedure of submitting a reasoned opinion is used indiscriminately. Instead, national parliaments appear to choose carefully when to submit a reasoned opinion.

The following sections first present each of the yellow cards and then explore each card's consequences for the future of each of the proposals.

A. The First 'Yellow Card'

The Commission proposal for the 'Monti II' regulation aimed to provide clarification of the EU rules regarding the exercise of the fundamental right to take collective action in the context of the freedom to provide services and the freedom of establishment, especially the necessity to reconcile these in practice in cross-border situations.[47] In the background of the proposal were two CJEU judgments: *Viking* and *Laval*, in which the Court recognised the right to strike as a fundamental right that can be, however, subject to limitations to ensure the protection of free-movement rights.[48] The draft regulation sought to address the tensions between the freedoms to provide services and of establishment, on the one hand, and the fundamental right to strike, exposed by those Court decisions.[49]

The proposal was based on Article 352 TFEU, 'the flexibility clause', applicable when the Treaties do not provide the necessary powers for actions necessary to achieve one of the objectives of the Treaties. The use of this legal basis implied a unanimous vote on the proposal in the Council. The Commission proposal enshrined the so-called 'Monti clause' that the regulation shall not affect, in purely internal situations, the exercise of the right to strike or other industrial action or the right to negotiate, conclude and enforce collective agreements, as provided by national law or practice.[50] The central provision of the proposal provided for mutual respect between the exercise of the EU economic freedoms of establishment and to provide services, on the one hand, and the exercise of the right to take collective action, on the other.[51] Moreover, for transnational disputes, the proposal established the principle of equal access to alternative dispute resolution mechanisms. Finally, Article 4 created an 'alert mechanism' for cases in which economic freedoms are affected in a way that would lead to 'grave disruption to the proper functioning of the internal

[47] For the context of the proposal see F Fabbrini and K Granat, 'Yellow card, but no foul: The role of the national parliaments under the subsidiarity protocol and the Commission proposal for an EU regulation on the right to strike' (2013) 50 *Common Market Law Review* 115, 125–30.

[48] Case C-438/05 *The International Transport Workers' Federation and The Finnish Seamen's Union (Viking)*, ECLI:EU:C:2007:772; Case C-341/05 *Laval un Partneri*, ECLI:EU:C:2007:809.

[49] Explanatory Memorandum of the proposal, 8.

[50] Art 1(2) of the proposal.

[51] Art 2 of the proposal.

market and/or which may cause serious damage to its industrial relations system or create serious social unrest'. In such a situation, concerned Member States were to inform both the Member State of the establishment or origin of the establishment or service provider and the Commission of the current position.

National parliaments did not assess any material or procedural aspect of the subsidiarity principle in their reasoned opinions.[52] Instead, in their argumentation, national parliaments focused mainly on the legal basis of the proposal. Concerns were raised about the application of the flexibility clause: the proposal did not fulfil the criteria for the use of Article 352 TFEU, for example, it did not identify the objective of the Treaties that it aimed to pursue.[53] Additionally, national parliaments maintained that Article 153(5) TFEU excludes EU action in the area of the right to strike, and the flexibility clause cannot be used as a legal basis where harmonisation of national laws is prohibited as indicated in Article 352(3) TFEU.[54] Labour law was seen a national question 'par excellence'.[55]

Regarding the proportionality principle, the Finnish Eduskunta observed that the Commission proposal was not suitable to achieve the objective of the Treaties. However, most arguments of national parliaments concerned the necessity of the proposal to achieve the goals of EU action.[56] In this vein, the UK House of Commons and the Maltese Kamra tad-Deputati pointed out that the proposal lacked evidence in the explanatory memorandum and in impact assessment on the necessity for EU action.[57]

Concerning the content of the proposal, specifically the general clause of Article 2, national parliaments highlighted incompatibility of the provision with the national constitutional tradition and its constitutional interpretation.[58] The Swedish Riksdag emphasised the lack of clarity and legal certainty of Article 2 which, according to the Dutch Tweede Kamer, could be detrimental to the well-functioning national labour law.

In the view of the Danish Folketing, EU intervention in the national mechanisms of dispute settlement and the requirement to inform the Commission about potential labour disputes was not necessary. Also, the other parliaments defended well-functioning domestic

[52] For a contrasting view, see I Cooper, 'A yellow card for the striker: national parliaments and the defeat of EU legislation on the right to strike' (2015) 22 *Journal of European Public Policy* 1406, 1411. Cooper argues that national parliaments 'objected to Monti II on the ground that it violated the principle of subsidiarity, although these objections frequently overlapped with broader objections on policy grounds, or to its legal basis'.

[53] Finnish Eduskunta, Reasoned opinion of 16.05.2012 on COM(2012) 130; Latvian Saeima, Reasoned opinion of 18.05.2012 on COM(2012) 130, point 3; Swedish Riksdag, Reasoned opinion of 11.05.2012 on COM(2012) 130; Belgian Chambre des représentants, Reasoned opinion of 30.05.2012 on COM(2012) 130; Luxembourg Chambre des Députés, Reasoned opinion of 15.05.2012 on COM(2012) 130; Portuguese Assembleia da República; Reasoned opinion of 18.05.2012 on COM(2012) 130.

[54] Dutch Tweede Kamer, Reasoned opinion of 22.05.2012 on COM(2012) 130; Luxembourg Chambre des Députés, Reasoned opinion of 15.05.2012 on COM(2012) 130; French Sénat, Reasoned opinion of 22.05.2012 on COM(2012) 130; Maltese Kamra tad-Deputati, Reasoned opinion of 22.05.2012 on COM(2012) 130, paras 1–2; Portuguese Assembleia da República, Reasoned opinion of 18.05.2012 on COM(2012) 130, Part II, let A; Danish Folketing, Reasoned opinion of 03.05.2012 on COM(2012) 130.

[55] Reasoned opinion of Belgian Chambre des représentants (n 53).

[56] Reasoned opinions of Maltese Kamra tad-Deputati (n 54), Finnish Eduskunta (n 53) and the UK House of Commons of 21.05.2012 on COM(2012) 130.

[57] Reasoned opinion of UK House of Commons (n 56) paras 14–15; Reasoned opinion of Maltese Kamra tad-Deputati (n 54) para 23. Although this could be seen as an argument concerning procedural subsidiarity, those chambers made this argument with regard to necessity of the proposal.

[58] Reasoned opinion of Portuguese Assembleia da República (n 54) Part II, let b.

models in this regard.[59] Finally, some national parliaments evaluated the content of the regulation by pointing to the relationship between the proposed regulation and other international tools for the protection of social rights, such as the European Social Charter or the European Convention on Human Rights.[60]

Some of the parliaments assessed the proposal within the political dialogue.[61] They were critical of a few aspects of the proposal, yet they did not declare a subsidiarity breach.[62] The Spanish Cortes Generales and the Italian Senato della Repubblica endorsed the proposal.[63]

On 6 June 2012, the Commission acknowledged that the first yellow card was triggered with regard to the Monti II proposal.[64] After reviewing the proposal, on 12 September 2012, the Commission communicated its withdrawal.[65] In a letter to national parliaments, the Commission stated that it still considered the proposal as compatible with the principle of subsidiarity. The Commission reasoned that the arguments of the national parliaments concerned the added value of the proposal, its legal basis, the EU competence to legislate on the matter, the implications of the general principle included in Article 2 of the proposal, the reference to the principle of proportionality in Article 3(4) and in recital 13 of the proposal, equal access to dispute resolution mechanisms, and the alert mechanism.[66] On the basis of those arguments, the Commission did not find a violation of the principle of subsidiarity. However, the Commission decided to withdraw the proposal because of the unlikelihood of sufficient support in the EP and the Council.

In light of lack of any formal communication from the Commission, in October 2012 the Conference of European Affairs Committees (COSAC) asked the Commission for individual responses to the reasoned opinions with an explanation of why, in the view of the Commission, the principle of subsidiarity had not been breached.[67] Hence, in March 2013 in an identical letter to all the national parliaments participating in the first yellow card, the Commission attempted to give a more thorough reply to the concerns raised in the reasoned opinions. Regarding the legal basis, the Commission explained that, because of the absence of an explicit provision in the Treaty, it had chosen Article 352 TFEU as an anchor for the proposal. Moreover, it upheld the earlier argument from the explanatory memorandum that the CJEU's rulings 'have clearly shown that the fact that Article 153 does not apply

[59] Polish Sejm, Reasoned opinion of 11.05.2012 on COM(2012) 130; the reasoned opinions of Swedish Riksdag (n 53), the Dutch Tweede Kamer (n 54), Maltese Kamra tad-Deputati (n 54), Portuguese Assembleia da República (n 54).

[60] The reasoned opinions of the Belgian Chambre des représentants (n 53), Finnish Eduskunta (n 53) and Latvian Saeima (n 53).

[61] The Czech Senát and the Czech Poslanecká sněmovna adopted a reasoned opinion after the elapse of the eight-week deadline.

[62] German Bundesrat, Opinion of 15.06.2012; Slovenian Državni zbor, Opinion of 25.05.2012; Polish Senat, Opinion of 08.05.2012; Lithuanian Seimas, Opinion of 02.05.2012.

[63] Spanish Cortes Generales, Opinion of 21.05.2012 on COM(2012) 130; Italian Senato della Repubblica, Opinion of 02.05.2012 on COM(2012) 130.

[64] See, eg, Commission reply of 06.06.2012 to the Belgian Chambre des représentants, Ares(2012) 775028.

[65] See the letter from President Barroso to the President of the European Parliament, Martin Schulz, Memo 12/661, 12 September 2012. On the interpretation of the Commission reply see also B Schima, 'Die Subsidiaritatskontrolle durch die nationalen Parlamente nach dem vertrag von Lissabon' (2013) 68 *Zeitschrift für öffentliches Recht* 384, 384–85.

[66] Commission reply of 12.09.2012 to the UK House of Commons, Ares(2012)1058907.

[67] COSAC, 19th Bi-annual Report, 26.

to the right to strike does not exclude collective action from the scope of EU law'.[68] On the choice of a regulation instead of a directive, the Commission underlined that a regulation 'would have reduced regulatory complexity and offered greater legal certainty'.[69] Finally, on the merits of the proposal, the Commission highlighted the enhanced role of national courts in adjudicating on the proportionality of collective actions, taking into account national laws and procedures on the exercise of the right to strike, and encompassing existing alternative dispute-settlement mechanisms. Notwithstanding the foregoing, the introduction of such mechanisms would remain facultative for the informal resolution of labour disputes at the national level.

B. The Second 'Yellow Card'

The EPPO proposal was based on Article 86 TFEU that explicitly foresees the establishment of such an office. The EPPO was designed as a decentralised integrated office,[70] consisting of the European Public Prosecutor (EPP) assisted by four deputies.[71] The European Delegated Prosecutors (EDPs) had the competence to conduct the investigations and prosecutions under the direction and supervision of the EPP.[72] The EDPs who would be national prosecutors were an integral part of the EPPO and remained under the exclusive authority of the EPP.[73] The first competence was to investigate and prosecute 'criminal offences affecting the financial interests of the Union'.[74] The second was an ancillary competence to pursue criminal offences 'inextricably linked' with EU fraud and where 'their joint investigation and prosecution are in the interest of a good administration of justice'.[75] For the EPPO to have an exclusive competence in these two cases, the offence had to be 'wholly or partly committed' either on the territory of one or several Member States or by one of their nationals, EU staff members or members of the institutions.[76]

Despite the fact that some national parliaments welcomed the creation of the EPPO in their reasoned opinions[77] or considered that the EPPO would be able to be 'assimilated' into the national judicial system and that it contributed to the objective of the proposal,[78] the message from the reasoned opinions was negative: the proposal is 'unnecessary, excessive and insufficiently justified'.[79] The main arguments of national parliaments concerned the competence of the EU to act, subsidiarity, proportionality and the merits of the proposal, especially the structure of the office and fundamental rights protection. Hence, in contrast to their actions for the first yellow card, parliaments were more careful in the drafting of their reasoned opinions and provided an assessment of the subsidiarity of the proposal.

[68] See, eg, Commission reply of 14.03.2013 to the Portuguese Assembleia da República on COM(2012) 130.
[69] ibid.
[70] Explanatory Memorandum, point 2.
[71] Arts 6(1) and 6(2) of the proposal.
[72] ibid, Art 6(3).
[73] ibid Art 6(5) and 6(6).
[74] ibid, Art 12.
[75] ibid, Art 13.
[76] ibid, Art 14.
[77] Maltese Kamra tad-Deputati, Reasoned opinion of 28.10.2013 on COM(2013) 534, point 2.1.
[78] Romanian Camera Deputaţilor, Reasoned opinion of 28.10.2013 on COM(2013) 534, point 3.
[79] UK House of Lords, Reasoned opinion of 24.10.2013 on COM(2013) 534, point 13.

Reviewing the compliance of the proposal with the subsidiarity principle, national parliaments argued that it failed the 'national insufficiency test'. The Slovenian Državni zbor stated that the national authorities in that Member State were successful in the investigation and prosecution of offences affecting the EU's financial interests and that improvements should, rather, be sought in the cooperation between the competent national authorities and the already existing EU bodies.[80] The UK House of Lords concluded that the Commission was too optimistic in forecasting the improved prosecution rate and that Member States are in a position to fight EU fraud by means of national criminal law.[81] Likewise, the Swedish Riksdag stated that the Commission did not show that the national level measures together with Eurojust could not better achieve the objectives of the proposal.[82] The idea of improving existing mechanisms, Eurojust and the European Anti-Fraud Office (OLAF),[83] and their cooperation with Member States, was also echoed in the opinions of other parliaments.[84]

Moreover, in the view of national parliaments, the Commission did not fulfil the second dimension of the subsidiarity principle, the 'comparative efficiency test'. For example, the Czech Senát argued that insufficiencies in the prosecution of criminal offences against the financial interests of the EU at the national level are caused by the deficiencies inherent in national systems and the difficulty in uncovering financial crimes that are not solved by the EPPO proposal'.[85] The objectives of the proposal, thus, could not be better achieved at the EU level.

The reasoned opinions also assessed the procedural aspect of the subsidiarity principle.[86] For example, the UK House of Commons argued that the draft legislative acts should incorporate a detailed statement on the subsidiarity and proportionality of a measure in the explanatory memorandum, which is available in all official languages of the EU, in contrast to an impact assessment, which usually contains only an executive summary in the Member State's official language.[87] In the view of the UK House of Lords, options other than the EPPO, for example, strengthening the powers of Eurojust, were not sufficiently examined by the Commission.[88] The impact assessment was seen as not solid in arguing that Member States' actions are insufficient.[89]

Many of the national parliaments voiced their concerns regarding the lack of competence of the EU to act in the area at stake. Namely, national parliaments opined that penal

[80] Slovenian Državni zbor, Reasoned opinion of 25.10.2013 on COM(2013) 534.

[81] UK House of Lords, Reasoned opinion (n 79) point 17.

[82] Swedish Riksdag, Reasoned opinion of 25.10.2013 on COM(2013) 534.

[83] Dutch Eerste Kamer, Reasoned opinion of 17.10.2013 on COM(2013) 534; Dutch Tweede Kamer, Reasoned opinion of 10.10.2013; UK House of Lords, Reasoned opinion (n 79) point 18.

[84] Irish Houses of the Oireachtas, Reasoned opinion of 16.10.2013 on COM(2013) 534, point 5b-c.

[85] Czech Senát, Reasoned opinion of 09.10.2013 on COM(2013) 534, point II 1.

[86] Cyprus Vouli ton Antiprosopon, Reasoned opinion of 23.10.2013 on COM(2013) 534, 3; Irish Houses of the Oireachtas, Reasoned opinion (n 84) point 5 c.

[87] UK House of Commons, Reasoned opinion of 22.10.2014 on COM(2013) 534, point 10. The Impact Assessment for the EPPO was drafted in English, see: Commission Staff Working Document, 'Impact Assessment, Accompanying the Proposal for a Council Regulation on the establishment of the European Public Prosecutor's Office' SWD(2013)274, whereas the Executive Summary was available in all EU official languages, SWD(2013) 275.

[88] UK House of Lords, Reasoned opinion (n 79) point 14.

[89] See reasoned opinions of Dutch Eerste Kamer and Tweede Kamer (n 83).

legislation is a matter of national sovereignty;[90] in other words, criminal law is 'primarily a national competence'.[91] In the view of the Hungarian Országgyűlés, the 'supranational model' of the Office limits the existing national sovereignty in the field of criminal law.[92] Finally, the Slovenian Državni zbor suggested that the far-reaching exclusive competence of the EPPO runs counter to Slovenian constitutional law.

National parliaments also highlighted the violation of the proportionality principle. For instance, the Cypriot and Maltese parliaments found violation of the necessity test by granting the EPPO an exclusive competence in the investigation and prosecution of PIF (protection of financial interests) offences.[93] The Swedish Riksdag concluded that the proposal, by exceeding what is necessary to achieve its objective, violated the proportionality criterion inherent to the subsidiarity check.[94]

Regarding the merits of the Commission proposal, the French and Romanian chambers maintained that the EPPO should have a collegial character (a chosen president with a rotation), which would anchor the EPPO better in the national systems.[95] Some parliaments found the notion of 'the Union's financial interest' unclear and leading to jurisdictional problems.[96] Concerning fundamental rights protection, some legislative chambers argued that the proposal does not provide for the necessary level of protection of rights of suspects as compared to the national level with regard to access to court and a fair trial,[97] or that some of the investigative measures listed in the proposal were not available in each Member State.[98]

In addition, some parliaments issued opinions within the political dialogue and claimed compatibility with the subsidiarity principle because of the efficacy of the proposal, efficacy which cannot be achieved by individual Member States, and the EPPO's fundamentally European dimension.[99] Other parliaments backed the EPPO yet demanded changes to its structure or competences.[100]

In the letters addressed to national parliaments, the Commission confirmed that the yellow card had been triggered.[101] Shortly afterwards, on 27 November 2013, the Commission communicated to national parliaments its decision to maintain the EPPO proposal.

[90] Maltese Kamra tad-Deputati, Reasoned opinion (n 77) point 2.3.

[91] Irish Houses of the Oireachtas, Reasoned opinion (n 84) point 5.

[92] Hungarian Országgyűlés, Reasoned opinion of 21.10.2013 on COM(2013) 534 (summary in English).

[93] Cyprus Vouli ton Antiprosopon, Reasoned opinion (n 86) 4; Maltese Kamra tad-Deputati, Reasoned opinion (n 77) point 2.2.

[94] Swedish Riksdag, Reasoned opinion (n 82).

[95] French Sénat, Reasoned opinion of 28.10.2013 on COM(2013) 534; Romanian Camera Deputaţilor, Reasoned opinion (n 78) point 10; Maltese Kamra tad-Deputati, Reasoned opinion (n 77) point 2.3.

[96] Romanian Camera Deputaţilor, Reasoned opinion (n 78) point 9; Reasoned opinions of Dutch Eerste and Tweede Kamer (n 83).

[97] Czech Senát, Reasoned opinion (n 85).

[98] Cyprus Vouli ton Antiprosopon, Reasoned opinion (n 86).

[99] Italian Senato della Repubblica, Risoluzione della Commissione Permanente of 19.11.2013 on COM(2013) 534; Portuguese Assembleia da República, Opinion of the European Affairs Committee of 22.10.2013 on COM(2013) 534, point 12(b); in general also Romanian Senat, Reasoned opinion (n 78).

[100] The French Assemblée nationale, Opinion of 31.01.2014 on COM(2013) 534; Croatian Hrvatski sabor, Opinion of 01.04.2014 on COM(2013) 534; Polish Senat, Opinion of 09.10.2013 on COM(2013) 534, Spanish Cortes Generales, Resolution of the Joint Committee for EU Affairs of 15.10.2014 on COM(2013) 534; Finish Eduskunta, Statement of the Grand Committee 1/2013 of 13.12.2013 on COM(2013) 534; German Bundesrat, Resolution of 11.10.2013 on COM(2013) 534, point 6.

[101] See, eg, Commission reply to the Romanian Camera Deputaţilor of 12.11.2013, Ares(2013) 3702525.

In the view of the Commission, the proposal complied with the principle of subsidiarity; hence there was no need to withdraw or amend it.[102] The Commission, while examining the reasoned opinions, decided to distinguish between 'arguments relating to the principle of subsidiarity, or that could be interpreted as subsidiarity concerns, and other arguments relating to the principle of proportionality, to policy choices unrelated to subsidiarity, or to other policy or legal issues'.[103] Providing arguments on subsidiarity, the Commission qualified those that concern the sufficient substantiation of the compatibility with the subsidiarity principle, the alleged sufficient character of existing mechanisms, the added value of the proposal, issues relating to the structure of the EPPO, and issues relating to the nature and scope of its competences.[104]

Concerning the 'national insufficiency test', the Commission maintained, basing its assessment on OLAF's annual statistics, that the '[sufficient] situation in particular Member States is therefore not decisive in itself, as long as it can be shown that action at the level of Member States is generally insufficient, and that Union action would generally better achieve the policy objective'.[105] The Commission rebutted the arguments on using the existing mechanisms of OLAF, Eurojust and Europol instead of introducing the EPPO by stating that their powers would be insufficient.[106] Likewise, the proposed PIF Directive,[107] which harmonises definitions of offences and sanction levels with regard to crimes against the EU's financial interests, has no impact on the compatibility of the EPPO proposal with subsidiarity. In sum, the Commission restated that Member States cannot sufficiently achieve the objective of the EPPO Regulation.

With regard to the 'EU's comparative efficiency test', labelled as the 'added value' of the proposal, the Commission underlined that the common EU-level prosecution will compensate for the differences among Member States on investigation and prosecution of EU fraud, additionally preventing forum shopping by perpetrators.[108] Moreover, the likelihood of discovering cross-border links in EU fraud crimes will increase in comparison to exclusively national-level investigations. Other 'added-value' elements concerned the simplification of procedures in obtaining information and evidence, the unconstrained admission of evidence lawfully collected in other Member States except for situations affecting fairness of the procedure and defence rights, and the merging of expertise on EU fraud. Taking into account these grounds, the Commission stated that the proposal fulfils the 'comparative efficiency test'.

Regarding procedural subsidiarity, the Commission argued that the explanatory memorandum and the accompanying legislative financial statement, together with the more detailed impact assessment, offer a sufficient justification of the proposal's compliance with the subsidiarity principle.[109]

[102] 'Communication from the Commission to the European Parliament, the Council, and the National Parliaments on the review of the proposal for a Council Regulation on the establishment of the European Public Prosecutor's Office with regard to the principle of subsidiarity, in accordance with Protocol No 2' COM(2013) 851, final.

[103] ibid, point 2.1.

[104] ibid.

[105] ibid, point 2.3.

[106] ibid.

[107] 'Proposal for a directive of the European Parliament and of the Council on the fight against fraud to the Union's financial interests by means of criminal law' COM(2012) 363 final.

[108] COM(2013) 851 final, point 2.4.

[109] ibid, point 2.2.

Next, still within the subsidiarity test, the Commission elaborated on the concerns of national parliaments with regard to the structure of the EPPO and its competences. Regarding the former, the Commission stated that the arguments concern more the proportionality principle than subsidiarity. Specifically, the choice of a decentralised model and the collegial structure favoured by national parliaments is not a question of preference of action at the national level over the EU level, but 'a comparison between two possible modes of action at the Union level' and therefore does not concern subsidiarity.[110] In the view of the Commission, the EPPO's structure is, however, pertinent to the subsidiarity principle with regard to the comparative efficiency of EU-level action: a collegial structure would make the EPPO less efficient. Nonetheless, the Commission proposal allows for a 'quasi-collegial' approval in some cases because of the cases' 'operational importance' without diminishing the EPPO's efficiency.

Replying to the arguments concerning the competence of the EPPO to deal with all cases of fraud, including the non-cross-border cases, the Commission pointed to issues such as consistency of investigation and prosecution policy across the EU and avoidance of duplicate proceedings.[111] Regarding the ancillary competence of the EPPO's being allowed to intervene in criminal offences inextricably linked with those affecting the EU's financial interests, the Commission underlined that the principle of subsidiarity is not violated because it allows for an efficient engagement in anti-fraud activities and does not violate the *ne bis in idem* principle.

In March 2014, the Commission, having learnt from the experience of the first yellow card, sent individual replies to each of the involved parliaments. The Commission defended the proposal as the least intrusive and the most effective for protection of the EU's financial interest after considering alternatives such as national action or strengthening of existing EU mechanisms.[112] The proposal did not exceed what is necessary to achieve the objective and, therefore, proportionality was given.[113]

The Commission maintained also that the proposal provides for the necessary fundamental rights protections. Although not all the investigative measures were provided in national systems, they were necessary for effective investigation and prosecution of offences.[114] Moreover, the most intrusive investigative measures demanded a prior judicial authorisation, even where such is not needed in national law. The proposal, in the view of the Commission, provides a comprehensive set of procedural rights for suspects and accused. Where national parliaments preferred a collegial character for the EPPO, the Commission argued that the proposal already foresees a college at the central level that will adopt internal rules of procedure.[115] The Commission remained open to consider other options that maintain the independence, accountability and efficiency of the EPPO.[116] Finally, in the view of the Commission, the notion of the 'Union's financial interest' was clearly defined in the proposal (Article 2c).[117]

[110] ibid, point 2.5.
[111] ibid, point 2.6.
[112] Commission reply of 13.03.2014 to the Maltese Kamra tad-Deputati on COM(2013) 534.
[113] Commission reply of 18.03.2014 to the Swedish Riksdag on COM(2013) 534.
[114] Commission reply of 13.03.2014 to the Cyprus Vouli ton Antiprosopon on COM(2013) 534.
[115] Commission reply to the Maltese Kamra tad-Deputati (n 112).
[116] ibid.
[117] Commission reply of 19.03.2014 to the Romanian Camera Deputaţilor on COM(2013) 534.

C. The Third 'Yellow Card'

The revision of the Posted Workers Directive aimed to tackle the unfair practices in the labour market and encourage the principle of equal pay for the same work at the same place.[118] The proposal, as was the directive it was amending, was based on Articles 53(1) and 62 TFEU concerning freedoms of establishment and services. Under the revised directive, collective agreements become applicable to posted workers in all sectors of the economy (previously, it was applicable only in the construction sector). The rules on remuneration applicable to local workers stemming from national law or collective agreements become applicable also to posted workers. The directive obliges the Member States to publish on a website the elements of remuneration applicable to posted workers. Member States should oblige undertakings to subcontract only to undertakings that grant workers certain conditions on remuneration applicable to the contractor. Member States had to apply the same conditions to the cross-border agencies that hire out workers as are applicable to national agencies. Finally, the labour law of the host Member State should apply to the employment contract of the posted worker if the anticipated or the effective duration of the posting exceeds two years.[119]

In their reasoned opinions, some national parliaments argued that whereas the current 1996 directive offered such a possibility, a number of Member States have already extended the rules applicable to posted workers.[120] In those cases, the collective labour agreements became applicable to all economy sectors or else equal treatment of temporary agency workers and subcontractors was provided. Therefore, those national parliaments pointed out that the Commission did not prove insufficiency of national regulations and that now, by making those rules obligatory, it violates the subsidiarity principle. The Czech Poslanecká sněmovna argued that industrial relations should be regulated at the national level because of their historical and social path dependency.[121] In the view of this chamber, the proposal substitutes the national mechanism of collective bargaining that reflects the needs of employees and employers. The Romanian Camera Deputaţilor questioned the EU added value of the proposal: posted workers comprise only a small part of mobile workers, and only 50 per cent of them come from low-wage Member States. The Estonian Riigikogu put in doubt whether the EU can better achieve the objective by taking into account the scale or the effects of the action and without harming the competitiveness of business.

The main subsidiarity related criticism, however, concerned the procedural aspect of the subsidiarity principle. National parliaments found the subsidiarity justification insufficient, a mere statement that the existing directive can only be amended by a new directive and no

[118] 'Proposal for a Directive of the European Parliament and of the Council amending Directive 96/71/EC of the European Parliament and of the Council of 16 December 1996 concerning the posting of workers in the framework of the provision of services' COM(2016) 128, point 1.1.

[119] Art 1 of the proposal.

[120] Polish Sejm, Reasoned opinion of 13.04.2016 on COM(2016) 128; Bulgarian Narodno sabranie, Reasoned opinion of 20.04.2016 on COM(2016) 128; Polish Senat, Reasoned opinion of 29.04.2016 on COM(2016) 128; Romanian Camera Deputaţilor, Reasoned opinion of 13.04.2016 on COM(2016) 128.

[121] Czech Poslanecká sneěmovna, Reasoned opinion of 31.04.2016 on COM(2016) 128.

information regarding the real impact of the introduction of remuneration.[122] Moreover, the Bulgarian chamber stated that the explanatory memorandum did not contain qualitative and quantitative evidence or the financial assessment to support the directive. The Lithuanian Seimas and the Romanian Senat criticised the impact assessment which, in their view, did not provide analysis on economic and social sectors, was not based on reliable data and did not include the financial impact of the proposal, and was not supported by quantitative and qualitative indicators.

Most of the reasoned opinions feared that the proposal would equalise wages between local and posted workers, removing the competitive advantage of posted workers.[123] It was also raised that the proposal aligns wages across Member States.[124] A few of the reasoned opinions maintained that the legal basis does not match the objective of the proposal, which is workers' protection.[125] The Slovakian Národná rada argued that compensation of workers is a national competence, while the Hungarian Országgyűlés maintained that the Treaty grants the EU a complementary competence with respect to social policy. The competence issue was also raised by the only parliament out of the Central Eastern European bloc. Specifically, the Danish Folketing maintained that the definition of pay and conditions applicable to posted workers remains a Member State competence.[126] Some reasoned opinions claimed that the revised directive violates the proportionality principle by significantly limiting the free movement of services[127] and introducing additional administrative burdens without affirming any benefits.[128] Some also underlined that since the implementation period of the IMI Regulation[129] has not expired yet, it creates over-regulation and uncertainty, and the effects of that directive should be evaluated first.[130] Other arguments raised in the reasoned opinions pointed out the violation of Article 2 of Protocol No 2 since

[122] Bulgarian Narodno sabranie, Reasoned opinion (n 120), Polish Sejm, Reasoned opinion (n 120); Romanian Camera Deputaţilor Reasoned opinion (n 120); Croatian Hrvatski sabor, Reasoned opinion of 05.05.2016 on COM(2016) 128; Czech Poslanecká sněmovna, Reasoned opinion (n 121); Czech Senát, Reasoned opinion of 27.04.2016 on COM(2016) 128; Hungarian Országgyűlés, Reasoned opinion of 10.05.2016; Latvian Saeima, Reasoned opinion of 05.05.2016 on COM(2016) 128; Romanian Senat, Reasoned opinion of 04.05.2016 on COM(2016) 128; Slovak Národná rada, Reasoned opinion of 10.05.2016 on COM(2016) 128.

[123] Bulgarian Narodno sabranie, Reasoned opinion (n 120), Czech Poslanecká sněmovna, Reasoned opinion (n 121); Latvian Saeima, Reasoned opinion (n 122); Hungarian Országgyűlés, Reasoned opinion (n 122); Polish Sejm, Reasoned opinion (n 120); Estonian Riigikogu, Reasoned opinion of 10.5.2016 on COM(2016) 128; Lithuanian Seimas, Reasoned opinion of 03.05.2016 on COM(2016) 128.

[124] Czech Senát, Reasoned opinion (n 122); Lithuanian Seimas, Reasoned opinion (n 123); Hungarian Országgyűlés, Reasoned opinion (n 122); Slovak Národná rada, Reasoned opinion (n 122).

[125] Slovak Národná rada, Reasoned opinion (n 122); Romanian Camera Deputaţilor, Reasoned opinion (n 120); Romanian Senat, Reasoned opinion (n 122).

[126] Danish Folketing, Reasoned opinion of 06.05.2016 on COM(2016) 128.

[127] Hungarian Országgyűlés, Reasoned opinion (n 122).

[128] Bulgarian Narodno sabranie, Reasoned opinion (n 123); Romanian Senat, Reasoned opinion (n 122).

[129] Directive 2014/67/EU of the European Parliament and of the Council of 15 May 2014 on the enforcement of Directive 96/71/EC concerning the posting of workers in the framework of the provision of services and amending Regulation (EU) No 1024/2012 on administrative cooperation through the Internal Market Information System (the IMI Regulation) [2014] OJ L159/11.

[130] Croatian Hrvatski sabor, Reasoned opinion (n 122); Czech Senát, Reasoned opinion (n 122); Romanian Camera Deputaţilor, Reasoned opinion (n 120); Romanian Senat, Reasoned opinion (n 122); Estonian Riigikogu, Reasoned opinion (n 123); Lithuanian Seimas, Reasoned opinion (n 123); Slovak Národná rada, Reasoned opinion (n 122); Latvian Saeima, Reasoned opinion (n 122).

the Commission, in the view of some parliaments, did not conduct in-depth consultations with social partners or did not take into account the regional and local dimensions of the problem.[131]

There were also a number of opinions submitted within the political dialogue that claimed compatibility of the proposal with the subsidiarity principle and made detailed comments and suggestions for improving the proposal.[132]

On 11 May 2016, the Commission acknowledged that the yellow card was triggered. The first Vice-President of the Commission, Frans Timmermans, met with national parliaments' representatives at COSAC meetings before, in July 2016, sending the reply to national parliaments deciding that it was not necessary to withdraw the proposal.[133] The Commission summarised the subsidiarity arguments of national parliaments into four groups. First, with regard to those claiming that existing rules are sufficient, the Commission underlined that the facultative extension of collective agreements to all sectors of the economy does not fully achieve the objective, and hence it can be better achieved at the EU level. Similar arguments concerned the obligation to apply the same conditions to cross-border temporary agency workers and national temporary agency workers. For instances in which national parliaments argued that the alignment of wages within the EU should be achieved through economic development, the Commission explained that this is not the aim of the proposal, as it ensures only that remuneration rules of a host Member State are applicable to the posted worker. Second, the Commission addressed the arguments that considered the national level as the adequate level of action or that indicated that the Commission has not sufficiently proved that action should be achieved at the EU level. The Commission defended the proposal by stating that if the Member States acted unilaterally, their action could lead to fragmentation of the internal market with regard to the freedom to provide services: the proposal enables posted workers to enjoy the same conditions as do national workers. Individual actions of Member States could not achieve legal consistency and clarity in this regard. Third, the Commission maintained that the proposal respects the Member States' competence for defining pay and conditions of employment. The proposal provides only that mandatory rules on remuneration as set by the Member States should apply to local and cross-border service providers and to local and posted workers. Fourth, regarding the lack of justification with regard to the principle of subsidiarity, the Commission relying on the Court's case law argued that while the explanatory memorandum is short, it is accompanied by both the recitals of the proposal making clear why EU action is required and by the impact assessment.

[131] Czech Senát, Reasoned opinion (n 122); Romanian Camera Deputaţilor, Reasoned opinion (n 120); Romanian Senat, Reasoned opinion (n 122); Slovak Národná rada, Reasoned opinion (n 122); Hungarian Országgyűlés, Reasoned opinion (n 122); Latvian Saeima, Reasoned opinion (n 122); Lithuanian Seimas, Reasoned opinion (n 123).

[132] French Sénat, Opinion of 26.05.2016 on COM(2016) 128; French Assemblée nationale, Opinion of 13.08.2016 on COM(2016) 128; Spanish Cortes Generales, Opinion of 27.04.2016 on COM(2016) 128; Italian Senato della Repubblica, Opinion of 03.05.2016 on COM(2016) 128; Italian Camera dei Deputati, Opinion of 12.05.2016 on COM(2016) 128; Portuguese Assembleia da República, Opinion of 05.05.2016 on COM(2016) 128; UK House of Commons, Business Innovation and Skills Committee, Opinion of 25.05.2016 on COM(2016) 128.

[133] 'Communication from the Commission to the European Parliament, the Council and the National Parliaments on the proposal for a Directive amending the Posting of Workers Directive, with regard to the principle of subsidiarity, in accordance with Protocol No 2' COM(2016) 505 final.

The Commission's replies within the Barroso initiative countered non-subsidiarity-related arguments raised in the reasoned opinions. For example, there will be no additional administrative burden for companies posting workers because the applicable rules will be published on a single national website.[134] Even though in the proposal the notion of 'remuneration' replaces the notion of 'minimum rate of pay' preferred by some of the national parliaments, in the Commission's view, thanks to that website, posting companies will be easily able to check the rules applicable to remuneration in the host Member State.[135] The Commission also underlined that the proposal does not restrict the freedom to provide services and that labour cost is a legitimate aspect of competitiveness: instead, it offers more equality.[136] Since the proposal does not address any issue addressed by the IMI Regulation, there is no legal uncertainty in the period for implementation, and the proposals are, in fact, complementary.[137] The proposal does not replace the national mechanism of collective bargaining by extensively determining the binding effect of collective agreements regarding remuneration, but it ensures that the universal collective agreements are applicable to posted workers to the extent foreseen in the proposed directive.[138] The Commission underlined that the proposal does not equalise pay between local and posted workers but, instead, gives an option to apply rules on remuneration that are mandatory for national workers and that offer more protection to posted workers than the 'minimum rate of pay' that is guaranteed under the current system.[139] The proposed directive ensures that work carried out by a national worker or a posted worker is remunerated according to the same rules.[140] Each Member State continues to decide on wages and rules of remuneration; the proposal does not align or harmonise wages or rules across the Member States.[141] The Commission admitted that the proposal may reduce the labour cost competitiveness, yet SMEs will be able to continue competing with regard to quality of service, specialisation and innovation, and their services will still be required because of skill and labour shortages in other Member States.[142] Regarding the consultation of social partners, the Commission underlined

[134] Commission reply of 20.07.2016 to the Bulgarian Narodno sabranie on COM(2016) 128; Commission reply of 20.07.2016 to the Latvian Seimas on COM(2016) 128; Commission reply of 20.07.2016 to the Romanian Camera Deputaţilor on COM(2016) 128; Commission reply of 20.07.2016 to the Polish Senat on COM(2016) 128.

[135] Commission reply of 20.07.2016 to Hungarian Országgyűlés on COM(2016) 128.

[136] Commission reply to the Hungarian Országgyűlés (n 135); Commission reply of 20.07.2016 to the Croatian Hrvatski sabor on COM(2016) 128.

[137] Commission reply to the Croatian Hrvatski sabor (n 136), Commission reply to the Latvian Seimas (n 134); Commission reply to the Romanian Camera Deputaţilor (n 134); Commission reply to the Polish Senat (n 134); Commission reply of 20.07.2016 to the Estonian Riigikogu on COM(2016) 128; Commission reply of 20.07.2016 to the Romanian Senat on COM(2016) 128.

[138] Commission reply of 20.07.2016 to the Czech Poslanecká sněmovna on COM(2016) 128.

[139] Commission reply to the Czech Poslanecká sněmovna (n 138); Commission reply to the Croatian Hrvatski sabor (n 136); Commission reply to the Bulgarian Narodno sabranie (n 134); Commission reply to the Estonian Riigikogu (n 137); Commission reply to the Hungarian Országgyűlés (n 135); Commission reply to the Latvian Seimas (n 134); Commission reply of 20.07.2016 to the Czech Senát on COM(2016) 128; Commission reply of 20.07.2016 to the Polish Sejm on COM(2016) 128; Commission reply of 20.07.2016 to the Slovak Národná rada on COM(2016) 128.

[140] Commission reply to the Czech Senát (n 139).

[141] Commission reply to the Czech Senát (n 139); Commission reply to the Latvian Seimas (n 134); Commission reply to the Romanian Camera Deputaţilor (n 134); Commission reply to the Polish Sejm (n 139); Commission reply to the Slovak Národná rada (n 139).

[142] Commission reply to the Czech Senát (n 139); Commission reply to the Estonian Riigikogu (n 137); Commission reply to the Hungarian Országgyűlés (n 135); Commission reply to the Latvian Seimas (n 134); Commission reply to the Romanian Camera Deputaţilor (n 134); Commission reply to the Romanian Senat (n 137); Commission reply to the Polish Senat (n 134); Commission reply to the Slovak Národná rada (n 139).

that social partners had enough time to react and that their views were taken into account; those that do not agree with the proposal can contribute to the debate at national and EU levels.[143] The proposal does not interfere with the competence of the Member States to decide on the temporary agency work, but rather obliges them to apply the same rules on working and employment conditions that are applicable to workers hired as national temporary workers.[144] The Commission maintained that despite the fact that some Member States use the option to extend the universal collective agreements to posted workers in all sectors of the economy, the Commission does not see it as adequate for providing equality for companies and Member States that may not have the same interest in protecting posted workers as they do national workers.[145]

D. Compatibility of the Proposals with the Subsidiarity Principle

Crucially, the Commission did not acknowledge a subsidiarity breach with regard to any of the three yellow cards. Were the proposals compatible with the subsidiarity principle?

Regarding the Monti II proposal, the transnational labour disputes that were the object of the Commission proposal have a cross-border dimension that cannot be regulated by Member States. While preserving national industrial relations regimes in purely internal situations, the Commission proposed a framework for the management of those conflicts between business and labour that fall outside the regulatory powers of a single Member State when one of the actors in the conflict is enjoying rights resulting from EU free-movement law. The Commission proposal acknowledged that only the EU by regulating the exercise of transnational industrial action can address, by reason of its scale and effects, the challenge posed by the *Viking* and *Laval* judgments. Because national action in this field would be insufficient and because EU action is comparatively more efficient, the Monti II proposal fulfilled the material requirement of the principle of subsidiarity.

Similarly, the introduction of an EPPO as an answer to the question of which level of government can best protect the EU budget appears compatible with the subsidiarity principle.[146] Single Member States might not have sufficient means to investigate financial crimes of a cross-border nature. Moreover, because of the intrinsically European character of the issue to be protected—the European budget—Member States might not show the same interest in its protection as they would in the case of national budgets. The scale and the effects of the protection of the EU budget speak in favour of comparatively more efficient EU action.

Finally, the revision of the Posted Workers Directive aimed to protect workers exercising their economic freedoms. Again, the issue at stake has a transnational character that has not

[143] Commission reply to the Czech Senát (n 139); Commission reply to the Latvian Seimas (n 134); Commission reply to the Romanian Senat (n 137).

[144] Commission reply of 20.07.2016 to Danish Folketing on COM(2016) 128.

[145] Commission reply to the Polish Sejm (n 139).

[146] See the evidence of Katalin Ligeti and Valsamis Mitsilegas, UK House of Lords, Unrevised transcript of evidence taken before the Select Committee on the European Union, Justice, Institutions and Consumer Protection (Sub-Committee E), Inquiry into the Establishment of a European Public Prosecutor's Office (EPPO), Evidence Session No 1, 24.03.2014, 9–11.

been satisfactorily regulated by the Member States; cases of social dumping persist. The EU, by promoting the principle that the same work at the same place should be remunerated in the same manner, can address those issues and contribute to the objective of mutual recognition and non-discrimination of Articles 53(1) and 62 TFEU.

As demanded by the case law of the CJEU, to avoid 'empty formulas', the national insufficiency and EU comparative efficiency have to be substantiated with evidence. The Court has indicated that the analysis commonly found in the impact assessments has a useful role to play here.[147] The review of the same proposals for their compliance with the procedural requirement of the subsidiarity principle also seems fulfilled. The impact assessments in the three yellow card cases all identify a problem in achieving an objective, such as internal market integration, that exists without EU action. In all cases, the problems arise in an environment in which policy is led by the Member States, and thus this analysis suggests that there is 'insufficiency' in addressing the problem, echoing one leg of the subsidiary test. The impact assessments then analyse a number of alternative options, including as a baseline the pre-existing regime and, invariably, a number of options with policy driven by the EU, from which one is picked to become the proposal. This analysis incorporates a number of aspects, including the extent to which each option would contribute to achieving the objective behind the proposal and the costs involved. The comparison between the Member State-driven baseline scenario and the EU-driven alternatives thus offers insights into the possible comparative advantage of action at the EU level, the second leg of the subsidiarity test.

The extent to which the impact assessments make the implications for subsidiarity explicit varies by proposal. In the first and third yellow card, there is little direct reference to subsidiarity, while in the second proposal on the EPPO an explicit case is made for why the EU is 'best placed' to act in this matter.[148] Furthermore, throughout the impact assessment, the language appears suffused by subsidiarity considerations, emphasising the case for EU action with its 'value added'.

The impact assessments in these three proposals thus appear to support the Court's view that they can act as a source of information in determining whether a proposal is consistent with the subsidiarity principle. However, it should be noted that the Court has so far refrained from a critical review of the analysis in the impact assessments for that purpose and has provided little guidance regarding what analysis would be required. The door is thus left open for the Commission to replace 'empty formulas' concerning subsidiarity in the preamble with similarly empty analysis in the impact assessment to serve its case for EU action.

IV. CONSEQUENCES OF THE 'YELLOW CARDS'

The Commission's withdrawal of the Monti II proposal might have encouraged national parliaments to continue the practice of extending their reasoned opinions well beyond subsidiarity. By withdrawing its proposal despite of a lack of subsidiarity violation in the case

[147] See ch 1.
[148] See section IV of this chapter.

at stake, the Commission might have unintentionally encouraged a further misuse of the subsidiarity review by the national parliaments with potentially negative effects on the delicate balance of power between Member States and the EU.

In fact, the withdrawal of the Monti II proposal was celebrated by some national parliaments as the effect of their reasoned opinions rather than a result of the unlikely support of the EU legislator.[149] The reaction of parliaments to the Commission's decision to maintain the proposal in the case of the second and third yellow cards was to some extent more measured. For instance, the Romanian Camera Deputaţilor, which issued a reasoned opinion on the EPPO, recognised the validity of the Commission's arguments for maintaining the proposal and made some additional observations.[150] Yet, a number of parliaments were dissatisfied with the Commission's reply.[151] They criticised the Commission's communication, especially with the fact that the Commission divided the arguments between those concerning subsidiarity and those that were unrelated to subsidiarity.[152] Moreover, the UK House of Lords pointed out that the Commission gave detailed replies to national parliaments only several months after its communication on maintaining the proposal, seemingly making it evident that the Commission made its decision first and only later considered the reasoned opinions.[153] The Commission subsequently changed its approach in this regard when the third yellow card was triggered. Specifically, it sent its decision to maintain the proposal together with detailed replies to national parliaments. Still, some of those parliaments that sent a reasoned opinion were dissatisfied with the Commission's communication to maintain the proposal.[154]

The decision of the Commission to withdraw the proposal in the case of the first yellow card and maintain it in the case of the second yellow card raises some concerns with regard to the consistency of the Commission. The Monti II and the EPPO proposals both demanded unanimity in the Council to become binding law. As a reason to withdraw the Monti II proposal, the Commission cited the possible problem with reaching such a decision in the Council; yet in the case of the EPPO, this did not seem problematic for the Commission. This inconsistency of the Commission's approach concerning the Monti II and the EPPO proposal yellow cards might be connected with how important the proposal is on the Commission's agenda and whether other ways of pursuing the objective exist, for example, through enhanced cooperation. The Commission seems to be willing to stay firm on its position and move forward with its 'plan B' in case the proposal fails to achieve the necessary support with the EU legislator.[155]

[149] See Press release of 13.09.2012 of the French Sénat, available at: www.senat.fr/presse/cp20120913.html; Press release of 18.09.2012 of the Latvian Saeima, available at: www.saeima.lv/en/news/saeima-news/20026-saeima-makes-eu-withdraw-its-proposed-regulation).

[150] Romanian Camera Deputaţilor, Opinion of 27.12.2013 on COM(2013) 534.

[151] See Report from the Commission, 'Annual Report 2014 on relations between the European Commission and National Parliaments' COM(2015) 316 final, 5.

[152] UK House of Lords on COM(2013) 851 of 10.01.2013; UK House of Commons, European Scrutiny Committee, *Thirty-first Report of Session 2013–14*, 8.32 and *45th Report of Session 2013–14*, 10.14; Croatian Hrvatski sabor, Opinion of 01.04.2014 on COM(2013) 851.

[153] UK House of Lords, Opinion of 02.04.2014 on COM (2013)851; Dutch Tweede Kamer on COM(2013) 534 of 16.04.2014; Dutch Eerste Kamer on COM(2013) 534 of 03.06.2014.

[154] Czech Poslanecká sněmovna, Opinion of 03.11.2016 on COM(2016) 505.

[155] See also C Fasone, 'Parliamenti nazionali e controllo di sussidiarietà: il secondo "cartellino giallo" sull'istituzione della Procura europea' (2014) 33 *Quaderni Constituzionali* 165, 166.

First, the EPPO proposal has enjoyed support within the Commission since the beginning.[156] However, the 'right to strike' proposal was very brief and ambiguous, and seemed to aim at satisfying the demands of the EP Socialist Group. From the beginning it was evident that the Commission would not accord it absolute priority, but had to provide a compromise solution.[157] The yellow card might have offered an opportunity for the Commission to abandon its proposal.[158]

Second, whereas lack of unanimity in the Council or lack of the EP's consent was a clear threat to the future of the Monti II proposal after the yellow card triggered by national parliaments, Article 86(1) TFEU allows such proposals to be restarted in the form of enhanced cooperation. Accordingly, because of the lack of unanimity in the Council, on 7 February 2017 steps to establish an enhanced cooperation for the EPPO were completed.[159] On 14 February 2017, 17 Member States asked for the proposal to be referred to the European Council.[160] In its meeting on 9 March 2017, the European Council did not reach a consensus. On 3 April 2017, 16 Member States[161] notified the EP, the Council and the Commission of their intention to launch the EPPO.[162] Those Member States were Belgium, Bulgaria, Croatia, Cyprus, the Czech Republic, Germany, Greece, Spain, Finland, France, Lithuania, Luxembourg, Portugal, Romania, Slovenia, and Slovakia. This indicates that despite the reasoned opinions of the Cypriot Vouli ton Antiprosopon, the Slovenian Državni zbor, the Czech Senát, the French Sénat, and the Romanian Camera Deputaţilor, their governments decided to participate in the EPPO. As provided by Article 86(1) TFEU, the authorisation to proceed with enhanced cooperation is deemed granted, meaning that there is no further need for the Council or the EP to authorise cooperation. Next, on 8 June 2017, the Member States participating in the enhanced cooperation agreed on a draft regulation setting the details of the EPPO.[163] Finally, on 5 October 2017, the EP granted consent to the draft regulation.[164]

Is the launch of the EPPO in the form of enhanced cooperation, however, less justifiable from the perspective of the subsidiarity principle? Indeed, the Commission has argued that an action at the EU level, covering all Member States, is necessary because of the cross-border character of EU fraud crimes.[165] Starting an enhanced cooperation of a limited number of Member States seems to go against the need for action at the EU level.[166]

[156] See 'Green Paper on criminal law protection of the financial interests of the Community and the establishment of a European Prosecutor' COM(2001) 715.

[157] EP debate of 15.09.2009, Statement by the President-designate of the Commission, point 11.

[158] G Barrett, 'Monti II. The Subsidiarity Review Process Comes of Age … Or Then Again Maybe It Doesn't' (2012) 19 *Maastricht Journal of European and Comparative Law* 595, 599. See also Schima (n 65) 385.

[159] Council of the EU, Press release 48/17 of 07.02.2017.

[160] European Council, 'Request for referral to the European Council in accordance with the procedure set out in the second subparagraph of Article 86(1) TFEU' EUCO 4/17 of 17.02.2017.

[161] The minimum number of Member States to launch an enhanced cooperation is nine.

[162] Council of the EU, Press release 184/17 of 03.04.2017.

[163] Council of the EU, Press release 333/17 of 08.06.2017. See that the number of Member States participating rose to 18 with two more Member States considering joining.

[164] European Parliament, Legislative Resolution of 5 October 2017 on the draft Council regulation implementing enhanced cooperation on the establishment of the European Public Prosecutor's Office, P8_TA(2017)0384.

[165] COM(2013) 534, Explanatory Memorandum, 2.

[166] In any case, it would be impossible to include all Member States in the EPPO project because of the UK, Irish and Danish opt-outs. See Art 1 of Protocol No 21 on the position of the United Kingdom and Ireland in respect to the Area of Freedom, Security and Justice; Art 1 of Protocol No 22 on the position of Denmark. The UK, Ireland and Denmark may, however, in accordance with Art 3 of the appropriate protocols, within three months of the proposal being presented to the Council, notify its president that they wish to take part in the adoption and application of the proposal.

The enhanced cooperation, however, is open to Member States to join, and joining can be expected. Moreover, the regulation implementing the enhanced cooperation on the EPPO will have to pass the subsidiarity test. Article 3 of Protocol No 2 includes in the notion of 'draft legislative acts', not only proposals from the Commission, but also, among others, initiatives from a group of Member States.[167]

The revision of the Posted Workers Directive has been under discussion since the Commission's communication to maintain the proposal. Shortly after that communication, some of the Member States' representatives in the Council demanded a withdrawal of the draft, putting forward arguments on the diminished competitiveness and good functioning of the internal market, invoking the yellow card, while others supported moving forward with the proposal.[168] The Council adopted a progress report focusing on long-term posting, the notion of remuneration, collective agreements, subcontracting and temporary agency workers.[169] In the EP, the responsible committee adopted a report that highlighted the need to extend the legal basis of the proposal to include Article 151 TFEU and points (a) and (b) of Article 153(1) TFEU on workers' rights and to offer Member States the freedom to determine the concept of remuneration at the national level, yet all due entitlements must be included.[170] As of September 2017 the proposal awaits a decision of the EP committee, after which the trilogue, informal meetings among the Commission, the EP and the Council on the proposal will begin. In sum, the proposal has been generally perceived as an improvement as compared with the existing Posted Workers Directive.[171] Legislative intervention of the EU in the field of social rights would bring benefits. It would offer a structure for the market participants, provide detail and certainty about what is lawful and what is not, allow for adaptation by constructing a special regime, provide a vehicle for consolidation of the Court's case law in the area, and deliver a democratic imprimatur needed in this controversial area.[172]

V. OBSERVATIONS ON THE PRACTICE OF THE EWS

In practice, the three 'yellow cards' show that national parliaments have become more conscious about the drafting of their reasoned opinions to clearly address subsidiarity issues. Similarly, in its communications, the Commission replied to subsidiarity-related

[167] As a comparable example, see the 'Proposal for a Council Directive implementing enhanced cooperation in the area of financial transaction tax' COM(2013) 71 final, in which case the *Letter de saisine* (SG-Greffe(2013) D/1947, 19.02.2013) clearly stated that the EWS applies. See the reasoned opinion of the Swedish Riksdag of 11.04.2013 on COM(2013) 71. Because in the EPPO's case authorisation is deemed to be granted, national parliaments will not assess the Commission proposal for a Council Decision *authorising* enhanced cooperation, as in the case of the 'Proposal for a Council Decision authorising enhanced cooperation in the area of the creation of unitary patent protection' COM(2010) 790 final and the political dialogue opinion of the Italian Senato della Repubblica.

[168] Council of the EU, Outcome of the Council Meeting, 26–27 May 2016, 9357/16.

[169] Council of the EU, Progress Report, 25.11.2016, 14368/16.

[170] EP, Committee on Employment and Social Affairs, Draft Report, 02.12.2016, 2016/0070.

[171] R Zahn, 'Revision of the Posted Workers Directive: A Europeanisation Perspective' (2017) 19 *Cambridge Yearbook of European Legal Studies* 1, 21.

[172] C Kilpatrick, 'Internal market architecture and the accommodation of labour rights: As good as it gets?' (2011) 4 EUI Working Papers, Department of Law, 2–3.

comments of national parliaments, while the other arguments were addressed within the political dialogue. The three yellow cards and the case studies presented in this book clearly show that national parliaments continue with a broad assessment of Commission proposals.[173] The reaction of the Commission to the first yellow card as mentioned above undoubtedly contributed to national parliaments' understanding of the EWS.

The practice also shows that national parliaments have adopted their own labels for the parts of the subsidiarity test. The UK House of Commons in its reasoned opinions conducts a subsidiarity test, the first limb of which consists of a 'necessity test' (questioning whether the EU Commission has established that legislative action at EU level is necessary at all) and 'insufficiency of Member State action test', the latter of which requires the Commission to prove that the action proposed cannot be sufficiently achieved by the Member States.[174] The second limb is whether the 'action is better achieved at EU level', a test which requires the Commission to provide evidence that the objective of the proposal 'would be better achieved, by reason of its scale or effects, by action at EU level'.[175] The Irish Parliament indicates that Article 5(3) TEU constitutes a 'comparative efficiency exercise', involving a 'necessity test' and a 'greater benefits test'.[176] Within the necessity limb, the Parliament attempts to answer the question of whether 'the action by the EU [is] necessary to achieve the objective of the proposal' and whether 'the objective of the proposal [can] only be achieved, or achieved to a sufficient extent, by EU action'. The 'greater benefits test' asks, in turn, whether the objective would be better achieved at EU level—'ie would EU action provide greater benefits than action at Member State level?' The problem of labelling the 'national insufficiency test' as a 'necessity test' is the confusion with the 'necessity test' that is a part of the proportionality principle expressed in Article 5(4) TEU. This provision states that 'the content and form of Union action shall not exceed what is necessary to achieve the objectives of the Treaties'. This is exactly the enquiry of the Irish Parliament within the scrutiny of Article 5(3) TEU.

There is also the question of how many Member States in which the achievement of an action would be 'insufficient' are necessary to fulfil the 'national insufficiency test'. In fact, national parliaments often underline in their reasoned opinions that the proposal violates the subsidiarity principle because Member States can achieve the objective on their own or because they already have some mechanisms implemented in this regard. For example, in reaction to the Commission proposal on periodic testing for motor vehicles and their trailers, the Swedish Riksdag underlined in its reasoned opinion that the system operating in Sweden is 'well organized and adapted to maintain high levels of road safety among the various vehicles used on the roads'.[177] In the same vein, both the Dutch Tweede and Eerste Kamer argued that this Commission proposal 'intervenes in well-functioning systems of the Member States'.[178] However, as was pointed out by the Court,

> the subsidiarity principle is not intended to limit the EU's competence on the basis of the situation of any particular Member State taken individually, but requires only that the proposed action can,

[173] See chs 6 and 7.
[174] UK House of Commons, Reasoned opinion of 12.02.2014 on COM(2013) 893, points 17 and 19.
[175] ibid, point 21.
[176] Irish Houses of the Oireachtas, Reasoned opinion of 06.11.2013 on COM(2013) 627.
[177] Swedish Riksdag, Reasoned opinion of 17.10.2012 on COM(2012) 380, 1.
[178] Dutch Tweede Kamer, Reasoned opinion of 09.10.2012 and Eerste Kamer of 11.10.2012, 4 on COM(2012) 380.

> by reason of its scale or effects, be better achieved at the level of the European Union in view of the objectives of the European Union set out in Article 3 TEU, and provisions specific to various areas … laid down in the Treaties.[179]

In other words, for the compliance of an EU legislative act with the principle of subsidiarity, the fact that a Member State sufficiently achieves an objective does not matter; the Court compares the efficiency of the EU level with the national level as such.

Another issue visible in the reasoned opinions concerns impact assessments. Since impact assessments are not translated into all official EU languages, national parliaments often rely on the executive summaries of impact assessments that are fully translated and on the explanatory memoranda included in the draft legislative acts. Those documents are much shorter and less elaborative than the impact assessments. In consequence, national parliaments may consider the justifications given in explanatory memoranda as not constituting a sufficient qualitative and quantitative substantiation of the compliance with the subsidiarity principle as foreseen by Protocol No 2.[180] However, national parliaments do also refer to impact assessments in their reasoned opinions.[181]

In addition to the examples indicated in the discussion of the yellow cards above, other instances show that national parliaments perceive the review of proportionality as an independent step of scrutiny. For example, the German Bundestag confirmed a violation of the proportionality principle in the Commission proposal on the Fund for European Aid to the Most Deprived 'because its content and form far exceed[ed] what [was] necessary to achieve the objectives of the treaties'.[182] The Hellenic Voulí ton Ellínon voiced reservations on the Tobacco Products Directive, as the objective could be achieved by 'means of milder measures' rather than by banning flavoured or slim cigarettes.[183] The Polish Sejm found the Commission proposal on 'Women on Boards' in breach of the principle of proportionality because 'in order to achieve the directive's objective it would suffice to adopt EU-wide measures aimed at standardising the criteria of appointing members of company boards, without the need to establish binding parities'.[184] Other parliaments explicitly see proportionality as an inherent part of the subsidiarity test, reviewing 'the proportionality aspect in the principle of subsidiarity'.[185] The Swedish Riksdag, in its analysis of the Commission proposal on the European Single Market for electronic communications, enquired whether the proposal 'is suited to its purpose, and argue[d] instead that there are other and less intrusive ways than those considered by the Commission to secure a harmonised market for e-com services'.[186] These examples show that national parliaments, while assessing proportionality of proposals, focus on the necessity and *stricto sensu* tests inherent to that principle. The Commission rightly addresses the proportionality violations highlighted by national

[179] Case C-358/14 *Poland v Parliament and Council*, EU:C:2016:323, para 119.

[180] See, eg, UK House of Commons, Reasoned opinion of 11.11.2013 on COM(2013) 618, 619, points 10 and 12.

[181] See, eg, UK House of Commons, Reasoned opinion of 21.05.2013 and the Romanian Camera Deputaţilor, Reasoned opinion of 28.05.2013 on COM(2013) 147.

[182] See, eg, German Bundestag, Reasoned opinion of 12.12.2012 on COM(2012) 617.

[183] Hellenic Vouli ton Ellinon, Reasoned opinion of 21.02.2013 on COM(2012) 788, similarly as in the opinion of 04.09.2013 on COM(2013) 472, 4.

[184] Polish Sejm, Reasoned opinion of 04.01.2013 on COM(2012) 614.

[185] Swedish Riksdag, Reasoned opinion of 07.11.2013 on COM(2013) 627.

[186] ibid.

parliaments in its answers within the political dialogue, maintaining that proportionality analysis 'goes beyond the scope of application of Article 6, Protocol No 2'.[187] A similar approach has been taken regarding cases in which the yellow card was triggered.

Besides the possible mix-up with the 'necessity test' inherent in the proportionality principle, a question as to whether any action is 'necessary at all' is often addressed as a subsidiarity issue. However, this is not a question about the right level of governance, because at the subsidiarity level, we assume that some action must be taken, and we decide on the more appropriate level of government. For example, the UK House of Commons, which notoriously checks the necessity of Commission proposals, states that 'necessity is a pre-requisite both for action at EU level and for conformity with the principle of subsidiarity'.[188] However, the 'necessity' question in the meaning implied by the UK House of Commons comes before subsidiarity and is decided upon by the Commission. It is a policy question, one that is not to be answered within the subsidiarity test.[189]

VI. CONCLUSION

The aim of this chapter was to provide an assessment of the understanding of the subsidiarity principle by the national parliaments. As an analytical framework, the chapter provided a set of textual, structural and functional arguments speaking against a wide scope of the EWS that often includes an assessment of the legal basis, proportionality, and contents of proposals. The analysis of the first three 'yellow cards' and other reasoned opinions issued by national parliaments shows that national parliaments in their reasoned opinions go beyond the assessment of the subsidiarity principle. In particular, the withdrawal of the Monti II proposal, despite a lack of subsidiarity violation, could be seen as an inadvertent encouragement of a broad review by the Commission. When triggering the following two yellow cards, national parliaments were more conscious about the drafting of their reasoned opinions, attempting to make the subsidiarity argument clearer. However, the Commission seemed inconsistent in its decision to withdraw the proposal in the Monti II case and to maintain the EPPO proposal when both demanded unanimitiy in the Council. This chapter explained that the support for the proposal within the Commission and the possibility to refer to the enhanced cooperation might explain the Commission's decision to maintain the EPPO proposal. However, as such, all three proposals to which the yellow cards were shown seemed to be compatible with the subsidiarity principle.

Based on a wider analysis of the reasoned opinions submitted by national parliaments, it is apparent that some national parliaments have provided their own labels and questions to be asked in the subsidiarity review. They often marry subsidiarity and the proportionality principle and understand the subsidiarity principle as a policy question. National legislators

[187] eg, Commission reply to Austrian Bundesrat of 13.02.2014 on COM(2013) 620, 2. See section II of this chapter.

[188] UK House of Commons (n 56) point 15.

[189] See, however, Emiliou, who argues that 'proportionality is concerned with the question whether Community action is necessary *at all*' (emphasis added). N Emiliou, 'Subsidiarity: An Effective Barrier Against "the Enterprises of Ambition"?' (1992) 17 *European Law Review* 383, 402.

have been focusing also on the justification of Commission proposals, and in their reviews, they refer to impact assessments. In sum, two issues became clear: national parliaments in their reasoned opinions conduct a broad scrutiny of Commission proposals, and the assessment of the subsidiarity principle as such is often conflated with the principles of conferral, proportionality, and contents of proposals.

4

Design of the Subsidiarity Review at the National Level

I. INTRODUCTION

FOR A LONG time, national parliaments have been 'slow and retarding adapters' to changes in the EU system.[1] The entry into force of the Treaty of Lisbon demanded further adjustments of national parliaments, especially for the new function of subsidiarity review. National parliaments maintained autonomy, however, with regard to the design of the subsidiarity scrutiny procedures; the requirement was that under the relevant national law, the reasoned opinions must be regarded as adopted by the parliament or a chamber thereof.[2]

This chapter reviews whether national parliaments are prepared to be 'responsible for integration'.[3] The responsibility for integration implies that '(i)f the legitimization of supranational secondary acts cannot be directly constructed, at least the institution with the greatest base of legitimacy should be involved'.[4] This institution is, primarily, the national parliament. Adjustments for subsidiarity scrutiny at the national level indicate the readiness of national parliaments to accept their new role and to improve their effectiveness at the EU level. Specifically, the internal organisation for subsidiarity scrutiny is a crucial point to be developed in the debate about the new role of national parliaments in the EU. Because the adaptation of the internal legislative organisation for the Early Warning System (EWS) is in the hands of the Member States, the effectiveness of national parliaments largely relies on how these procedures are designed at the national level.

This chapter is structured as follows. Section II offers an overview of the institutional reforms at the national level that took place following the changes in EU Treaties. Section III presents the judgments of some of the national constitutional courts that triggered changes at the national level following EU reforms. The core of this chapter, in section IV, provides a review of all the national systems of subsidiarity review, to demonstrate all possible types of scrutiny: centralised, decentralised, mixed and 'subsidiarity-oriented' models. Section V

[1] A Maurer and W Wessels, 'National Parliaments after Amsterdam: From Slow Adapters to National Players?' in A Maurer and W Wessels (eds), *National Parliaments on their Ways to Europe: Losers or Latecomers?* (Baden-Baden, Nomos, 2001) 461. See also O Rozenberg and C Hefftler, 'Introduction' in C Hefftler et al (eds), *The Palgrave Handbook of National Parliaments and the European Union* (Basingstoke, Palgrave Macmillan, 2015) 16–20.

[2] P Kiiver, *The Early Warning System for the Principle of Subsidiarity: Constitutional Theory and Empirical Reality* (London, Routledge, 2012) 25.

[3] BVerfG, 2 BvE 2/08, judgment of 30.06.2009, para 245 (English version).

[4] F Schorkopf, 'The European Union as an Association of Sovereign States: Karlsruhe's Ruling on the Treaty of Lisbon' (2009) 10 *German Law Journal* 1219, 1235.

compares the institutional adjustments for the EWS based on the following variables: the moment of detection of a subsidiarity violation, the role of the government, and the role of the plenary session and the possibility for the regional parliaments to state its view regarding subsidiarity of Commission proposals. What follows in section VI is a study of the latest Commission reports on the activity of national parliaments in the EWS. This analysis shows that the choice of the scrutiny procedure is not the decisive element for a large number of reasoned opinions of a national parliament in the EWS.

II. INSTITUTIONAL EVOLUTION OF NATIONAL PARLIAMENTS

National parliaments of the founding Member States did not alter their internal structures in response to the process of European integration. At the time, governments were in a strong position at the EU level, and although some national parliaments (namely, the German, Belgian, Italian and Dutch parliaments) had established European committees, such committees wielded only marginal influence.[5] Subsequently, parliaments in the UK and Denmark established European Affairs Committees (EACs) in order to safeguard the strong constitutional position of their parliaments after accession to the Community.[6]

The shift of many competences from the national level to the EU level was another trigger for reform in national parliaments. The White Paper on the completion of the internal market (1985) and the Single European Act (1986) mark an important stage in this process, because the Act established new areas of Community competence and broad powers for the Community to adopt legislation on the internal market with a qualified majority, instead of unanimity, in the Council.[7] Subsequently, the attitude of national parliaments towards European integration changed with regard to three issues.[8] First, because of the establishment of the EACs, the members of national parliaments started to specialise in particular EU policy areas. Second, committees became more involved in the management of European affairs, as indicated by the increase in time dedicated to the analysis of documents for Council meetings and the implementation of directives. Third, national parliaments underwent 'segmentation and fragmentation' (developments connected to the greater involvement of EACs), and MEPs became involved in the work of advisory committees.[9]

The Maastricht Treaty brought about a need for further adjustments at the national level, strengthening the participation rights of parliaments, especially regarding information rights. For example, in 1992, France and Germany regulated the position of the national parliament in EU affairs at the constitutional level.[10] Concomitantly, sectoral committees became more involved in EU affairs, particularly as a result of the growing workload of EACs.[11] The following reform treaties, while referring to national parliaments, did not have

[5] Maurer and Wessels (n 1) 437.

[6] P Norton, 'Introduction: Adapting to European Integration' in P Norton (ed), *National Parliaments and the European Union* (London, Frank Cass, 1996) 24.

[7] 'Completing the Internal Market', White Paper from the Commission to the European Council COM(85) 310 final; Single European Act [1987] OJ L169.

[8] Norton (n 6) 25; Maurer and Wessels (n 1) 435.

[9] Maurer and Wessels (n 1) 435.

[10] Art 4 La loi constitutionnelle no92-554 du 25 juin 1992; Art 1 Gesetz zur Änderung des Grundgesetzes v 21.12.1992 BGBl. I 92, 2086.

[11] J O'Brennan and T Raunio, 'Introduction: deparliamentarization and European integration' in J O'Brennan and T Raunio (eds), *National Parliaments within the Enlarged European Union: from 'victims' of integration to competitive actors?* (London, Routledge, 2007) 12.

the same effects as the Single European Act or the Maastricht Treaty.[12] With the Constitutional Treaty, some parliaments saw an incentive to reform their internal organisation in order to accommodate new powers; however that treaty did not come into force.[13]

The new powers that national parliaments gained through the ratification of the Treaty of Lisbon triggered procedural changes, while no new committees needed to be created. National laws were amended to incorporate the new competences of national parliaments, for example, the participation of national parliaments in the treaty change procedure.[14] To participate in the EWS, Member States reformed their scrutiny procedures, with some of these changes made via constitutional amendment. In 2008, Germany and France amended their constitutions to accommodate the participation rights of national parliaments in subsidiarity scrutiny.[15] This level of reform reflected the importance of national parliaments' participation in the EU legislative process for national constitutional systems. In addition to the amendment of constitutions of some Member States, most Member States introduced reforms of infra-constitutional law, especially to the rules of procedure of their parliaments, in order to accommodate subsidiarity review. This chapter aims to establish how national procedures were amended to allow national parliaments the control of the subsidiarity principle and whether some scrutiny systems and their particular elements can be highlighted.

III. ANALYSIS OF CONSTITUTIONAL JURISPRUDENCE

Besides the treaties reforming the EU, constitutional courts played an important role in shaping the extent to which national parliaments participate in EU affairs. Constitutional courts demanded constitutional or infra-constitutional adjustments for this purpose. This section examines the decisions of the German, French and Polish constitutional courts concerning the new functions of national parliaments.

A. Germany

The judgment of the German Federal Constitutional Court in June 2009 held that the new institutional role of national parliaments introduced by the Treaty of Lisbon does not compensate the legitimacy deficit based on EP elections and does not rectify the legitimacy deficit in the EU, as the reduced number of decisions demanding unanimity and supranationalisation of police and judicial cooperation in criminal matters diminishes the role played by national parliaments in the EU decision-making process.[16] In the view of the Constitutional Court, only the national parliaments, and not the European Parliament (EP),

[12] See ch 2.

[13] See, eg, the UK House of Commons, Modernisation Committee *Second Report, Session 2004–2005*, paras 113–18.

[14] K Granat, 'Interparliamentary Cooperation and the Simplified Revision Procedures' in N Lupo and C Fasone (eds), *Interparliamentary Cooperation in the Composite European Constitution* (Oxford, Hart Publishing, 2016).

[15] Art 1 Gesetz zur Änderung des Grundgesetzes Artikel 23, 45 und 93 v 08.10.2008 BGBl. I 2009, 1926; Art 43 and 47 Loi constitutionnelle no 2008-724 du 23 juillet 2008 de modernisation des institutions de la Ve République.

[16] BVerfG, 2 BvE 2/08, judgment of 30.06.2009, paras 293–94.

may safeguard democracy at the European level. In this respect, the Court introduced the new concept of 'responsibility for integration' (*Integrationsverantwortung*), applicable to all state organs, which are obliged to ensure that the political systems of Germany and the EU remain in compliance with the principle of democracy according to the German Basic Law.[17] The 'responsibility for integration' should be understood as a counterbalance to the dynamic developments of European integration and the lack of direct legitimacy of secondary legislation.[18] In such a situation, the national parliament, as the state organ with the most legitimacy, should assume the responsibility for integration. The responsibility for integration guarantees the participation of the Bundestag and the Bundesrat, not only for treaty changes, but it also compels these parliamentary chambers to 'politically accompany' decisions taken by the EU.[19]

Changes of national provisions had to be introduced in order to meet the obligation of 'the responsibility for integration'. The Federal Constitutional Court ruled that both the Act Approving the Treaty of Lisbon[20] and the Act Amending the Basic Law (Articles 23, 45 and 93)[21] were compliant with the Basic Law, yet the Act Extending and Strengthening the Rights of the Bundestag and the Bundesrat, regulating the participation of the Bundestag and the Bundesrat in EU affairs, contradicted Article 38(1) in connection with Article 23(1) of the Basic Law.[22] The latter Act did not offer sufficient participation rights to the German Parliament.[23] According to the Federal Constitutional Court, a new legal act should 'take into account that [the Bundestag and the Bundesrat] must exercise their responsibility for integration in numerous cases of dynamic development of the treaties'.[24] Regarding the subsidiarity review, the Constitutional Court specifically stated that the effectiveness of the EWS 'depends on the extent to which the national parliaments will be able to make organisational arrangements that place them in a position to make appropriate use of the mechanism within the short period of eight weeks'.[25] The Court also expressed concern regarding the scope of the subsidiarity action (ex post subsidiarity scrutiny of a EU legislative act), specifically whether the action of the national parliaments and of the Committee of the Regions before the Court of Justice of the European Union (CJEU/the Court) will be extended to assessing 'whether the European Union has competence for the specific lawmaking project'.[26] For the ex post subsidiarity scrutiny, the Basic Law was amended to enable the Bundestag and the Bundesrat to bring a subsidiarity action before the Court.[27]

[17] ibid, paras 238–45.
[18] Schorkopf (n 4) 723.
[19] M Nettesheim, 'Die Integrationsverantwortung-Vorgaben des BVerfG und gesetzgeberische Umsetzung' (2010) 63 *Neue Juristische Wochenschrift* 177.
[20] Zustimmungsgesetz zum Vertrag von Lissabon, Gesetz v 08.10.2008 zum Vertrag von Lissabon v 13.12.2007 BGBl. II 2008, 1038.
[21] Gesetz zur Änderung des Grundgesetzes Artikel 23, 45 und 93 v 08.10.2008 BGBl. I 2009, 1926.
[22] Gesetz über die Ausweitung und Stärkung der Rechte des Bundestages und des Bundesrates in Angelegenheiten der Europäischen Union, BT-Dr 16/8489.
[23] BVerfG, 2 BvE 2/08, judgment of 30.06.2009, paras 411–19. However, the failure of the Act Extending and Strengthening the Rights of the Bundestag and the Bundesrat was connected with the treaty amendment procedures and not the subsidiarity review.
[24] BVerfG, 2 BvE 2/08, judgment of 30.06.2009, para 411.
[25] ibid, para 305.
[26] ibid.
[27] Art 23.1a of the Basic Law.

After the Federal Constitutional Court issued its judgment, Germany introduced new laws regulating the participation of the Bundestag and the Bundesrat in EU affairs. Nevertheless, these changes were assessed as failing to satisfy the core idea of the responsibility for integration, since the changes are limited to the direct consequences of the judgment and do not include, for example, the parliamentary oversight of the EU energy policy (Article 194 TFEU).[28] Moreover, since three different laws regulate the matter, the procedure is not sufficiently transparent,[29] and for this reason, some propose that the Parliament should draw up a 'German Code on European Law' consolidating the existing laws.[30]

B. France

In France, the Conseil constitutionnel considered, in response to a request from the president pursuant to Article 54 of the Constitution of France (on references concerning the constitutionality of international treaties), whether the authorisation to ratify the Treaty of Lisbon required prior revision of the Constitution. In its decision, the Conseil constitutionnel recognised the new role of national parliaments in the activities of the EU. However, the power of the French Parliament to oppose certain aspects of family law subject to the ordinary legislative procedure and to ensure compliance with the principle of subsidiarity required a constitutional amendment.[31] As a consequence, France added Article 88–6 to Title XV on the EU in order to provide for a mechanism to conduct subsidiarity review.[32]

C. Poland

In Poland, as early as 2005, the Constitutional Court stressed the need to ensure that both the Sejm and the Senat participate in EU affairs.[33] The Constitutional Court stated that exercising influence on the position of the government in EU affairs is, in fact, a legislative function. In the view of the Constitutional Court, both chambers should be guaranteed equal participation in activities concerning the shaping position of Poland in the field of adopting EU law. However, until the Treaty of Lisbon the necessary changes to Polish law were not introduced because of a lack of political will.[34] As a consequence, in its judgment concerning the Lisbon Treaty, the Constitutional Court emphasised the role of the reasoned opinions that allow the Parliament to shape the content of EU law 'to the extent … that it

[28] Nettesheim (n 19) 182.

[29] ibid 183.

[30] C Calliess and T Beichelt, 'The Europeanization of the Bundestag: From Observer to Player?' [2013] *Bertelsmann Stiftung* 31.

[31] Conseil constitutionnel, Décision no 2007-560 DC, 20 January 2007 (Treaty of Lisbon amending the Treaty on European Union and the Treaty establishing the European Community) 28–32.

[32] Loi constitutionnelle no 2008-724 du 23 juillet 2008 de modernisation des institutions de la Ve République.

[33] Trybunał Konstytucyjny, K 24/04 judgment of 12.01.2005, inequality in competences of the Sejm and Senat committees in respect of European Union legislative proposal. See A Łazowski, 'The Polish parliament and EU affairs: An effective actor or an accidental hero?' in J O'Brennan and T Raunio (eds), *National Parliaments within the Enlarged European Union: from 'victims' of integration to competitive actors?* (London, Routledge, 2007) 212–14.

[34] A Fuksiewicz, 'Sejm i Senat rok po wejściu w życie Traktatu Lizbońskiego-dostosowanie do reformy instytucjonalnej' [2011] *Instytut Spraw Publicznych* 1, 1s1.

is possible to narrow down the scope of its "external character" in relation to the Polish state'.[35] In this respect, the Constitutional Court left it to the legislature to take the legal measures to accommodate the EWS and to establish the principles of the cooperation of government with the Sejm and the Senat in EU affairs.[36] An amendment of the Constitution was not necessary in this respect.

The decisions of constitutional courts in Germany, France and Poland underlined the importance of national parliaments for the participation of these Member States in the affairs of the EU. Whereas the role of national parliaments, including their scrutiny of the subsidiarity principle, was elevated to the level of a constitutional amendment in Germany (albeit only for ex post scrutiny) and France, in Poland this procedure remained at the level of infra-constitutional law, probably because of the inflexibility of the Constitution of Poland.[37] The next section explores the details of Member States' institutional design concerning subsidiarity scrutiny.

IV. OVERVIEW OF SCRUTINY TYPES

An analysis of the systems in place in the Member States indicates the existence of four broad types of scrutiny of the principle of subsidiarity: centralised, mixed, decentralised and 'subsidiarity-focused'. First, a single dominant committee, the EAC, characterises the centralised system. There is no delegation of scrutiny to sectoral committees. This type of procedure was adopted by the Austrian Bundesrat[38] and the Polish Sejm[39] as well as the Croatian Hrvatski sabor,[40] Hungarian Országgyűlés,[41] Latvian Saeima[42] and Maltese Kamra tad-Deputati.[43] The scrutiny system may also be double-centralised in the sense that there is one joint committee for two parliamentary chambers, as is the case in Spain.[44] Another type includes subcommittees of the EAC specialising in particular aspects of EU affairs, as in the UK.[45] In the Austrian Nationalrat, the Main Committee on EU Affairs can

[35] Trybunał Konstytucyjny, K 32/09 judgment of 24.11.2010, 31. The Court, following the Polish doctrine, sees EU law as an order that is 'partially external' to Polish law. Even though the Polish legal system is generally seen by the Court as 'multicentric' meaning that EU legal acts have a legal force in Poland, the Court underlines that EU primary law comes into force as accepted by all Member States, while EU secondary law by the national representatives in the Council and the representatives of European citizens (including Polish) in the EP. The element of 'externality' is hence that it is not the Polish legislator which constitutes EU law.

[36] Trybunał Konstytucyjny, K 32/09, 31.

[37] Art 235 of the Polish Constitution.

[38] Art 23g(1) of the Austrian Constitution; and §13a(5) of the Bundesrat Rules of Procedure.

[39] Art 148b par 1 and 148cc par 1 of the Sejm Rules of Procedure.

[40] Art 4 of the Act on the Co-Operation of the Croatian Parliament and the Government of the Republic of Croatia in European Affairs.

[41] § 134/D(1) of the Rules of Procedure.

[42] 185[1] (1) of the Saeima Rules of Procedure. Theoretically the EAC may send the proposal to other Saeima committees, but it is not practiced. Information received from the EAC of the Latvian Saeima, 04.07.2016.

[43] Art 120F of the Standing Orders.

[44] Ley 24/2009, de 22 de diciembre, de modificación de la Ley 8/1994, de 19 de mayo, por la que se regula la Comisión Mixta para la Unión Europea, para su adaptación al Tratado de Lisboa de 13 de diciembre de 2007. For the history of this regulation see S Piedrafita, 'The Spanish Parliament and EU Affairs in the Post Lisbon Treaty Era: All Change?' (2014) 20 *Journal of Legislative Studies* 18.

[45] House of Commons, *European Scrutiny Committee, Reforming the European Scrutiny System in the House of Commons, Twenty-Fourth Report of Session 2013–14, Volume* I, point 22; House of Lords, *The Role of National Parliaments in the European Union, 9th Report of Session 2013–14*, point 30.

delegate its powers with regard to the scrutiny of EU draft legislative acts to the Standing Sub-Committee on EU Affairs.[46]

Second, a scrutiny system may take a decentralised form, in which only a sectoral committee conducts scrutiny. This procedure is quite rare among the Member States' scrutiny systems: only the Belgian Parliament, both the Chambre des représentants[47] and the Sénat,[48] the Dutch Eerste and Tweede Kameren,[49] and the Swedish Riksdag[50] apply it. The sectoral committees of the houses of the Irish Parliament meet as a joint committee to adopt a reasoned opinion.[51]

Third, subsidiarity scrutiny may have a mixed character if it combines aspects of both centralised and decentralised systems. This is the most popular system among the national parliaments. Depending on the interaction between the EAC and the sectoral committees the following constellations are possible:

a. The EAC adopts the reasoned opinion after consultation of sectoral committees (the Bulgarian Narodno sabranie,[52] Finnish Eduskunta,[53] German Bundesrat,[54] Italian Camera dei Deputati,[55] Lithuanian Seimas,[56] Portuguese Assembleia da República,[57] Romanian Camera Deputaţilor and Senat,[58] Cypriot Vouli ton Antiprosopon,[59] Danish

[46] Arts 23(g)(1) and 23k(2) of the Austrian Constitution.

[47] Art 37bis (1) of the Rules of Procedure of the Chambre des représentants. See also T Delreux and F Randour, 'Belgium: Institutional and Administrative Adaptation but Limited Political Interest' in C Hefftler et al (eds), *The Palgrave Handbook of National Parliaments and the European Union* (Basingstoke, Palgrave Macmillan, 2015) 161.

[48] COSAC, 16th Bi-annual Report on EU Practices and Procedures (October 2011).

[49] See: www.houseofrepresentatives.nl/how-parliament-works/europe-house-representatives-and-senate. See also A-L Högenauer, 'The Dutch Parliament and EU Affairs: Decentralizing Scrutiny' in C Hefftler et al (eds), *The Palgrave Handbook of National Parliaments and the European Union* (Basingstoke, Palgrave Macmillan, 2015) 260.

[50] §9:20 (2) of the Riksdag Act provides that the Riksdag decides on compliance of the proposal with subsidiarity. In practice, the Chamber refers them to sectoral committees. See A Jonsson Cornell, 'The Swedish Riksdag as Scrutiniser of the Principle of Subsidiarity' (2016) 12 *European Constitutional Law Review* 294, 303.

[51] G Barrett, 'Long Train Running: The Slowly Developed (and Slowly Developing) Role of Ireland's Oireachtas in EU Affairs' in C Hefftler et al (eds), *The Palgrave Handbook of National Parliaments and the European Union* (Basingstoke, Palgrave Macmillan, 2015) 298.

[52] Art 121 (1)–(3) of the Rules of Procedure of the Narodno sabranie.

[53] s 30 of the Rules of Procedure of the Eduskunta, see also T Raunio, 'The Finnish Eduskunta and the European Union: The Strengths and Weaknesses of a Mandating System' in C Hefftler et al (eds), *The Palgrave Handbook of National Parliaments and the European Union* (Basingstoke, Palgrave Macmillan, 2015) 416.

[54] IV a, § 45 a (1) of the Rules of Procedure of the Bundesrat.

[55] The rapporteur of a sectoral committee is invited to attend the meeting of the EAC, but under the EWS the sectoral committees are competent only regarding the content and proportionality of proposals. The procedure is based on two interpretative decisions of the Rules Committee of the Camera dei Deputati. See N Lupo, 'The Scrutiny of the Principle of Subsidiarity in the Procedures and Reasoned Opinions of the Italian Chamber and Senate' in A Jonsson Cornell and M Goldoni (eds), *National and Regional Parliaments in the EU-Legislative Procedure Post-Lisbon: The Impact of the Early Warning Mechanism* (Oxford, Hart Publishing, 2017) 233; S Cavatorto, 'Italy: Still Looking for a New Era in the Making of EU Policy' in C Hefftler et al (eds), *The Palgrave Handbook of National Parliaments and the European Union* (Basingstoke, Palgrave Macmillan, 2015) 220.

[56] Art 180^6 of the Seimas Rules of Procedure.

[57] Art 3(2) of Law no 43/2006 of 25 August 2006 as amended by Law no 21/2012 of 17 May 2012, COSAC, 19th Bi-Annual Report—Annex, Section on Portugal.

[58] See: www.cosac.eu/subs-romania/.

[59] The subsidiarity check is done by the EAC, without precluding the involvement of the sectoral committees. See COSAC, Annex to 13th Bi-annual Report, 74.

Folketing,[60] Estonian Riigikogu,[61] Slovak Národná rada,[62] Slovenian Državni zbor,[63] and Czech Poslanecká sněmovna and Senát).[64]

b. The EAC adopts a reasoned opinion, but the sectoral committee retains the 'last word' (French Assemblée nationale[65] and French Sénat).[66]
c. The sectoral committee adopts a reasoned opinion with a sifting or coordinating role for the EAC (the Luxembourg Chambre des Députés).[67]
d. The sectoral committee adopts a reasoned opinion with an opinion from the EAC (the German Bundestag[68] and the Italian Senato della Repubblica).[69]
e. Both the EAC and sectoral committees scrutinise the proposal and adopt a reasoned opinion at a joint session (the Greek Vouli ton Ellinon[70] and the Polish Senat).[71]

The fourth 'subsidiarity focused' form includes a specific committee that deals exclusively with subsidiarity issues; such an organ, the Temporary Committee on Subsidiarity (Tijdelijke Commissie Subsidiariteitstoets), has only functioned between 2006 and 2009 in the Netherlands.[72]

Those types of scrutiny systems built around the degree of centralisation, although oriented towards scrutiny of the subsidiarity principle, correspond with a pre-Lisbon study by Kiiver who also distinguishes both more- and less-centralised scrutiny systems.[73] Kiiver explores the parliamentary committees that scrutinise EU affairs in general before the entry into force of the Lisbon Treaty with its EWS. This study describes centralised systems, such as in Denmark and Finland, with varying degrees of involvement of the sectoral committees and decentralised systems with sectoral specialisation of EU affairs, such as in the UK, along with hybrids with varying degrees of stimulation and coordination of sectoral committees by the EAC.

[60] See at: www.thedanishparliament.dk/Committees_and_delegations/Committees/EUU.aspx.

[61] § 152[3] and § 152[6](2) of the Riigikogu Rules of Procedure and Internal Rules Act. Note that a sectoral committee can propose amendments to the draft reasoned opinion.

[62] s 58a(3)(a) and (d) of the Act on the National Council of the Slovak Republic, No 350/1996 on Rules of Procedure as amended.

[63] Art 154m (5) and (6) of the Rules of Procedure of the Državni zbor.

[64] In both chambers, the consultation of a sectoral committee is facultative. See §109a(2) of the Rules of Procedure of the chamber and s 119(d)4 of the Rules of Procedure of the Senát.

[65] If a sectoral committee does not react in time, the EAC's opinion is considered as adopted. Art 151-6 of the Rules of Procedure of the Assemblée nationale. See also D Fromage, *Les parlements dans l'Union Européenne après le Traité de Lisbonne: la participation des parlements allemands, britanniques, espagnols, français et italiens* (Paris, L'Harmattan, 2015) 292.

[66] Art 73 octies para 3 and para 4 of the Rules of Procedure of the Sénat. If the relevant committee does not respond in due time, the reasoned opinion of the EAC is considered as adopted.

[67] Art 168 (5) of the Rules of Procedure of the Chambre des Députés. The Committee on Foreign and European Affairs, Defence, Cooperation and Immigration conducts the initial selection. See at: www.chd.lu/wps/portal/public/Accueil/ChambreEtUE/UETravailCommissionsParlementaires/LirePlus.

[68] §93a (1) of the Rules of Procedure of the Bundestag.

[69] If the sectoral committee does not adopt an opinion in a timely manner, the resolution of the EAC is sent to the Commission. The letter of the Speaker of the Senato della Repubblica, which is the basis for this procedure is not public. See Lupo (n 55) 233.

[70] Art 41B(2) and (3) of the Standing Orders of the Hellenic Vouli ton Antiprosopon.

[71] Art 75a(3) and 75d(1) of the Senat Rules of Procedure.

[72] See at: www.eerstekamer.nl/eu/thema/tijdelijke_commissie.

[73] P Kiiver, *The National Parliaments in the European Union: A Critical View on EU Constitution-Building*, vol 50 (The Hague, Kluwer Law International, 2006) 47–54.

In terms of effectiveness in scrutinising the EU, each of the different systems mentioned has its advantages and disadvantages. The main benefits of a centralised scrutiny system are its efficiency, EU-related expertise, confidentiality and promptitude.[74] The centralised scrutiny also implies that the interpretation of the subsidiarity principle that the committee adopts will remain constant throughout the scrutiny process and the reasoned opinions. The main drawback, however, is that only a small number of parliamentarians remain informed of EU affairs. Nonetheless, this can be remedied by the composition of the EAC committees often characterised by a dual membership, meaning that a member of the EAC is simultaneously a member of a sectoral committee; this is the case, for example, in the Croatian, Hungarian and Latvian parliaments and the Polish Sejm.[75] Similarly, in the UK House of Commons, each of the ad hoc European committees includes at least two members of the European Scrutiny Committee and two members of the Departmental Select Committee.[76] In the House of Lords, each Lord member of the EU select committees sits at one of the subcommittees.[77]

In the decentralised subsidiarity scrutiny system, the sectoral committees, even when lacking profound knowledge of EU affairs, may competently contribute in their specific policy areas, such as agriculture or the environment. For example, all the Swedish Riksdag's sectoral committees that conduct subsidiarity scrutiny are represented in the EAC.[78] Such a system allows a link and exchange of information between the sectoral committees and the EAC, which does not participate in the subsidiarity scrutiny. In the Belgian Chambre des représentants, which applies decentralised subsidiarity scrutiny, in order to increase awareness of EU issues, each sectoral committee establishes a Europromoter.[79] These are recruited from the Federal Advisory Committee that deals with the broader issues of Belgium's EU policy but does not participate in the subsidiarity review.[80] However, in the decentralised scrutiny system, there can also be an evident level of disregard of European documents by MPs.[81]

A mixed system, by fully involving the sectoral committees and EAC, and not just a couple of their members, may therefore present the most appropriate form of subsidiarity scrutiny. This system connects the expertise on EU affairs of the EAC and the insights of sectoral committees. Still, even this system raises the issue of time requirements and the possibilities of conflict between different committees, two significant drawbacks of the mixed system. One solution may be to confer scrutiny power to an EAC within which EU subcommittees focus on specific policies, as in the UK.

Overall, from a theoretical perspective, it is unclear which approach may perform best. Section VI examines the impact of the different scrutiny models on the actual participation in the subsidiarity review procedure by national parliaments. Before moving to this

[74] ibid 49.

[75] Based on a survey of the websites of those parliaments.

[76] A Huff and J Smith, 'Westminster and the European Union: Ever-Increasing Scepticism?' in C Hefftler et al (eds), *The Palgrave Handbook of National Parliaments and the European Union* (Basingstoke, Palgrave Macmillan, 2015) 316.

[77] ibid 317.

[78] See information on the Swedish Riksdag at: www.cosac.eu/national-parliament-european-c/.

[79] Delreux and Randour (n 47) 158.

[80] ibid 156.

[81] Kiiver, *The National Parliaments in the European Union* (n 73) 51.

enquiry, the following section further explores the specificities of national procedures for subsidiarity scrutiny.

V. COMPARISON OF PROCEDURES

This section studies the forms of subsidiarity scrutiny in national parliaments by taking into account the following variables: screening EU proposals for a subsidiarity violation; the initiative to adopt a reasoned opinion; the function of the government; and the role of the plenary. The variety of approaches taken across these dimensions demonstrate that there is no 'one-size-fits-all' system for the subsidiarity scrutiny.

A. The Initial Detection of Subsidiarity Breaches

The first element of a subsidiarity scrutiny procedure is the question as to whether there is an a priori examination process or whether the detection of breaches is largely random. The scrutiny systems explored in this chapter reveal that different possibilities for identifying problematic draft legislative acts are in use. These can be roughly grouped into 'ex ante' and 'ongoing' sections.

By now, almost all national parliaments scrutinise the Work Programme of the Commission. For example, on the basis of the document annually received from the Commission, the Dutch Eerste Kamer prepares its European Work Programme,[82] and the UK House of Commons conducts a preliminary subsidiarity assessment on this basis.[83] In fact, the majority of national parliaments used the Commission Work Programme for 2016[84] for setting their scrutiny priorities for 2016.[85] The Commission Work Programme for 2017[86] was again scrutinised by 'the vast majority' of national parliaments.[87] Moreover, in 2015 the Dutch Tweede Kamer launched an action in which national parliaments inform each other about which Commission's initiatives they chose to scrutinise based on the Commission Work Programme. A large number of national parliaments shared their priorities and highlighted those Commission initiatives for which the parliament plans to conduct a subsidiarity check.[88] The chair of the EAC of the Dutch Tweede Kamer forwarded to the Commission the overview of the initiatives that national parliaments plan to scrutinise.[89]

[82] Dutch Eerste Kamer, Letter to Minister President of 05.01.2010, concerning the Adoption of the Lisbon Treaty, Vergaderjaar 2009–10, 30 953 en 31 384, H, 1.

[83] See, eg, documents considered by the European Scrutiny Committee on 16.12.2015.

[84] 'Communication from the Commission to the European Parliament, the Council, the European Economic and Social Committee and the Committee of the Regions, Commission Work Programme 2016, No time for business as usual' COM(2015) 610 final.

[85] COSAC, 26th Biannual Report, 6.

[86] 'Communication from the Commission to the European Parliament, the Council, the European Economic and Social Committee and the Committee of the Regions, Commission Work Programme 2017, Delivering a Europe that protects, empowers and defends' COM(2016) 710 final.

[87] COSAC, 27th Bi-annual Report, 7.

[88] For the priorities based on the Commission Work Programme 2015, see: www.eerstekamer.nl/eu/documenteu/_priorities_national_parliaments/f=/vjuffts0i4r4.pdf.

[89] See: ec.europa.eu/dgs/secretariat_general/relations/relations_other/npo/docs/netherlands/2015/com20150610/com20150610_tweedekamer_opinion_en.pdf.

The identification of potentially controversial acts in parliament is also possible on an ongoing basis. Many national parliaments pursue this approach, and the parliamentary body responsible in this respect varies. For example, the UK House of Lords' chairman of the EU Committee examines all EU documents on a weekly basis to identify which of them demands further scrutiny.[90] In the French Sénat, a working group on subsidiarity within the EAC preliminarily examines the EU documents every 15 days.[91] In the Swedish Riksdag, the Secretariat of the Chamber upon the receipt of the *lettre de saisine* alerts sectoral committees that the EU proposal will undergo a subsidiarity scrutiny.[92] At the Latvian Saeima the detection of subsidiarity violation is conducted by the EAC on a continuous basis, when an EU draft proposal arrives.[93]

Some parliaments rely on their administrative staff to identify the subsidiarity breach at an early stage. The Spanish Cortes Generales' legal service sends a list twice a month to the Joint Committee for the EU that includes EU legislative proposals that may create problems from the point of view of subsidiarity, as along with those against which the subsidiarity action could be brought.[94] In the Austrian Nationalrat and the Bundesrat, the administrative staff conduct a pre-check for subsidiarity violations and once a week send preparatory lists to members of the EU committees.[95] Some other parliaments that rely on their administrative staff are the Cypriot,[96] Greek,[97] Latvian[98] and Slovak[99] parliaments. The Polish Senat is also assisted by a staff analyst who offers a subsidiarity assessment at an early stage.[100] In the Polish Sejm, the Bureau of Research conducts a preliminary analysis of EU draft proposals usually once a week and provides an opinion for the selected proposal that includes an assessment of subsidiarity principle.[101] In contrast, for example, the Italian Senato della Repubblica did not adopt any procedure for selection of the proposals for the EWS.[102]

If national parliaments scrutinise EU proposals for the identification of subsidiarity violations on an ongoing basis, problematic Commission proposals may come as a surprise to national parliaments. Thus, parliaments' analysis of the Commission Work Programme may be more advantageous and offer some focus to that scrutiny. Moreover, an 'early warning' in the form of the Commission Work Programme may help to ensure that parliaments have sufficient time to submit a fully developed reasoned opinion within the eight-week period allotted. Nevertheless, the significance of the Commission Work Programme should

[90] House of Lords, European Union Committee, *9th Report of Session 2013–14*, point 33.

[91] L Guilloud-Colliat, *L'action normative de l'Union européenne* (Bruxelles, Brulyant, 2014) 280. See, eg, French Sénat, Reasoned opinion of 14.02.2014 on COM(2013) 894 and the role of the group: www.senat.fr/leg/ppr13-309.html.

[92] See: www.ipex.eu/IPEXL-WEB/parliaments/institution/serik.do.

[93] Information received from the EAC of the Latvian Saeima, 04.07.2016.

[94] Piedrafita (n 44).

[95] Scrutiny of documents coming from the European Union and monitoring compliance with the principle of subsidiarity, available at: www.ipex.eu/IPEXL-WEB/parliaments/institution/atbun.do.

[96] See: www.ipex.eu/IPEXL-WEB/parliaments/institution/cyvou.do.

[97] See: www.ipex.eu/IPEXL-WEB/parliaments/institution/grvou.do.

[98] At the EAC one adviser is responsible for the subsidiarity scrutiny and conducting an early scrutiny. Information received from the EAC of the Latvian Saeima, 04.07.2016.

[99] A Figulová, 'The Slovak Parliament and EU Affairs: In Need of a Wake-Up Call' in C Hefftler et al (eds), *The Palgrave Handbook of National Parliaments and the European Union* (Basingstoke, Palgrave Macmillan, 2015) 640.

[100] See: www.ipex.eu/IPEXL-WEB/parliaments/institution/plsen.do.

[101] See: oide.sejm.gov.pl/oide/en/images/files/badanie_pomocniczosci/subsidiarity_sejm_table_en.pdf.

[102] Fromage, *Les parlements dans l'Union Européenne après le Traité de Lisbonne* (n 65) 277; Lupo (n 55) 234.

not be exaggerated, since the proposed initiatives often have a very broad character at that stage, and it may be difficult to assess compatibility with the principle of subsidiarity on the basis of the programme itself. If engaged at this point, national parliaments may tend to challenge the idea of the proposal itself rather than acting according to the vision of national parliament participation in the EU decision-making process. In fact, this problem might be increasing with the Juncker Commission in office since 1 November 2014, as some members of national parliaments have underlined the difficulty with the assessment of the proposals on the basis of the Commission Work Programmes since then as, in contrast to the Barroso Commissions, the Juncker Commission focuses on broader ideas rather than enlisting specific proposals.[103]

B. The Role of the Government in Subsidiarity Review

There are various degrees of the national government's involvement in the EWS. At one end of the spectrum some national parliaments receive the opinion of the government, including a subsidiarity assessment, automatically. For instance, the Estonian Riigikogu obtains an explanatory memorandum discussing a number of issues of an EU proposal, including an analysis of the conformity of that proposal with the subsidiarity principle.[104] Other examples include the UK, where both Houses of Parliament receive explanatory memoranda from the government for EU documents deposited in the Parliament within 10 working days of the receipt of a draft legislative act.[105] The same procedure is in place for the Polish Sejm and Senat, both of which should receive an explanatory memorandum no later than 14 days after the receipt of the EU draft legislative act.[106] The German Bundestag receives a comprehensive appraisal of an EU draft legislative act within two weeks of the receipt of the draft by the committees or before the start of Council negotiations.[107] In Lithuania, the government sends its position including a subsidiarity statement within 15 working days.[108] In Ireland and Italy, the government sends an opinion including a subsidiarity assessment within 20 days,[109] while in Slovakia that time frame is three weeks.[110] In France, the government committed to submitting a simplified impact assessment within three weeks of the transmission of any draft proposal.[111] In Romania the government sends its opinion with regard to the proposals pre-selected on the basis of the Commission Work Programme within 10 days of the act's submission to the Parliament.[112]

[103] B van Apeldoorn, Chair of the Standing Committee on European Affairs of the Dutch Senate: www.eerstekamer.nl/eu/intern_stuk/20170126/speech_van_het_lid_van_apeldoorn.

[104] § 152^{2} (1) of the Riigikogu Rules of Procedure and Internal Rules Act.

[105] House of Commons, The European Scrutiny System in the House of Commons, *A short guide by the staff of the House of Commons European Scrutiny Committee* (May 2015) 10.

[106] Art 7 of Cooperation Act.

[107] §13 (6) of IntVG, § 7 (2) of EUZBBG.

[108] Art 180^{7}(3) of the Statute of Seimas.

[109] Scrutiny of documents coming from the European Union and monitoring compliance with the subsidiarity principle, Irish Parliament (IPEX), for Italy see Art 6(4)(a) Law N 234/2012.

[110] s 58a(8) of the Act on the National Council of the Slovak Republic, No 350/1996 on Rules of Procedure as amended.

[111] Circulaire du 21 juin 2010 relative à la participation du Parlement national au processus décisionnel européen, JORF no 0142 du 22 juin 2010, 11232.

[112] Art 14(2) of the Act on the cooperation between the Parliament and the Government in EU Affairs.

At the other end of the spectrum are systems in which the government is less involved: in Hungary, the government is not obliged to provide a written opinion, but is invited to the committee meeting upon request.[113] Intermediate approaches include a possibility for national parliaments to request an opinion of the government. This is the prerogative of, for example, the Spanish Cortes Generales,[114] the Austrian Nationalrat and Bundesrat,[115] and the Luxemburg Chambre des Députés.[116]

The variation in the involvement of governments in the EWS is also reflected in data collected in the 27th Bi-annual Report of COSAC in 2017. Of the 37 parliaments or their chambers responding to COSAC's questionnaire, 17, that is, only slightly less than half, always received the government's position on a new draft legislative act within the eight-week deadline.[117] The Belgian Chambre des représentants reported that it received the government's opinion only sometimes, while the Belgian Sénat indicated that it never received such a position.[118] In sum, these data suggest there is room for improvement in the support that Member State governments provide to their national parliaments when exercising their scrutiny of the subsidiarity principle under the EWS.

Having said that, the obligation of governmental participation at an early stage may be somewhat surprising as it runs counter to the fact that subsidiarity review is a competence specifically created for national parliaments. In addition, governments already dispose of a possibility to state their views on the principle of subsidiarity through participation in the discussions on draft EU acts in the Council. However, two arguments speak in favour of the governments' involvement in parliamentary scrutiny. First, the executive body may possess greater research resources, in particular when parliaments are small or have smaller administrative support. Second, an early signal by the government of a subsidiarity breach may provide an incentive for parliaments that are relatively inactive on EU affairs to examine a proposal more closely. Certainly, the usefulness of the government's opinion depends on a timely submission.

C. The Role of the Plenary

The analysis of Member States' regulations implies three different attitudes towards the involvement of the parliamentary chamber as a whole in subsidiarity scrutiny: the plenary session may have a facultative or an obligatory character, or the national provisions provide that only a committee is responsible for adoption of the reasoned opinion.

First, some national procedures foresee that a reasoned opinion can be adopted by the plenary. In the Belgian Chambre des représentants, the plenary gets involved only if one-third of the members of the sectoral committee demand it; otherwise, the reasoned opinion adopted by a committee is sent to the Commission.[119] The same is true in the

113 COSAC, 27th Biannual Report, 226.
114 Art 3 (j) of Ley 24/2009.
115 Art 23(g)(2) of the Austrian Constitution.
116 Annexe 3 III(3) to the Rules of Procedure (2017).
117 COSAC, 27th Bi-annual Report, 14.
118 ibid, Annex 16 and Annex 29.
119 Art 37bis (5) of the Rules of Procedure of the Chambre des représentants (2016).

French Sénat: the reasoned opinions may be adopted by the plenary, if requested by the chamber's president, president of a group, chair of a sectoral committee or of the EAC, or by the government.[120] If no such request is made, the committee's reasoned opinion is considered as the Sénat's resolution and sent to EU institutions.[121] Also in the Swedish Riksdag, on the request of five committee members, the plenary has to deliver the reasoned opinion.[122] In the Czech Poslanecká sněmovna, a committee or the plenary[123] can adopt a reasoned opinion, while in the German Bundestag, it is either the EAC or the plenary.[124] Other parliaments where the plenary can be involved include the Austrian Bundesrat,[125] French Assemblée nationale,[126] Greek Vouli ton Ellinon,[127] Italian Camera dei Deputati and Senato della Repubblica,[128] Luxembourg Chambre des Députés,[129] Slovenian National Assembly,[130] and the Spanish Cortes Generales.[131]

Second, several of the national scrutiny systems demand the adoption of the reasoned opinion by the parliament's plenary. For example, the reasoned opinion has to be approved by the plenary in the UK House of Commons[132] and the House of Lords,[133] the Belgian Sénat,[134] the Czech Senát,[135] in the Dutch Tweede Kamer and Eerste Kamer,[136] the Estonian Riigikogu,[137] the Finnish Eduskunta,[138] the German Bundesrat,[139] the Hungarian Országgyűlés,[140] the Irish Dáil Éireann and Seanad Éireann,[141] the Lithuanian Seimas,[142]

[120] Art 73 octies par 5 of the Sénat Rules of Procedure.

[121] Art 73 octies par 4 of the Sénat Rules of Procedure.

[122] Jonsson Cornell (n 50) 304.

[123] §109a(4) of the Rules of Procedure.

[124] §93c of the Rules of Procedure.

[125] Art 23(k) 3 of the Austrian Constitution. See also E Miklin, 'The Austrian Parliament and EU Affairs: Gradually Living Up to Its Legal Potential' in C Hefftler and others (eds), *The Palgrave Handbook of National Parliaments and the European Union* (Basingstoke, Palgrave Macmillan, 2015) 397.

[126] Art 151-7 of the Assemblée nationale Rules of Procedure.

[127] Art 41B(4) of the Standing Orders of the Hellenic Parliament.

[128] The plenary has so far not been involved. See Lupo (n 55) 236.

[129] Art 168(5) of the Rules of Procedure of the Chambre des Députés.

[130] Art 154m (6) and (9–12) of the Rules of Procedure of the National Assembly of 02.04.2012.

[131] Art 5.1. and 5.2 of Ley 24/2009, de 22 de diciembre, de modificación de la Ley 8/1994, de 19 de mayo, por la que se regula la Comisión Mixta para la Unión Europea, para su adaptación al Tratado de Lisboa de 13 de diciembre de 2007.

[132] If the debate has taken place on the floor of the European Committee, the question on the reasoned opinion will be put to the floor of the House without a debate. See House of Commons, *Short Guide by the Staff* (n 105) 23–24.

[133] See: www.ipex.eu/IPEXL-WEB/parliaments/institution/uklor.do.

[134] Delreux and Randour (n 47) 157.

[135] §119f (3) of the Standing Rules of the Senát.

[136] See: www.houseofrepresentatives.nl/how-parliament-works/europe-house-representatives-and-senate.

[137] § 152[6](7) of the Riigikogu Rules of Procedure and Internal Rules Act.

[138] s 30(4) of Finland's Constitution.

[139] Art 52(3a) of the Basic Law. The Bundesrat can also decide in the Chamber for European Affairs (Europakammer), whose decisions shall be considered decisions of the Bundesrat. See also C Mellein, 'Die Rolle von Bundestag und Bundesrat in der Europäischen Union' [2011] *Zeitschrift Europarecht-Beiheft* 13, 58.

[140] § 134/D(4) of the Rules of Procedure.

[141] Order 114(3)(b) of the consolidated version of all the Standing Orders of the Dáil Éireann currently in effect, as of 9 May 2017 and Order 107(3)(b) of the Standing Orders of Seanad Éireann (2016).

[142] 180[6] (5–8) of the Seimas Statute.

the Maltese Kamra tad-Deputati,[143] the Portuguese Assembleia da República,[144] the Polish Sejm[145] and Senat,[146] and the Romanian Camera Deputaţilor and Senat.[147]

Finally, some of the national procedures for the EWS endow only a parliamentary committee with the adoption of the reasoned opinion. In Bulgaria, the Committee on European Affairs and Oversight of the European Funds forwards the reasoned opinion to the president of the National Assembly who then sends it to the Commission.[148] The plenary is not involved. Similar procedures that delegate power to act on behalf of the parliament are foreseen in the Austrian Nationalrat,[149] Croatian Hrvatski sabor,[150] Cypriot Vouli ton Antiprosopon,[151] Danish Folketing,[152] Latvian Saeima,[153] and the Slovak Národná rada.[154]

Debating the adoption of reasoned opinions in a plenary session, on the one hand, raises and demonstrates MPs' awareness of current EU affairs. This argument is especially applicable in the cases of centralised scrutiny as the applicable model. Nonetheless, only some of the national parliaments that adopt the centralised subsidiarity scrutiny demand involvement of the plenary. On the other hand, the involvement of the entire chamber, especially if the plenary session includes a debate and not just a vote, may not fit well in the strict eight-week deadline for the submission of a reasoned opinion.[155] Although national parliaments often criticise the strict eight-week rule, they do not reduce this obstacle to the timely submission of reasoned opinions. Although a vote in the plenary could give the reasoned opinion more publicity than when adopted in a committee, this would be the case only if there is a debate and when it is not automatic.[156] In addition, as underlined by a British MP, discussing subsidiarity in committee rather than in the plenary allows 'go[ing] into considerable detail, which has been highly advantageous for an understanding of all the issues that have come up'.[157]

[143] R Pace, 'The Maltese Parliament and EU Affairs: A Slow Awakening to Its Responsibilities' in C Hefftler et al (eds), *The Palgrave Handbook of National Parliaments and the European Union* (Basingstoke, Palgrave Macmillan, 2015) 587.

[144] Art 3(3) of Law no 43/2006 of 25 August 2006 as amended by Law no 21/2012 of 17 May 2012.

[145] Art 148cc(5) of the Sejm Rules of Procedure.

[146] Art 75d(1) of the Senat Rules of Procedure.

[147] Art 14(5) of the Act on cooperation between the Parliament and the Government in EU affairs.

[148] Art 121(4) of the Rules of Procedure.

[149] Art 23k(2) of the Austrian Constitution.

[150] Art 158 of Standing Orders (2013).

[151] A Emilianides, O Christou and C Ioannou, 'The Cypriot Parliament and EU Affairs' in C Hefftler et al (eds), *The Palgrave Handbook of National Parliaments and the European Union* (Basingstoke, Palgrave Macmillan, 2015) 486.

[152] See: www.thedanishparliament.dk/Committees_and_delegations/Committees/EUU.aspx.

[153] 185^1 (1) of the Saeima Rules of Procedure.

[154] s 58a of the Act of the National Council of the Slovak Republic 350/1996 on Rules of Procedure of the National Council of the Slovak Republic as amended.

[155] Z Cieślik and B Pawłowski, 'Zmiana roli parlamentów narodowych w Unii Europejskiej (według Traktatu reformującego Unię Europejską, przyjętego w Lizbonie, w dniach 17–18 października 2007 r), Mozliwosc badania zasady pomocniczosci w polskim parlamencie' (2007) 16 *Zeszyty Prawnicze* 37.

[156] Fromage, *Les parlements dans l'Union Européenne après le Traité de Lisbonne* (n 65) 400.

[157] See the statement of MP Jacob Rees-Mogg in the House of Commons European Committee: Communication Networks, 20.05.2013, Column 19.

D. The Accommodation of Regional Parliaments' Views

The following section explores the extent to which the national scrutiny of the subsidiarity principle takes into account the views of the regional parliaments. The Lisbon Treaty indicates that each national parliament should consult, 'where appropriate', regional parliaments with legislative powers.[158] The regional parliaments with legislative powers may participate in the EWS in two ways: through their national parliaments or through the Subsidiarity Monitoring Network of the Committee of the Regions.[159] The procedures through which the national parliament and the regional parliament interact are presented below.

The Austrian Bundesrat informs the Austrian regional parliaments (Landtage) about all the EU draft legislative acts and offers them the possibility to take a position.[160] When adopting a reasoned opinion, the Bundesrat should consider the regional parliaments' positions and inform them about its decision.

In Belgium, the Agreement on Cooperation (2017) elaborates on Declaration 51 to the Lisbon Treaty that states that the parliamentary assemblies of the Communities and the Regions act, in terms of the competences exercised by the EU, as components of the national parliamentary system or chambers of the national parliament. The agreement provides first for the procedures on transmission of information from the Belgian Sénat to the Belgian regional parliaments.[161] With regard to the subsidiarity scrutiny, the agreement regulates the procedure of issuing a reasoned opinion and the distribution of votes. Specifically, if a parliament considers an EU draft legislative act in violation of the subsidiarity principle and if the draft act concerns the sphere of competence of that parliament, that parliament may issue a reasoned opinion.[162] The two votes for the Belgian Parliament under the EWS are distributed in a way that depends on how many and which (federal or regional) parliaments issue a reasoned opinion and whether they have an exclusive competence in the matter at stake.[163] The Secretariat of the Conference of Presidents of the parliamentary assemblies gathers the reasoned opinions and communicates them and the number of votes which those opinions represent to the EU institutions.[164]

In Germany, the Basic Law does not provide for the direct participation of regional parliaments in EU affairs, including subsidiarity review.[165] German regional parliaments

[158] Art 6 of Protocol No 2.

[159] K Borońska-Hryniewiecka, 'Regions and Subsidiarity after the Treaty of Lisbon: Overcoming the "Regional Blindness"' in M Cartabia, N Lupo and A Simoncini (eds), *Democracy and Subsidiarity in the EU* (Bologna, Il Mulino, 2013). On REGPEX see ch 2.

[160] Art 23g(3) of the Austrian Constitution.

[161] Art 3 of the Accord de coopération entre l'État fédéral, les Régions, les Communautés, la Commission communautaire française et la Commission communautaire commune relatif à l'exercice des compétences attribuées aux parlements nationaux par le Traité sur l'Union européenne, le Traité sur le fonctionnement de l'Union européenne et les protocoles y annexés, Annexes au Règlement de la Chambre des représentants—Dernière mise à jour: le 29 mars 2017 (the Agreement).

[162] Art 4 of the Agreement.

[163] ibid, Art 5 of the Agreement.

[164] ibid, Art 6.

[165] S Delgado del Saz, 'Die Rolle der nationalen Parlamente nach dem Vertrag von Lissabon—ein Vergleich zwischen spanischem und deutschem Recht' (2011) 67 *Berliner Online-Beiträge zum Europarecht* 30.

may participate only through their governmental representatives in the Bundesrat.[166] Thus, the Länder's power concerning subsidiarity scrutiny depends on relations with the regional executive power.[167]

In Italy, the EWS enabled the creation of a relationship between the regional councils and the Italian Parliament, especially the Italian Senato della Repubblica.[168] Both chambers of the Italian Parliament can consult regional councils within the EWS.[169] However, it is the Italian government that transmits EU draft legislative acts to the regional councils.[170] The regional councils can send their opinions on compliance of the proposals with the subsidiarity principle to the Italian Parliament.[171] Nonetheless, the Italian Parliament is under no legal obligation to take those opinions into account.[172]

In Portugal, the Portuguese Assembleia da República should consult the parliaments of the autonomous regions of the Azores and Madeira Archipelagos if the EU draft legislative act concerns an issue within their competence.[173] Moreover, the representatives of the regional parliaments participate in the annual meeting with the Portuguese Assembleia da República to choose initiatives for further scrutiny on the basis of the Commission Work Programme.[174]

In Spain, the national parliament transmits any EU draft legislative act to one of the 17 regional parliaments without prejudging the existence of a regional competence for a matter.[175] From the moment of the receipt of the draft legislative act from the Cortes Generales, regional parliaments have four weeks to submit an opinion.[176] However, the Joint Committee is not obliged to discuss an opinion of a regional parliament after this period has elapsed.[177] A reasoned opinion submitted in due time shall be incorporated into the reasoned opinion of the national parliament if the Cortes Generales decides to issue a reasoned opinion.[178] Still, the position of the regional parliaments in the EWS is considered very limited.[179]

In asymmetrically regionalised Finland, where the Åland Islands have an autonomous status, the parliament is eligible to participate in subsidiarity review. All the EU draft

[166] Art 23(2) of the Basic Law.

[167] G Vara Arribas and D Bourdin, *The Role of Regional Parliaments in the Process of Subsidiarity Analysis within the Early Warning System of the Lisbon Treaty* (EIPA and ECR, 2011) 48–49, available at: cor.europa.eu/en/documentation/studies/Documents/Role-Regional-Parliaments-in%20Process-of-Subsidiarity-Analysis-within-Early-Warning-System-of-Lisbon-Treaty/EN.pdf.

[168] C Fasone, 'Italian Regional Councils and the Positive Externalities of the Early Warning Mechanism for National Constitutional Law' in A Jonsson Cornell and M Goldoni (eds), *National and Regional Parliaments in the EU-Legislative Procedure Post-Lisbon* (Oxford, Hart Publishing, 2017) 156.

[169] Art 8.3 Law no 234/2012.

[170] Fasone (n 168) 164.

[171] Art 25 Law no 234/2012.

[172] Fasone (n 168) 166.

[173] Art 3.4. Law no 43/2006 of 25.08.2006 as amended by Law no 21/2012 of 17.05.2012.

[174] See: www.en.parlamento.pt/EuropeanAffairs/EuropInitiativesScrutiny.html.

[175] Art 6, para 1 of Ley 24/2009.

[176] ibid, para 2.

[177] Vara Arribas and Bourdin (n 167) 77.

[178] Ley 24/2009, Art 6, para 3.

[179] TA Vandamme, 'From Federated Federalism to Harmonized Federalism? The Case of EU Subsidiarity Scrutiny in Spain and Belgium' (2011) Amsterdam Law School Research Paper 2011/05, 22.

legislative proposals are sent to the Åland Lagtinget, and the Autonomy Committee takes the decision whether an opinion on subsidiarity is necessary.[180] However, the Eduskunta should receive any opinion, which is not binding, from the Åland Lagtinget within six weeks.[181] In addition, a reasoned opinion of the Åland Islands is an obligatory incentive for the Eduskunta to start subsidiarity review at the national level.[182]

Finally, the three devolved UK legislative bodies (the Scottish Parliament, the National Assembly for Wales, and the Northern Ireland Assembly) participate in subsidiarity review in the United Kingdom. These parliaments may issue their own reasoned opinion, but neither of the Houses is bound by their requests.[183] The House of Commons, however, can ask devolved legislatures to comment on its own reasoned opinions, and it may take into account the opinions of these legislatures in its own scrutiny.[184]

This overview reveals that the roles of regional parliaments are all similar, insofar as their opinions are not binding on the national parliaments. The only exception is Belgium, where the parliamentary assemblies of the Communities and the Regions can issue a reasoned opinion that will be forwarded to the Commission. Nevertheless, recommendations of regional parliaments may incentivise the closer examination of some of the EU draft legislative acts. In this respect, the regional parliament in Finland plays an important role because a reasoned opinion causes a 'snowball effect' and obliges the Eduskunta to pursue subsidiarity review. In other Member States, the position of the regional parliaments is rather weak. The Spanish and the UK parliaments will incorporate the opinions of the regional parliaments in their own reasoned opinions. The Italian, Austrian and Portuguese parliaments only consider the opinions of the regional assemblies, without any obligation to take such opinions on board. Finally, in Germany the regional parliaments have to work with the regional governments. In sum, this overview confirms that the empowerment of regional parliaments in EU affairs and, more precisely, the degree of accommodation of their views on subsidiarity by the national parliaments, is conditioned upon a number of national institutional factors.[185] This may explain why in 2016 some regional parliaments informed the Commission directly in their opinions that they also submitted to their national parliaments as a part of the subsidiarity scrutiny.[186] The Commission takes those opinions into consideration 'where appropriate'.[187]

The participation of the regional parliaments in the EWS raises some questions concerning its added value. First, the EU draft legislative acts, if not pre-selected, for example, on the basis that they concern a regional competence, might create an administrative burden on the regional parliaments. This is why a systematic scrutiny of all EU proposals by the

[180] Committee of the Regions, The Subsidiarity Early Warning System of the Lisbon Treaty—the role of regional parliaments with legislative powers and other subnational authorities (2013) 44.

[181] Vara Arribas and Bourdin (n 167) 100.

[182] COSAC, Annex to the 13th Bi-annual Report, 135.

[183] Committee of the Regions, The Subsidiarity Early Warning System of the Lisbon Treaty (n 180) 95.

[184] ibid 98.

[185] K Borońska-Hryniewiecka, 'Regional parliamentary empowerment in EU affairs. Building an analytical framework' (2017) 23 *The Journal of Legislative Studies* 144, 157.

[186] See Commission, 'Annual Report 2016 on Subsidiarity and Proportionality' COM(2017) 600 final, 8.

[187] ibid.

regional parliaments is discouraged, while the use of the political dialogue might present a more appropriate tool allowing them to raise issues more freely.[188] Second, it is also additional work for the national parliament to consider the reasoned opinion of a regional parliament even if not bound by it, taking into account the eight-week deadline to submit a reasoned opinion.

VI. THE IMPACT OF THE EX ANTE SUBSIDIARITY REVIEW DESIGN ON THE NUMBER OF REASONED OPINIONS

The following section will analyse the reports of the Commission concerning the application of the principle of subsidiarity. These reports provide a thorough survey of the application of ex ante review.[189] What are the implications of institutional design decisions by national parliaments regarding subsidiarity scrutiny processes on the outcomes of such activity?

The institutional design around the subsidiarity scrutiny in the Member States can be very complex, as this chapter shows. The three main scrutiny types—centralised, mixed and decentralised—may not play the pivotal role for the number of the reasoned opinions issued by chambers. Table 1 presents the number of reasoned opinions issued by each parliamentary chamber between 2010 and 2016 and the type of procedure adopted by each of them (centralised, mixed, decentralised).[190] What can be observed in Table 2 is that between 2010 and 2016, parliaments applying mixed scrutiny issued the highest number of reasoned opinions, with 159 out of a total of 350, while centralised and decentralised chambers issued 94 and 97, respectively. However, once one takes into consideration the fact that chambers applying mixed scrutiny also account for the largest share of chambers in Members States in total, a different picture emerges. Each mixed chamber on average issued only about 7.2 reasoned opinions, while centralised and decentralised chambers were significantly more active (9.4 and 13.9 reasoned opinions per chamber, respectively). However, some of these results are sensitive to the exclusion of individual chambers. For example, among the decentralised chambers, the Swedish Riksdag issued 57 of the 97 reasoned opinions of this type. It is thus hard to draw any robust conclusions about the relationship between the type of chamber's scrutiny and its activity in the EWS. In addition, the absence of a reasoned opinion as an outcome of the subsidiarity procedure does not necessarily suggest lack of effectiveness of the procedure at stake. The parliament could have conducted the scrutiny and decided in the end that no subsidiarity violation is at stake.

[188] D Fromage, 'Regional Parliaments and the Early Warning System: An Assessment and Some Suggestions for Reform' in A Jonsson Cornell and M Goldoni (eds), *National and Regional Parliaments in the EU-Legislative Procedure Post-Lisbon* (Oxford, Hart Publishing, 2017) 132.

[189] COSAC also prepared one of the early reports on the activity of national parliaments. However, this chapter relies on the reports provided by the Commission that gather the most up-to-date information.

[190] See the Commission Reports on Subsidiarity and Proportionality for 2010–16: COM(2011) 344; COM(2012) 373; COM(2013) 566; COM(2014) 506; COM(2015) 316, Annex 1; COM(2016) 469, Annex 1; COM(2017) 600, Annex 1.

Table 1: Reasoned Opinions by Chamber

Member State	Chamber	Type	2010	2011	2012	2013	2014	2015	2016
Austria	Bundesrat	Centralised	2	1	3	6	3	0	4
Austria	Nationalrat	Centralised	1	0	1	0	1	0	0
Belgium	Chambre des représentants	Decentralised	0	1	3	1	0	0	0
Belgium	Sénat	Decentralised	0	1	0	1	0	0	0
Bulgaria	Narodno Sabrania	Mixed	0	2	0	0	0	0	3
Croatia	Hrvatski Sabor	Centralised	/	/	/	/	1	0	1
Cyprus	House of Representatives	Mixed	0	1	1	1	0	0	0
Czech Republic	Poslanecká sněmovna	Mixed	1	0	0	2	0	1	4
Czech Republic	Senát	Mixed	1	0	0	2	1	1	3
Denmark	Folketinget	Mixed	2	1	3	1	1	0	2
Estonia	Riigikogu	Mixed	0	0	0	1	0	0	1
Finland	Eduskunta	Mixed	0	1	1	1	0	0	0
France	Assemblée Nationale	Mixed	0	1	0	1	1	0	0
France	Sénat	Mixed	3	1	7	4	2	0	3
Germany	Bundesrat	Mixed	1	1	5	3	0	0	0
Germany	Bundestag	Mixed	1	1	1	0	0	0	0
Greece	Chamber of Deputies	Mixed	0	0	0	3	0	0	0
Hungary	Országgyülés	Centralised	0	0	0	1	0	1	2
Ireland	Dáil Eireann	Decentralised	/	1	0	0	0	0	2
Ireland	Dáil Eireann and Seanad Eireann (both chambers)[191]	Decentralised	0	/	0	3	0	0	0
Ireland	Seanad Eireann	Decentralised	/	/	/	/	/	/	1
Italy	Camera dei Deputati	Mixed	0	2	0	0	0	0	0
Italy	Senato della Repubblica	Mixed	1	3	1	2	1	1	3
Latvia	Saeima	Centralised	0	0	1	1	0	0	1

(continued)

[191] For 2010, the Commission Report refers to 'Oireachtas (both chambers)'.

Table 1: ***(Continued)***

Member State	Chamber	Type	2010	2011	2012	2013	2014	2015	2016
Lithuania	Seimas	Mixed	2	0	1	6	1	0	1
Luxembourg	Chambre des Députés	Mixed	3	7	3	2	1	0	2
Malta	Kamra tad-Deputati	Centralised	0	2	1	5	0	0	5
The Netherlands	Eerste Kamer and Tweede Kamer (both chambers)	Decentralised	2	2	1	0	0	0	0
The Netherlands	Eerste Kamer	Decentralised	0	0	2	3	0	0	1
The Netherlands	Tweede Kamer	Decentralised	0	1	3	5	2	1	3
Poland	Sejm	Centralised	2	5	3	2	0	0	2
Poland	Senat	Mixed	4	4	1	2	0	0	2
Portugal	Assembleia da Republica	Mixed	0	1	1	1	0	0	1
Romania	Camera Deputaţilor and Senatul (both chambers)	Mixed	0	1	/	0	0	0	0
Romania	Camera Deputaţilor	Mixed	0	2	0	2	0	1	2
Romania	Senatul	Mixed	0	2	0	3	0	0	1
Slovakia	Národná rada	Mixed	0	2	1	0	0	1	2
Slovenia	Državni svet	Not participating	0	0	0	0	0	0	0
Slovenia	Državni zbor	Mixed	0	0	0	1	0	0	0
Spain	Congreso de los Diputados and Senado (both chambers)	Centralised	0	2	2	5	1	1	0
Sweden	Riksdag	Decentralised	3	11	20	9	2	0	12
United Kingdom	House of Commons	Centralised	3	3	3	5	3	0	1
United Kingdom	House of Lords	Centralised	2	1	1	3	0	0	0
		Total	**34**	**64**	**70**	**88**	**21**	**8**	**65**

Source: Own compilation on the basis of the Commission Reports on Subsidiarity and Proportionality for 2010–16.

Table 2: Reasoned Opinions by Chamber Type

	Number of Chambers	2010	2011	2012	2013	2014	2015	2016	Total
Centralised	10	10	14	15	28	9	2	16	94
Mixed	22	19	33	26	38	8	5	30	159
Decentralised	7	5	17	29	22	4	1	19	97
Total		**34**	**64**	**70**	**88**	**21**	**8**	**65**	**350**

Source: Own compilation on the basis of the Commission Reports on Subsidiarity and Proportionality for 2010–16.

Nonetheless, qualitative studies of some of the national parliaments indicate indeed that the type of procedure adopted for a subsidiarity scrutiny does play a role in the number of reasoned opinions issued. For example, the vast number of reasoned opinions of the Swedish Riksdag is explained by the decentralised subsidiarity scrutiny in addition to the fact that this parliament scrutinises all EU draft legislative acts.[192] In the Italian Senato della Repubblica, each EU draft legislative act goes to a sectoral committee competent in the given subject area and to the EAC, while in the Italian Camera preselected EU draft proposals reach only the EAC.[193] The 'kick off' of the subsidiarity scrutiny procedure is potentially one of the explanations of the different number of reasoned opinions issued by each of the chambers.[194]

The findings of this chapter are connected to the results of Gattermann and Heftler, who study a sample of 342 Commission legislative acts and investigate the variation in national parliaments' decisions to act or not to act. They find that it is not institutional capacity, but rather the political motivation of chambers that explains whether a reasoned opinion is issued or not. They point in particular to the degree of contestation over EU integration among parties in the national system as a predictor for EWS action and whether a Commission proposal is contentious and highly visible.[195]

Moreover, the assessment of efficiency of national systems through the lens of the number of reasoned opinions issued is not the most crucial aspect of the exercise of the EWS at the national level. It is the scrutiny of EU documents itself that counts, rather the number of opinions issued. Studies that explore other aspects of Europeanisation of national parliaments indicate that factors such as the increasing transnational interaction among parliaments or technical expertise and administrative support need to be taken into account.[196] These elements may also play an important role for the subsidiarity scrutiny: more cooperation between parliaments can raise the possibility of raising a 'yellow' or 'orange card', whereas bureaucratic, expertise-oriented assistance may increase the quality of reasoned

[192] C Neuhold and J Smith, 'Conclusion: From "Latecomers" to "Policy Shapers"?—The Role of National Parliaments in the "Post-Lisbon" Union' in C Hefftler et al (eds), *The Palgrave Handbook of National Parliaments and the European Union* (Basingstoke, Palgrave Macmillan, 2015) 676.

[193] Lupo (n 55) 233–34.

[194] ibid 234.

[195] K Gattermann and C Hefftler, 'Beyond Institutional Capacity: Political Motivation and Parliamentary Behaviour in the Early Warning System' (2015) 38 *West European Politics* 305.

[196] T Christiansen, A-L Högenauer and C Neuhold, 'National Parliaments in the post-Lisbon European Union: Bureaucratization rather than Democratization?' (2014) 12 *Comparative European Politics* 121.

opinions. Summarising the analysis of this section, the mechanics of the control mechanisms may influence the activity of national parliaments less than the content of proposals and their salience.

VII. CONCLUSION

The purpose of this chapter has been to analyse the internal legislative organisation for ex ante subsidiarity scrutiny in different EU Member States. EU institutional reforms have always demanded reorganisation in national-level scrutiny, and the major change in the position of national parliaments introduced by the Lisbon Treaty again required suitable scrutiny procedures. Constitutional courts supported this view and recognised the new role of national parliaments in the EU legislative process. The German Federal Constitutional Court even conferred upon the German Parliament the responsibility for further European integration. Thus, as a consequence of the Lisbon Treaty and, in some cases of the constitutional jurisprudence, constitutional and infra-constitutional changes had to be introduced in order to accommodate the process of subsidiarity review.

This chapter demonstrated that Member States have offered different models for the regulation of their respective subsidiarity review processes allowing national parliaments to fulfil their role of responsibility for European integration. While some parliaments have entrusted EACs with this task, others have delegated responsibilities to sectoral committees, or both types of committee in a mixed type of scrutiny model. Within the established procedures for subsidiarity scrutiny, the chapter further enquired into aspects such as the moment of detection of a breach, the role of the government and the role of the plenary session, and the extent to which national parliaments take on board the views of the regional parliaments. National parliaments have been scrutinising the Commission Work Programme, in addition to ongoing scrutiny by, for example, chairs of the committees or the administrative staff. National governments contribute to the subsidiarity scrutiny in the national parliaments by submitting explanatory memoranda on the Commission proposals, memoranda which include an assessment of the principle. This is a useful tool for national parliaments, especially if the government sends in the contribution in a timely manner. The involvement of the parliaments' plenaries in the adoption of the EWS varies across the scrutiny systems. Although it can increase the knowledge of members of national parliaments in EU affairs, it can also slow down the submission of a reasoned opinion. Finally, the regional parliaments have a rather weak position in the EWS. The relevant national parliaments are not obliged to consult the regional assemblies and take their views on board when issuing a reasoned opinion. The exceptions are the Belgian regional assemblies, which can even provide their own reasoned opinions counted under Protocol No 2.

This chapter also explored the correlation between the subsidiarity scrutiny procedure and the number of reasoned opinions adopted by the national parliament at stake; the study established that the form of scrutiny is not the decisive point in assessing participation. Further research should take into account the constitutional traditions of the Member States and the content of the Commission proposals.

5

The EWS Within National Political Systems

I. INTRODUCTION

THIS BOOK HAS thus far focused on the design of the Early Warning System (EWS) at the EU level—its scope, operation, and consequences—and at the national level—by analysing how national procedures accommodate the subsidiarity review. No attention has so far been devoted to the debates and voting on the reasoned opinions in the national parliaments. This aspect of the EWS has also not yet been studied in the relevant literature.

This chapter will therefore analyse four questions regarding the interaction between national executive and legislative bodies in the EWS. First, the chapter considers to what extent the EWS has allowed the national parliamentary chambers to act independently from their respective governments. Second, this chapter investigates whether the decision to pursue subsidiarity violations through the EWS reflects the division between the parliamentary majority and the opposition or whether there is unanimity between the parties on reasoned opinions. Third, the chapter examines to what extent the EWS permits the expression of regional interests independently from such institutions as the Committee of the Regions.[1] Fourth, based on the available plenary and committee debates, the chapter establishes the reasons that may lead a national parliament to issue a reasoned opinion, such as the redistributive character of EU policies or idiosyncratic national interests at stake. This sheds some light on the motivation of national parliaments to participate in the EWS.

This chapter takes the parliamentary chambers of the UK, Germany, Poland and Belgium as case studies. Although not fully representative of all political and constitutional configurations within the EU, this group enables us to enquire into a number of relevant features of the parliamentary process such as federal and centralised structures, majoritarian (Westminster model) and consensus models of executive–legislative relations, and variety within the bicameral structure of parliaments. Hence, the sample can be used to look into how the EWS operates in different institutional and political formations.

The primary source of data for this chapter comes from the analysis of the position of the government on the subsidiarity violation and from the debates in national parliaments. The access to the relevant information is differentiated among the Member States studied in this chapter.[2] The information on the opinion of government on the

[1] See ch 2.

[2] In general, on transparency of work of parliaments see C Fasone and N Lupo, 'Transparency vs Informality in Legislative Committees: Comparing the US House of Representatives, the Italian Chamber of Deputies and the European Parliament' (2015) 21 *The Journal of Legislative Studies* 342, 342–59.

compliance of a proposal at stake with the subsidiarity principle is freely available in the UK from the government's website, while in Germany, Poland and Belgium, only in some cases could it be found in the parliamentary debates.[3] Similarly, while the positions of the majority and opposition parties are in most cases sufficiently and clearly stated in the debates of the Commission proposals at stake, only in Poland is a detailed name vote record accessible.

The chapter is structured as follows. Section II reviews current studies on the government, majority and opposition in EU affairs to indicate the gap in the relevant literature. Section III then discusses the research approach taken in this chapter, specifically the justification of the study sample, and provides the collected data on government's, parliamentary majority's, and opposition's views on the compliance of EU draft legislative acts. Section IV offers an analysis of the data with regard to the central questions of this chapter. As mentioned previously, those include the independence of parliaments from their government in the EWS, the division between the majority and opposition on reasoned opinions, and the expression of regional interests under the EWS. Section V, by focusing on the content of the debates, enquires into two issues. First, by referring to the notions of 'debating' and 'working' parliaments, this section explores the use of the EWS by the parliamentary opposition. Second, this section, on the basis of the available debates on the adoption of reasoned opinions, investigates possible motivations that led national parliaments to issue reasoned opinions.

II. GOVERNMENT, MAJORITY AND OPPOSITION IN EU AFFAIRS

The relationship between the parliamentary majority and opposition in EU affairs and in particular in the scrutiny of the government has been the subject of several studies. These look beyond the national parliament as a single unit and emphasise lines of conflict between different actors within the chamber, such as political parties. Holzhacker offers one of the first systematic analyses of the role of opposition party groups within EU scrutiny by national parliaments.[4] He sets out the benefits that active and effective opposition confers on the political system and then presents a framework to measure the strength of the opposition in scrutinising EU affairs, applying the framework to parliaments with a majority government, coalition government, and minority government.

In a study, Auel and Benz focus on the dilemma that national parliaments, and in particular members of the majority, face in scrutinising the government in EU matters.[5] Pursuing the control function too aggressively may incapacitate one's government's ability to negotiate at the EU level, thereby possibly foreclosing advantageous outcomes, while overly permissive scrutiny can make the parliament appear powerless and thus ultimately undermine the legitimacy of EU policymaking. Within this context,

[3] For the opinions of the UK government on EU proposals see: europeanmemoranda.cabinetoffice.gov.uk.

[4] R Holzhacker, 'The power of opposition parliamentary party groups in European scrutiny' (2005) 11 *The Journal of Legislative Studies* 428.

[5] K Auel and A Benz, 'The politics of adaptation: The Europeanisation of national parliamentary systems' (2005) 11 *The Journal of Legislative Studies* 372.

opposition parties, even though they generally cannot formally constrain the government, are seen as important in providing public debate on the position taken by the executive body.

In a different contribution, Auel revisits the role of the majority and opposition in EU affairs and argues that national parliaments behave in EU affairs similarly to domestic politics in terms of public deliberation and holding the government publicly accountable.[6] Accordingly, it should not be expected that the majority party will publicly criticise the government's position and that this will remain in the domain of the opposition.[7] Auel emphasises the additional functions of scrutiny of the government by the national parliament that work through the political competition between majority and opposition parties.

Another set of studies focuses on the motivation of the majority and opposition to scrutinise EU draft legislation. For example, Finke and Dannwolf, focusing on coalition governments in Germany and the Czech Republic and using data on EU legislative proposals, enquire into the reasons why parties might initiate scrutiny of the government in EU affairs.[8] Concerning the majority coalition, this study finds that the salience of a proposal can explain whether scrutiny was initiated to strengthen the bargaining position of the government ('Schelling conjecture') or to weaken the relevant minister for domestic gain ('whistle-blowing'). In contrast, the study finds that opposition parties may trigger scrutiny to gain access to information from the government in order to support the activities of their fellow party members in the EP.

Winzen presents an empirical analysis of the factors driving EU scrutiny institutions in national parliaments.[9] He finds that Euroscepticism and internal party divisions in the governing majority influence the degree to which parliaments provide for oversight institutions for EU affairs.

Finally, Miklin explores the position of the opposition parties within the interparliamentary cooperation in EU affairs in the example of the Austrian Parliament.[10] Interparliamentary cooperation has more importance for opposition parties as compared with the governing majority, allowing the opposition to obtain information on EU issues and offering an outlet for its views. However, cooperation is conditioned on whether the party ideology (the left–right division or position on EU integration) allows the opposition party to integrate into a European party network or EP group.

In this light, this book offers a new angle for studies on the relations between different parliamentary actors in EU affairs. None of the earlier studies has focused on the EWS and the relationship among the government, the majority and the opposition when a

[6] K Auel, 'Democratic Accountability and National Parliaments: Redefining the Impact of Parliamentary Scrutiny in EU Affairs' (2007) 13 *European Law Journal* 487.

[7] ibid 502.

[8] D Finke and T Dannwolf, 'Domestic scrutiny of European Union politics: Between whistle blowing and opposition control' (2013) 52 *European Journal of Political Research* 715.

[9] T Winzen, 'European integration and national parliamentary oversight institutions' (2013) 14 *European Union Politics* 297.

[10] E Miklin, 'Inter-Parliamentary Cooperation in EU affairs and the Austrian Parliament: Empowering the Opposition?' (2013) 19 *The Journal of Legislative Studies* 22, 36.

reasoned opinion is debated. In addition, this chapter attempts to understand whether the EWS confirms or challenges any of the assumptions about the involved parliamentary actors.

III. RESEARCH APPROACH

The following section presents the data collected on all reasoned opinions concerning Commission proposals made from the entry into force of the Lisbon Treaty until the end of 2016.[11] The study is limited to the debates and voting in which the respective parliaments decided to issue a reasoned opinion. While the selected parliaments of the UK, Germany, Poland and Belgium are not fully representative of all possible political and constitutional configurations across Member States, the sample nonetheless allows us to cover substantial ground regarding the research questions of this chapter.

A. Justification of the Sample Choice

First, the sample includes both centralised and federal constitutional systems. The national parliaments of the chosen Member States operate in federal (Germany, Belgium) or centralised Member States (Poland), while in the UK, the parliaments have been governed via the devolution principle since 1999.[12] The varying degree of centralisation may be expected to correlate with the degree to which regional interests are captured and reflected within the EWS where possible.

Second, the sample contains representatives of both majoritarian (Westminster model) and consensus models of executive–legislative relations. In the former, the executive tends to dominate the legislative; the latter model presents a more balanced relationship.[13] In consequence, within the majoritarian model, the parliament will have less independence, as compared with the consensus model, to issue reasoned opinions when the government does not see a subsidiarity violation.

In a close relationship to executive–legislative relations, Max Weber's division between the 'debating' and 'working' chambers offers an additional avenue to discuss the EWS.[14] All the parliaments explored in this chapter have established committees to scrutinise EU legislative proposals, a classic feature of a 'working' parliament.[15] However, the debates on

[11] In consequence, some of the reasoned opinions were issued in 2017.

[12] Devolution means a transfer of power to a subnational authority (Scotland, Wales, or Northern Ireland) in a unitary system of government. In contrast to federalism, the powers of subnational authorities can be withdrawn by the central government at any time. See CA Carter, 'Rethinking UK Parliamentary Adaptation in EU Affairs: Devolution and Europeanisation' (2013) 19 *The Journal of Legislative Studies* 392; R Hazell, 'Westminster as a Three-in-One Legislature for the United Kingdom and its Devolved Territories' (2007) 13 *The Journal of Legislative Studies* 254.

[13] A Lijphart, *Patterns of Democracy: Government Forms and Performance in Thirty-Six Countries* (New Haven, CT, Yale University Press, 2012) 105.

[14] M Weber, *Weber: Political Writings* (Cambridge, Cambridge University Press, 2003).

[15] See ch 4.

the EWS, be it in the committee or in the plenary session of the parliament, in some cases discussed below, present an opportunity for the parliament (especially the opposition) to scrutinise the government. This aspect points towards some of the 'debating' characteristics of national parliaments when participating in the EWS.

Third, this chapter examines both elected and unelected chambers. While the UK House of Lords members are appointed or hereditary, the members of the German Bundesrat represent regional entities. The senators in the Polish Senat are directly elected and, finally, the members of the Belgian Sénat (until 2014) were selected in a combination of appointment and election. The expectation is that directly elected chambers will act more politically, suggesting that the majority will align with the government, while unelected or indirectly elected chambers may act more independently. In addition, political cleavages between parties can be expected to be more prominent in elected chambers, and such conflicts may also be reflected in the views expressed on reasoned opinions under the EWS.

B. Data Collected on Debates and Votes in the EWS

The next section presents the data on the reasoned opinions issued by national parliaments in the UK, Germany, Poland and Belgium.[16] Each of the sections starts with a summary of the main parliamentary features and current political situation in each of the Member States. Next, each of the four tables presents the votes of the majority and the opposition on the adoption of a reasoned opinion. The information on their positions is drawn from records of debates in parliamentary committees and plenary debates of the parliaments. Only in the case of Poland was a detailed record of votes available online. The position of each national government is retrieved from the following: in the UK, from the explanatory memoranda, and in Germany, Poland and Belgium, from the position of the government representative, as stated during a parliamentary committee meeting or during plenary debates.

i. The UK

The British system is characterised by 'the close union, the nearly complete fusion, of the executive and legislative powers'.[17] The UK Parliament consists of the directly elected House of Commons and of the House of Lords, the latter, on the contrary, not being elected. In the House of Commons, 650 constituencies are represented by one Member of Parliament (MP). The House of Commons has a legislative function and a function as that of a government scrutiniser; the government has to retain the confidence of the House of Commons. The House of Commons also keeps government spending in check.

[16] For a similar study of the reasoned opinions issued by the Czech parliament see K Granat, 'Like Two Peas in a Pod? The Functioning of the Early Warning Mechanism in the Czech Republic and Poland' in A Jonsson Cornell and M Goldoni (eds), *National and Regional Parliaments in the EU-Legislative Procedure Post-Lisbon* (Oxford, Hart Publishing, 2017).

[17] W Bagehot, *The English Constitution*, 2nd edn (Boston, MA, Little, Brown and Company, 1873).

House of Lords members include hereditary peers (whose titles are inherited), life peers (appointed for their lifetimes) and archbishops and bishops of the Church of England. The majority of the lords are life peers, since the House of Lords Act 1999 deprived most hereditary peers of the right to sit and vote in the House of Lords. The House of Lords, as does the House of Commons, also considers Bills, which have to pass both Houses to become law. The House of Lords has no veto power; it can only delay, for a certain period, Bills originating from the House of Commons. Moreover, the House of Lords holds the government to account only during debates and question time. Today, the House of Lords scrutinises the government and functions as a 'revising chamber with more time available and, in many cases, more expertise to perform this task' than the directly elected House of Commons.[18] In particular, the 'working peers' (mainly the life peers) regularly and actively participate in select committees, working in a much more 'non-partisan, technical, expert' manner than members of the House of Commons.[19]

Between May 2010 and May 2015, the Conservatives under the leadership of David Cameron formed a coalition with the Liberal Democrats, with the Labour Party as the main opposition party in the House of Commons. Between May 2016 and June 2017, the Conservative Party formed a majority government, first as Cameron's government and then as the government of his successor, Theresa May.

The House of Lords reform of 1999 first stopped the domination of the Conservatives in the chamber and in consequence the number of seats of the Conservative and Labour Parties almost equalised.[20] As Tony Blair had appointed a large number of peers during his government, Labour peers started to dominate the chamber in 2006.[21] In 2010, when David Cameron became the Prime Minister, the government depended on the votes of the Conservatives and the Liberal Democrats to have sufficient support to outnumber the Opposition.[22] An important role was also played by the crossbenchers (members without party affiliation) who, post-2010, contributed to the Cameron–Clegg coalition's defeats in the House of Lords.[23] The domination of Labour Lords has diminished over time because of the new appointments of Conservative peers,[24] and since October 2013, the Conservative Party again has the highest number of affiliated Lords.[25]

In the House of Lords, with much weaker whips than in the Commons, the peers largely vote as cohesive party blocs and choose to abstain rather than dissent.[26] Therefore, the House of Lords exemplifies a case of distinctive cohesion without the discipline tools provided by party leadership, as in the House of Commons.[27]

[18] P Leyland, *The Constitution of the United Kingdom: A Contextual Analysis (Constitutional Systems of the World)* (Oxford, Hart Publishing, 2012) 127.

[19] D Oliver, 'Reforming the United Kingdom Parliament' in J Jowell and D Oliver (eds), *The Changing Constitution*, 7th edn (Oxford, Oxford University Press, 2011) 180. See also M Russell, *The Contemporary House of Lords: Westminster Bicameralism Revived* (Oxford, Oxford University Press, 2013) 90.

[20] Russell (n 19) 69.

[21] ibid 74.

[22] ibid 96.

[23] ibid 119.

[24] ibid 96.

[25] See at: myparliament.info/Historical/Lords.

[26] Russell (n 19) 114.

[27] P Norton, 'Cohesion without discipline: Party voting in the House of Lords' (2003) 9 *The Journal of Legislative Studies* 57.

Table 1: Overview of the Positions of the Government, Majority and Opposition on the Commission proposals in the UK

Commission proposal	Opinion of the government	Vote of the parliamentary majority	Vote of the parliamentary opposition
House of Commons			
COM(2010) 371[28]	(–)[29]	(+)	(+)[30]
COM(2011) 121[31]	(+)[32]	(+)	(+)[33]
COM(2011) 452[34]	(+)[35]	(+)	(+)[36]
COM(2011) 635[37]	(–)[38]	(+)	(+)[39]
COM(2011) 895 + COM(2011) 896[40]	(+)[41]	(+)	(+)[42]
COM(2012) 130[43]	(–)[44]	(+)	(+)[45]

(continued)

[28] 'Proposal for a Directive of the European Parliament and of the Council amending Directive 97/9/EC of the European Parliament and of the Council on investor-compensation schemes' COM(2010) 371 final.

[29] Explanatory Memorandum submitted by HM Treasury of 17 September 2010, pt 24. The EM of the government is in general negative, but 'based on national sovereignty, rather than specifically on subsidiarity', as the government's representative explains in the House of Commons European Committee Debate of 21.10.2010, Column 9.

[30] The Labour Party members supported issuing a reasoned opinion at the Committee stage. See House of Commons European Committee: Investor Compensation Schemes of 21.10.2010, col 12. The House agreed to the motion without a debate. See House of Commons Hansard Debates for 25.10.2010, Column 26.

[31] 'Proposal for a Council Directive on a Common Consolidated Corporate Tax Base (CCCTB)' COM(2011) 121 final.

[32] Explanatory Memorandum Supplement 7263/11, point 6.

[33] The Opposition was pointing out that the coalition partner—the Liberal Democrats—had a different position in its party programme on the corporate taxation (in favour). Yet, the Conservatives argued that the position of the coalition is uniform. See HC Deb 11 May 2011, col 1288.

[34] 'Proposal for a Regulation of the European Parliament and the Council on prudential requirements for credit institutions and investement firms (Text with EEA relevance)' COM(2011) 452 final.

[35] Explanatory Memorandum submitted by HM Treasury of 05.09.2011, point 59.

[36] See positions of the Labour Party Members in HC Deb 8 November 2011.

[37] 'Proposal for a Regulation of the European Parliament and the Council on a Common European Sales Law' COM(2011) 635 final.

[38] Explanatory Memorandum submitted by the Ministry of Justice of 31.10.2011, point 23. However, see HC Deb 7 December 2011, col 315, where the government agrees with the Parliament on the lack of necessity of the proposal.

[39] See HC Deb 7 December 2011, col 322.

[40] 'Proposal for a Directive of the European Parliament and of the Council on procurement by entities operating in the water, energy, transport and postal services sectors' COM(2011) 895 final; 'Proposal for a Directive of the European Parliament and of the Council on public procurement' COM(2011) 896 final.

[41] See HC Deb 6 March 2012, col 755 (EM not found).

[42] ibid.

[43] 'Proposal for a Council Regulation on the exercise of the right to take collective action within the context of the freedom of establishment and the freedom to provide services' COM(2012) 130 final.

[44] See House of Commons European Committee: Right to Take Collective Action on 21.05.2012, col 5. According to the government the CJEU's jurisprudence on the balance between fundamental freedoms and the right to strike is clear and the regulation only repeats that.

[45] See House of Commons European Committee: Right to Take Collective Action on 21.05.2012, col 8.

Table 1: (*Continued*)

Commission proposal	Opinion of the government	Vote of the parliamentary majority	Vote of the parliamentary opposition
COM(2012) 614[46]	(+)[47]	(+)	(+)[48]
COM(2012) 617[49]	(+)[50]	(+)	(+)[51]
COM(2013) 147[52]	(+)[53]	(+)	(+)[54]
COM(2013) 534[55]	(+)[56]	(+)	(+)[57]
COM(2013) 619, 618[58]	(+)[59]	(+)	(+)[60]
COM(2013) 641[61]	(+)[62]	(+)	(+)[63]

(continued)

[46] 'Proposal for a Directive of the European Parliament and of the Council on improving the gender balance among non-executive directors of companies listed on stock exchanges and related measures' COM(2012) 614.

[47] Explanatory Memorandum submitted by the Department for Business, Innovation & Skills on 04.12.2012, stating that the UK government is 'still considering' the compatibility with subsidiarity, point 23. In the government's reply to the House of Lords on 20.12.2012, the minister agreed in this context that the government should consider 'adherence of any legislation to the principle of subsidiarity in the light of the extensive efforts made domestically' and 'oppose any such measure strongly'.

[48] The opposition supports the motion, but does also criticise the government's reforms on equality in companies' boards. See HC Deb 7 January 2013, col 60.

[49] 'Proposal for a Regulation of the European Parliament and the Council on the Fund for European Aid to the Most Deprived' COM(2012) 617 final.

[50] Explanatory Memorandum submitted by the Department for Work and Pensions of 23.11.2012, points 14–15.

[51] See HC Deb 18 December 2012, col 13.

[52] 'Proposal for a Regulation of the European Parliament and the Council on measures to reduce the cost of deploying high-speed electronic communications networks' COM(2013) 147 final.

[53] Explanatory Memorandum submitted by the Department for Culture, Media and Sport on 22.04.2013, points 17–18.

[54] The opposition supports the motion, but does also criticise the government's actions with regard to infrastructure sharing. See House of Commons European Committee: Communication Networks, 20.05.2013, col 12.

[55] 'Proposal for a Council Regulation on the establishment of the European Public Prosecutor's Office' COM(2013) 534 final.

[56] Explanatory Memorandum submitted by the Home Office on 7.08.2013, point 45.

[57] HC Deb 22 November 2013, col 265.

[58] 'Proposal for a Directive of the European Parliament and of the Council amending Council Framework Decision 2004/757/JHA of 25 October 2004 laying down minimum provisions on the constituent elements of criminal acts and penalties in the field of illicit drug trafficking, as regards the definition of drug' COM(2013) 618 final; 'Proposal for a Regulation of the European Parliament and the Council on new psychoactive substances' COM(2013) 619 final.

[59] Explanatory Memorandum submitted by the Home Office on 08.10.2013, point 19. Additional explanation in the letter from the Minister for Crime Prevention, Norman Baker MP, to Bill Cash MP, Chairman of the European Scrutiny Committee (11.11.2013).

[60] The opposition supports the motion, but does also criticise the government failure in response to 'legal highs'. HC Deb 11 November 2013, col 764.

[61] 'Proposal for a Regulation of the European Parliament and the Council on indices used as benchmarks in financial instruments and financial contracts' COM(2013) 641 final.

[62] Explanatory Memorandum submitted by HM treasury in October 2013 states that '[t]he Government is concerned that this proposal and its scope may raise subsidiarity issues'. See point 14. In its letter to the Chairman of the European Scrutiny Committee (07.11.2013), the Financial Secretary to the Treasury further explained that '[a]fter further consideration, I consider that this proposal does not comply with the principle of subsidiarity under Article 5(3) of the TEU'. This view was confirmed in the House of Commons, European Committee B, Financial Services Benchmarks debate of 28.11.2013.

[63] House of Commons, European Committee B, Financial Services Benchmarks, 28.11.2013, 6.

Table 1: (*Continued*)

Commission proposal	Opinion of the government	Vote of the parliamentary majority	Vote of the parliamentary opposition
COM(2013) 821[64]	(+)[65]	(+)	(+)[66]
COM(2013) 893[67]	(+)[68]	(+)	(–)[69]
COM(2014) 221[70]	(+)[71]	(+)	(+)[72]
2015/0907/APP[73]	(+)[74]	(+)	(+)[75]

(continued)

[64] 'Proposal for a Directive of the European Parliament and of the Council on the strengthening of certain aspects of the presumption of innocence and of the right to be present at trial in criminal proceedings' COM(2013) 821 final.

[65] The initial position of the government changed under the influence of the Parliament. Explanatory Memorandum submitted by the Ministry of Justice on 09.01.2014 states no subsidiarity violation (points 18–19). The UK government states, however, that 'there is limited statistical quantifiable evidence of insufficient mutual trust which may raise a question about the necessity of the proposal'. In the letter of 20.01.2014 to William Cash, Chairman of European Scrutiny Committee, Chris Grayling, Secretary of State for Justice states that the proposal complies with the principle of subsidiarity (p 4). In a later letter of 06.02.2014 to the Chairman of the European Scrutiny Committee, the government seems to agree with the opinion of the House of Commons and admits that the Commission has failed to satisfy Art 5 of Protocol No 2 requirement of a detailed statement on subsidiarity and proportionality (p 2). In the House of Commons debate (HC Deb 10 February 2014) on the reasoned opinion the opposition underlined that '[t]he Government, taxed by the European Scrutiny Committee, have fallen in line with that view at the eleventh hour' (col 671), whereas the coalition 'welcome[d] the fact that in that letter the Government have belatedly accepted that "a lack of evidence of necessity renders a proposal in breach of subsidiarity principle"' (col 673).

[66] HC Deb 10 February 2014, col 672.

[67] 'Proposal for a Council Directive on the placing on the market of food from animal clones' COM(2013) 893 final.

[68] Explanatory Memorandum submitted by the Department for Environment, Food and Rural Affairs on 14.01.2014, point 6, states no subsidiarity violation. The UK government does not believe, however, that the proposal is necessary, 'given the absence of human health concerns associated with cloning and the protection already offered by the existing EU animal welfare and novel food regimes'. This position of the government has changed, and it supported the Committee in the view that the proposal does not meet the subsidiarity requirements. See European Committee A of the House of Commons on 11.02.2014, col 11.

[69] The Reasoned opinion was agreed to without debate on the floor of the House of Commons on 12.02.2014 (Business without Debate). The reasoned opinion was discussed in the European Committee A of the House of Commons on 11.02.2014.

[70] 'Proposal for a Directive of the European Parliament and of the Council on establishing a European Platform to enhance cooperation in the prevention and deterrence of undeclared work' COM(2014) 221 final.

[71] Explanatory Memorandum submitted by the Department for Business, Innovation and Skills on 30.04.2014, point 12. See, however, that the UK government had less certainty on the subsidiarity violation because the proposal had been negotiated and the only obligatory requirement would remain to attend the platform, while taking action would be voluntary. But in the end, the UK government was in favour of sending the Reasoned opinion. See HC Deb 9 June 2014, Undeclared work, cols 379–80.

[72] The opposition agreed with issuing a reasoned opinion. HC Deb 9 June 2014, col 377.

[73] Reform of the electoral law of the European Union, 14.12.2015.

[74] European Scrutiny Committee, *Nineteenth Report, Session 2015–16*, point 1.7.

[75] European Committee B, Electoral Law, 02.02.2016, col 13. The government was criticised for the quality of the subsidiarity assessment.

Table 1: (*Continued*)

Commission proposal	Opinion of the government	Vote of the parliamentary majority	Vote of the parliamentary opposition
COM(2016) 491[76]	(+)[77]	(+)	(+)[78]
House of Lords			
COM(2010) 379[79]	(–)[80]	(+)	(+)[81]
COM(2010) 486[82]	(+)[83]	(+)	(+)[84]
COM(2011) 634[85]	(+)[86]	(+)	(+)[87]
COM(2012) 614	(+)[88]	(+)	(+)[89]
COM(2012) 617	(+)[90]	(+)	(+)[91]

(continued)

[76] 'Proposal for a Regulation of the European Parliament and of the Council establishing a Union certification system for aviation security screening equipment' COM(2016) 491 final.

[77] The Explanatory Memorandum states that the government does not believe that the proposal is compatible with subsidiarity. See EM of Department for Transport on 19.10.2016, point 14. In the committee debate, the Minister of State, Department for Transport stated, however, that the proposal conflicts with the subsidiarity principle. See European Committee A, 31.10.2016.

[78] The Reasoned opinion was presented by a Labour MP on behalf of the European Scrutiny Committee. European Committee A, Aviation Security (Reasoned Opinion), 31 October 2016, cols 1–12.

[79] 'Proposal for a Directive of the European Parliament and of the Council on the conditions of entry and residence of third-country nationals for the purposes of seasonal employment' COM(2010) 379.

[80] Explanatory Memorandum submitted by the Home Office on 20.07.2010, point 13. The UK government agrees that in regard to situations in which the decision of one Member State on the rights of third-country nationals affects other Member States and distorts migratory flows, the subsidiarity principle is met. The same argument was raised in the House of Lords debate. See further HL text 20 October 2010, col 879.

[81] Labour Party and UK Independence Party Lords were in favour of a Reasoned opinion. See HL text 20 October 2010, cols 873–75.

[82] 'Amended proposal for a Regulation of the European Parliament and the Council amending Council Regulations (EC) No 1290/2005 and (EC) No 1234/2007, as regards distribution of food products to the most deprived persons in the Union' COM(2010) 486 final.

[83] The Explanatory Memorandum submitted by the Department for Environment, Food and Rural Affairs of 04.10.2010, point 7 under title 'subsidiarity' states that 'the government remains unconvinced as to the merits or appropriateness of the proposal'; 'social measures should be taken by Member States'. The debate seems to point at a clearer position of the government. See HL text 3 November 2010, col 1689.

[84] HL text 3 November 2010, cols 1684, 1686.

[85] 'Amended proposal for a Regulation of the European Parliament and the Council amending Council Regulation (EC) No 1290/2005 and Council Regulation (EC) No 1234/2007 as regards distribution of food products to the most deprived persons in the Union' COM(2011) 634 final.

[86] Explanatory Memorandum submitted by the Department for Environment, Food and Rural Affairs on 17.10.2011, pt 9. Confirmed later also in the letter of the Minister of State for Agriculture and Food to the House of Lords on 15.11.2011, EM 15054/11.

[87] HL text 28 November 2011, col 91.

[88] Explanatory Memorandum submitted by the Department for Business, Innovation & Skills on 04.12.2012, stating that the UK government is 'still considering' the compatibility with subsidiarity, point 23. In the government's reply to the House of Lords on 20.12.2012, the minister agreed in this context that the government should consider 'adherence of any legislation to the principle of subsidiarity in the light of the extensive efforts made domestically' and 'oppose any such measure strongly'.

[89] HL text 10 January 2013, cols 342, 349–50.

[90] Explanatory Memorandum submitted by the Department for Work and Pensions of 23.11.2012, points 14–15.

[91] HL text 13 December, col 406.

Table 1: (*Continued*)

Commission proposal	Opinion of the government	Vote of the parliamentary majority	Vote of the parliamentary opposition
COM(2013) 534[92]	(+)[93]	(+)	(+)[94]
COM(2013) 618, 619	(+)[95]	(+)	(+)[96]
2015/0907/APP	(+)[97]	(+)	(+)[98]

Note: (+) subsidiarity violation; (–) no subsidiarity violation.

Table 1 lists the Commission proposals that the House of Commons and the House of Lords assessed as contrary to the subsidiarity principle. Table 1 reflects the government's opinion on the compatibility of proposals with the subsidiarity principle as stated in explanatory memoranda and the views of the majority and opposition which were reconstructed on the basis of the transcripts of the debates in the Houses.[99]

Table 1 shows that the House of Commons and the House of Lords issued three reasoned opinions and one reasoned opinion, respectively, in cases in which the government did not believe that the Commission proposal was in violation of subsidiarity. In the House of Commons, there was a consensus between the majority and the opposition on almost all reasoned opinions except for the reasoned opinion on the proposed directive on the placing on the market of food from animal clones; in this instance, the views of the majority and opposition diverged.[100] Although the coalition claimed that there was 'almost' a cross-party coalition on the subsidiarity issue, the position presented by two Labour MPs clearly indicated that the issue should be approached at EU level.[101] The underlying grounds such as consumer protection, animal health and welfare and food safety—uncovered by the horse meat scandal in the UK—were seen as best dealt with at the EU level. In a grey area was the reasoned opinion on the right to strike proposal,[102] in which Labour MPs were in favour

[92] 'Proposal for a Council Regulation on the establishment of the European Public Prosecutor's Office' COM (2013) 534 final.

[93] Explanatory Memorandum submitted by the Home Office on 07.08.2013, point 45.

[94] HL text 28 October 2013, col 1404.

[95] Explanatory Memorandum submitted by the Home Office on 8.10.2013, point 19. Additional explanation in the letter from the Minister for Crime Prevention, Norman Baker MP, to Bill Cash MP, Chairman of the European Scrutiny Committee (11.11.2013).

[96] HL text 11 November 2013, col 583.

[97] HL text 4 February 2016, col 1951.

[98] HL text 4 February 2016, cols 1948 and 1953. Only one Labour peer voted against the Reasoned opinion, while the Labour Party supported the Reasoned opinion.

[99] Note that during a debate in the House of Commons on a reasoned opinion, when a question is 'put and agreed to' it means that the chair has 'put' the question, and those present have generally shouted 'Aye' in response. So when the chair then says, 'I think the Ayes have it, the Ayes have it' no one has then challenged the decision and called a vote (known as a division). There is therefore no count or registration of votes in these cases. See House of Commons, Standing Orders 2013, No 38. Similar rules apply in the House of Lords when a motion is 'moved and agreed to'. There is no vote unless a division takes place. See House of Lords, Standing Orders 2013, No 53.

[100] 'Proposal for a Council Directive on the placing on the market of food from animal clones' COM(2013) 893 final.

[101] European Committee A of the House of Commons on 11.02.2014, cols 10–12.

[102] 'Proposal for a Council Regulation on the exercise of the right to take collective action within the context of the freedom of establishment and the freedom to provide services' COM(2012) 130 final.

of the reasoned opinion, not because of the subsidiarity violation, but to support the position of trade unions.[103] In contrast to those cases of disagreement, the House of Lords was unanimous on the reasoned opinions to be adopted.

ii. Germany

The Bundestag comprises at least 598 members elected in a system that combines a plurality voting system with a proportional one. Specifically, half of the Bundestag members are elected directly and half from party lists; the 'overhang seats' for which a party won more constituency seats than it would have been entitled to based on its share of the second votes increase the number of Bundestag members.[104]

The Bundesrat consists of members of the Länder governments; thus its composition changes via elections in the Länder.[105] It consists of 69 members. Each Land has at least three votes, the number of which can increase up to six depending on population. Each of the Länder in the Bundesrat votes through its representative (*Stimmführer*) in order to avoid situations when during the vote two ministers from the same Land present two contrary votes.[106] A more important issue is that the Bundesrat provides a means for the Länder to represent their territorial interests and influence federal government policy.[107] Hence, the representatives of two different Länder that are governed by the same party may vote differently in the Bundesrat.

Both the Bundestag and the Bundesrat have legislative competences for federal legislation: they can both initiate legislation.[108] The Bundestag scrutinises the government, scrutiny which includes a constructive vote of no confidence, and consents to the federal budget.[109] The Bundesrat also has a suspensive veto and an absolute veto on federal legislation. In practice, the veto power from the latter provision has been interpreted relatively widely so that the Bundesrat and the Länder representatives that comprise its membership have been important veto players in German legislative politics.[110]

Between 2009 and 2013, the composition of the Bundestag allowed the formation of a coalition government of the Liberal-Conservative Christlich Demokratische Union Deutschlands (CDU) and the Christlich-Soziale Union in Bavaria (CSU) with the Liberal Freie Demokratische Partei (FDP), while the Social-Democratic Sozialdemokratische Partei Deutschlands (SPD), Democratic Socialist Die Linke, and the Greens Bündnis 90/Die Grünen remained in opposition. Following the 2013 parliamentary elections, the CDU/CSU remained in power, forming a 'grand coalition' with the SPD from 2013 to 2017.

[103] House of Commons, European Committee: Right to Take Collective Action on 21.05.2012, col 8.

[104] The reform of the electoral law of 21.02.2013 changed the 'overhang seats' (*Überhangmandat*') into 'balance seats' (*Ausgleichmandate*), a situation which means that for every 'overhang mandate' for one party, the other will be compensated. With the reform, voters will be better represented, as the *Überhängmandate* differentiated the value of votes.

[105] Art 51 I of the Basic Law.

[106] K Reuter, *Praxishandbuch Bundesrat: Verfassungsrechtliche Grundlagen, Kommentar zur Geschäftsordnung, Praxis des Bundesrates* (Heidelberg, CF Müller, 2007) 508.

[107] M Russell, 'The Territorial Role of Second Chambers' (2001) 7 *The Journal of Legislative Studies* 105, 110.

[108] Art 76 II of the Basic Law.

[109] Arts 67 and 110 of the Basic Law.

[110] W Heun, *The Constitution of Germany: A Contextual Analysis* (Oxford, Hart Publishing, 2011) 70.

Since 2010, the federal government has been without a majority in the Bundesrat, both during the CDU/CSU and FDP coalitions and the grand coalition in place after the elections of 2013. Between 2010 and 2013, the opposition parties on the Left, including the SPD, Die Grünen, and Die Linke, had a narrow majority in the Bundesrat. Since the election of 2013, neither the government nor the opposition have had a majority of votes in the Bundestag, in part because of the variety of coalitions in the Länder, including traditional combinations on the Left (SPD–Greens) and Right (CDU–FDP) that under the federal 'grand coalition' belonged to neither government nor opposition.

Table 2: Overview of the Positions of the Government, Majority and Opposition on the Commission proposals in Germany

Commission proposal	Opinion of the federal government	Vote of the parliamentary majority	Vote of the parliamentary opposition
Bundestag			
COM(2010) 368[111]	(?)	(+)	(–)[112]
COM(2011) 635[113]	(–)[114]	(+)	(+)[115]
COM(2012) 617[116]	(+)[117]	(+)	(–)[118]
COM(2016) 821+822+823+824[119]	(–)[120]	(+)	(+)[121]
COM(2016) 861 + 863[122]	(–)[123]	(+)	(+)[124]

(continued)

[111] 'Proposal for a Directive of the European Parliament and of the Council on Deposit Guarantee Schemes' COM(2010) 368 final.

[112] CDU/CSU, FDP and Die Linke voted in favour of the Reasoned opinion, SPD and die Grünen against. Deutscher Bundestag, Stenografischer Bericht, 07.10.2010, Plenarprotokoll 17/65, 6866.

[113] 'Proposal for a Regulation of the European Parliament and the Council on a Common European Sales Law' COM(2011) 635 final.

[114] Berichtsbogen gemäß Anlage zu § 7 Absatz 1 EUZBBG und Ziffer II. 3 der Anlage zu § 9 EUZBLG, Landtag von Baden-Württenberg, Drucksache 15/848, 07.11.2011, 6.

[115] Unanimity. Deutscher Bundestag, Stenografischer Bericht, 01.12.2011, Plenarprotokoll 17/146, 17507.

[116] 'Proposal for a Regulation of the European Parliament and the Council on the Fund for European Aid to the Most Deprived' COM(2012) 617 final.

[117] Deutscher Bundestag, Stenografischer Bericht, 13.12.2012, Plenarprotokoll 17/214, 26500.

[118] CDU/CSU and FDP voted in favour. SPD and Die Linke voted against. Die Grünen abstained. Deutscher Bundestag, Stenografischer Bericht, 13.12.2012, Plenarprotokoll 17/214, 26427.

[119] Services Package, 10.01.2017, COM(2016) 821, 822, 823, 824.

[120] Deutscher Bundestag, Stenografischer Bericht, 09.03.2017, Plenarprotokoll 18/221, 22241.

[121] CDU/CSU, SPD and Die Linke voted in favour of the reasoned opinion. Die Grünen abstained. Deutscher Bundestag, Stenografischer Bericht, 09.03.2017, Plenarprotokoll 18/221, 22242.

[122] 'Proposal for a Regulation of the European Parliament and of the Council on the internal market for electricity' COM(2016) 861 final; and 'Proposal for a Regulation of the European Parliament and of the Council establishing a European Union Agency for the Cooperation of Energy Regulators (recast)' 2016 COM(2016) 863 final.

[123] Deutscher Bundestag, Stenografischer Bericht, 30.03.2017, Plenarprotokoll 18/228, 23049.

[124] CDU/CSU and SPD voted in favour of the reasoned opinion, while Die Linke and Die Grünen abstained. Deutscher Bundestag, Stenografischer Bericht, 30.03.2017, Plenarprotokoll 18/228, 23008.

Table 2: (*Continued*)

Commission proposal	Opinion of the federal government	Vote of the chamber
Bundesrat		
COM(2010) 368	(?)	(+)[125]
COM(2011) 654[126]	(?)	(+)[127]
COM(2011) 793[128]	(?)	(+)[129]
COM(2011) 828[130]	(?)	(+)[131]
COM(2011) 897[132]	(–)[133]	(+)[134]
COM(2012) 10[135]	(–)[136]	(+)[137]

(continued)

[125] See Deutscher Bundesrat, Stenografischer Bericht, 24.09.2010, Plenarprotokoll 874, 307–09. The representative of the Bayern government (CSU) and Baden-Württenberg government (CDU) supported issuing a reasoned opinion, while the representative of Nordrhein-Westfallen government (SPD) voted against. Similarly, the Landtag von Baden-Württenberg, Drucksache 15/1323, 01.03.2012, found a subsidiarity breach.

[126] 'Proposal for a Directive of the European Parliament and of the Council on criminal sanctions for insider dealing and market manipulation' COM(2011) 654 final.

[127] No information on the votes, but the Reasoned opinion has been issued.

[128] 'Proposal for a Directive of the European Parliament and of the Council on alternative dispute resolution for consumer disputes and amending Regulation (EC) No 2006/2004 and Directive 2009/22/EC (Directive on consumer ADR)' COM(2011) 793 final.

[129] The Thüringer Landtag dominated by the CDU found a subsidiarity breach. See Unterrichtung durch die Präsidentin des Landtags, 20.01.2012, Drucksache 5/3932. The Europakammer of the Bundesrat issued the Reasoned opinion in this case. The record of voting was not public. See Bundesrat, Europakammer, 24.01.2012, Umfrage 19.

[130] 'Proposal for a Regulation of the European Parliament and the Council on the establishment of rules and procedures with regard to the introduction of noise-related operating restrictions at Union airports within a Balanced Approach and repealing Directive 2002/30/EC of the European Parliament and of the Council' COM(2011) 828 final.

[131] The Europakammer of the Bundesrat issued the Reasoned opinion in this case. The record of voting was revealed on the motion of the State Hessen. See Bundesrat, Europakammer, 07.02.2012, Umfrage 21. The CDU and FDP motion in the Hessen Landtag pointed at a violation of subsidiarity by Art 10 of the proposal. See Hessischer Landtag, 17.01.2012, Drucksache 18/5154.

[132] 'Proposal for a Directive of the European Parliament and of the Council on the award of concession contracts' COM(2011) 897 final.

[133] Stenografischer Bericht, 02.03.2012, Plenarprotokol 893, 110.

[134] The opinions of regional parliaments underlined that there is a subsidiarity breach. Bayerischer Landtag, 26.01.2012, Drucksache 16/11067 on COM (2011) 897; Landtag von Baden-Württemberg, 03.02.2012, Drucksache 15-1323; Thüringer Landtag, 17.02.2012, Drucksache 5/4082 (all CDU/CSU). The SPD Minister of Rheinland-Pfalz expressed support for the Bundesrat's Reasoned opinion at a later stage. See Bundesrat, Stenografischer Bericht, 30.03.2012, Plenarptokoll 895, 175.

[135] 'Proposal for a Directive of the European Parliament and of the Council on the protection of individuals with regard to the processing of personal data by competent authorities for the purposes of prevention, investigation, detection or prosecution of criminal offences or the execution of criminal penalties, and the free movement of such data' COM(2012) 10 final.

[136] Berichtsbogen gemäß Anlage zu § 7 Absatz 1 EUZBBG und Ziffer II 3 der Anlage zu § 9 EUZBLG, Landtag von Baden-Württenberg, Drucksache 15/1302, 20.02.2012, 12.

[137] Bundesrat, Stenografischer Bericht, 30.03.2012, Plenarprotokoll 895, 178–80. Also the Bayerischer Landtag, 01.03.2012, Drucksache 16/11706 (CSU, SPD, FDP, Freie Wähler), Thüringer Landtag, 16.03.2012, Drucksache 5/4206, Schleswig-Holsteinischer Landtag, 12.03.2012, Drucksache 17/2413 (CDU, SPD, FDP voted in favour) found a subsidiarity breach.

Table 2: (*Continued*)

Commission proposal	Opinion of the federal government	Vote of the chamber
COM(2012) 11[138]	(–)[139]	(+)[140]
COM(2013) 133[141]	(?)	(+)[142]
COM(2013) 173[143]	(?)	(+)[144]
COM(2013) 721[145]	(+)[146]	(+)[147]
COM(2016) 861[148]	(–)[149]	(+)[150]

Notes: (+) subsidiarity violation; (–) no subsidiarity violation; (?) position unknown.

Table 2 illustrates, where obtainable, the position of the federal government for each of the Commission proposals for which the chambers issued a reasoned opinion and the stances

[138] 'Proposal for a Regulation of the European Parliament and the Council on the protection of individuals with regard to the processing of personal data and on the free movement of such data (General Data Protection Regulation)' COM(2012) 11 final.

[139] Berichtsbogen gemäß Anlage zu § 7 Absatz 1 EUZBBG und Ziffer II 3 der Anlage zu § 9 EUZBLG, Landtag von Baden-Württenberg, Drucksache 15/1302, 20.02.2012, 7.

[140] Bundesrat, Stenografischer Bericht, 30.03.2012, Plenarprotokoll 895, 178–80. Also Thüringer Landtag, 16.03.2012, Drucksache 5/4207; Schleswig-Holsteinischer Landtag, 07.03.2012, Drucksache 17/2350 (CDU, FDP); Bayerischer Landtag, 01.03.2012, Drucksache 16/22705 (CSU, SPD, FDP, Freie Wähler); Hessischer Landtag (Dricksache 18/5396), 13.03.2012 (motion of CDU and FDP) pointed out subsidiarity concerns and instructed their respective governments to argue for a reasoned opinion in the Bundesrat.

[141] 'Proposal for a Directive of the European Parliament and of the Council establishing a framework for maritime spatial planning and integrated coastal management' COM(2013) 133 final.

[142] Only the SPD Ministerpräsident of Mecklenburg-Vorpommern did directly support the Reasoned opinion. Bundesrat, Stenografischer Bericht, 03.05.2013, Plenarprotokol 909, 252. However, the Thüringer Landtag (Drucksache 5/5987), 19.04.2013 and the Bayerischer Landtag (Drucksache 16/16592) of 24.04.2013 (moved by CSU, Freie Wähler, Die Grünen, FDP) pointed out subsidiarity concerns and instructed their respective governments to argue for a Reasoned opinion in the Bundesrat. The Thüringer Landtag underlined that even though the Land is not directly affected by the Commission proposal, the EU does not have a competence to act.

[143] 'Proposal for a Regulation of the European Parliament and the Council on the European Union Agency for Law Enforcement Cooperation and Training (Europol) and repealing Decisions 2009/371/JHA and 2005/681/JHA' COM(2013) 173 final.

[144] Positions unknown. Bundesrat, Stenografischer Bericht, 07.06.2013, Plenarprotokol 910, 320. However, the Thüringer Landtag (Drucksache 5/6114), 17.05.2013; Landtag of Baden-Württenmberg (Drucksache 15/3555), 05.06.2013; and the Bayerischer Landtag (Drucksache 16/16956), 04.06.2013 (moved by CSU, SPD, Freie Wähler, Die Grünen, FDP) pointed out subsidiarity concerns and instructed their respective governments to argue for a Reasoned opinion in the Bundesrat.

[145] 'Proposal for a Council Directive amending Directive 2006/112/EC on the common system of value added tax as regards a standard VAT return' COM(2013) 721 final.

[146] Berichtsbogen gemäß Anlage zu § 7 Absatz 1 EUZBBG und Ziffer II 3 der Anlage zu § 9 EUZBLG, Landtag von Baden-Württenberg, Drucksache 15/4328, 13.11.2013, 5.

[147] Positions taken in the Bundesrat unknown. Bundesrat, Stenografischer Bericht, 29.11.2013, Plenarprotokol 917, 551. However, the Thüringer Landtag (Drucksache 5/6905), 15.11.2013 and the Bayerischer Landtag (Drucksache 17/121), 26.11.2013 (moved by SPD, CSU, Freie Wähler, Die Grünen) pointed out subsidiarity concerns and instructed their respective governments to argue for a Reasoned opinion in the Bundesrat.

[148] 'Proposal for a Regulation of the European Parliament and of the Council on the internal market for electricity' COM(2016) 861 final.

[149] Deutscher Bundestag, Stenografischer Bericht, 30.03.2017, Plenarprotokoll 18/228, 3049.

[150] Detailed positions unknown. Bundesrat, Stenografischer Bericht, 31.03.2015, Plenarprotokol 956, 196.

of the majority and opposition accordingly. The views of the government, the majority and the opposition on the compatibility of the proposals with subsidiarity were established by analysing the protocols of Bundestag and Bundesrat sittings. The opinion of the federal government is not openly accessible, as it is in the UK. In the Bundestag, in three out of five cases in which the Parliament issued a reasoned opinion, the government did not see a subsidiarity violation by the proposal. Based on the available information for the Bundesrat, the Parliament has issued several reasoned opinions on proposals for which the federal government did not see such a violation. Yet, the reactions to one of the proposals show a division between different Länder, depending on their regional interests and the protection of their own prerogatives.[151] In the German Bundesrat, the vote usually takes place by the raising of hands, and only the fact that there was a necessary majority is reflected in the protocol.[152] Hence, an analysis of whether there is a convergence of views between the majority and opposition is not feasible from the protocols unless one of the Länder urges that the vote is recorded.

Regarding the positions of the majority and opposition in the Bundestag, only in one case of five, in which the reasoned opinion was issued on the proposed regulation on a Common European Sales Law, was there unanimity on its adoption.[153] In two cases, there was a clear cleavage between the majority and opposition. Specifically, this disagreement concerned the proposals on deposit guarantee schemes and on the Fund for European Aid to the Most Deprived.[154] In the latter case, the SPD did not support the reasoned opinion proposed by the coalition, and voted against sending it to the EU institutions. As one of the SPD MPs underlined, '[i]t was always a matter for the social-democrats to support the ideas and actions in science and society that aim at strengthening of the principles of sustainability and solidarity. In securing the nutrition, we see a safeguard of basic human right'.[155] Die Linke sided with the SPD and, in a similar vein, underlined its party position, which supports social rights.[156] Die Grünen also saw the Commission proposal as constituting support for social solidarity, yet abstained because of the administrative costs connected with the creation of the fund.[157] Finally, the two remaining cases were qualified

[151] See section IV.C. of this chapter.

[152] Proceedings in the main chamber are recorded in the Plenarprotokoll (protocol of the plenary). For the reasoned opinions listed here, the protocols rarely record a substantial discussion in the plenary. Results of votes are recorded simply by stating acceptance by the majority without listing votes of individual Länder, consistent with §29 of the Rules of Procedure of the Bundesrat (see Reuter (n 106) 508). Representatives can elect to submit their votes or statements to the protocol, and in some cases did so on the matters discussed here. Detailed discussions appear to take place in the committees. Proceedings in the committees of the Bundesrat are as a rule confidential unless otherwise determined by vote of the committee (§37 (2) Rules of Procedure of the Bundesrat). In cases of urgency and in cases in which confidentiality needs to be persevered, the specific Europakammer is used (§45 d of Rules of Procedure of the Bundesrat). Proceedings are confidential if the Europakammer was used for that reason (§45 f of Rules of Procedure of the Bundesrat). If the chairperson of the Europakammer considers discussion unnecessary, the procedure allows for a simplified *Umfrageverfahren* without discussion (§45 i of Rules of Procedure of the Bundesrat).

[153] 'Proposal for a Regulation of the European Parliament and the Council on a Common European Sales Law' COM(2011) 635 final.

[154] 'Proposal for a Directive of the European Parliament and of the Council on Deposit Guarantee Schemes' COM(2010) 368 final; 'Proposal for a Regulation of the European Parliament and the Council on the Fund for European Aid to the Most Deprived' COM(2012) 617 final.

[155] Own translation. Deutscher Bundestag, Stenografischer Bericht, 13.12.2012, Plenarprotokoll 17/214, 26503.

[156] ibid 26504.

[157] ibid 26505.

as a consensus between the majority and opposition since none of the parties voted against the reasoned opinion, yet some of the opposition parties abstained from voting. The proposals at stake were the Services package and the Commission's initiative 'Clean Energy for All Europeans'.[158]

Similar data that allows the clear establishment of the positions of the majority and opposition in the Bundesrat were not available. Accordingly, Table 2 on the Bundesrat indicates only the position of the federal government and some information on which Länder governments supported the reasoned opinion, in cases in which that information was available.

The obtainable information confirms that the representatives vote in the Bundesrat primarily according to the interests of their respective Länder. The analysis of the vote on the reasoned opinion on the Commission proposal on the introduction of noise-related restrictions at EU airports[159] shows that the representatives of the Länder do not vote according to party lines in the sense that two Länder governed by the CDU may vote differently on the subsidiarity issue.[160] The reasoned opinion of the Bundesrat specifically pointed out that Article 10 of the proposal may confer upon the Commission a direct influence on all planned operating restrictions in airports in Member States and allow it to demand changes to these restrictions.[161] Interestingly, the Länder voting in favour of issuing the reasoned opinions included those with big airports in their territories, for example, Hessen, which contains Frankfurt airport. Moreover, an important political issue in Hessen was the night flight limits imposed by the Hessen Administrative Court and confirmed by the Federal Administrative Court in Leipzig.[162]

iii. Poland

The Polish Parliament consists of 460 members (Sejm) and 100 members (Senat). The Sejm and the Senat are not equal chambers: whereas the Polish Constitution confers the legislative competence upon both chambers, only the Sejm fulfils a controlling function over the government and approves the state's budget.[163] Hence Polish bicameralism is unequal or incomplete, with the Senat as a chamber of reflection.[164] Nonetheless, both chambers are elected in universal, direct and secret ballot elections, though only those ballot elections in the Sejm are equal and proportional.[165] The Senat, reinstated after the fall

[158] 'Proposal for a "Services Package"' COM(2016) 821 final 822, 823, 824; 'Proposal for a Regulation of the European Parliament and of the Council on the internal market for electricity' COM(2016) 861 final; and 'Proposal for a Regulation of the European Parliament and of the Council establishing a European Union Agency for the Cooperation of Energy Regulators (recast)' COM(2016) 863 final.

[159] Proposal for a Regulation of the European Parliament and the Council on the establishment of rules and procedures with regard to the introduction of noise-related operating restrictions at Union airports within a Balanced Approach and repealing Directive 2002/30/EC of the European Parliament and of the Council' COM(2011) 828 final.

[160] Bundesrat, Europakammer, Umfrage 21, 07.02.2012, Abstimmungsverhalten der Länder zu BR-Drucksache 799/1/11, Ziffer 1.

[161] German Bundesrat, Reasoned opinion of 07.02.2012 on COM(2011) 828.

[162] BVerwG 4 C 8.09, judgment of 4 April 2012.

[163] Arts 95 and 219 of the Polish Constitution.

[164] See L Garlicki, *Polskie Prawo Konstytucyjne: Zarys Wykadu* (Warsaw, Liber, 2006) 199.

[165] Arts 96 and 97 of the Polish Constitution.

of communism in 1989, was first elected in a non-proportional voting system of plurality bloc voting. Since the 2011 reform that introduced the first-past-the-post method into the Senat's electoral system, 100 constituencies elect one senator each.

Between 2007 and 2015, the governing coalition consisted of the liberal–conservative Platforma Obywatelska (PO) and the centrist Polskie Stronnictwo Ludowe (PSL), a force reflected in the composition of the Sejm and Senat. The opposition included the Conservative Prawo i Sprawiedliwość (PiS), Liberal Ruch Palikota (RP), Social-Democratic Sojusz Lewicy Demokratycznej (SLD), and right-wing Solidarna Polska.[166] In the autumn of 2015, PiS gained the majority in the parliamentary elections, enabling it to create a government on its own. The opposition parties included PO, PSL and the newly established Liberal Nowoczesna party and the right-wing movement Kukiz'15.[167]

Table 3: Overview of the Positions of the Government, Majority and Opposition on the Commission proposals in Poland

Commission proposal	Opinion of the government	Vote of the parliamentary majority	Vote of the parliamentary opposition[168]
Sejm			
COM(2010) 537[169]	0[170]	(+)	(+)[171]
COM(2010) 539[172]	0[173]	(+)	(+)[174]
COM(2010) 728[175]	0[176]	(+)	(+)[177]

(continued)

[166] Ruch Palikota and SLD had no representatives in the Senat, similar to the period of 2007–11.

[167] Only PiS (majority) and PO (opposition) have representatives in the Senat.

[168] Because the number of MPs who usually abstained or voted against in both the Sejm and Senat, even though from opposition parties, was relatively low in relation to the total number of votes and also did not represent the position of the party at stake, I qualified the Reasoned opinion as taken consensually.

[169] 'Proposal for a Regulation of the European Parliament and the Council amending Council Regulation (EC) No 1698/2005 on support for rural development by the European Agricultural Fund for Rural Development (EAFRD)' COM(2010) 537 final.

[170] The government did not take a specific stance on subsidiarity, yet criticised the lack of precision of delegation. Komisja do Spraw Unii Europejskiej, 05.11.2010, Biuletyn Nr 4349/VI.

[171] 369 in favour, 1 against (PO). Sejm, Sprawozdanie Stenograficzne z 93. Posiedzenia Sejmu Rzeczypospolitej Polskiej, 25.11.2010, 135.

[172] 'Proposal for a Regulation of the European Parliament and the Council amending Council Regulation (EC) No 73/2009 establishing common rules for direct support schemes for farmers under the common agricultural policy and establishing certain support schemes for farmers' COM(2010) 539 final.

[173] The government did not take a specific stance on subsidiarity, yet criticised the lack of precision of delegation. Komisja do Spraw Unii Europejskiej, 05.11.2010, Biuletyn Nr 4349/VI.

[174] Unanimity. Sejm, Sprawozdanie Stenograficzne z 93. Posiedzenia Sejmu Rzeczypospolitej Polskiej, 25.11.2010, 135.

[175] 'Proposal for a Regulation of the European Parliament and the Council amending Council Regulation (EC) No 1234/2007 as regards contractual relations in the milk and milk products sector' COM (2010) 728 final.

[176] No position of the government on subsidiarity, but it seconds the EU Affairs Committee in the criticism of extensive implementation powers to the Commission. Komisja do Spraw Unii Europejskiej, 21.01.2011, 7.

[177] 418 in favour, 2 against (PiS). Sejm, Sprawozdanie Stenograficzne z 84. Posiedzenia Sejmu Rzeczypospolitej Polskiej, 03.02.2011, 259.

Table 3: (*Continued*)

Commission proposal	Opinion of the government	Vote of the parliamentary majority	Vote of the parliamentary opposition
COM(2010) 738[178]	(+)[179]	(+)	(+)[180]
COM(2010) 799[181]	0[182]	(+)	(+)[183]
COM(2011) 121[184]	(–)[185]	(+)	(+)[186]
COM(2011) 127[187]	(+)[188]	(+)	(–)[189]
COM(2012) 130[190]	(+)[191]	(+)	(+)[192]
COM(2012) 369[193]	(–)[194]	(+)	(+)[195]
COM(2012) 372[196]	(–)[197]	(+)	(+)[198]

(continued)

[178] 'Proposal for a Regulation of the European Parliament and the Council amending Council Regulation (EC) No 1234/2007 as regards marketing standards' COM(2010) 738 final.

[179] Sejm, Sprawozdanie Stenograficzne Sejmu z Stenograficzne z 84. Posiedzenia Sejmu Rzeczypospolitej Polskiej, 03.02.2011, 285.

[180] 428 in favour, 1 against (PO), Sejm, Sprawozdanie Stenograficzne z 84. Posiedzenia Sejmu Rzeczypospolitej Polskiej, 04.02.2011, 379.

[181] 'Proposal for a Regulation of the European Parliament and the Council establishing a common organisation of agricultural markets and on specific provisions for certain agricultural products (Single CMO Regulation)' COM(2010) 799 final.

[182] The government does not assess subsidiarity, but expressed critiscism in regard to merits similar to the Parliament. See Biuletyn z posiedzenia Komisji do Spraw Unii Europejskiej, 18.02.2011.

[183] Unanimity. Sejm, Sprawozdanie Stenograficzne z 86. Posiedzenia Sejmu Rzeczypospolitej Polskiej, 04.03.2011, 238.

[184] 'Proposal for a Council Directive on a Common Consolidated Corporate Tax Base (CCCTB)' COM(2011) 121 final.

[185] According to the government there are transparency problems, which the directive will resolve. See Pełny zapis przebiegu posiedzenia Komisji do Spraw Unii Europejskiej, 26.09.2012, 5.

[186] 419 in favour, 2 against (1 PiS, 1 Socjaldemokracja Polska). Sejm, Sprawozdanie Stenograficzne 92. Posiedzenia Sejmu Rzeczypospolitej Polskiej, 13.05.2011, 204.

[187] 'Proposal for a Council Regulation on jurisdiction, applicable law and the recognition and enforcement of decisions regarding the property consequences of registered partnerships' COM (2011) 127 final.

[188] Komisja do Spraw Unii Europejskiej, 11.05.2011, Biuletyn Nr 5035/VI.

[189] 379 in favour, 41 against (SLD), 3 abstained (2 PO, 1 PiS). Sejm, Sprawozdanie Stenograficzne z 93. Posiedzenia Sejmu Rzeczypospolitej Polskiej, 27.05.2011, 238.

[190] 'Proposal for a Council Regulation on the exercise of the right to take collective action within the context of the freedom of establishment and the freedom to provide services' COM(2012) 130 final.

[191] Sejm, Sprawozdanie Stenograficzne z 14. Posiedzenia Sejmu Rzeczypospolitej, 10.05.2012, 252.

[192] Unanimity. Sejm, Sprawozdanie Stenograficzne z 14. Posiedzenia Sejmu Rzeczypospolitej Polskiej, 11.05.2012, 323.

[193] 'Proposal for a Regulation of the European Parliament and the Council on clinical trials on medicinal products for human use, and repealing Directive 2001/20/EC' COM(2012) 369 final.

[194] Sprawozdanie Stenograficzne z 23. Posiedzenia Sejmu Rzeczypospolitej Polskiej, 10.10.2012, 8.

[195] Unanimity. Sejm, Sprawozdanie Stenograficzne z 23. Posiedzenia Sejmu Rzeczypospolitej Polskiej, 10.10.2012, 11.

[196] 'Proposal for a Directive of the European Parliament and of the Council on collective management of copyright and related rights and multi-territorial licensing of rights in musical works for online uses in the internal market' COM(2012) 372 final.

[197] Sejm, Sprawozdanie Stenograficzne z 23. Posiedzenia Sejmu Rzeczypospolitej Polskiej, 11.10.2012, 243.

[198] 445 in favour, 4 abstained (2 Ruch Palikota, 2 Solidarna Polska, 1 against (PSL)). Sejm, Sprawozdanie Stenograficzne 23. Posiedzenia Sejmu Rzeczypospolitej Polskiej, 12.10.2012, 331.

Table 3: (*Continued*)

Commission proposal	Opinion of the government	Vote of the parliamentary majority	Vote of the parliamentary opposition
COM(2012) 614[199]	(–)[200]	(+)	(–)[201]
COM(2013) 296[202]	(+)[203]	(+)	(+)[204]
COM(2016) 128[205]	(+)[206]	(+)	(+)[207]
COM(2016) 270[208]	(+)[209]	(+)	(+)[210]
COM(2016) 861[211]	(+)[212]	(+)	(+)[213]
Senat			
COM(2010) 61[214]	(+)[215]	(+)	(+)[216]

(continued)

[199] 'Proposal for a Directive of the European Parliament and of the Council on improving the gender balance among non-executive directors of companies listed on stock exchanges and related measures' COM(2012) 614 final.

[200] Sejm, Sprawozdanie Stenograficzne z 31. Posiedzenia Sejmu Rzeczypospolitej Polskiej, 03.01.2013, 86.

[201] 333 in favour, 60 against (3 PO, 24 Ruch Palikota, 23 SLD), 35 abstained (31 PO, 3 PSL, 1 indep.). Sejm, Sprawozdanie Stenograficzne z 31. Posiedzenia Sejmu Rzeczypospolitej Polskiej, 04.01.2013, 133.

[202] 'Proposal for a Regulation of the European Parliament and the Council establishing a framework on market access to port services and financial transparency of ports' COM(2013) 296 final.

[203] Pełny zapis przebiegu posiedzenia Komisji, Komisja do Spraw Unii Europejskiej Nr 169, 4.

[204] 448 in favour, 1 abstained (1 indep). Sejm, Sprawozdanie Stenograficzne z 46 posiedzenia Sejmu, 26.07.2013, 438.

[205] 'Proposal for a Directive of the European Parliament and of the Council amending Directive 96/71/EC of the European Parliament and of the Council of 16 December 1996 concerning the posting of workers in the framework of the provision of services' COM(2016) 128 final.

[206] Pełny zapis przebiegu posiedzenia Komisji do Spraw Unii Europejskiej Nr 40, 30.03.2016, 12.

[207] 443 in favour, 1 against (1 PO), 3 abstained (1 Kukiz, 1 Nowoczesna, 1 indep) Sprawozdanie stenograficzne z 16 posiedzenia Sejmu, 13.04.2016, 203.

[208] 'Proposal for a Regulation of the European Parliament and of the Council establishing the criteria and mechanisms for determining the Member State responsible for examining an application for international protection lodged in one of the Member States by a third-country national or a stateless person' COM(2016) 270 final.

[209] The government's representative stated generally violation of Treaty principles. Pełny zapis przebiegu posiedzenia Komisji, Komisja do Spraw Unii Europejskiej Nr 79, 22.09.2016, 9.

[210] 431 in favour, 1 abstained (1 PO). Sejm, Sprawozdanie Stenograficzne z 28 posiedzenia Sejmu, 21.10.2016, 343.

[211] 'Proposal for a Regulation of the European Parliament and of the Council on the internal market for electricity' COM(2016) 861 final.

[212] The position of the government was not clearly stated in the Sejm's debates, yet was stated in the Senat. Zapis Stenograficzny, Wspólne posiedzenie Komisji Gospodarki Narodowej i Innowacyjności (82) oraz Komisji Spraw Zagranicznych i Unii Europejskiej (99), 25.04.2017, 3.

[213] 413 in favour, 2 against (2 PO), 1 abstained (1 ind), Sejm, Sprawozdanie stenograficzne z 41. Posiedzenia Sejmu, 11.05.2017, 141.

[214] 'Proposal for a Regulation of the European Parliament and the Council amending Council Regulation (EC) No 2007/2004 establishing a European Agency for the Management of Operational Cooperation at the External Borders of the Member States of the European Union (FRONTEX)' COM(2010) 61 final.

[215] Sprawozdanie Stenograficzne z 53. Posiedzenia Senatu, 28.04.2010, 49.

[216] 80 in favour, 1 abstained (PO). Sprawozdanie stenograficzne z 53. Posiedzenia Senatu, 29.04.2010, 59.

Table 3: (***Continued***)

Commission proposal	Opinion of the government	Vote of the parliamentary majority	Vote of the parliamentary opposition
COM(2010) 379[217]	(+)[218]	(+)	(+)[219]
COM(2010) 537	0[220]	(+)	(+)[221]
COM(2010) 539	0[222]	(+)	(+)[223]
COM(2010) 738	(+)[224]	(+)	(+)[225]
COM(2010) 745[226]	0[227]	(+)	(+)[228]
COM(2010) 799	(+)[229]	(+)	(+)[230]
COM(2011) 127	(+)[231]	(+)	(+)[232]
COM(2012) 48 + 49[233]	(+)[234]	(+)	(+)[235]

(continued)

[217] 'Proposal for a Directive of the European Parliament and of the Council on the conditions of entry and residence of third-country nationals for the purposes of seasonal employment' COM(2010) 379 final.

[218] Zapis Stenograficzny, 117. Posiedzenie Komisji Spraw Unii Europejskiej, 06.10.2010, 19.

[219] 84 in favour, 1 abstained (PiS), Sprawozdanie Stenograficzne z 63. Posiedzenia Senatu, 21.10.2010, 149.

[220] The government did not take a specific stance on subsidiarity, yet criticised the lack of precision of delegation. Zapis stenograficzny, 122. Posiedzenie Komisji Spraw Unii Europejskiej, 16.10.2010, 12.

[221] 80 in favour, 1 abstained (PiS), 1 against (PiS). Sprawozdanie Stenograficzne z 66. Posiedzenia Senatu, 25.11.2010, 29.

[222] The government did not take a specific stance on subsidiarity, yet criticised the lack of precision of delegation. Zapis stenograficzny, 122. Posiedzenie Komisji Spraw Unii Europejskiej, 16.10.2010, 12.

[223] Unanimity. Sprawozdanie Stenograficzne z 66. Posiedzenia Senatu, 25.11.2010, 29.

[224] Sprawozdanie Stenograficzne z 70. Posiedzenia Senatu, 03.02.2011, 73.

[225] 87 in favour, 2 abstained (1 PO, 1 indep), Sprawozdanie stenograficzne z 70. Posiedzenia Senatu, 04.02.2011, 108.

[226] 'Proposal for a Regulation of the European Parliament and the Council amending Council Regulation (EC) No 1290/2005 on the financing of the common agricultural policy and repealing Council Regulation (EC) No 165/94 and Council Regulation (EC) No 78/2008' COM(2010) 745 final.

[227] Not specified. Zapis Stenograficzny, Wspólne posiedzenie Komisji Rolnictwa I Rozwoju Wsi oraz Komisji Spraw Unii Europejskiej, 03.02.2011.

[228] 88 in favour, 2 abstained (1 PO, 1 indep), Sprawozdanie Stenograficzne z 70. Posiedzenia Senatu, 04.02.2011, 108.

[229] Zapis stenograficzny, 135. Posiedzenie Komisji Spraw Unii Europejskiej, 08.02.2011, 10.

[230] Unanimity. Sprawozdanie Stenograficzne z 71. Posiedzenia Senatu, 03.03.2011, 237.

[231] See Sprawozdanie Stenograficzne z 77. Posiedzenia Senatu, 26.05.2011, 28.

[232] 67 in favour, 1 against (1 indep). Sprawozdanie Stenograficzne z 77. Posiedzenia Senatu, 26.05.2011, 63.

[233] 'Amended proposal for a Directive of the European Parliament and of the Council amending Directive 2001/83/EC as regards information to the general public on medicinal products subject to medical prescription amending, as regards information to the general public on medicinal products subject to medical prescription, Directive 2001/83/EC on the Community code relating to medicinal products for human use' COM(2012) 48 final; 'Amended proposal for a Regulation of the European Parliament and the Council amending Regulation (EC) No 726/2004 as regards information to the general public on medicinal products for human use subject to medical prescription' COM(2012) 49 final.

[234] 19. Posiedzenie Komisji Spraw Unii Europejskiej, 13.03.2012, 8.

[235] 85 in favour, 2 against (PO), 2 abstained (1 PO, 1 indep). Sprawozdanie Stenograficzne z 8. Posiedzenia Senatu, 29.03.2012, 75.

Table 3: (*Continued*)

Commission proposal	Opinion of the government	Vote of the parliamentary majority	Vote of the parliamentary opposition
COM(2012) 614	(–)[236]	(+)	(+)[237]
COM(2013) 133[238]	(+)[239]	(+)	(+)[240]
COM(2016) 128	(+)[241]	(+)	(+)[242]
COM(2016) 270	(+)[243]	(+)	(–)[244]
COM(2016) 861	(+)[245]	(+)	(+)[246]
COM(2016) 864[247]	(+)[248]	(+)	(+)[249]

Notes: (+) subsidiarity violation; (–) no subsidiarity violation; 0 position not required.

Drawing on committee and plenary protocols and the register of votes, Table 3 reflects the views of the coalition and the opposition on Commission proposals violating the subsidiarity principle,[250] along with the position of the government when it was under the legal obligation to present it to the Parliament.[251] In four out of 15 cases, the Sejm issued

[236] The government's representative states that the position of the government is favourable to the aim of the directive, but the way to achieve this aim should be more flexible. No stance on subsidiarity. See Sprawozdanie Stenograficzne z 25. Posiedzenia Senatu, 09.01.2013, 151.

[237] 80 in favour, 6 against (1 PO, 3 indep, 2 PSL), 3 abstained (3 PO). Sprawozdanie Stenograficzne z 25. Posiedzenia Senatu, 09.01.2013, 172.

[238] 'Proposal for a Directive of the European Parliament and of the Council establishing a framework for maritime spatial planning and integrated coastal management' COM(2013) 133 final.

[239] 63. Posiedzenie Komisji Spraw Unii Europejskiej, 17.04.2013, 8.

[240] 80 in favour, 2 against (1 PO, 1 indep), Sprawozdanie Stenograficzne z 32. Posiedzenia Senatu, 25.04.2013, 94.

[241] Zapis Stenograficzny, Wspólne posiedzenie, 23. Komisji Rodziny, Polityki Senioralnej i Społecznej, 29. Komisji Spraw Zagranicznych i Unii Europejskiej oraz 22. Komisji Gospodarki Narodowej i Innowacyjności, 27.04.2016, 4.

[242] Unanimity. Sprawozdanie stenograficzne z 16. Posiedzenia Senatu Rzeczypospolitej Polskiej, 28–29.04.2016, 153.

[243] Zapis Stenograficzny, Wspólne posiedzenie Komisji Praw Człowieka, Praworządności i Petycji (86) oraz Komisji Spraw Zagranicznych i Unii Europejskiej (67), 19.10.2016, 4.

[244] 57 in favour (PiS), 27 against (26 PO, 1 indep.), 1 abstained (1 PO). Sprawozdanie Stenograficzne z 28. Posiedzenia Senatu Rzeczypospolitej Polskiej, 19–21.10.2016, 130.

[245] Zapis Stenograficzny, Wspólne posiedzenie Komisji Gospodarki Narodowej i Innowacyjności (82) oraz Komisji Spraw Zagranicznych i Unii Europejskiej (99), 25.04.2017, 3.

[246] 69 in favour (52 PiS, 16 PO, 1 indep), 1 against (PO), 9 abstained (8 PO, 1 indep). Sprawozdanie Stenograficzne z 40. Posiedzenia Senatu, 26–27.04.2017, 144.

[247] 'Proposal for a Directive of the European Parliament and of the Council on common rules for the internal market in electricity (recast)' COM(2016) 864 final.

[248] Sprawozdanie Stenograficzne z 40. Posiedzenia Senatu, 26–27.04.2017, 121.

[249] 68 in favour (52 PiS, 15 PO, 1 indep), 2 against (2 PO), 7 abstained (6 PO, 1 indep). Sprawozdanie Stenograficzne z 40. Posiedzenia Senatu, 26–27.04.2017, 144.

[250] For the purposes of the study on the Polish Parliament, I disregarded single votes of MPs or senators who were not in favour of issuing a reasoned opinion or else abstained, unless it was a clear party position to vote against or abstain. The voting results in Table 3 reflect this approach.

[251] Until the new cooperation law was introduced in February 2011, there was no obligation for the government to inform the chambers of its position regarding compatibility of Commission proposals with subsidiarity principle. Art 7 par 3 no 3 of the Act of 8 October 2010 on the Cooperation of the Council of Ministers with

reasoned opinions even though the government did not see a subsidiarity violation. In the Senat, this proportion was one out of 15 cases.

Moreover, Table 3 shows a major convergence of views on subsidiarity violations between the majority and the opposition in the Sejm. They disagreed on the proposal on 'jurisdiction, applicable law and the recognition and enforcement of decisions regarding the property consequences of registered partnerships' and the 'Women on Boards' proposal.[252] In the first case, the Social-Democrats did not support the reasoned opinion on the Commission proposal on registered partnerships, as the proposal was compatible with the political programme of the party that supports the legalisation of partnerships in Poland.[253] In the second case, the Liberal opposition did not sustain the reasoned opinion on the 'Women on Boards' proposal that aimed at introducing more women to non-executive boards of companies. In fact, those MPs underlined the need for gender balance and the lack of national means that can help achieve this aim.[254] Interestingly, in this case also a reasonable number of the more progressive MPs from the governing majority abstained; however enough MPs still supported the reasoned opinion, which the chamber later sent to the EU institutions.[255]

In the Senat, the majority and the opposition were in agreement with regard to all the reasoned opinions except for one. This outlier concerned the proposed regulation offering a new mechanism of refugee allocation.[256] The senators opposing the reasoned opinion argued that a solution at the EU level is necessary to manage the refugee crisis. Interestingly, in the Sejm, while considering the same proposal, the PO Party, also in the opposition, voted with the parliamentary majority. The PO's vote in favour of the reasoned opinion in the Sejm reflects how highly politicised the issue of refugees is in Poland. It seems to have been a vote to satisfy anti-refugee sentiments in Poland. In contrast, the senators in opposition showed more independence from current political debates.

iv. Belgium

The Belgian federal system consists of two different types of unit: three communities (Flemish-, French- and German-speaking) and three regions (Flanders, Wallonia and

the Sejm and the Senate in Matters Relating to the Republic of Poland's Membership of the European Union, as published in *Dziennik Ustaw* of 2010, No 213, item 1395 in force since 13.02.2011. Hence the reasoned opinions on the following proposals: COM(2010) 537; COM(2010) 539; COM(2010) 728; COM(2010) 738; and COM(2010) 799 did not demand the official assessment of the government.

252 'Proposal for a Council Regulation on jurisdiction, applicable law and the recognition and enforcement of decisions regarding the property consequences of registered partnerships' COM(2011) 127 final; and 'Proposal for a Directive of the European Parliament and of the Council on improving the gender balance among non-executive directors of companies listed on stock exchanges and related measures' COM(2012) 614 final respectively.

253 Sejm, Sprawozdanie Stenograficzne z 93. Posiedzenia Sejmu Rzeczypospolitej Polskiej, 25.05.2011, 92.

254 Sejm, Sprawozdanie Stenograficzne z 31. Posiedzenia Sejmu Rzeczypospolitej Polskiej, 03.01.2013, 83.

255 Sejm, Sprawozdanie Stenograficzne z 31. Posiedzenia Sejmu Rzeczypospolitej Polskiej, 04.01.2013, 133.

256 'Proposal for a Regulation of the European Parliament and of the Council establishing the criteria and mechanisms for determining the Member State responsible for examining an application for international protection lodged in one of the Member States by a third-country national or a stateless person (recast)' COM(2016) 270 final.

Brussels).[257] The 150 members of the Chambre des représentants are elected directly.[258] In the Sénat, 71 senators were selected by a number of bodies between 1993 and 2014. Forty senators were elected directly in either Flemish or French electoral colleges. Twenty-one senators were appointed from within the existing parliaments: the Flemish and French community parliaments appointed 10 senators each, whereas the German community designated one. The remaining senators were co-opted: language groups in Flemish and French communities designated six and four senators each, respectively. The 2014 reform reduced the number of senators to the total of 60 seats.[259] The direct election of the senators was abolished, while the co-option mechanism of 10 senators remained intact. The novel aspect is the increase from 21 to 50 in the number of senators that represent subnational parliaments. The reform allowed the Sénat to better reflect the views of subnational entities.[260]

Regarding the competences of the chambers, the federal government is accountable only before the Chambre des représentants.[261] The Chambre des représentants is also competent in the budgetary procedure.[262] Before the 2014 reform, the Sénat had a legislative initiative and could amend the most bills coming from the other chamber. Since then, the role of the Sénat has been weakened, making the default procedure the monocameral procedure that involves only the Chambre des représentants, leaving some limited competences for the Sénat in other types of legislative procedures.[263]

The Belgian political system represents one of the most fragmented party systems in modern democracy.[264] Nonetheless, Belgian political parties maintain a high level of party discipline.[265] The Di Rupio government (December 2011–May 2014) was supported by a coalition of the Dutch-speaking parties, the social-democratic Socialistische Partij Anders (sp.a), the liberal Open Vlaamse Liberalen en Democraten (Open Vld) and the Christian-democratic Christen-Democratisch en Vlaams (CD&V), and their French-speaking counterparts, le Parti Socialiste (PS), the conservative-liberal Mouvement Réformateur (MR), and the Centre démocrate humaniste (cdH). The biggest party in opposition was the centre-right, nationalist Nieuw-Vlaamse Alliantie (N-VA). For the electoral term during the period studied in this book, the first reasoned opinion being issued in 2011 and the last one (and latest one as of August 2017) in 2013, the parties that formed the government controlled a total 96 of 150 seats in the Chambre des représentants

[257] RL Watts, *Comparing Federal Systems* (Montreal & Kingston, McGill-Queen's University Press, 2008) 43; A Lecours, 'Belgium' in A Griffiths (ed), *Handbook of Federal Countries* (Montreal & Kingston, McGill-Queen's Press, 2005). Moreover, it should be noted that the Brussels Region is weaker than the two others in terms of autonomy and competences.

[258] Art 63 of the Belgian Constitution.

[259] ibid, Art 67.

[260] P Popelier and K Lemmens, *The Constitution of Belgium. A Contextual Analysis* (Oxford, Hart Publishing, 2015) 117.

[261] Art 101 of the Belgian Constitution.

[262] ibid, Art 174.

[263] Popelier and Lemmens (n 260) 124–25.

[264] Lijphart (n 13) 35.

[265] T Delreux and F Randour, 'Belgium: Institutional and Administrative Adaptation but Limited Political Interest' in C Hefftler et al eds (eds), *The Palgrave Handbook of National Parliaments and the European Union* (Basingstoke, Palgrave Macmillan, 2015) 153.

(with the N-VA having 27 seats during that time) and 44 of 71 seats in the Sénat (with the N-VA having 14 seats during that time). After the 2014 federal and regional elections, Charles Michel became the Prime Minister supported by a centre-right coalition of four parties: CD&V, OPEN Vld, MR and N-VA.

Table 4: Overview of the Positions of the Government, Majority and Opposition on the Commission proposals in Belgium

Commission proposal	Opinion of the government	Vote of the parliamentary majority	Vote of the parliamentary opposition
Chambre des représentants			
COM(2011) 779[266]	(+)[267]	(+)[268]	(+)[269]
COM(2012) 10+11[270]	(+)[271]	(+)	(−)[272]
COM(2012) 130[273]	(+)[274]	(+)	(+)[275]
COM(2013) 173[276]	(+)[277]	(+)	(+)[278]

(continued)

[266] 'Proposal for a Regulation of the European Parliament and the Council on specific requirements regarding statutory audit of public-interest entities' COM(2011) 779 final.

[267] Rapport fait au nom de la Commission charge des problèmes de droit commercial et économique 16.02.2012, DOC 53 2068/001, 11, 14.

[268] The coalition seems to be supported by the Greens (Ecolo Groen, 12–13).

[269] 10 in favour, 4 abstained (one of them was an N-VA MP). Rapport fait au nom de la Commission charge des problèmes de droit commercial et économique 16.02.2012, DOC 53 2068/001, 16.

[270] 'Proposal for a Directive of the European Parliament and of the Council on the protection of individuals with regard to the processing of personal data by competent authorities for the purposes of prevention, investigation, detection or prosecution of criminal offences or the execution of criminal penalties, and the free movement of such data' COM (2012) 10 final; 'Proposal for a Regulation of the European Parliament and the Council on the protection of individuals with regard to the processing of personal data and on the free movement of such data (General Data Protection Regulation)' COM(2012) 11.

[271] The minister spoke in favour of the Reasoned opinion proposed by the coalition, explaining that it is similar to the negotiating position of the government. Rapport fait au nom de la Commission de la Justice, DOC 53 2145/001, 12.

[272] 8 in favour, 1 against, 2 abstentions. Presumably two N-VA MPs abstained, whereas an MP from Ecolo-Groen was against. See Rapport fait au nom de la Commission de la Justice, DOC 53 2145/001, 13.

[273] 'Proposal for a Council Regulation on the exercise of the right to take collective action within the context of the freedom of establishment and the freedom to provide services' COM(2012) 130 final.

[274] Annex to the Rapport fait au nom de la Commission des Affaires Sociales, DOC 53 2221/001, 30.05.2012, 8.

[275] 10 votes in favour, 1 abstained (N-VA). Rapport fait au nom de la Commission des Affaires Sociales, DOC 53 2221/001, 30.05.2012, 6.

[276] 'Proposal for a Regulation of the European Parliament and the Council on the European Union Agency for Law Enforcement Cooperation and Training (Europol) and repealing Decisions 2009/371/JHA and 2005/681/JHA' COM(2013) 173 final.

[277] The representative of the Vice-Prime Minister and of the Internal Affairs and Equality Minister advocated caution in the formulation of the reasoned opinion, as the Belgian government is a strong supporter of Europol: the Reasoned opinion should not be interpreted as a sign of mistrust in the agency. It was, however, underlined that the government will support the 'legitimate concern' of the Parliament that national parliaments should have a possibility to scrutinise Europol. Rapport fait au nom de la Commission de l'Intérieur des Affaires Générales et de la Fonction Publique, Doc 53 2910/001, 26.06.2013, 6–7.

[278] Unanimity. Rapport fait au nom de la Commission de l'Intérieur des Affaires Générales et de la Fonction Publique, Doc 53 2910/001, 26.06.2013, 7.

Table 4: (*Continued*)

Commission proposal	Opinion of the government	Vote of the parliamentary majority	Vote of the parliamentary opposition
Sénat			
COM(2011) 635[279]	(–)[280]	(+)	(+)[281]
COM(2013) 133[282]	(?)	(+/–)	(+/–)[283]

Notes: (+) subsidiarity violation; (–) no subsidiarity violation; (?) position unknown.

Table 4 illustrates the views of the government and the votes of the majority and the opposition on Commission proposals, as interpreted on the basis of protocols from committee or plenary meetings. First, with regard to the relationship between government and parliament, the opinion of the government was similar to that of the majority in the Chambre des représentants. In contrast, the Sénat, in the period of study, had issued two reasoned opinions. In one of the two cases this was despite the fact that the government did not find the Commission proposal contrary to the subsidiarity principle.[284] Second, in the Chambre des représentants, the disagreement between the majority and opposition is reflected in MPs' abstentions. Only in the case concerning the Data Protection package did an opposition MP vote against.[285] Regarding the Sénat, when the reasoned opinion on a draft directive on 'establishing a framework for maritime spatial planning and integrated coastal management' was issued by the Flemish Parliament on behalf of the Sénat, there was a disagreement both within the majority and within the opposition.[286] In the other case,

[279] 'Proposal for a Regulation of the European Parliament and the Council on a Common European Sales Law' COM(2011) 635 final.

[280] See Sénat de Belgique, Rapport fait au nom de la Commission de la Justice, 06.12.2011, 3.

[281] 45 in favour, 2 abstained (1 Open Vld, 1 CD&V). Séances plénières, 12.12.2011, Annales no 5-39, 5. Because it was the members from the coalition that abstained, I qualified the reasoned opinion as supported by the opposition. Abstaining senators highlighted unclear difference between the EWS and the political dialogue, as well as the cross-border character of the directive and hence lack of a subsidiarity violation.

[282] 'Proposal for a Directive of the European Parliament and of the Council establishing a framework for maritime spatial planning and integrated coastal management' COM(2013) 133 final.

[283] The Reasoned opinion has been issued by the Flemish Parliament, which has an equal position as the parliamentary chambers to issue a Reasoned opinion on behalf of the Senate. Vlaams Parlement, 85 in favour (Open Vld, CD&V, N-VA andt LDD), 8 against (2 sp.a, 6 Greens), 17 abstained (16 SP.A, 1 UF). Plenaire vergadering nr 34 (2012–2013), 8 mei 2013, Stemming nr 3, 66. One of the governing parties (sp.a) voted against adoption of the reasoned opinion proposal; whereas two opposition parties Open Vld and LDD voted in favour of the adoption of the reasoned opinion.

[284] In the other case, concerning COM(2013) 133 (n 282) final, the position of the government was not specified.

[285] 'Proposal for a Directive of the European Parliament and of the Council on the protection of individuals with regard to the processing of personal data by competent authorities for the purposes of prevention, investigation, detection or prosecution of criminal offences or the execution of criminal penalties, and the free movement of such data' COM(2012) 10 final; 'Proposal for a Regulation of the European Parliament and the Council on the protection of individuals with regard to the processing of personal data and on the free movement of such data (General Data Protection Regulation)' COM(2012) 11 final.

[286] COM(2013) 133 (n 282).

concerning a Common European Sales Law, the majority and the opposition members were in agreement on issuing a reasoned opinion.[287]

IV. ANALYSIS OF THE DATA

This section revisits the questions listed at the beginning of the chapter in light of the data presented above.

A. Independence of Parliaments from the Governments

The first question addressed here is to what extent the EWS has allowed the national parliamentary chambers to act independently from their respective governments. Before the entry into force of the Lisbon Treaty, there was some distrust in that a national parliament's majority and the government would differ on the issue of subsidiarity.[288] It was perceived as dubious that parliament would issue a reasoned opinion without the consent of its government, since the '[g]overnment frequently cajole their backbenchers into supporting them using the possible loss of a parliamentary majority as a threat'.[289]

The data presented in this chapter confirm that the parliaments followed their governments under the EWS. However, the study of the UK, German, Polish and Belgian parliaments shows that there are at least 17 instances in which parliaments took a view different from the government on the question of the subsidiarity violation. This outcome contradicts the view that under the EWS national parliaments dominated by parliamentary majorities could have a low incentive to challenge their governments on EU affairs, in addition to little electoral benefit from engaging in those matters.[290]

There appear to be no clear distinctions between the different chambers analysed concerning their propensity to act independently from their respective governments. Indeed, the analysis of the positions of each government and its parliament in the UK, Germany, Poland and Belgium shows that the division between the Westminster and consensus models seems to disappear. It is only the lower chamber of the Belgian Parliament that has always followed the line of the federal government on the subsidiarity violation, a situation which could be explained by strong party discipline. Hence, except for this case, every upper and lower chamber displays at least one instance of independence. Therefore, neither the model of relations between the government and legislature nor the differences between the upper and lower chambers seems to strongly influence the independence of parliaments in the EWS.

[287] 'Proposal for a Regulation of the European Parliament and the Council on a Common European Sales Law' COM(2011) 635 final.

[288] FC Mayer, 'Competences—Reloaded? The vertical division of powers in the EU and the new European constitution' (2005) 3 *International Journal of Constitutional Law* 493, 502.

[289] P de Wilde, 'Why the Early Warning Mechanism does not Alleviate the Democratic Deficit' (2012) OPAL Online Paper Series 6/2012, 9.

[290] I Cooper, 'A "Virtual Third Chamber" for the European Union? National Parliaments after the Treaty of Lisbon' (2012) 35 *West European Politics* 441, 449.

Specifically analysing the power-sharing models, the legislatures have gained an independent voice on EU affairs from the national-level perspective in both the executive-dominated Westminster model and the power-sharing consensus model. Within the Westminster model, as many as three differences between the position of the government and Parliament are visible in the case of the House of Commons, which managed to issue reasoned opinions when the government did not see a subsidiarity violation. This was the case with regard to the Commission proposal on the right to strike:[291] according to the government, the proposed regulation only repeated the jurisprudence of the Court of Justice of the European Union, which was sufficiently clear according to the government's explanatory memorandum. Yet, the independence of the House of Commons could also be seen as undermined by the fact that the government found the proposed regulation unnecessary.

Moreover, the total number of opinion differences could even rise by three, because whereas the explanatory memorandum did not state a subsidiarity violation in the cases of the Commission proposals on the presumption of innocence,[292] food from cloned animals,[293] and a certification system for aviation security screening equipment,[294] the government's representative changed that position in the parliamentary debate.[295] However, the findings about the increased independence of the UK House of Commons must be qualified, as is the case, for example, with regard to the Commission proposal on investor compensation schemes.[296] In this case, the government, similarly to the UK House of Commons, took a negative stance on the Commission's proposal, but for a different reason: the government argued that the Commission's proposal infringed 'national sovereignty'. Finally, the relative independence of the UK Parliament under the EWS might be explained by the fact that, under a coalition government, the domination of the executive is not possible to the same extent as in the classic situation of a majority government. Under the majority government, the UK House of Commons and the government agreed that there was a subsidiarity violation by the two EU draft acts considered by the Parliament. However, this evidence based on only two reasoned opinions might be too anecdotal to offer a definitive explanation.

Against the expectations based on the consensus model, the Polish and German lower chambers gained some independence from their respective governments. This irregularity—that the position of the parliament is not always automatically adjusted to that of the government with regard to subsidiarity—presents an interesting impact of the EWS on national parliamentary system.

[291] COM(2012) 130 (n 43).

[292] 'Proposal for a Directive of the European Parliament and of the Council on the strengthening of certain aspects of the presumption of innocence and of the right to be present at trial in criminal proceedings' COM(2013) 821 final.

[293] 'Proposal for a Council Directive on the placing on the market of food from animal clones' COM(2013) 893 final.

[294] 'Proposal for a Regulation of the European Parliament and of the Council establishing a Union certification system for aviation security screening equipment' COM(2016) 491 final.

[295] In Table 1, I qualified the position of the government as stating a subsidiarity violation, even though the EM did not mention a subsidiarity violation. In contrast to that, in the case of COM(2011) 635, even though the government agreed with the House of Commons during the debate that there is a violation of necessity, a direct statement on violation of subsidiarity was not made as in cases of proposals COM(2013) 821, COM(2013) 897 and COM(2016) 491.

[296] 'Proposal for a Directive of the European Parliament and of the Council amending Directive 97/9/EC of the European Parliament and of the Council on investor compensation schemes' COM(2010) 371 final.

Finally, within the consensus model, the Belgian example presents a convergence of views on subsidiarity compliance between the Belgian lower chamber and the Belgian government. One explanation might be that the fragmentation of the political system in Belgium forces the government to consider the coalition view already at the stage of formulating its own view on a Commission proposal. Another reason might be the general weakness of the Belgian Parliament in EU affairs and a greater obedience to the government's lead,[297] following the general institutional weakness of the Belgian Parliament[298] and the fact that the coalitions adopt a *déclaration gouvernementale* at the beginning of a period of legislation.[299] Finally, overall strong control by the political parties on both the government and the parliament could provide an explanation for the consistency of views of the Belgian lower chamber and the government.

Some diversity in the independent decisions of the national parliaments is visible from the perspective of the distinction between lower and upper chambers. Surprisingly, the upper chambers—the UK House of Lords and the Polish Senat—could have been expected to act more independently because they do not have the responsibility link with the government. Nonetheless, the Polish Senat, which issued as many reasoned opinions as the Polish Sejm, differed from the government's opinion in only one case, while the Sejm differed in four cases. In the case of the UK Parliament, the House of Commons diverged from the government's opinion in four cases out of 17 reasoned opinions, while the House of Lords differed in only one out of eight reasoned opinions.

The case of the German Bundesrat is slightly different. As Table 2 shows, in four known instances the federal government did not find a subsidiarity breach, while the Bundesrat did. This in part reflects the fact that the Bundesrat consists of representatives of the governments of the Länder. These are elected in separate Länder elections, often taking place at different times from the Bundestag election and reflecting regional issues. Thus, they can result in governments formed by different parties and with different views on the compliance of EU proposals with the subsidiarity principle. Furthermore, in some case the Länder interest may simply diverge from that of the federal government.

The overlap of views of the government and the parliament on whether a proposal breaches the subsidiarity principle is helpful for the government in the process of further negotiation of proposals in the Council. While the UK House of Commons European Scrutiny Committee, for example, considers its role in subsidiarity review as not only trying to protect its parliamentary sovereignty, but also the interests of the country, the MPs view their opinions as a way for the government to 'back up' its arguments during Council's negotiations of the proposal.[300] In fact, the UK government confirms that the reasoned opinion of the parliament may 'help strengthen the Government's hand in negotiation with Brussels'.[301] A reasoned opinion in such a situation presents a new aspect of the relationship

[297] J Karlas, 'National Parliamentary Control of EU Affairs: Institutional Design after Enlargement' (2012) 35 *West European Politics* 1095, 1102.

[298] Delreux and Randour (n 265).

[299] See, eg: premier.fgov.be/fr/d%C3%A9claration-gouvernementale.

[300] House of Commons, European Committee: Financial Services: Prudential Requirements, 14.03.2012, col 15.

[301] HC Deb 8 November 2011, col 212, 196.

between government and parliamentary majority, strengthening the negotiating position of the government.

Yet a different position on the proposal expressed by the government and the reasoned opinion may also put the former in a 'strange position'.[302] Therefore, when the executive's position on subsidiarity differs from that of the parliamentary majority, which in fact occurred in a number of cases indicated in this chapter, a reasoned opinion can restrict the government's negotiating position at EU level. This corresponds with the aforementioned findings of Auel and Benz.

However, in some cases the government may use the difference in the executive's and parliament's views on the subsidiarity violation for its own purposes. For example, in the debate on the reasoned opinion of the Polish Sejm on the Commission regulation on clinical trials on medicinal products for human use, the government's representative explained the government's stance in favour of the proposal, because '[the government] does not want to be seen as blocking all the initiatives'.[303] It could thus be hypothesised that a national government might be willing to shift the blame for the lack of support for a proposal onto a reasoned opinion of the national parliament.

B. Division Between the Majority and Opposition on Subsidiarity Issues

The second question concerns whether the decision to pursue a subsidiarity violation through the EWS reflects divisions between the parliamentary majority and the opposition or whether it is to a large extent a unanimous decision. Starting with the UK, as Table 1 shows, the coalition and opposition in both Houses agree that a reasoned opinion should be issued. The only exception concerned the reasoned opinion in the UK House of Commons on the proposed directive on placing on the market food from animal clones.

Also in Poland (Table 3), there is a striking convergence between the coalition and opposition in both the Sejm and the Senat. Nevertheless, the underlining principle here is that as long as the coalition is willing to pursue a reasoned opinion, it will be submitted to the EU institutions. Specifically, the example of an ill-fated reasoned opinion regarding the Commission proposal for the programme FISCUS, which supports cooperation between the customs and tax authorities and other parties concerned, but at the same time, safeguards the particularities of customs and taxation of Member States, confirms this argument.[304] The opposition party PiS, the sponsor of the reasoned opinion, argued that the proposal was unlawfully based on Article 114 of the Treaty on the Functioning of the European Union, which excludes the harmonisation of taxes, claiming also that it would deeply interfere in the national fiscal system.[305] The government, the coalition and a couple

[302] ibid.

[303] In response, one of the MPs proposed that the consequence of the reasoned opinion should change the position of the government in the future. See Pełny zapis przebiegu posiedzenia Komisji do Spraw Unii Europejskiej, 29.08.2012, 12.

[304] 'Proposal for a Regulation of the European Parliament and of the Council establishing an action programme for customs and taxation in the European Union for the period 2014–2020 (FISCUS) and repealing Decisions No 1482/2007/EC and No 624/2007/EC' COM(2011) 706 final.

[305] Sejm, Sprawozdanie Stenograficzne z 5. Posiedzenia Sejmu, 13.01.2012, 238.

of the opposition parties rejected this argument as invalid and, in consequence, the parliament did not send the reasoned opinion.

Germany (Table 2) represents a less clear case. The information on the debates and votes in the Bundestag and the Bundesrat is much more limited than in the other cases explored in this chapter, mainly because of the internal rules of the German chambers.[306] In the Bundestag, a clear cleavage between the majority and opposition was present in two out of five cases for which the parliament issued a reasoned opinion. The remaining three cases, although the vote on only one reasoned opinion was approved unanimously, confirm a consensual decision-making of the Bundestag under the EWS.

In the case of the German Bundesrat, the parliamentary records do not allow a clear attribution of votes to the different parties. In addition, the Länder representatives often reflect governments that fall into neither the government nor the opposition camp at the national level. Table 2, therefore, records only the final outcome regarding the issuance of a reasoned opinion by the Bundesrat.

Finally, in the Belgian Chambre des représentants (Table 4), the opposition parties in the chamber usually abstain, a situation which leads to a major consensus on issuing a reasoned opinion. The Flemish Parliament, which issued a reasoned opinion for the Sénat, showcased a disagreement both within the majority and within the opposition.[307] The other reasoned opinion of the Sénat was supported by the majority and the opposition.

In sum, in all of the parliaments studied in this chapter, there is a major convergence of views between the political parties with regard to whether the parliament should issue a reasoned opinion. Where a cleavage between the majority and opposition exists, it is indeed more prominent in elected lower chambers: the House of Commons (one case), the Sejm (two cases), the Bundestag (two cases) and the Chambre des représentants (one case). In the upper chambers, such cases are even more rare. The available data allow pointing out one case of political cleavage in the Polish Senat, one in the Belgian Sénat and none in the UK House of Lords.

A closer analysis of the cases of disagreement between the majority and opposition points to the left–right cleavage and socio-economic cleavage characteristic of day-to-day political life.[308] That is to say, in cases in which the views of whether to issue a reasoned opinion differed between the majority and opposition in parliaments, those political actors remained faithful to their own political positions, similar to how they would vote on national issues.

The examples from the Polish Sejm depict the traditional left–right cleavage. The contentious proposals at stake in the Sejm concerned the property consequences of registered

[306] § 69 Rules of Procedure of the Bundestag; § 34 and § 37 Rules of Procedure of the Bundesrat.

[307] COM(2013) 133 (n 282).

[308] Gattermann and Heftler present a statistical analysis of the process of issuing reasoned opinions. They find that a greater degree of left–right contestation in Parliament is weakly associated with a lower probability of a reasoned opinion being issued, holding all else constant. Their result is complementary to the point presented here. In all the cases presented in this chapter, reasoned opinions were issued. The analysis of the content of the parliamentary debates shows that arguments along the traditional left–right division are, in fact, regularly invoked in the discussion of EU legislative proposals. See K Gattermann and C Hefftler, 'Beyond Institutional Capacity: Political Motivation and Parliamentary Behaviour in the Early Warning System' (2015) 38 *West European Politics* 305, 320.

partnerships and gender balance on company boards, both issues supported by the social-democrats, while the conservative majority voted in favour of the reasoned opinions.

The socio-economic cleavage is visible in the Bundestag debate on the Commission proposal on the Fund for the Aid to the Most Deprived Persons, where the SPD, the Linke and Die Grünen cited their support for social solidarity as a reason to vote against or abstain from the adoption of the reasoned opinion. The socio-economic cleavage is also visible in the Polish Senat during the debate on the new allocations system of refugees, where the PO opposition voted against the reasoned opinion, arguing that an action at EU level is necessary to solve the refugee crisis. In the UK House of Commons, similarly, the discussion of the Commission proposal on the food from cloned animals shows that such reasons as consumer safety and animal welfare led the Labour MPs not to support the reasoned opinion in the case at stake. However, the socio-economic cleavage can in some cases lead to casting a vote in favour of a reasoned opinion on both sides of the political spectrum. For example, the opposition in the UK House of Commons was in favour of the reasoned opinion on the Commission proposal on the right to strike, but for a different reason from the coalition: the Commission right to strike proposal did not safeguard the rights of trade unions to a sufficient degree.

C. Reflection of Regional Interests

The third question concerns the extent to which the EWS permits the expression of regional interests independently of national governments. This was expected: in particular the German Länder saw the subsidiarity mechanism as 'enhanced protection against interference with their own legislative and enforcement powers'.[309]

i. Germany

In Germany, the reasoned opinions of the Bundesrat should be explored together with the instructions issued by Länder Landtage.[310] The latter instruct the respective Länder governments to support a reasoned opinion in the Bundesrat.[311] Yet, the competences that the Länder highlight and that are later expressed in the Bundesrat's reasoned opinions do not necessarily concern only the infringement of their own powers by a Commission proposal. The reasoned opinions issued in the Bundesrat can reflect both encroachment on federal and on Länder powers.

[309] A von Bogdandy and J Bast, 'The Federal Order of Competences' in A von Bogdandy and J Bast (eds), *Principles of European Constitutional Law* (Oxford, Hart Publishing, 2010) 276.

[310] Available on REGPEX.

[311] The opinions of Landtage may influence the position of the regional government during its vote in the Bundesrat. Yet, in principle the ministers in the Bundesrat are not bound by these opinions because of the constitutional principle of own political responsibility of the executives (*Prinzip der Eigenverantwortung der Regierung*). Nonetheless, the government will have to explain why it did not follow the recommendation of the Landtag. So far only in Baden-Württemberg might the Landtag issue a decision binding on the government, while in Bavaria and Saxony the state governments committed to take into account the position of the Parliament in cases of a subsidiarity violation. See Committee of the Regions, *The Subsidiarity Early Warning System of the Lisbon Treaty— the role of regional parliaments with legislative powers and other subnational authorities* (2013) 55.

First, as some examples show, the focus is often on the protection of a federal competence. For instance, the Thüringer Landtag and the Bayerischer Landtag instructed their governments to highlight subsidiarity issues and influence the decision of the Bundesrat in that direction, as the Commission proposal on the EU Agency for Law Enforcement Cooperation and Training[312] affected the national training of police officers, an area which falls within the 'national sovereignty' of the Member States.[313] This view was later reflected in the opinion of the Bundesrat.[314]

Second, the Data Protection package shows that the competences of both the Länder and the federal state may be violated by the Commission's proposals. The Hessischer Landtag argued that Germany offers a much higher level of protection than the EU proposal, a point later reflected in the reasoned opinion of the Bundesrat.[315] Moreover, the Bundesrat argued that the Commission's Data Protection package proposal extends EU substantive competences in a way 'particularly detrimental to the sovereignty of the federal states (Länder) in matters pertaining to the police'.[316] Similarly, with regard to the Commission proposal amending the Deposit Guarantee Schemes, an act which already set the coverage level of deposits at €100,000 but now required all banks to join the Deposit Guarantee Schemes, the Bundesrat stressed the specificities of the German banking system, connected to its regional and local dimensions. In the view of the Bundesrat, the proposed directive especially affected these banks, which already participated in the institutional warranties scheme (institutions provide security to associated institutions) and which have strong roots in the regions.[317] In the same case, members of the Bundestag emphasised that 'Europe has to take into account the inherent structures and specificities of Member States'.[318]

Finally, an EU draft legislative act might violate the competences of the Länder. For instance, the German Bundesrat negatively opined on the draft directive, which aimed at introducing clear legal rules governing the award of concessions contracts.[319] The parliament maintained that, in particular, the provisions of the proposal could infringe on the competence of the Länder to grant service concessions for services of general economic interest. Specifically, the proposal affected the exclusive competence of the Länder regarding emergency services, a vital guarantee of internal security, and may thus violate the principle of regional and local self-administration.[320]

In sum, the reasoned opinions of the Bundesrat highlight the protection of both Länder and federal competences against EU intervention.

[312] 'Proposal for a Regulation of the European Parliament and the Council on the European Union Agency for Law Enforcement Cooperation and Training (Europol) and repealing Decisions 2009/371/JHA and 2005/681/JHA' COM(2013) 173 final.

[313] Thüringer Landtag, Unterrichtung, Drucksache 5/6114, Bayerischer Landtag (Drucksache 16/16945).

[314] German Bundesrat, Reasoned opinion of 07.06.2013 on COM(2013) 173, 346/13, point 3.

[315] Hessischer Landtag, opinion of 13.03.2012 on COM(2012) 11, Drucksache 18/5396, points 1 and 2; German Bundesrat, Reasoned opinion of 30.03.2012 on COM(2012) 11, 52/12, points 2 and 10.

[316] Reasoned opinion of the German Bundesrat of 30.03.2012 on COM(2012) 10 final, 4. See Bundesrat, 895. Sitzung, Plenarprotokoll, 30.12.2012, 175–80.

[317] German Bundesrat, Reasoned opinion of 24.09.2010 on COM(2010) 368 final, point 2. See Bundesrat, Stenografischer Bericht of 24.09.2010, Erklärung von Minister Prof D. W Reinhart (Baden-Württemberg) 330.

[318] Bundestag, Plenarprotokoll of 07.10.2010, 6865 (own translation).

[319] 'Proposal for a Directive of the European Parliament and of the Council on the award of concession contracts' COM(2011) 897 final.

[320] German Bundesrat, Reasoned opinion of 02.03.2012 on COM(2011) 897, point 10.

ii. Belgium

Declaration No 51 'by the Kingdom of Belgium on national Parliaments to the Lisbon Treaty' clarifies that, in accordance with Belgian constitutional law, not only the Chambre des représentants and the Sénat but also the parliamentary assemblies of the communities and the regions should be conceived of as 'components of the national parliamentary system or chambers of the national Parliament'.[321] In fact, the Flemish Parliament took stock of this declaration and issued its reasoned opinion on the Commission proposal for 'a framework for maritime spatial planning and integrated coastal management'. The declaration, therefore, enables parliamentary assemblies of the communities and regions to argue a violation of subsidiarity principle directly at EU level. This possibility for the parliamentary assemblies under the EWS enables them to directly check whether EU action fulfils the premise of Article 5(3) of the Treaty on the European Union, which allows EU action only if its objective cannot be reached at national or regional and local level. In fact, in 2017, an agreement was signed between the relevant parties that incudes rules on the participation in the EWS, especially the division of the two Belgian votes between the parliaments.[322]

Nonetheless, that Declaration No 51 was invoked only once so far seems to show that the interests of the regional entities do not play much of a role in the subsidiarity scrutiny procedure. This may not be surprising, taking into account the lack of appropriate administrative equipment of regional assemblies to participate in the EWS.[323] The Sénat after the 2014 reform more adequately represents the regions and may therefore offer an appropriate forum to coordinate and cooperate on the issuing of reasoned opinions.[324]

iii. The UK

The application of the EWS in the UK, where the devolution principle governs the process of decentralisation, has been shown to take into consideration the prerogatives of the devolved territories of Scotland, Wales, and Northern Ireland. This is visible in reasoned opinions of the House of Commons that often include the arguments of the devolved parliaments. For instance, such a case concerns two draft directives regarding public procurement and procurement by public entities, one which aimed at establishing a single national authority in charge of procurement oversight and empowered with reviewing the decisions of contracting entities.[325] In the view of the UK House of Commons, the

[321] On Declaration No 51 and its impact on the EWS see further, M Romaniello, 'Beyond the Constitutional "Bicameral Blueprint": Europeanisation and National Identities in Belgium' in M Cartabia, N Lupo and A Simoncini (eds), *Democracy and Subsidiarity in the EU* (Bologna, Il Mulino, 2013) 304–08.

[322] Accord de coopération entre l'État fédéral, les Régions, les Communautés, la Commission communautaire française et la Commission communautaire commune relatif à l'exercice des compétences attribuées aux parlements nationaux par le Traité sur l'Union européenne, le Traité sur le fonctionnement de l'Union européenne et les protocoles y annexes, Annexes au Règlement de la Chambre des représentants—Dernière mise à jour le 29 mars 2017.

[323] W Vandenbruwaene and P Popelier, 'Belgian Parliaments and the Early Warning System' in A Jonsson Cornell and M Goldoni (eds), *National and Regional Parliaments in the EU-Legislative Procedure Post-Lisbon* (Oxford, Hart Publishing, 2017) 181.

[324] ibid 195.

[325] 'Proposal for a Directive of the European Parliament and of the Council on procurement by entities operating in the water, energy, transport and postal services sectors' COM(2011) 895 final; 'Proposal for a Directive of the European Parliament and of the Council on public procurement' COM(2011) 896 final.

Commission proposal, by obliging the UK to create a single oversight body for the breach of procurement rules that would have replaced the High Court's jurisdiction in England, Wales, and Northern Ireland, did not sufficiently take into account the legal traditions of the Member States.[326]

Similarly, the reasoned opinion of the House of Commons on the Proposal for a Council Regulation on the establishment of the European Public Prosecutor's Office (EPPO proposal) underlines that the Commission did not sufficiently take into account the issue that the devolved territories have their separate criminal justice systems.[327] In this respect, the House of Commons referred to the opinion received from the Scottish Parliament, which found the EPPO proposal in violation of the subsidiarity principle.

Finally, the reasoned opinion of the House of Commons on the Commission proposal on strengthening of the principle of the presumption of innocence takes into account the view of the Scottish Parliament.[328] In this case, the Scottish Parliament questioned the necessity of EU action to ensure that the Member States' judicial authorities cooperate with each other by highlighting lack of evidence in the proposal that Scottish authorities are reluctant to cooperate.

V. ANALYSIS OF THE DEBATES

A. The 'Debating' and 'Working' Features of Parliaments in the EWS

This section studies to what extent the EWS offers a forum for a critical assessment of the government by the opposition. The notions of a 'debating' as opposed to a 'working' parliament are used here to illustrate rather than explain the behaviour of national parliaments.[329]

Max Weber first applied the notion of a 'working' parliament in his criticism of the German Reichstag. He preferred reform in the direction of a working type of parliament, which he contrasted with parliaments described as 'talking shops'.[330] In Weber's view, the parliament should have stronger control of the executive ('officialdom'); it should possess 'specialist knowledge' received in the course of 'cross-examination (under oath) by experts before a parliamentary commission with powers to summon the relevant departmental officials' and obtain 'official information', normally protected by government officials.[331]

[326] House of Commons, Reasoned opinion of 06.03.2012 on COM(2011) 895 and 896, point 21. The House of Commons repeats this issue after the subsidiarity report from the Welsh Assembly, annexed to the reasoned opinion.

[327] UK House of Commons, Reasoned opinion of 22.10.2013 on COM(2013) 534, point 15 and the annexed opinion of the Scottish Parliament.

[328] House of Commons, Reasoned opinion of 10.02.2014 on COM(2013) 821, point 18.

[329] As such, those notions have, however, a limited explanatory value in EU affairs, since all national parliaments have adopted a committee-based approach, typical for 'working' parliaments. See K Auel and T Raunio, 'Debating the State of the Union? Comparing Parliamentary Debates on EU Issues in Finland, France, Germany and the United Kingdom' (2014) 20 *The Journal of Legislative Studies* 13, 15.

[330] Weber (n 14) 177–96 and 181.

[331] ibid 178.

Weber contrasted the Reichstag with the status of the British Parliament. For Weber, the House of Commons represented the best characteristics of a working parliament: the sole existence of parliamentary enquiry kept the public constantly well informed and officials under its control. Moreover, Weber advocated the introduction of parliamentary committees to the German Reichstag for greater oversight of officials through the right to enquiry. Finally, according to Weber, a working parliament demanded 'cooperation between specialist officials and professional politicians'.[332]

Winfred Steffani elaborated on the Weber model and added the notion of the 'debating' parliament, describing it as 'the most important forum of public opinion'.[333] According to Steffani, the debates serve to justify decisions taken, criticise the choices of the other party, publicly scrutinise the government, and obtain information. The working parliament, on the contrary, relies on the work of committees with its experts, who pose questions to experts representing the government.

The differences between 'debating' and 'working' chambers in general seem to diminish in the current parliamentary world.[334] In fact, the subsidiarity scrutiny mechanism manages to marry the 'working' style, visible especially in high-level reports and reasoned opinions of committees, with the 'debating' style of scrutiny and criticism of the government during committee or plenary sittings in both chambers. This is quite evident in the debates preceding agreement on a reasoned opinion.[335] In Germany and the UK, the opposition used the EWS as an opportunity to criticise the government. In particular in the case of proposals on the Aid to the Most Deprived People or gender balance on corporate boards,[336] in the UK House of Commons, the Labour opposition singled out the lack of appropriate action to improve the situation in the UK by the government.[337] Similarly, while scrutinising this proposal, the German opposition in the Bundestag attacked the government for not paying enough attention to the social problems in the EU.[338]

Finally, the 'debating' features of the Polish Sejm and Senat, where the opposition has opportunities to criticise the coalition and the government while discussing reasoned opinions, are much less present than in the UK. In the Polish Sejm, even in those debates in which

[332] ibid 182.

[333] W Steffani, 'Amerikanischer Kongreß und Deutscher Bundestag' in W Steffani (ed), *Parlamentarische und präsidentielle Demokratie* (Opladen, Westdt Verlag, 1979) 333 (own translation).

[334] P Dann, 'Looking through the federal lens: The semi-parliamentary democracy of the EU' (2002) Jean Monnet Working Paper 5/02, 22. Dann who applies Weber's notions of the 'debating' and 'working' parliament to assess the EP, points out that these notions are 'ideal types'. Dann labels the House of Commons as a debating parliament. In this model there is a 'fusion of majority party and government'; the opposition uses the plenary to attack the government and to put forward its own proposals. The US Congress is an example of a working parliament. This model is characterised by its 'fair' separation of Parliament from the government, as well as by its concentration of parliamentary work in strong, specialised committees. In addition, some chambers such as the French lower chamber cannot even qualify under any of them.

[335] I refer here only to those Member States for which the full stenographic protocols of the debates are accessible.

[336] HC Deb 18 December 2012 (especially on food banks); HC Deb 7 January 2013 (eg, col 60).

[337] Nonetheless, quite similar, but less intensive disputes might be observed in the UK House of Lords, despite more often described as a 'working' chamber. See, eg, HL text for 10 January 2013, col 350.1; also the debates on the EPPO proposal or 'Broadcasting networks' proposal.

[338] Deutscher Bundestag, Stenografischer Bericht, 13.12.2012, Plenarprotokoll 17/214, 26502. For the opposition's criticism of the EU politics of the German governments, see also Deutscher Bundestag, Stenografischer Bericht, 7.10.2010, Plenarprotokoll 17/65, 6866.

the opposition did not support the reasoned opinion, such as on the proposal regarding the property consequences of registered partnerships, the criticism was marginal.[339] Hence, at least for the review of subsidiarity, the Polish Sejm turns out to be more of a working chamber. This is visible to an even greater degree in the Polish Senat, with a high consistency of views on reasoned opinions among the coalition, opposition and government; no major criticism of the government was visible.

The notions of 'debating' and 'working' parliaments have more of a descriptive rather than explanatory value in the study of the EWS. The central features of the debating parliament—the debates and criticism of the government—are especially visible in the debates on the reasoned opinions, while the reasoned opinions themselves, which are often an overall assessment of the proposal, and not only of the subsidiarity question, prepared usually at the committee level underline the 'working' side of the parliaments in the EWS.

In sum, in a limited number of cases, the opposition parties, although they cannot stop the adoption of the reasoned opinions, provide some criticism of the government. Since to a large extent, however, the parliaments adopted reasoned opinions unanimously, this agreement proves the relationship between majority and opposition to be consensual. The diminished role of the opposition in criticising the government remains in contrast to the usual behaviour of the opposition in EU affairs.[340] This could be possibly explained by how the opposition views the EWS: more as a new tool enhancing the position of the parliament vis-a-vis the EU legislator rather than remaining in the traditional lines of government–opposition relationship.

B. Motivation of National Parliaments

The examination of the debates that led to issuing a reasoned opinion in the UK, Germany, Poland and Belgium highlights two main ideas on why a reasoned opinion against a Commission proposal was necessary. While these arguments are not always expressed in the reasoned opinions, they are stated in the debates or can be interpreted on the basis thereof. The arguments against Commission proposals raised by the parliamentarians can be divided into arguments on the redistributive character of EU policies and on the idiosyncratic interests of Member States.

Current EU policies and the dominating majoritarian form of decision-making bring forth redistributive effects that can be seen as exceeding the notion of the EU as a regulatory authority.[341] National parliaments, when scrutinising EU legislative proposals, consider a proposal's redistributive aspects and their impact on the Member State concerned.

A clear example of this problem is a series of Commission proposals regarding the distribution of food products to the most deprived persons in the EU, a series which aimed at formalising Common Agricultural Policy (CAP) funds to purchase goods not only from

339 Sejm, Sprawozdanie Stenograficzne z 93. Posiedzenia Sejmu Rzeczypospolitej Polskiej, 25.05.2011, 92.

340 Auel and Benz (n 5); Auel (n 6).

341 M Poiares Maduro, *A New Governance for the European Union and the Euro: Democracy and Justice* (Florence, European University Institute, 2012) 18.

intervention stocks but also on the open market.[342] While discussing the Commission's initiatives, some of the Lords stressed the fact that the UK has not benefited from the aid in recent years, with its contribution to the EU budget later being used for this scheme.[343] The latest proposal in this series, creating the Fund for European Aid to the Most Deprived, designed to promote social cohesion and no longer based on agricultural policy, makes the participation of the Member States obligatory.[344] It imposed a requirement on Member States to set up a single national programme to implement the scheme, where the EU will contribute 85 per cent. However, this time the Lords focused more on the administrative burden connected to the operation of the Fund in its reasoned opinion; further the redistributive character of the proposal might have influenced the attitude of the House towards the Commission proposal.[345] With regard to the same proposal, the Bundestag's majority also raised analogous objections about the financing of the Fund. According to the Bundestag, the €2.5 billion might have been used in the framework of the existing Social Fund, which would have also provided for a democratic supervision by national parliaments.[346] Finally, in the same vein, some of the Polish senators raised concerns about the methods of the division of means for specific actions in CAP, a significant issue for Poland.[347]

National interests endangered by a Commission proposal present another reason for expressing a reasoned opinion. In the debate on the Commission proposal on prudential requirements, an MP in the House of Commons maintained Britain's 'unique interest in financial services'.[348] Therefore, the parliament should fight any encroachment on the ability of the UK to manage financial services, as presented by the Commission proposal in question.

Furthermore, the Polish Parliament issued a notable number of reasoned opinions on Commission proposals in the field of CAP. Accordingly, in the discussion of these reasoned opinions, emphasis was placed on the national interest of agriculture, calling it the Polish 'apple of the eye'.[349] The members of the parliament very often underlined that Poland is the biggest producer in their area of Europe, or the most agriculture-oriented Member State of those that have recently acceded.[350] Hence, conferral of powers to the Commission in this sphere seems extremely unfavourable,[351] and Poland's aim should be to defend the influence of Member States on this policy.[352] Beyond the proposals on CAP, the Polish MPs

[342] 'Amended proposal for a Regulation of the European Parliament and the Council amending Council Regulations (EC) No 1290/2005 and (EC) No 1234/2007, as regards distribution of food products to the most deprived persons in the Union' COM(2010) 486 final; and amended 'Proposal for a Regulation of the European Parliament and the Council amending Council Regulation (EC) No 1290/2005 and Council Regulation (EC) No 1234/2007 as regards distribution of food products to the most deprived persons in the Union' COM(2011) 634 final.

[343] HC Deb 3 November 2010, col 1693 and of 28 November 2011, col 89.

[344] COM(2012) 617 final.

[345] House of Lords, European Union Committee, *6th Report of Session 2012–13*, point 11.

[346] Bundestag Plenarprotokol of 13.12.2012, 26504.

[347] Senat, Zapis Stenograficzny, 135. Posiedzenie Komisji Spraw Unii Europejskiej, 08.02.2011, 8.

[348] House of Commons European Committee, Financial Services: Prudential Requirements, 14.03.2012, col 24. See also House of Commons, European Committee B, Financial Services Benchmarks, col 8.

[349] Own translation. Komisja do Spraw Unii Europejskiej, 02.02.2011, Nr 4659/VI, 12.

[350] Komisja do Spraw Unii Europejskiej, 18.02.2011, Nr 4692/VI, 11; Senat, Zapis Stenograficzny, Wspólne posiedzenie Komisji Rolnictwa i Rozwoju Wsi oraz Komisji Spraw Unii Europejskiej, 03.02.2011, 6.

[351] Komisja do Spraw Unii Europejskiej, 21.01.2011, Nr 4628/VI, 7.

[352] Sejm, Sprawozdanie Stenograficzne z 78. Posiedzenia Sejmu Rzeczypospolitej Polskiej, 24.11.2010, 110.

and senators pointed to national interest in areas such as services,[353] the refugee crisis[354] and energy policy.[355]

Moreover, national parliaments understand a reasoned opinion as a signal both to Brussels and to the national voters. In this regard, the German Bundestag MPs perceived the proposed Services package as a deregulation of services that is 'not good for Germany', and a reasoned opinion sends a signal to Brussels that the proposal is problematic.[356] In contrast, a Member of the Belgian pro-European N-VA in the Chambre des représentants stated that issuing the reasoned opinion creates a negative image of Belgium at the European level and should be avoided, in particular, as there would not be enough opinions from national parliaments for the Commission to change its proposal in this case.[357] Finally, focusing on national voters, the Polish senators claimed that the refugee crisis cannot be solved at national or regional level, yet lack of Polish objection on this matter was seen as hard to explain to public opinion.[358]

While the redistributive character of EU policies and the idiosyncratic national interests may shed some light on why the chambers in question decided to issue a reasoned opinion, it also signals that the members of national parliaments do not necessarily think in subsidiarity terms when conducting scrutiny under the EWS. Naturally the EWS did not grant national parliaments veto power over EU draft legislative acts. However, the reasoning of national parliaments based on national interest or contesting EU redistributive policy goes against the task with which the Lisbon Treaty endowed the national parliaments, namely, the review of compliance of EU draft legislative acts with the subsidiarity principle. In this sense, the subsidiarity principle serves as a cover for the protection of national conditions. In fact, in some of the debates analysed in this chapter, MPs have underlined that no subsidiarity violation is at stake and condemned issuing a reasoned opinion in such cases.[359] For example, debating the Commission proposal for an internal market on electricity, the rapporteur of the Senate's committee raised doubt as to whether the proposal was indeed incompatible with the subsidiarity principle, yet for the sake of the protection of Polish national interests, he urged the parliament to adopt a reasoned opinion.[360] Such a use of subsidiarity may indeed lead to 'instrumentalisation of this principle for other purposes than its own, and its use by pressure groups, passed on by parliaments, which are more concerned with defending national positions than fighting against excessive EU legislation'.[361]

[353] Sprawozdanie Stenograficzne z 16. Posiedzenia Senatu, 28–29.04.2016, 137.

[354] Sprawozdanie Stenograficzne z 28. Posiedzenia Sejmu, 20.10.2016, 298.

[355] Sprawozdanie Stenograficzne z 41. Posiedzenie Sejmu, 10.05.2017, 57 and 60.

[356] German Bundestag, Stenografischer Bericht 221. Sitzung, Plenarprotokoll 18/221, 9.03.2017, 22238–39.

[357] Rapport fait au nom de la Commission charge des problèmes de droit commercial et économique 16.02.2012, DOC 53 2068/001, 16.

[358] Posiedzenie Komisji Spraw Zagranicznych i Unii Europejskiej, Nr 57, 28.09.2016.

[359] See Senat, Zapis Stenofraficzny, Wspólne posiedzenie Komisji Praw Człowieka, Praworządności i Petycji (86) oraz Komisji Spraw Zagranicznych i Unii Europejskiej (67) 19.10.2016, 4–5; HL 4 February 2016, col 1943.

[360] Posiedzenie Komisji Spraw Zagranicznych i Unii Europejskiej, Nr 97, 20.04.2016. On the support for a reasoned opinion despite a lack of subsidiarity violation see also Sejm, Sprawozdanie Stenograficzne z 28 posiedzenia Sejmu, 20.10.2016, 299.

[361] V Constantinesco, 'Les compétences et le principe de subsidiarité' (2005) 2 *Revue trimestrielle de droit européen* 305 (own translation).

VI. CONCLUSION

This chapter tackled four questions regarding the interaction of executive and legislative actors in the EWS on the basis of debates and votes taken in the UK, German, Polish and Belgian parliaments. Despite the fact that this sample is not fully representative of all possible political and constitutional configurations within the EU, it allowed a comparison based on a number of relevant characteristics of national political systems.

The analysis of the data collected on the debates and votes on reasoned opinions in four national case studies provided some preliminary indications with regard to the questions posed in this chapter. First, the study of activity in the Member States showed that in a considerable number of cases a reasoned opinion was issued, even though the government did not find a subsidiarity violation.[362] This was the case in both the executive-dominated Westminster model and the power-sharing consensus model. Only the Belgian Chambre des représentants always followed the line of the federal government on subsidiarity violations, a situation which was explained by its generally weak position in EU affairs vis-a-vis the government. Moreover, the distinction between upper and lower chambers did not much affect the independence of the legislative from the executive branches under the EWS. Each of the upper chambers took part in issuing reasoned opinions despite the acquiescence of the executive branch. This may not be a surprise, taking into account the fact that the upper chambers tend not to have such strong political links to the executive branch as the lower chambers.

The study of the positions of the majority and opposition under the EWS shows a major convergence of views between the political parties with regard to whether the parliament should issue a reasoned opinion. In the rare cases of a cleavage between the majority and opposition, this is more visible in elected lower chambers: the UK House of Commons, the Polish Sejm, the German Bundestag, and the Belgian Chambre des représentants, than in the upper chambers. The different stance on issuing a reasoned opinion between the majority and opposition shows the left–right cleavage and socio-economic cleavage characteristic of day-to-day political life, similar to their positions on national political issues.

This chapter also explored the extent to which the EWS permits the expression of regional interests independently from institutions such as the Committee of the Regions. In fact, as expected, the protection of the prerogatives of the Länder played an important role in the reasoned opinions of the German Bundesrat. However, it is important to point out that the members of the Bundesrat, often following the instructions of the state Landtage, also raised questions of federal importance. In sum, the reasoned opinions reflect the protection of both regional as well as federal matters. In Belgium, the Flemish Parliament has also made use of its prerogative, in accordance with Declaration No 51, to issue a reasoned opinion. This, per se, can be seen as a reflection of a regional matter in the EWS. Finally, in the UK in a number of cases the House of Commons in its reasoned opinions took into account the reports of the parliaments of devolved entities.

Finally, by exploring the parliamentary and committee debates this chapter shows that the EWS tends to combine the 'working' and 'debating' features of national parliaments.

[362] Possibly the number of cases where the parliament and the government agree could have been higher if the study included also cases in which national parliaments at stake did not issue reasoned opinions.

Moreover, only to a limited extent would the opposition use the EWS as an opportunity to criticise the government. A closer analysis of the debates that led to issuing reasoned opinions indicated that the redistributive character of a policy that the Commission proposal pursues or an idiosyncratic national interest at stake might represent some of the causes why national parliaments issue reasoned opinions under the EWS. In some of those cases, national parliaments sent a reasoned opinion despite the loudly voiced concerns that, in fact, an EU draft legislative act complies with the subsidiarity principle.

Beyond the reasons for participation in the EWS that were signalled here, further points raised by national parliaments will be analysed in the forthcoming chapters. They include the scrutiny of the competence for the EU to act and the analysis of delegations to adopt delegated and implementing acts. These chapters show how the participation in the EWS allows national parliaments to increase their review powers beyond the function to scrutinise subsidiarity as granted by the Lisbon Treaty.

6

Principle of Conferral Under Protocol No 2

I. INTRODUCTION

EU LAW HAS been alarmingly successful in forcing its way into all areas of national competence in the past few decades.[1] The phenomenon of 'competence creep' demanded a search for a more precise account to the question of existence and policing of EU competence.[2] The adopted Lisbon Treaty that accumulated a number of provisions limiting the EU's competence represents the idea of containment and rationalisation of competences.[3] The 'federal order of competence' enshrined in the Lisbon Treaty was designed to provide 'a stable set of rules for determining the existence of and co-ordinating the exercise of the respective powers'[4] for the EU.[5] The principles of Article 5 of the Treaty on the European Union (TEU) govern the 'existence' of EU competence (principle of conferral) and the 'exercise' of EU competence (subsidiarity and proportionality).[6] The principle of conferral demands that 'the EU acts only within the limits of the competences conferred upon it by the Member States in the Treaties to attain the objectives set out therein'.[7] Competences that were not conferred on the EU remain with the Member States.[8]

The proximity of two principles of EU law—conferral and subsidiarity, both enshrined in Article 5 TEU—justifies an in-depth study of their relationship. This particular question has been animating national parliaments under the Early Warning System (EWS). In as much as the question of the EU competences and their limits in fact concerns the reach and the purpose of European integration,[9] this chapter aims to present and assess the views of national parliaments on the compliance of EU proposals with the principle of conferral.[10]

[1] L Azoulai, 'Introduction' in L Azoulai (ed), *The Question of Competence in the European Union* (Oxford, Oxford University Press, 2014) 9.

[2] S Weatherill, 'Competence Creep and Competence Control' (2004) 23 *Yearbook of European Law* 1.

[3] Azoulai (n 1) 11. For a critical appraisal see R Schütze, 'Lisbon and the federal order of competences: A prospective analysis' (2008) 33 *European Law Review* 709.

[4] A von Bogdandy and J Bast, 'The Federal Order of Competences' in A von Bogdandy and J Bast (eds), *Principles of European Constitutional Law* (Oxford, Hart Publishing, 2010) 275.

[5] Art 2-6 TFEU.

[6] P Craig, *EU Administrative Law* (Oxford, Oxford University Press, 2012) 391.

[7] Art 5(2) TEU.

[8] ibid.

[9] FC Mayer, 'Competences—Reloaded? The vertical division of powers in the EU and the new European constitution' (2005) 3 *International Journal of Constitutional Law* 493.

[10] The notions of 'competence' and 'power' used in the treaties or the terms 'enabling norm' and 'legal base' do not seem to have distinct legal meanings and, as such, are used interchangeably in this chapter. See A von Bogdandy and J Bast, 'The European Union's Vertical order of Competences: The Current Law and Proposals for its Reform' (2002) 39 *Common Market Law Review* 227, 229.

To explore the limits of EU competence from the national parliaments' perspective, section II elaborates on the understanding of the principle of conferral under the Lisbon Treaty and its links to the subsidiarity principle. Next, section III examines the reasoned opinions of national parliaments, which aim to control the principle of conferral. Section IV focuses on the problematic Articles 114 and 352 of the Treaty on the Functioning of the European Union (TFEU). The case study pursued in section V provides an analysis of the right to strike proposal based on the flexibility clause, wherein the main concern of national parliaments was the lack of competence of the EU to act.

II. THE QUESTION OF EU COMPETENCE

The limit of Community competences has been eroded since the revitalisation of the Community in the mid-1970s.[11] Article 235 EEC (Article 308 EC, current Article 352 TFEU) was 'the key' to this revival.[12] It stipulated that if action on the part of the Community in the common market was necessary to achieve the treaty objectives but the Treaty did not explicitly provide such power, the Council could, via a unanimous vote, and after consultation with the European Parliament (EP), approve legislation in that area. The frequent application of Article 235 EEC when the Community did not have a specific legislative power in a certain area 'opened up practically any realm of state activity to the Community, provided the governments of the Member States found accord among themselves'.[13]

It was not until the Single European Act that specific legal bases were introduced for the cases in which Article 235 EEC was applicable earlier. The Single European Act included a new Article 100a EEC (Article 95 EC, current Article 114 TFEU), allowing for qualified majority voting for measures, the objective of which is the establishment and functioning of the internal market. This amendment, however, caused further growth in centralised EU policies; Member States especially contested 'the Community's competence to regulate in sensitive national areas such as culture, education, and public health'.[14] Taken together, the two provisions—Article 95 EC and Article 308 EC, the predecessors of Articles 114 TFEU and 352 TFEU—were perceived as the 'principal problem cases in the corrosive trajectory of "competence creep"'.[15]

A. The 'New Order of Competences' in the Lisbon Treaty and its Assessment

The Treaty of Lisbon eventually provided some clarity on the question 'qui fait quoi, that is, which level(s) of governments may be responsible for which kinds of policy action'.[16]

[11] JHH Weiler, 'The Transformation of Europe' (1991) 100 *Yale Law Journal* 2403, 2449. Weiler explains that the Paris Summit of 1972 attempted a fresh start for the Community, after the Luxembourg Crisis ('empty chair crisis') and the twice unsuccessful application of the UK to join the Community.

[12] ibid.

[13] ibid 2450.

[14] MA Pollack, 'The End of Creeping Competence? EU Policy-Making Since Maastricht' (2000) 38 *Journal of Common Market Studies* 519, 525.

[15] S Weatherill, 'The Limits of Legislative Harmonization Ten Years after Tobacco Advertising: How the Court's Case Law has Become a Drafting Guide' (2011) 12 *German Law Journal* 827, 851.

[16] G de Búrca and B de Witte, 'The Delimitation of Powers Between the EU and its Member States' in A Arnull and D Wincott (eds), *Accountability and Legitimacy in the European Union* (Oxford, Oxford University Press, 2002) 203.

Building upon the categories of the Constitutional Treaty,[17] the Lisbon Treaty classifies competences as EU exclusive competences (Article 3 TFEU), shared competences (Article 4 TFEU), and competences to support, coordinate, or supplement Member State action (Article 6 TFEU).

Commentators welcomed this new catalogue with varying degrees of satisfaction. The division allows for more clarity, yet issues with delineating the boundaries of each of the competence categories were anticipated.[18] Others perceive the reforms as useful but conservative.[19] On the one hand, Articles 2–6 TFEU are more transparent when it comes to the scope, nature and effect of the EU legislative competence; on the other hand, the change in substance is limited.[20] In addition, Article 114 TFEU, together with subsidiarity and proportionality, underwent only 'cosmetic' textual changes, without an effort to put a limit on EU competence.[21] Some view the Treaty of Lisbon as not extending EU competences, but, rather, reflecting the existing case law of the Court of Justice of the European Union (CJEU/Court).[22] More negatively, the competence categorisation was described as retrograde in terms of 'constitutional clarity'.[23] This was visible in the lack of distinct competence categories. Instead, the Lisbon Treaty provided three 'official' and a number of 'unofficial' competences, and the distinction between the competence types remained unclear.[24]

B. Links Between the Principles of Conferral and Subsidiarity

Article 5 TEU, which deals with the existence of EU competence and with its exercise, closely links the principle of conferral to the principle of subsidiarity.[25] The close relationship renders the competence question not a simple 'yes-or-no question'.[26] In consequence, a number of scholars and national parliaments alike suggest that the assessment of Commission proposals under the EWS includes the scrutiny of the principle of conferral as the first step. This argument is often based on the logical assumption that 'if the Union already fails the competence test, a subsidiarity test even if conducted cannot possibly be positive'.[27] For example, the German Bundesrat, which habitually reviews the principle of conferral, justifies its scrutiny with the logical interrelation between competence and subsidiarity: the

[17] On the division of competences under the Constitutional Treaty, see V Constantinesco, 'Les compétences et le principe de subsidiarité' (2005) 2 *Revue trimestrielle de droit européen* 305. For a critical assessment see Mayer (n 9) 493.

[18] Craig, *EU Administrative Law* (n 6) 398.

[19] Weatherill, 'The Limits of Legislative Harmonization' (n 15) 850.

[20] ibid.

[21] ibid.

[22] See Minutes of Evidence taken before the Select Committee on the European Union, 20.11.2007, oral evidence given by D Chalmers, *10th Report of Session 2007–08, The Treaty of Lisbon: an impact assessment, Volume II: Evidence*, S3.

[23] Schütze (n 3).

[24] ibid 709.

[25] Craig, *EU Administrative Law* (n 6) 391.

[26] de Búrca and de Witte (n 16) 205.

[27] P Kiiver, *The Early Warning System for the Principle of Subsidiarity: Constitutional Theory and Empirical Reality* (London, Routledge, 2012) 99.

subsidiarity principle is also breached if there is no EU competence in the area in question.[28] Similarly, the Spanish Parliament first considers the principle of conferral, as '[i]n the wording of Article 5 of the TFEU, the principle of conferral precedes, not by pure chance, the definition of the principle of subsidiarity'.[29]

The second argument sometimes put forward to support the inclusion of the principle of conferral under the EWS is the Court's case law, which has been seen as not offering a sufficient safeguard of the distribution of competences. This has been observed especially with regard to the Court's judgments regarding the EU's legislative competence in the internal market.[30] The Commission has adopted the Court's vague language on the limits of Article 114 TFEU, shedding EU legislative acts from their annulment by the Court.[31] Up to the date of writing, there has been only one case—*Tobacco Advertising*—wherein the Court has found the directive in question in violation of the legal basis.[32]

The third argument is that allowing national parliaments to conduct scrutiny of the principle of conferral under the EWS will contribute to alleviating the democratic deficit and increasing EU's legitimacy.[33] Similarly, a review of a Commission proposal that includes the check of its legal basis allows for a more representative political space at the national level.[34]

In contrast, a number of arguments can be raised against the inclusion of a check on the EU competence in the reasoned opinions. First, a textual interpretation of Article 5 TEU does not support this view. Article 5 TEU refers to Protocol No 2 only in paragraphs 3 (on subsidiarity) and 4 (on proportionality). This provision obliges EU institutions to apply the principles of subsidiarity and proportionality in accordance with Protocol No 2. National parliaments, however, safeguard compliance (only) with the subsidiarity principle, according to Article 5(3) TEU. Second, from a historic perspective, the emphasis that the Lisbon Treaty puts on the task of separation of competences in comparison to previous treaties implies that the subsidiarity principle cannot settle the question of competence, even though that question might be related to the more general idea of subsidiarity.[35]

Third, the comparative institutional analysis, conducted in chapter three, supports a limited role for national parliaments under Protocol No 2. The Court is more apt to review the compatibility of EU draft legislative acts with the principle of conferral. The Court, as the final interpreter of the EU Treaties, with an explicit function to review the legality of EU legislative acts, appears to be better endowed with the technical expertise on EU law needed

[28] German Bundesrat, Reasoned opinion of 16.12.2012 on COM(2011) 654, point 2 of 30.03.2012 on COM(2012) 10 and of 07.06.2013 on COM(2013) 173. Also the Polish Sejm perceives a violation of the conferral principle as a violation of subsidiarity (scrutiny of competence supplements subsidiarity). See Polish Sejm, Reasoned opinion of 13.05.2011 on COM(2011) 121 and of 15.09.2012 on COM(2012) 369. However, some parliaments, like the Italian Camera dei Deputati assess that the legal basis is wrong, but the proposal still complies with the subsidiarity principle. See Italian Camera dei Deputati, Reasoned opinion of 15.12.2011 on COM(2011) 615.

[29] Spanish Cortes Generales, Reasoned opinion of 13.06.2012 on COM(2012) 167.

[30] S Weatherill, *The Internal Market as a Legal Concept* (Oxford, Oxford University Press, 2017) 175.

[31] ibid 175.

[32] Case C-376/98 *Germany* v. *Parliament and Council*, ECLI:EU:C:2000:544.

[33] D Jančić, 'The Game of Cards: National Parliaments in the EU and the Future of the Early Warning Mechanism and the Political Dialogue' (2015) 52 *Common Market Law Review* 939, 942.

[34] M Goldoni, 'The Early Warning System and the Monti II Regulation: The Case for a Political Interpretation' (2014) 10 *European Constitutional Law Review* 90, 102.

[35] T von Danwitz, 'Subsidiaritätskontrolle in der Europäischen Union' in K Hansmann, K-P Dolde, S Paetow and E Schmidt-Assmann (eds), *Verfassung-Umwelt-Wirtschaft Festschrift für Dieter Sellner zum 75 Geburtstag* (München, CH Beck, 2010) 41.

to review whether the EU has the power to act within a certain domain. In addition, the EU legislator conducts a review of the legal basis of proposals.[36] Section III below focuses on the quality of national parliaments' scrutiny of the principle of conferral and highlights its superficial character.

Finally, in defence of the Court, commentators maintain that it is not true that the Court adopts an expansive interpretation of the competences or that its judgments are favouring (short-term) integration-friendly solutions.[37] Since the beginning of the 1990s, the Court's case law concerning EU competences was not always favourable to the EU, the *Tobacco Advertising* case being again the relevant judgment here, in which the Court ruled against the broad political consensus of EU legislative institutions and Member States.[38]

III. REASONED OPINIONS CONCERNING VIOLATION OF THE PRINCIPLE OF CONFERRAL

This section focuses on the question of how national parliaments in their reasoned opinions frame a violation of the conferral principle. In theory, this principle has both positive and negative dimensions that delimit and enable EU actions accordingly.[39] The negative aspect underlines the hierarchical order of EU law and means that any EU act must be compatible with EU primary law.[40] The positive aspect, in turn, demands an enabling provision—a legal basis—for every act of EU secondary law, either in the treaties or in secondary law, itself anchored in the treaties.[41] In general, national parliaments focus on the positive aspect of the principle of conferral. The scrutiny of the negative aspect of the principle of conferral, in the sense that any EU act must be compatible with the treaties, is less common.[42] Occasionally, some national parliaments test whether the legal basis has been chosen correctly as one of the steps in their scrutiny.[43]

This section focuses on the competence issues raised by national parliaments concerning treaty provisions other than Articles 114 and 352 TFEU, which are the focus of section IV. There are two strands of arguments of competence violation that national parliaments follow. First, the principle of conferral might be violated because the area under regulation falls outside the ambit of the treaty's legal basis. Second, the Commission proposal may pursue an objective that is different from the one indicated in the legal basis. Finally, this section lists the areas that national parliaments indicate as being of exclusive national competence or remaining under national sovereignty.

[36] Rule 39 of the Rules of Procedure of the European Parliament (2017); Art 19(1)(a) of the Rules of Procedure of the Council (2016). See also the Interinstitutional Agreement between the European Parliament, the Council of the European Union and the European Commission on Better Law-Making [2016] OJ L123, para 25.

[37] von Bogdandy and Bast, 'The Federal Order of Competences' (n 4) 257.

[38] ibid.

[39] ibid 229.

[40] ibid.

[41] ibid 231.

[42] Swedish Riksdag, Reasoned opinion of 17.10.2013 on COM(2013) 520.

[43] Greek Parliament, Reasoned opinion of 21.02.2013 on COM(2012) 788 and Italian Senato della Repubblica, Reasoned opinion of 30.01.2013 on COM(2012) 788; Dutch Eerste Kamer, Reasoned opinion of 24.01.2012 on COM(2011) 793, 794; Both Dutch chambers, Reasoned opinion of 17.02.2011 on COM(2010) 748; Romanian Camera Deputatilor, Reasoned opinion of 24.10.2011 on COM(2011) 453.

A. The Area that the Draft Legislative Act Regulates Falls Outside the Treaty's Legal Basis

The dominant type of competence scrutiny concerns situations in which the action pursued by a Commission proposal falls outside the treaty's legal basis in the view of national parliaments. However, this claim is different from the allegation that the issue at stake falls 'outside (overall) EU competence', as presented in section C below.

The first illustration of a draft proposal with an allegedly incorrect legal basis is the Commission proposal establishing a set of rules of international private law applicable to the property consequences of registered partnerships in the area of judicial cooperation in civil matters.[44] The proposal was based on Article 81(3) TFEU, which allows the Council members acting unanimously after consulting the EP to establish measures concerning family law with cross-border implications. The Italian Senato della Repubblica questioned the legal basis of the proposal by arguing that 'family law' does not cover the notion of 'registered partnership'.[45] In its reply to the Italian Senato della Repubblica, the Commission plausibly indicated that the notion of 'registered partnership' stems from a family relationship between the persons involved, and as it is closely linked with the family, it is understood to be part of family law.[46] The Commission has, however, withdrawn the proposal, as it was replaced by proposals under the procedure of enhanced cooperation.[47]

With regard to another draft legislative act, the Polish Sejm highlighted problems with the legal basis concerning the Commission proposal 'Women on Boards' introducing a 40 per cent quota for women on non-executive company boards.[48] The chamber argued that board members who are not employed within the meaning of the TFEU are not covered by the principle of equal pay for male and female workers for equal work or work of equal value because this principle applies only in relationships of employment (Article 157(3) TFEU).[49] As the Commission rightly pointed out in the reply to the Polish Sejm, Article 157(3) TFEU is not limited to 'workers', and the CJEU offers a broad interpretation of that notion.[50] The Commission convincingly invoked the *Danosa* case, according to which a member of a capital company's board of directors who provides services to that company and is an integral part of it must be, under specific conditions, regarded as having the status of a worker.[51]

These examples show that the national parliaments' assessment of the legal basis of Commission proposals is not necessarily correct. The fact that national parliaments seem to reserve 'exclusive national competence' in areas such as family law (see section C below) appears to be one of the explanations as to why they are quick to judge a legal basis of a proposal as wrong.

44 'Proposal for a Council Regulation on jurisdiction, applicable law and the recognition and enforcement of decisions regarding the property consequences of registered partnerships' COM(2011) 127 final.

45 Italian Senato della Repubblica, Reasoned opinion of 25.05.2011 on COM(2011) 127.

46 Commission reply of 12.03.2012 to the Reasoned opinion of the Italian Senato on COM(2011) 127.

47 See Commission Work Programme 2017, Annex 4, COM(2016) 710, 4.

48 'Proposal for a Directive of the European Parliament and of the Council on improving the gender balance among non-executive directors of companies listed on stock exchanges and related measures' COM(2012) 614 final. See ch 8.

49 Polish Sejm, Reasoned opinion of 04.01.2013 on COM(2012) 614.

50 Commission reply of 17.07.2013 to the Reasoned opinion of the Polish Sejm on COM(2012) 614.

51 Case C-232/09 *Danosa*, ECLI:EU:C:2010:674, para 56.

B. The Draft Legislative Act Pursues a Different Objective from that Indicated in the Legal Basis

The second strand of arguments regarding competence violations relies on Article 5(2) TEU, which states that the EU may take action 'only within the limits of the competences conferred upon it by the Member States in the treaties to attain the *objectives* set out therein' (emphasis added). Following the wording of the treaty, national parliaments argue that the Commission anchors its proposals in an incorrect legal basis, as the draft legislative act pursues a different objective than that stipulated in the treaty provision in question.

The series of Commission proposals on aid to the most deprived people in the EU illustrates this problem well. In 2010, following the reform of the Common Agricultural Policy (CAP), the Commission proposed a regulation on the distribution of food products to the most deprived persons in the EU.[52] The proposal, amending the existing legislation in this area, was supposed to guarantee the aims of the CAP and help achieve cohesion objectives.[53] Its aim was to establish a scheme to distribute food products to the most deprived persons in the EU through Member State organisations. The products were to be made available from intervention stocks, but they could have also been purchased on the market. The national parliaments, in their reasoned opinions, questioned the extent to which purchases from the market contribute to the objectives of the CAP, maintaining instead that the objective shifted from having been an agricultural policy measure to a social policy measure.[54] The Commission withdrew the proposal because of a CJEU judgment, stating that purchases from the market for deprived persons could not be made under the auspices of agricultural legislation.[55] In consequence, the Commission revised the proposal and added Article 175(3) TFEU as the legal basis, relating to economic, social and territorial cohesion, now as a joint legal basis together with Articles 42 and 43(2) TFEU on the fulfilment of the objectives of the CAP.[56] National parliaments maintained, however, that the proposal's objective is extended to social policy.[57] Nevertheless, the proposal was adopted, and the supply of food to the most deprived people was extended to the end of 2013.[58]

[52] 'Amended proposal for a Regulation of the European Parliament and the Council amending Council Regulations (EC) No 1290/2005 and (EC) No 1234/2007, as regards distribution of food products to the most deprived persons in the Union' COM(2010) 486, final.

[53] Motive (2) of the preamble.

[54] See, eg, the Danish Folketing, Reasoned opinion of 15.11.2011; Swedish Riksdag, Reasoned opinion of 10.11.2010; Dutch Eerste Kamer, Reasoned opinion of 30.11.2010, all on COM(2010) 486. The Danish Folketing (07.03.2011) and the Swedish Riksdag (09.03.2011) maintained the same position with regard to COM(2010) 799 on common organisation of agricultural markets and on specific provisions for certain agricultural products, which included provision regarding distribution of food products to the most deprived persons in the Union. Other examples include the Reasoned opinion of the Czech Poslanecká sněmovna of 14.10.2015 on COM(2015) 450 (the proposal pursues adoption of emergency measures for migration flows, while the legal basis concerns standard situations).

[55] Case T-576/08 *Germany v Commission*, ECLI:EU:T:2011:166.

[56] 'Amended proposal for a Regulation of the European Parliament and the Council amending Council Regulation (EC) No 1290/2005 and Council Regulation (EC) No 1234/2007 as regards distribution of food products to the most deprived persons in the Union' COM(2011) 634, final.

[57] Swedish Riksdag, Reasoned opinion of 01.12.2011; UK House of Lords, Reasoned opinion of 11.11.2011 both on COM(2011) 634.

[58] Regulation (EU) No 121/2012 of the European Parliament and of the Council of 15 February 2012 amending Council Regulations (EC) No 1290/2005 and (EC) No 1234/2007 as regards distribution of food products to the most deprived persons in the EU [2012] OJ L44/1.

In the meantime, in 2012 the Commission proposed a new instrument, namely, the Fund for European Aid to the Most Deprived, based on Article 175(3) TFEU, which enables the EU to make provisions for specific actions outside the Structural Funds and is therefore no longer anchored in the CAP.[59] Nonetheless, the German Bundestag maintained that the legal basis provided by the Commission does not include a competence for combating poverty, and the proposal concerns the implementation of social policy, which falls within the remit of the Member States of the EU.[60] The Commission, however, replied that the proposal aims to contribute to enhancing the social cohesion of the EU, and as foreseen by Article 175 TFEU, the fund will complement the EU financial mechanisms promoting social cohesion that are already in place.[61] In other words, the Commission did not consider the fund a part of the social policy and left the legal basis of the proposal intact. The proposal was adopted in 2014 with its legal basis—Article 175(3) TFEU—also unchanged by the EU legislator.[62]

Overall, the saga on aid for the most deprived persons depicts the critical approach of national parliaments to the Commission's choice of a treaty anchor and the argument that the proposal allegedly pursues objectives other than those stated in that legal basis.[63] Nonetheless, national parliaments are not quite correct in their assessment of this issue. In fact, the Lisbon Treaty added 'mainstreaming clauses' that oblige EU institutions to take into account in defining and implementing its policies and activities requirements linked to, among others, the guarantee of adequate social protection and the fight against social exclusion (Article 9 TFEU).[64]

C. List of the Areas of 'Exclusive National Competence'

The examples presented above show a sensitivity of national parliaments to the validity of the legal basis chosen by the Commission for its proposals. This is not just a purely legal control of the principle of conferral. In fact, the use of the EWS for the review of issues other than subsidiarity, and specifically for the scrutiny of EU competence to act, is quite telling when it comes to the reach and the purpose of European integration as seen from the perspective of national parliaments. Their views, previously voiced only through their respective governments in the Council, inform the debate on the division of competence in the EU. Specifically, in the view of national parliaments, the criticised Commission proposals breach the principle of conferral as they touch upon an 'exclusive competence of Member States'.

[59] 'Proposal for a Regulation of the European Parliament and the Council on the Fund for European Aid to the Most Deprived' COM(2012) 617 final. See Impact Assessment, SWD(2012) 350, 25.

[60] German Bundestag, Reasoned opinion of 12.12.2012 on COM(2012) 617.

[61] Commission reply of 23.5.2013 to the German Bundestag on COM(2012) 617.

[62] Regulation (EU) No 223/2014 of the European Parliament and of the Council of 11 March 2014 on the Fund for European Aid to the Most Deprived [2014] OJ L72/1.

[63] Similarly, national parliaments maintained that a proposal introducing the Common Financial Transaction Tax aims to create a new EU budget income resource and is not directed at a smooth functioning of the internal market. See Cypriot Parliament, Reasoned opinion of 02.12.2011; Swedish Riksdag, Reasoned opinion of 01.12.2011; Maltese Parliament, Reasoned opinion of 12.12.2011, all on COM(2011) 594.

[64] B de Witte, 'A competence to protect. The pursuit of non-market aims through internal market legislation' in P Syrpis (ed), *The Judiciary, the Legislature and the EU Internal Market* (Cambridge, Cambridge University Press, 2012) 32.

The notion of exclusive competence, often used by national parliaments, cannot be found in the same wording in the Treaties, which instead speak of an exclusive Member State competence in the sense that 'competences not conferred upon the Union in the Treaties remain with the Member States'.[65] However, some of the treaty provisions bar certain matters from EU regulation, for example, Article 153(5) TFEU, which is drafted as excluding the EU's support and complementation of the activities of the Member States with regard to pay, the right of association, the right to strike, and the right to impose lock-outs.

Areas that reasoned opinions consistently qualify as an 'exclusive competence', as a 'national competence', or as remaining under national sovereignty are the following: corporate tax,[66] combating poverty,[67] substantive family law,[68] maritime spatial plans and integrated coastal management strategies (substantive spatial planning law),[69] some aspects of criminal law,[70] emergency services,[71] management of the national statistical system,[72] management and assignment of radio spectrum,[73] maintaining public order and internal security,[74] security policy and social rights,[75] permanent residency in the Member State,[76] operating restrictions and noise abatement at EU airports,[77] access to and sharing of benefits from genetic resources and traditional knowledge concerning genetic resources,[78] management of spectrum in electronic communications,[79] access to information on economic operators,[80] registering geographical indication of spirit drinks,[81] and the functioning and supervision of pensions systems.[82] Moreover, national parliaments argue that deciding on expenditure and revenue in the national budget is a national concern.[83]

[65] Art 5(2) TEU.

[66] Irish Dail Eireann, Reasoned opinion of 17.05.2011; Slovak Národná Rada, Reasoned opinion of 12.05.2012; Polish Sejm, Reasoned opinion of 13.05.2011, all on COM(2011) 121; Swedish Riksdag, Reasoned opinion of 10.06.2016 on COM(2016) 198; Danish Folketing, Reasoned opinion of 22.12.2016 on COM(2016) 683 and 685; Irish Houses of the Oireachtas, Reasoned opinion of 14.12.2016 on COM(2016) 683 and 685; Swedish Riksdag, Reasoned opinion of 15.12.2016 on COM(2016) 687.

[67] Swidish Riksdag, Reasoned opinion of 04.03.2011 on COM(2010) 799; Swidish Riksdag, Reasoned opinion of 01.12.2011 on COM(2011) 634; German Bundestag, Reasoned opinion of 12.12.2012 on COM(2012) 617.

[68] Polish Sejm, Reasoned opinion of 26.05.2011 on COM(2011) 127.

[69] Lithuanian Seimas, Reasoned opinion of 07.05.2013; Finish Eduskunta, Reasoned opinion of 08.05.2013; Dutch Twede Kamer, Reasoned opinion of 25.04.2013; Dutch Erste Kamer, Reasoned opinion of 25.04.2013; and German Bundesrat, reasoned opinion of 03.05.2013 all on COM(2013) 133.

[70] Swidish Riksdag, Reasoned opinion of 17.10.2012 on COM(2012) 363; German Bundesrat, Reasoned opinion of 30.03.2012 on COM(2012) 10.

[71] As a competence of German Länder; German Bundesrat, Reasoned opinion of 02.03.2012 on COM (2011) 897.

[72] As a competence of Spanish regions and Austrian Länder; Spanish Cortes Generales, Reasoned opinion of 13.06.2012 and Austrian Bundesrat, Reasoned opinion of 12.06.2012 both on COM(2012) 167.

[73] Swedish Riksdag, Reasoned opinion of 16.12.2016 on COM(2016) 590.

[74] Portuguese Assembleia da República, Reasoned opinion of 04.11.2011; Swedish Riksdag, Reasoned opinion of 10.11.2011 and Dutch Eerste and Tweede Kamer, Reasoned opinion of 08.11.2011, all on COM (2011) 560.

[75] Polish Senat, Reasoned opinion of 21.10.2016 on COM(2016) 270.

[76] Czech Poslanecká sněmovna, Reasoned opinion of 22.09.2016 on COM(2016) 270.

[77] German Bundesrat, Reasoned opinion of 07.02.2011 on COM(2011) 828.

[78] Swedish Riksdag, Reasoned opinion of 20.12.2012 and French Sénat, Reasoned opinion of 20.12.2012, both on COM(2012) 576.

[79] Irish Parliament, Reasoned opinion of 23.10.2013 and Maltese Kamra tad-Deputati, Reasoned opinion of 07.11.2013, both on COM(2013) 627.

[80] Spanish Cortes Generales, Reasoned opinion of 21.01.2014 on COM(2013) 796.

[81] Italian Senato della Repubblica, Reasoned opinion of 03.03.2017 on COM(2016) 750.

[82] Tweede Kamer, Reasoned opinion of 15.05.2014 on COM(2014) 147.

[83] Swedish Riksdag, Reasoned opinion of 25.01.2012 on COM(2011) 821.

What do we learn from this list? First, the competences selected by national parliaments significantly vary, a situation which shows that Member States may have different sensibilities. Second, national parliaments perceive issues such as family and criminal law and their security as reserved for Member States, similar to social measures—the fight against poverty or supervision of pensions or close to the budgetary prerogatives: taxation and decisions on expenditure and revenue. The main problem, however, is the quality of the criticism of national parliaments; the notions such as 'family', 'criminal', 'social', or 'tax' seem to be 'buzz words' for national parliaments, leading to some simplifications. The reasoned opinions appear to generalise and be rather superficial with regard to the assessment of competences. The clearest example is the draft regulation of recognition and enforcement of decisions concerning property consequences of registered partnerships that, in the view of the Polish Sejm, implied the violation of exclusive national competence on substantive family law and the introduction of partnerships into national law through the 'back door'.[84]

IV. SPECIAL CASES: ARTICLE 114 AND ARTICLE 352 TFEU

This section discusses, first, whether the Lisbon Treaty endows national parliaments with special scrutiny powers to review draft legislative acts based on Articles 114 and 352 TFEU. Second, focusing on Article 114 TFEU, this section demonstrates how the scrutiny of the internal market clause is pursued by national parliaments without being anchored in an enabling provision in the Treaty. Third, this section puts forward the reasons why, instead, some national parliaments argue for Article 352 TFEU as a more appropriate basis.

A considerable number of reasoned opinions concern draft legislative acts based on Articles 114 TFEU and 352 TFEU. The former provision concerns the approximation of laws in the internal market, and the latter provides the EU with a foundation to legislate when EU action is necessary to attain one of the treaty objectives in cases in which the Treaty did not foresee such a power for the EU (the so-called 'flexibility clause').[85] As a consequence of these 'functional competences', the EU may legislate in fields wherein a specific policy legal basis is not given.[86]

The opposition of national parliaments to Commission proposals based on Articles 114 and 352 TFEU does not come as a surprise. The Laeken Declaration saw the predecessors of both provisions as guilty of 'competence creep'.[87] However, the drafters of the Constitutional Treaty proposed some role for national parliaments only with regard to control of Article 308 EC (current Article 352 TFEU).[88] The omission to grant the national parliaments involvement with regard to Article 95 EC (current Article 114 TFEU) arguably seems not to be a conscious design but, rather, a consequence of spreading the question of competences between different working groups within the Convention on the Future of Europe.[89]

[84] Polish Sejm, Reasoned opinion of 27.05.2011 on COM(2011) 127 and the Commission reply to the Polish Sejm of 26.01.2012 on COM(2011) 127.

[85] On the history of Art 352 TFEU in legislative practice see Weiler (n 11) 2444.

[86] de Búrca and de Witte (n 16) 214.

[87] Weatherill, 'The Limits of Legislative Harmonization' (n 15) 855.

[88] Art I-18(2) of the Constitutional Treaty. Its wording is the same as Art 352(2) TFEU.

[89] Weatherill, 'The Limits of Legislative Harmonization' (n 15) 856.

Under the Lisbon Treaty, which did not significantly change the internal market provision or the 'flexibility clause', no specific, legal-basis-oriented control rights are conferred upon the national parliaments, especially with regard to Article 114 TFEU. Only Article 352(2) TFEU refers to national parliaments: 'Using the procedure for monitoring the subsidiarity principle referred to in Article 5(3) of the Treaty on European Union, the Commission shall draw national Parliaments' attention to proposals based on this Article'.

Despite the quite strict, but clear, wording of Article 352(2) TFEU on 'drawing attention of national parliaments', some commentators note that the EWS procedure should be used to alert national parliaments in this respect, including the legal basis of the proposal at stake.[90] This approach has been championed, for example, by the UK House of Commons, which labelled Article 352(2) TFEU as an 'extra ground' for challenging Commission proposals.[91]

Another reading of the phrasing of Article 352(2) TFEU is that the Commission has only to highlight to national parliaments that the proposal is anchored in the flexibility clause, without changing the original role of national parliaments in the EU legislative process. This 'more natural interpretation' is grounded in the fact that the 'flexibility clause' involves an exceptional use of EU legislative power, and therefore the Commission should highlight such proposals to a national parliament which, in turn, might challenge those proposals on the grounds of subsidiarity violation.[92] This is also the interpretation of the Commission which, by rejecting the first 'yellow card', excluded that the EWS should involve scrutiny of the legal base in the case of proposals based on Article 352 TFEU.[93]

The internal market provision is even less friendly to national parliaments. Article 114 TFEU does not even include a 'national parliaments clause' comparable to that in Article 352 TFEU. In consequence, by not providing specific scrutiny rights for Article 114 TFEU, the Lisbon Treaty with Protocol No 2 opened opportunities for national parliaments to reprimand the Commission's choice of legal basis.[94]

Indeed, on a number of occasions national parliaments have raised questions with regard to Commission proposals based on the internal market clause. In those cases, national parliaments pointed out that the internal market regulation was not the main objective of the proposal,[95] the proposal aimed at harmonisation of purely national situations,[96]

[90] A Rosas and L Armati, *EU Constitutional Law: An Introduction* (Oxford, Hart Publishing, 2010) 42; Weatherill, 'The Limits of Legislative Harmonization' (n 15) 853.

[91] See UK House of Commons, Reasoned opinion of 12.02.2014 on COM(2013) 893, point 8. In the case at stake, although the Art 352 as the proposal's legal basis seemed 'highly doubtful' to the chamber it relied on other arguments to challenge the proposal in question.

[92] Craig, *EU Administrative Law* (n 6) 388.

[93] See section V of this chapter.

[94] Weatherill, 'The Limits of Legislative Harmonization' (n 15) 855–57 and S Weatherill, 'Better Competence Monitoring' (2005) 30 *European Law Review* 23, 37.

[95] UK House of Commons, Reasoned opinion of 09.11.2011 on COM(2011) 452. It was argued that the primary objective is the prudential supervision of banks. Similarly, see the reasoned opinions of the Bulgarian Narodno Sabranie (28.02.2013), Italian Camera dei Deputati (19.02.2013), Czech Poslanecká sněmovna (24.01.2013) on COM (2012) 788. These chambers argued that the proposal aims at regulating public health, which is under the scope of Art 168 TFEU.

[96] German Bundesrat, Reasoned opinion of 24.01.2012 on COM(2011) 793 stated that 'in the case of purely domestic transactions, there is no sound reason for obliging Member States to adopt measures for a legal protection system for alternative dispute settlement with a view to promoting cross-border trade'.

the proposal's reference to Article 114 was insufficient,[97] or harmonisation in a specific field was excluded.[98] Moreover, according to national parliaments, cases wherein the Commission introduces a system in parallel to existing national provisions do not fall within the scope of Article 114 TFEU.[99]

The draft of the Common European Sales Law illustrates the concerns of national parliaments with regard to Article 114 TFEU as a legal basis.[100] In October 2011, the Commission proposed a regulation to reduce differences between Member States in contract law, which hinder traders and consumers from engaging in cross-border trade within the internal market.[101] The Common European Sales Law, as a 'self-standing uniform set of contract law rules including provisions to protect consumers', would run as 'a second contract law regime within the national law of each Member State'.[102] In their replies to the Commission, national parliaments criticised the legal basis of the proposal. The Austrian Bundesrat and the German Bundesrat argued that Article 114 TFEU could not be used as a legal basis for legal acts that exist in parallel to national laws.[103] Similarly, the Belgian Chambre des représentants and the Belgian Sénat opined that the proposal did not aim to approximate national sales law provisions, as it neither replaces nor harmonises them.

Interestingly, in the Common European Sales Law case, the Austrian Bundesrat, the German Bundesrat and the Belgian Sénat proposed that a more appropriate legal basis for the proposal would be Article 352 TFEU. The Commission replied that Article 114 TFEU is the correct legal basis in the case at stake because the aim of the proposal is to remove obstacles to cross-border transactions in the internal market, a situation which can be achieved even with an optional instrument.[104] In contrast, the Commission rejected Article 352 TFEU as an alternative legal basis for the proposal, basing the argumentation on the Court's case law that the flexibility clause can be applied only 'if no other legal basis, in particular Article 114 TFEU, is applicable'.[105]

Sometimes national parliaments suggest to the Commission a correct legal basis for its proposal.[106] In a number of cases, national parliaments put forward specifically

[97] Austrian Nationalrat, Reasoned opinion of 17.04.2012 on COM(2012) 84 argued that Art 114 is not sufficient to cover the organisation of statutory health systems of Member States, which the proposal intends to do.

[98] Polish Sejm, Reasoned opinion of 10.10.2012 on COM(2012) 369 argued that Art 179(3) TFEU excludes harmonisation of clinical trials.

[99] Italian Senato della Repubblica, Reasoned opinion of 30.01.2013 on COM(2012) 788.

[100] 'Proposal for a Regulation of the European Parliament and of the Council on a Common European Sales Law' COM(2011) 635 final.

[101] Explanatory Memorandum, 1.

[102] ibid 4 and 6.

[103] Austrian Bundesrat, Reasoned opinion of 30.11.2011; German Bundestag, Reasoned opinion of 01.12.2011; Belgian Chambre des représentants, Reasoned opinion of 09.12.2011; and Belgian Sénat, Reasoned opinion of 09.12.2011, all on COM(2011) 635.

[104] See, eg, the Commission reply of 10.01.2013 to the Austrian Bundesrat on COM(2011) 635.

[105] ibid.

[106] Both Dutch chambers, Reasoned opinion of 08.11.2011; Portuguese Assembleia da República, Reasoned opinion of 04.11.2011; Swedish Riksdag, Reasoned opinion of 10.11.2011 and Romanian Senatul, Reasoned opinion of 09.11.2011, all on COM(2011) 560. They propose substituting Art 77(1)(2) with Art 72 TFEU. See also Spanish Cortes Generales, Reasoned opinion of 14.06.2011 on COM(2011) 216. It proposes exchanging Art 118(1) with Art 118(2) TFEU. In none of those cases did the Commission's reply suggest that it will amend the legal basis accordingly. See, eg, the Commission reply of 05.06.2012 to the Dutch Eerste and Tweede Kamer on COM(2011) 560; and the Commission reply of 11.01.2012 to the Spanish Cortes Generales on COM(2011) 216.

Article 352 TFEU as an appropriate legal basis for the contested EU draft legislative act.[107] The reason for the suggestion of Article 352 TFEU as the legal basis is twofold. First, the Council has to unanimously agree to the legal acts based on Article 352 TFEU. Second, in some Member States, the national provisions demand that the national parliament has to consent to a Commission proposal based on Article 352 TFEU before a national minister votes in the Council. For example, in such a case, German law demands that the German representative in the Council receives the consent of the Bundestag expressed in a legal act before that representative can agree to the proposal in the Council.[108] Similarly, the UK Parliament has to consent in an Act of Parliament before a minister can agree to the proposal in the Council.[109] Milder means, such as those in Poland, include that a minister asks for the opinion of the parliament before consenting in the Council to a legal act based on Article 352 TFEU.[110]

Despite the suggestions of national parliaments to change the legal basis of the EU draft legislative acts to Article 352 TFEU, the Commission remained firm on its position. The Commission's argumentation against such an amendment of the legal basis to Article 352 TEU is the same as in the case of the proposal for a Common European Sales Law, namely, that this provision applies only to the cases wherein treaties do not confer necessary powers on the EU.[111]

The following section discusses the first 'yellow card' triggered by national parliaments. In their reasoned opinions, national parliaments focused to a large extent on the lack of competence of the EU to act and to apply the flexibility clause.

V. CASE STUDY: THE 'YELLOW CARD' ON THE RIGHT TO STRIKE PROPOSAL

Chapter three has already dealt with the Commission proposal on the right to strike: its background, the content of the proposal, the reasoned opinions issued by the national parliaments, and the reply of the Commission. The aim of this section is to comment on the outcome of the first 'yellow card' and its meaning for the relationship between the principles of conferral and subsidiarity.

A. The Legal Basis of the Proposal

In 2012, the Commission put forward a proposal for a Council regulation 'on the exercise of the right to take collective action within the context of the freedom of establishment and

[107] Danish Folketing, Reasoned opinion of 15.11.2010 and Swedish Riksdag, Reasoned opinion of 10.11.2010, both on COM(2010) 486; Danish Folketing, Reasoned opinion of 07.03.2011 and Swedish Riksdag, Reasoned opinion of 09.03.2011, both on COM(2010) 799; Austrian Nationalrat, Reasoned opinion of 28.05.2014 and Austrian Bundesrat, Reasoned opinion of 27.05.2014, both on COM(2014) 212; Hungarian Országgyűlés, Reasoned opinion of 03.11.2015 on COM(2015) 450.

[108] §8 Integrationsverantwortungsgesetz vom 22 September 2009 (BGBl I S 3022), geändert durch Artikel 1 des Gesetzes vom 1 Dezember 2009 (BGBl I S 3822). This provision, introduced at the request of the German Federal Constitutional Court in the Lisbon judgment is criticised as going 'too far', because of the 'danger of lack of flexibility'. See C Calliess and T Beichelt, 'The Europeanization of the Bundestag: From Observer to Player?' [2013] *Bertelsmann Stiftung* 12.

[109] P Craig, 'The European Union Act 2011: Locks, limits and legality' (2011) 48 *Common Market Law Review* 1881, 1884.

[110] Art 10 of the Act on Cooperation.

[111] See the Commission reply of 12.08.2014 to the Austrian Nationalrat on COM(2014) 212; Commission reply of 23.02.2016 to the Hungarian Parliament on COM(2015) 450.

the freedom to provide services'.[112] The aim of the proposal was to 'lay down the general principles and rules applicable at Union level with respect to the exercise of the fundamental right to take collective action within the context of the freedom of establishment and the freedom to provide services'.[113]

The explanatory memorandum in the proposal provided a clarification of its legal elements.[114] The Commission proposal was based on Article 352 TFEU, with a short justification of lacking 'explicit provision in the Treaty for the necessary powers'.[115] In addition, the Commission explained that, although 'Article 153(5) TFEU excludes the right to strike from the range of matters that can be regulated across the EU by way of minimum standards through Directives', 'the Court rulings have clearly shown that the fact that Article 153 does not apply to the right to strike does not as such exclude collective action from the scope of EU law'.[116]

The Commission argued that the stated objective of clarifying the general principles and EU rules applicable to the right to strike and fundamental freedoms demands EU action and cannot be achieved by Member States alone.[117] Additional aspects ensuring the subsidiarity compliance included the role of national courts in deciding on the proportionality of actions; national laws on the exercise of the right to strike were not affected by the proposal, and no changes in the existing alternative dispute-settlement institutions at national level were foreseen.[118]

In sum, seeking to achieve the aim of reconciling the protection of the right to strike with the fundamental freedom of establishment and the fundamental freedom to provide services, and to provide legal certainty in this respect at EU level, the regulation highlighted the question of the EU's competence to act. The questions were whether the Commission proposal was founded on a correct legal basis and whether the sidestepping of Article 153(5) TFEU was well justified.

B. The Reasoned Opinions of the National Parliaments

The Commission proposal for a regulation on the exercise of the right to take collective action was the first to trigger the 'yellow card' procedure. Twelve national parliaments issued reasoned opinions, and the opinions of seven unicameral (14 votes) and five bicameral (five votes) parliaments amounted to 19 votes.

The main issue that national parliaments criticised was the legal basis of the proposal.[119] The reasoned opinions raised concerns about both the application of the flexibility clause

[112] 'Proposal for a Council Regulation on the exercise of the right to take collective action within the context of the freedom of establishment and the freedom to provide services' COM(2012) 130 final. The proposal drew from the report of 09.05.2010 by former Commissioner Mario Monti (M Monti, *A New Strategy for the Single Market*) and is hence often labelled as the Monti II Regulation. The Monti report was the basis for a number of proposals. See Communication from the Commission, 'Towards a Single Market Act. For a Highly Competitive Social Market Economy' COM(2010) 623, proposal No 30.

[113] Art 1(1) of the proposal.

[114] Explanatory Memorandum, 10.

[115] ibid 11.

[116] ibid.

[117] ibid.

[118] ibid.

[119] For a detailed discussion of other arguments of reasoned opinions see ch 3.

(Article 352 TFEU) and Article 153(5) TFEU. Some of the national parliaments argued that the proposal did not satisfy the conditions for the use of Article 352 TFEU, for instance, it did not identify the objective of the treaties that it aimed to pursue.[120] Furthermore, national parliaments sustained that Article 153(5) TFEU excludes EU action in the area of the right to strike, while the flexibility clause cannot serve as a legal basis in cases in which harmonisation of national laws is excluded according to Article 352(3) TFEU.[121] Finally, a reasoned opinion claimed that labour law is a national question 'par excellence'.[122]

C. Outcome

The Commission decided to withdraw the draft regulation on the right to strike; however it maintained that the proposal complies with the principle of subsidiarity. As the reason for the withdrawal, the Commission cited the potential difficulties in the EP and the Council.[123] Moreover, the Commission explained that the opinions of the national parliaments had raised a number of issues, but they had essentially failed to identify a subsidiarity violation in the Commission proposal.[124]

Later, the Commission justified the use of Article 352 TFEU as the legal basis of the proposal with the absence of an explicit provision in the Treaty.[125] The Commission maintained its previous argument, expressed in the explanatory memorandum of the proposal, that the Court's judgments 'have clearly shown that the fact that Article 153 does not apply to the right to strike does not exclude collective action from the scope of EU law'.[126]

The compliance of this proposal with the subsidiarity principle was discussed in more detail in chapter three. With regard to the legal basis, it is clear that the Commission did not spend much effort in its arguments concerning the suitability of the legal basis. Basically, in its replies to national parliaments participating in the first yellow card procedure, it repeated the arguments from its explanatory memorandum. The Commission interpreted Article 153(5) TFEU as only prohibiting the harmonisation of national labour laws,[127] without impairing the EU from the ability 'to clarify the general principles and EU rules applicable to the exercise of the fundamental right to take industrial action within the

[120] Finnish Eduskunta, Reasoned opinion of 16.05.2012 on COM(2012) 130; Latvian Saeima, Reasoned opinion of 18.05.2012 on COM(2012) 130, point 3; Swedish Riksdag, Reasoned opinion of 11.05.2012 on COM(2012) 130; Belgian Chambre des représentants, Reasoned opinion of 30.05.2012 on COM(2012) 130; Luxembourg Chambre des Députés, Reasoned opinion of 15.05.2012 on COM(2012) 130; Portuguese Assembleia da República, Reasoned opinion of 18.05.2012 on COM(2012) 130; Dutch Tweede Kamer, Reasoned opinion of 22.05.2012 on COM(2012) 130, 2.

[121] Luxembourg Chambre des Députés, Reasoned opinion of 15.05.2012 on COM(2012) 130; French Sénat, Reasoned opinion of 22.05.2012 on COM(2012) 130; Maltese Kamra tad-Deputati, Reasoned opinion of 22.05.2012 on COM(2012) 130, paras 1–2; Portuguese Assembleia da República, Reasoned opinion of 18.05.2012 on COM(2012) 130, Part II let A; Danish Folketing, Reasoned opinion of 03.05.2012 on COM(2012) 130.

[122] Belgian Chambre des représentants, Reasoned opinion of 30.05.2012 on COM(2013) 130.

[123] See as letter of 12.09.2012 from the Commission to the Italian Senato, Ares(2012) 1058907.

[124] ibid.

[125] See, eg, the Commission reply of 14.03.2013 to the Portuguese Parliament on COM(2012) 130.

[126] ibid.

[127] EU harmonization of national strike laws was proposed in the 1970s by Antoine Jacobs: A Jacobs, 'Towards Community Action on Strike Law?' (1978) 15 *Common Market Law Review* 129.

context of the [single market]'.[128] Instead, the Commission could have used a teleological argument, namely, that Article 153(5) TFEU, drafted by a number of Member States with comparatively well-developed systems of protection of industrial action, aimed to defend their national systems from the influence of EU law.[129] The *Viking* and *Laval* judgments, however, removed this expectation by denying that Article 153(5) TFEU may limit the application of the EU free movement rules in cases in which action by trade unions obstructed the freedom of establishment or freedom to provide services.[130] In this context, the original aim to shield Member State industrial relations systems from EU law pursued by Article 153(5) TFEU has to be abandoned, and the EU can act to safeguard a better protection of labour rights.

VI. CONCLUSION

This chapter explored how national parliaments acting within the EWS also verify whether EU legislative acts remain within the limits of the principle of conferral. Such a check upon the existence of EU competence to act is not unexpected, especially taking into account the close links between the principles of conferral and subsidiarity. National parliaments often find Commission proposals as aiming to regulate an area that remains outside the legal basis suggested in the proposal and as pursuing an additional, different objective from that indicated in the legal basis. Moreover, the reasoned opinions, which assess the principle of conferral, provide a first account of the areas in which national parliaments call for national sovereignty or ascertain an 'exclusive competence' of the Member States. While the reasoned opinions of national parliaments may be interpreted as giving a new perspective on the limits of EU integration from the bottom-up point of view, this chapter pointed out that their assessment of the legal basis of Commission proposals often misses the point.

Moreover, this chapter analysed the reasoned opinions concerning proposals based on Articles 114 and 352 TFEU, always perceived as a main source of EU 'competence creep'. The proposals based on the internal market clause have attracted the special interest of national parliaments and, in addition, the first yellow card was triggered with regard to the Commission proposal on the right to strike, based on the flexibility clause. With regard to proposals based on Article 114 TFEU, national parliaments maintained, among other arguments, that the internal market regulation was not the main objective of the proposal or that the proposal aimed at harmonisation of purely national situations. Within the first yellow card, the national parliaments criticised the use of Article 352 TFEU as its legal basis and argued that the EU cannot legislate on the right to strike. The *Viking* and *Laval* judgments, however, have shown that the right to strike is not insulated from EU law and that the EU can act to safeguard a better protection of labour rights.

As in the case of the yellow card on the right to strike proposal, the Commission remains unconvinced of the criticism of national parliaments regarding the legal basis of the legislative proposals. The study of Commission replies to the reasoned opinions

[128] Explanatory Memorandum, 10.

[129] F Fabbrini, 'Europe in Need of a New Deal: On Federalism, Free Market, and the Right to Strike' (2012) 43 *Georgetown Journal of International Law* 1175, 1243.

[130] ibid.

and of the follow-ups to reasoned opinions in the 'Commission Reports on Subsidiarity and Proportionality' shows that thus far the Commission has never been influenced by the arguments raised by national parliaments concerning the compliance of its proposals with the principle of conferral. The Commission remains firm in its position, maintaining that proposals contribute to the pursued objectives[131] or do not call into question Member States' competences.[132] Over the years, in a positive development, the Commission has, however, started to offer a more detailed explanation with regard to the legal basis.[133]

[131] See, eg, the Commission reply of 18.04.2011 to the Danish Folketing, or of 04.04.2011 to the Swedish Riksdag on COM(2010) 486.

[132] See, eg, the Commission reply of 07.11.2011 to the Swedish Riksdag on COM(2011) 121 and of 29.05.2012 on COM(2011) 821.

[133] Compare the Reasoned opinion of 07.03.2011 of the Danish Folketing on COM(2010) 799 and the Commission reply to the Danish Folketing of 18.04.2011 on COM(2010)799 with Commission replies of 07.03.2016 to the Czech Poslanecká Sněmovna and Czech Senát on COM(2015) 450. In the first case, the Commission addresses the criticism of the legal basis only indirectly, while in the second case it offers a direct and longer justification of the legal basis of the proposal in the Annex.

7

Subsidiarity and the Delegation of Power in the EU

I. INTRODUCTION

THROUGH THEIR ACTIVE participation in the Early Warning System (EWS), national parliaments have claimed a new role with regard to the delegation of power to the Commission by means of delegated and implementing acts. When assessing EU legislative proposals, national parliaments often raise concerns about the delegations contained in the legislative proposal under review that allow the Commission to adopt a delegated or implementing act. A total of 62 reasoned opinions out of a total of 379 have evaluated delegations provided for in the drafts of EU legislative acts submitted by the Commission. Yet, this activity of national parliaments has been barely taken note of.[1]

The main aim of this chapter is to offer an overview and assess the concerns of national parliaments on delegations included in Commission proposals. Section II presents the concept of delegated and implementing acts as introduced by the Lisbon Treaty. Section III moves to an examination of the reasoned opinions issued by national parliaments, encompassing their concerns with regard to both types of delegated legislation—delegated and implementing acts. The case study of the Commission proposal on the Tobacco Products Directive highlights the main points raised by national parliaments with regard to delegations to the Commission to adopt a delegated act.[2] Beyond this case study, this section provides examples of other concerns voiced by national parliaments. Specifically, it discusses the issues raised with regard to delegations by means of implementing acts, along with the distinction between the two types of delegation. Next, this section analyses the Commission's replies to the national legislatures. It presents the Commission's arguments rebutting the concerns voiced in the reasoned opinions. Furthermore, this section examines the concerns of the national parliaments in light of the Court of Justice of the European Union (CJEU/Court) judgments of 2016 on the adopted Tobacco Products Directive.[3] Finally,

[1] See, however, that the COSAC 16th Bi-annual Report of October 2011 mentions this type of scrutiny of national parliaments. With regard to the Polish Parliament's scrutiny of the delegations by means of delegated acts (only), see A Grzelak and J Łacny, 'Kontrola przestrzegania unijnej zasady pomocniczości przez parlamenty narodowe–pierwsze doświadczenia' (2011) 32 *Zeszyty Prawnicze* 11, 28.

[2] 'Proposal for a Directive of the European Parliament and of the Council on the approximation of the laws, regulations and administrative provisions of the Member States concerning the manufacture, presentation and sale of tobacco and related products' COM(2012) 788 final.

[3] Directive 2014/40/EU of the European Parliament and of the Council of 3 April 2014 on the approximation of the laws, regulations and administrative provisions of the Member States concerning the manufacture, presentation and sale of tobacco and related products and repealing Directive 2001/37/EC [2014] OJ L127/1.

section IV examines the broader question of whether under the EWS national parliaments should assess the delegations of power conferred on the Commission.

II. DELEGATED AND IMPLEMENTING ACTS

Comitology came into existence in the 1960s, when the Council delegated some of its implementing powers to the Commission. An implementing act was an act based on a legislative act; it implemented the legislative act.[4] The committees staffed with representatives of Member States offered the Commission some input into the creation of implementing acts.[5]

The Single European Act formally recognised comitology: the Council shall 'confer on the Commission the powers for the implementation of the rules which the Council lays down'.[6] The Comitology Decisions of 1987 and 1999 set out for the first time the procedures for the exercise of implementing powers in which the Commission was assisted by an advisory, management, or regulatory committee.[7] In 2006, a new regulatory procedure with scrutiny was added, allowing the European Parliament (EP) to block draft implementing measures.[8] The complexity of the comitology system led some to label it 'an apt neologism—a phenomenon that requires its very own science, which no single person has mastered'.[9]

The Lisbon reform introduced Article 290 of the Treaty on the Functioning of the European Union (TFEU), which deals with delegated acts, while Article 291 TFEU governs implementing acts.[10] Article 290(1) TFEU states that a legislative act can delegate to the Commission the power to 'adopt non-legislative acts of general application to supplement or amend certain non-essential elements of the legislative act'. Moreover, as provided by Article 290(2) TFEU, the legislative act should contain the 'objectives, content, scope and duration of the delegation of power'. Only the legislative act can provide for the 'essential elements' of an area under regulation.[11] Article 290(3) TFEU abandoned the comitology regime for the delegated acts and introduced two safeguards instead. First, the EP or the Council may decide to revoke the delegation; second, the EP or the Council may express an objection within a period stipulated in the legislative act.

[4] Case 25/70 *Köster*, ECLI:EU:C:1970:115.

[5] On the development of the comitology system see A Héritier et al, *Changing Rules of Delegation: A Contest for Power in Comitology* (Oxford, Oxford University Press, 2013) 4–7.

[6] Art 202 of the EC Treaty.

[7] Council Decision of 13 July 1987, laying down the procedures for the exercise of implementing powers conferred on the Commission [1987] OJ L197/33 and Council Decision 1999/468/EC of 28 June 1999 laying down the procedures for the exercise of implementing powers conferred on the Commission [1999] OJ L184/23.

[8] Council Decision 2006/512/EC of 17 July 2006 amending Decision 1999/468/EC [2006] OJ L200/11.

[9] JHH Weiler, UR Haltern and FC Mayer, 'European Democracy and its Critique' (1995) 18 *West European Politics* 4, 9.

[10] See A Héritier, 'Institutional Change in Europe: Co-decision and Comitology Transformed' (2012) 50 *Journal of Common Market Studies* 38; B Driessen, 'Delegated legislation after the Treaty of Lisbon: An analysis of Article 290 TFEU' (2010) 35 *European Law Review* 837.

[11] Case C-355/10 *Parliament v Council*, ECLI:EU:C:2012:516, para 84.

In 2011, the Common Understanding, which builds on the Commission Communication of 2009,[12] introduced practical provisions and offered some clarifications to delegations of legislative power under Article 290 TFEU.[13] In 2016, the Interinstitutional Agreement on Better Law-Making replaced the Common Understanding of 2011 with a new Common Understanding.[14] The main novelty is the strengthened role of Member States' experts during the preparation and drawing up of delegated acts.[15] The Commission should report on the conclusions from the discussions with national experts that would take place in existing expert groups or during ad hoc meetings. Specifically, the Commission should report on how those conclusions will be taken into consideration in the planned delegated act. The experts will be able to react to the changes in the content of the draft delegated act. Although the involvement of national experts in the drafting of the delegated acts seems to benefit the Member States, it is at odds with the idea of abandoning the comitology system for that type of act. In addition, the Interinstitutional Agreement foresees an alignment of existing acts to the Lisbon Treaty by the end of 2016 and the establishment of a joint register of delegated acts by the end of 2017.[16]

Article 291 TFEU deals with implementing acts. Accordingly, implementation of EU law can take place either by the Member States themselves or by the Commission (or in some cases by the Council) 'where uniform conditions for implementing legally binding Union acts are needed'. Following Article 291(3) TFEU, the EP and the Council enacted Regulation 182/2011, which allows Member States to control the exercise of implementing powers by the Commission.[17] Regulation 182/2011 adopted two procedures: an examination procedure and an advisory procedure, applicable depending on the nature or impact of the implementing act.[18] Within the examination procedure, when the committee delivers a negative opinion, the Commission cannot adopt the draft implementing act. The Commission can appeal to the appeals committee; but, again, in the case of a negative opinion, the Commission is barred from adopting the measure at stake.[19] This veto power of the committee over the Commission presents a new, direct involvement of the Member States in the decision-making process.[20] In justified cases, the Commission can also adopt an implementing act applicable immediately without first submitting it to a committee.[21]

[12] 'Communication from the Commission to the European Parliament and the Council, Implementation of Article 290 of the Treaty on the Functioning of the European Union'COM(2009) 673 final.

[13] Council of the European Union, 'Common Understanding' 8753/11, 14.04.2011.

[14] Interinstitutional Agreement between the European Parliament, the Council of the European Union and the European Commission on Better Law-Making [2016] OJ L123/1 (Interinstitutional Agreement of 2016). See the annexed Common Understanding between the European Parliament, the Council and the Commission on Delegated Acts (Common Understanding of 2016).

[15] Common Understanding of 2016, paras 4–12.

[16] Interinstitutional Agreement of 2016, paras 27 and 29. See also Commission proposals COM(2016) 798 and COM(2016) 799 regarding the alignment of legislative acts which contain references to the regulatory procedure with scrutiny.

[17] Regulation No 182/2011 of the European Parliament and of the Council of 16 February 2011 laying down the rules and general principles concerning mechanisms for control by Member States of the Commission's exercise of implementing powers [2011] OJ L55/13.

[18] Art 2 of Regulation No 182/11.

[19] Art 6 of Regulation No 182/11.

[20] R Schütze, '"Delegated" Legislation in the (new) European Union: A Constitutional Analysis' (2011) 74 *Modern Law Review* 661, 689.

[21] Art 8 of Regulation No 182/11.

In practice, the choice between a delegated and an implementing act has been a problematic issue for EU institutions. Specifically, the Commission brought an action of annulment of a provision that conferred an implementing power on the Commission to specify fees payable to the European Chemicals Agency for the operation of Regulation 528/2012 on the marketing and use of biocidal products.[22] The question before the CJEU concerned the precise distinction between supplementation and implementation of a legislative act and in consequence the conferral of either delegated or implementing power. However, the Court did not provide such an explicit criterion and merely held to the wording of Articles 290 and 291 TFEU.[23] The CJEU pointed to the discretion of the EU legislature in conferring on the Commission either a delegated or an implementing power limiting the judicial review to manifest errors in the EU legislature's assessment.[24] The Court confirmed that in the case at stake, the EU legislature could reasonably take the view that the provision in question conferred implementing power to provide further detail in relation to the normative content of that act and that it did not supplement certain non-essential elements of a legislative act.[25] As this chapter will show, national parliaments do also take issue with a choice between conferral of power to adopt a delegated or an implementing act; however their reasoning is less nuanced.

Before embarking on specific analysis of the opinions of national parliaments, it should be recalled that Protocol No 2 of the Lisbon Treaty invests national parliaments with subsidiarity scrutiny of draft legislative acts only.[26] Specifically, Protocol No 2 defines 'draft legislative acts' as proposals from the Commission, initiatives from a group of Member States and the European Parliament, requests from the Court of Justice, recommendations from the European Central Bank, and requests from the European Investment Bank for the adoption of a legislative act.[27] Article 290 TFEU describes delegated acts as 'non-legislative acts of general application', reflecting the formal position[28] that under the Lisbon Treaty legislative acts are those made in accordance with the legislative procedure according to Article 289(3) TFEU.[29] In contrast, the Lisbon Treaty remains silent on the character of implementing acts. Article 291 TFEU does not label them 'non-legislative'. However, their 'executive nature' is not called into question.[30] Since under the Lisbon Treaty neither delegated nor implementing acts are legislative acts, national parliaments cannot put them under the subsidiarity review of Protocol No 2. In fact, if at all, national parliaments receive only the already enacted delegated or implementing act.[31] National parliaments do,

[22] Case C-427/12 *Commission v Parliament and Council (Biocides)*, ECLI:EU:C:2014:170.

[23] ibid, paras 38–39. See D Ritleng, 'The dividing line between delegated and implementing acts: the Court of Justice sidesteps the difficulty in *Commission v Parliament and Council (Biocides)*' 52 *Common Market Law Review* 243, 251.

[24] C-427/12 *Commission v Parliament and Council*, para 40.

[25] ibid, para 51.

[26] Additionally, Art 1 of Protocol No 1 grants national parliaments information rights, as they receive consultation documents directly from the Commission (green and white papers and communications and the annual legislative programme) and any other instruments of legislative planning or policy.

[27] Art 3 of Protocol No. 2.

[28] For a 'material' or 'functional' concept of legislation, see Schütze (n 20) 662.

[29] P Craig, 'Delegated Acts, Implementing Acts and the New Comitology Regulation' (2011) 36 *European Law Review* 671, 672.

[30] ibid 672.

[31] See, eg, §5 (1)b Gesetz über die Zusammenarbeit von Bundesregierung und Deutschem Bundestag in Angelegenheiten (BGBl 2012 II S 1006), according to which the German federal government forwards to the Bundestag legal acts adopted by the Commission on the basis of Art 290 TFEU.

however, assess the delegations to adopt a delegated or implementing act, delegations which are enshrined in the 'basic' draft legislative act. This assessment takes place at the moment of scrutiny of that 'basic' draft legislative act. Such scrutiny, however, cannot amount to an assessment of the substance of a future delegated or implementing act.

III. CASE STUDY OF THE PROPOSAL FOR A TOBACCO PRODUCTS DIRECTIVE

This section takes the Commission proposal for a Tobacco Products Directive as a case study for the national parliaments' scrutiny of the delegations to adopt delegated acts. Section A presents the merits of this Commission proposal. Section B turns to the reasoned opinions of national parliaments that provide a vivid illustration of the national parliaments' main criticisms with respect to Article 290 TFEU requirements: the non-essential elements, the duration of the delegation of power and the large number of delegations. Beyond the proposal on the Tobacco Products Directive, this section deals with the delegations by means of implementing acts. Specifically, it delves into the concerns of national parliaments with regard to subject matters that can be regulated by means of implementing acts and the distinction between the two types of delegation as understood by national parliaments. Section C then studies the replies of the Commission to national parliaments. An assessment of the exchange of views on delegations between the national parliaments and the Commission is presented in section D. Finally, section E presents the Court's assessment of the adopted Tobacco Products Directive.

A. The Commission Proposal

In December 2012, the Commission proposed a directive that updates and replaces the current Tobacco Products Directive and that, in general terms, aims to improve the functioning of the internal market with regard to tobacco products.[32] The novelty of the Commission proposal involved a number of its elements.[33] With regard to the ingredients, the proposal forbids tobacco products with characterising flavours such as fruit or chocolate flavours and additives associated with energy and vitality (eg, caffeine and taurine), along with those characterisations creating the impression that such products have health benefits. Further, in relation to labelling and packaging, the Commission proposal envisaged large health warnings covering 75 per cent of the package, displayed on both sides of the package of cigarettes and of roll-your-own tobacco, whereas it exempts other tobacco products from the larger health warnings. The Commission also projected an EU tracking and tracing system at packet level throughout the supply chain, excluding retail. Moreover, the proposal upheld the ban of tobacco for oral use, with the exception of Sweden. Novel tobacco products had to be introduced through a new notification system. Finally, products containing nicotine and herbal products for smoking could be sold only with adapted health warnings.

[32] MJ Elsmore and V Obolevich, 'Thank You for Not Smoking: The Commission's Proposal for a New Tobacco Products Directive—Legally Sound, but Does it Hit the Spot?' (2013) 38 *European Law Review* 552.

[33] The directive was adopted in 2014 and differed quite substantially from the Commission proposal: the text health warnings will cover 65% instead of 75% of the front and the back of cigarette packs, while the controversial prohibition of menthol cigarettes (a characterising flavour) will start after a phase-out period of four years.

In relation to the subsidiarity principle, the Commission argued that, as the previous Tobacco Products Directive[34] had already harmonised some of the areas included in the proposal, Member States could not act unilaterally and, hence, only an EU directive could, for example, increase the visual size of the health warnings.[35] According to the Commission, the proposal was compatible with the principle of subsidiarity since the legal regimes of the Member States differed with regard to some of the relevant areas of the proposal, such as labelling and ingredients, that in consequence imposed obstacles to the functioning of the internal market.

B. Reasoned Opinions of National Parliaments

Nine chambers in total issued a reasoned opinion to the Commission proposal: the unicameral Bulgarian Narodno sabranie, the Portuguese Assembleia da República, the Danish Folketing, the Hellenic Vouli ton Ellinon, the Swedish Riksdagen, and four chambers of bicameral parliaments, namely, the Czech Poslanecká sněmovna, the Italian Camera dei Deputati and the Senato della Repubblica, and the Romanian Camera Deputaţilor. These together represented 14 votes out of the 18 required to raise a 'yellow card'.[36]

i. Essential Elements

Most of the reasoned opinions focused to a large extent on the delegated acts foreseen by the Commission proposal and the prohibition of the regulation of essential elements of the legislative act by means of delegated acts.[37] As the Bulgarian Narodno sabranie stated, the essential elements of the act must be included in the legislative proposal and cannot therefore be subject to delegation of power.[38] In its opinion, the proposal was in breach of the principles of subsidiarity and proportionality. The Bulgarian Narodno sabranie listed a number of problematic provisions. One of them was the application of delegated acts allowing the Commission to adapt the maximum permitted yields of tar, nicotine and carbon monoxide to reflect scientific development and internationally agreed upon standards. Another highlighted provision contained the delegation to the Commission to adopt delegated acts to set maximum levels of additives or combinations of additives that cause, as forbidden by the directive, the characteristic flavour of a tobacco product. Also problematic was the use of delegated acts to adapt the wording, position, format, layout

[34] Directive 2001/37/EC of the European Parliament and of the Council of 5 June 2001 on the approximation of the laws, regulations and administrative provisions of the Member States concerning the manufacture, presentation and sale of tobacco products [2001] OJ L194/26.

[35] COM(2012) 788 final, point 3.9.2.

[36] The Bulgarian Narodno sabranie and the Italian Camera dei Deputati failed to submit their Reasoned opinions on time and the Commission did not count them towards a 'yellow card' threshold. See Report from the Commission, *Annual Report 2013 on Subsidiarity and Proportionality* COM(2014) 506, 11. Those Reasoned opinions are however available on IPEX and included in this chapter.

[37] The Italian Camera dei Deputati, the Italian Senato della Repubblica, the Bulgarian Narodno sabranie, the Czech Poslanecká sněmovna, and the Czech Senát reviewed the legal basis of the proposal. In addition, the Danish Folketing and the Swedish Riksdagen addressed the prohibition of distribution and sales of oral tobacco.

[38] Bulgarian Narodno sabranie, Reasoned opinion of 28.02.2013 on COM(2012) 788, point 3.

and design of the health warnings to scientific and market developments. The Bulgarian Narodno sabranie also listed the delegation of power to the Commission with regard to the appearance of a unit packet of cigarettes. Specifically, in the case of substantial changes of circumstances, as established in a Commission report, the Commission could by means of delegated acts offer more detailed rules on the obligatory cuboid shape and size of a packet of cigarettes. In the view of the Bulgarian Narodno sabranie, the approach presented in the proposed directive deprived the Member States of 'the opportunity to implement a policy tuned to their national specificities and societal and cultural differences, in accordance with national health policies'.[39]

Likewise, the Hellelnic Vouli ton Ellinon and the Italian Senato della Repubblica were critical about the delegations by means of delegated act in their reasoned opinions. The Hellenic Vouli ton Ellinon put forward reservations corresponding to those of the Bulgarian Narodno sabranie concerning the maximum yields, claiming that they were 'substantial elements' of the Commission proposal.[40] The Italian Senato della Repubblica stated that some instances of delegation concern essential elements of the proposal and present 'an excessive and unjustified' conferral of power on the Commission.[41] In doing so, the Commission proposal offers 'an excess of federal over national regulatory authority' and encroaches on the competence of national parliaments by denying them the possibility to assess the subsidiarity and proportionality of the delegated acts.[42] Finally, the Portuguese Assembleia da República simply stated that 'delegation of powers affects essential matters which are the responsibility of Member States and is carried out in an imprecise manner unclearly related to the Commission's objectives'.[43]

In general, when national parliaments criticise delegations of power in draft legislative proposals, they focus on the prohibition of delegation of essential elements of the legislative proposal. This also goes beyond the case study discussed here. A broader analysis of all the reasoned opinions issued by national parliaments indicates that national parliaments offer some suggestions on how to deal with the delegations by means of delegated acts:

1. Delegate power by means of implementing acts.
2. Use the ordinary legislative procedure.
3. Refer to national measures instead.

First, some national parliaments suggested that the Commission proposals should delegate power to the Commission by means of implementing acts instead of delegated ones when the essential elements are at stake.[44] For example, the Polish and the Lithuanian chambers furnished this proposal. The Polish Senat focused on the conditions when, in the trade between the EU and third countries, imported agricultural products (which have a special character) are considered to provide an equivalent level of compliance with EU requirements concerning marketing standards. In the view of the Senat, these conditions,

[39] Bulgarian Narodno sabranie, Reasoned opinion of 28.02.2013 on COM(2012) 788, point 3.

[40] Hellenic Vouli ton Ellinon, Reasoned opinion of 20.02.2013 on COM(2012) 788, 5.

[41] Italian Senato della Repubblica, Reasoned opinion of 30.01.2013 on COM(2012) 788, 1–2.

[42] ibid.

[43] Portuguese Assembleia da República, Reasoned opinion of 01.03.2013 on COM(2012) 788, point 4.

[44] This is an obvious legal mistake; only a legislative act can provide for the 'essential elements' of an area under regulation. See section II of this chapter.

expected to be defined by the Commission in a delegated act, should be adopted by means of implementing acts since they represented a 'significant element' of the regulation.[45] Similarly, the Lithuanian Seimas argued in favour of an implementing act instead of a delegated act to set the principles of controls, sanctions, exclusions and recovery of undue payments to ensure their efficient application and the equal treatment of all beneficiaries in the European Agricultural Fund for Rural Development (EAFRD) programme. In the case at stake, the Commission decided to amend the provision in the existing regulation in order to align it to the introduction of the delegated and implementing acts by the Lisbon Treaty.[46] Yet, in the view of the Lithuanian Seimas, the change concerned an 'essential' part of the Commission proposal; in consequence, these issues should be regulated by means of implementing acts.[47] This represented a way, according to the Lithuanian Seimas, to take into account any possible administrative burden on national authorities, operators and citizens.

Second, national parliaments argued that issues that are an essential element of the proposal but were supposed to be delegated instead should be regulated in the basic act, and the EU ordinary legislative procedure should apply, ensuring the participation of the EP and the Council. As the Spanish Cortes Generales posited, in arguing for the engagement of the EP and the Council, many of the delegated powers disregard the specific interests of some sectors of the agricultural or fishing policies and present 'an impoverishment of the decision making process without a greater effectiveness in the implementation of legislative acts'.[48] With regard to the Tobacco Advertising Directive, discussed earlier, the Bulgarian Narodno sabranie argued that essential elements 'must be included in the legislative acts and cannot therefore be subject to delegation of power'.[49]

Third, another possibility foreseen by national parliaments is that the matters in which power was conferred on the Commission could rather be decided by the Member States through national measures. The Polish Senat frequently raised the point that Member States have 'better knowledge of the local conditions' and they are more apt to provide the measures initially foreseen in the delegations.[50] Finally, in a combination of the first and second options, some chambers, such as the French Sénat in its reasoned opinion on the General Data Protection Regulation, divided the issues at stake into those demanding regulation by the EU legislator (eg, 'the right to be forgotten') and other aspects that should be decided at the national level.[51]

ii. Duration and Number of Delegations

Coming back to the proposed Tobacco Products Directive, the reasoned opinions of the Bulgarian Narodno sabranie and the Italian Senato della Repubblica also objected to the

45 Polish Senat, Reasoned Opinion of 04.02.2011 on COM(2010) 738.

46 'Proposal for a Regulation of the European Parliament and the Council amending Council Regulation (EC) No 1698/2005 on support for rural development by the European Agricultural Fund for Rural Development (EAFRD)' COM(2010) 537 final, Explanatory Memorandum, 2.

47 Lithuanian Seimas, Reasoned opinion of 17.11.2010 on COM(2010) 537.

48 Spanish Cortes Generales, Reasoned opinion of 04.02.2013 on COM(2012) 724, point 10. See also Luxembourg Chambre des Députés, Reasoned opinion of 08.02.2011 on COM(2010) 738.

49 Bulgarian Narodno sabranie, Reasoned opinion of 28.02.2013 on COM(2012) 788, point 3.

50 Polish Senat, Reasoned opinions of 25.11.2010 on COM(2010) 537 and COM(2010) 539.

51 French Sénat, Reasoned opinion of 04.03.2012 on COM(2012) 11, 3. See also Polish Senat, Reasoned opinion of 03.03.2011 on COM(2010) 799, point 16.

unlimited duration of the empowerment to adopt delegated acts. In general, parliaments often stress the absence of limits to the period granted to the Commission to exercise the delegation at stake.[52]

In addition, an excessive number of delegations—16 in this case—within one legislative act seemed problematic for some national parliaments.[53] Some national parliaments, for example, the Hellenic Vouli ton Ellinon and the Romanian Camera Deputaţilor, objected to such a large conferral of powers to adopt non-legislative acts on substantial provisions of the proposal to the Commission.[54] In consequence, as highlighted by the Danish Folketing, this impedes the subsidiarity review of the proposal.[55]

iii. Delegation by Means of Implementing Acts

The delegations by means of implementing acts received only a marginal level of attention on the part of national parliaments in the case of the Tobacco Products Directive.[56] Nonetheless, beyond this case study, national parliaments expressed concerns with regard to delegations by means of implementing acts:[57]

1. Which matters can be regulated by means of implementing acts?
2. Is there a more appropriate procedure for the issues at stake than adopting them by means of implementing acts?
3. How should one distinguish between the issues that should be regulated by means of delegated acts and those that demand an implementation by means of implementing acts?

The main focus of national parliaments was on the delegation of issues they perceived as essential elements, as seen earlier, or on the substance of delegation of power. The reasoned opinions remained unaware of the subtleties of supplementation and implementation in the *Biocides* case highlighted earlier in this chapter. Some examples of matters that the national parliaments excluded from delegating to the Commission by means of implementing acts are provided below.

[52] See, eg, Spanish Cortes Generales, Reasoned opinion of 04.02.2013 on COM(2012) 724, point 8; Austrian Bundesrat, Reasoned opinion of 24.05.2012 on COM(2012) 150, 1.

[53] Another example of a legislative proposal with a large number of delegations is the General Data Protection Regulation, in which the French Sénat and the German Bundesrat in their Reasoned opinions underlined that the number of delegations extended far beyond the objective of comprehensive regulation of European data protection law exclusively by the European legislator. See French Sénat, Reasoned opinion of 04.03.2012 and German Bundesrat, Reasoned opinion of 30.03.2012 on COM(2012) 11. See similar cases: Austrian Bundesrat, Reasoned opinion of 02.07.2013 on COM(2013) 267; Austrian Bundesrat, Reasoned opinion of 05.06.2013 and the Dutch Tweede Kamer, Reasoned opinion of 2.07.2013, both on COM(2013) 262; Luxembourg Chambre des Députés, Reasoned opinion of 20.05.2014 and Austrian Bundesrat, Reasoned opinion of 14.05.2014, both on COM(2014) 180; Italian Senato della Repubblica, Reasoned opinion of 26.03.2014 on COM(2014) 4, 5 and of 18.02.2016 on COM(2015) 613.

[54] Hellenic Vouli ton Ellinon, Reasoned opinion of 20.02.2013, 5; Romanian Camera Deputaţilor, Reasoned opinion of 26.02.2013, 1, both on COM(2012) 788.

[55] Danish Folketing, Reasoned opinion of 04.03.2013 on COM(2012) 788, 3.

[56] See the opinion of the German Bundesrat of 22.03.2013 on COM(2012) 788.

[57] Also, national parliaments expressed concerns of a formal character. Specifically, at the moment when the Commission was sending legislative proposals that prescribed an implementing act, the regulation foreseen by Art 291(3) TFEU was not yet in force. See, eg, the Reasoned opinions of the Polish Sejm of 25.11.2010 on COM(2010) 539. This criticism lost its relevance as Regulation No 182/2011 entered into force on 01.03.2011. The Commission indicated this in its replies to national parliaments. See, eg, the Commission reply to the Polish Sejm of 04.05.2011 on COM(2010) 539.

The German Bundesrat assessed the Commission proposal to amend the VAT Directive by introducing standardisation of the VAT return obligation.[58] The chamber stated that provisions on corrections to VAT returns concerned aspects of procedural and criminal law and as such cannot be determined by implementing acts.[59] In another reasoned opinion concerning the Commission proposal on information to the general public on medicinal products subject to medical prescription, the French Sénat disagreed with the delegation of power by means of implementing acts.[60] Specifically, implementing acts were to provide the measures that the marketing authorisation holder should fulfil with regard to the content and presentation of information on authorised, prescription-only medicines. The French Sénat criticised the delegation of power, as there was no agreement among the Member States on a common distinction between advertising and information with regard to the marketing of prescription-only medicines.[61]

National parliaments also weighed in on the choice of a procedure that would be more appropriate than delegation of power by means of implementing acts. The reasoned opinions suggested that the identified problematic issues should be dealt with in the basic legislative act rather than delegated by means of implementing acts.[62] The reference to the ordinary legislative procedure enables the participation of the EP and of Member States via the Council. In contrast, the reasoned opinions did not suggest the delegation by means of delegated act. This approach can be explained by the fact that changing the delegation from implementing to delegated act would decrease the Member States' influence on the shape of such acts.

Finally, going beyond the case study, the question that national parliaments often dealt with in their reasoned opinions is the distinction between delegated and implementing acts. For example, the Polish Sejm issued a reasoned opinion concerning the draft regulation on the Single Common Market Organisation that aimed at aligning the existing regulation with the differentiation between delegated and implementing acts as introduced by the Lisbon Treaty.[63] The Polish Sejm argued that the proposal did not set criteria governing whether an area will be regulated by means of delegated or implementing acts.[64] The Lithuanian Seimas with regard to two of the Commission's proposals on rural development reform and on the support scheme for farmers went a step further and considered that the choice to regulate in the form of a delegated act or implementing act should depend on the delegation of 'more' essential powers to the Commission.[65]

[58] 'Proposal for a Council Directive amending Directive 2006/112/EC on the common system of value added tax as regards a standard VAT return' COM(2013) 721 final.

[59] German Bundesrat, Reasoned opinion of 29.11.2013 on COM(2013) 721.

[60] 'Amended proposal for a Directive of the European Parliament and of the Council amending Directive 2001/83/EC as regards information to the general public on medicinal products subject to medical prescription' COM(2012) 48 final.

[61] French Sénat, Reasoned opinion of 10.04.2012 on COM(2012) 48 and 49.

[62] See Belgian Chambre des représentants, Reasoned opinion of 06.04.2012 on COM(2012) 11, 14; Romanian Camera Deputaţilor, Reasoned opinion of 24.10.2011 on COM(2011) 453, point 6; Czech Poslanecká sněmovna, Reasoned opinion of 01.09.2016 on COM(2016) 283, point 7.

[63] 'Proposal for a Regulation of the European Parliament and of the Council establishing a common organisation of agricultural markets and on specific provisions for certain agricultural products (Single CMO Regulation)' COM(2010) 799 final.

[64] Polish Sejm, Reasoned opinion of 04.03.2011 on COM(2010) 799.

[65] Lithuanian Seimas, Reasoned opinion of 17.11.2010 on COM(2010) 537 and Reasoned opinion of 17.11.2010 on COM(2010) 539.

C. The Commission's Replies

The following section explores the replies of the Commission to the reasoned opinions of national parliaments regarding the conferral of delegated and implementing powers. The replies were divided into those concerning characteristics of the delegated and implementing acts (essential elements, duration and number of delegations, and distinction between delegated and implementing acts) on the one hand, and the explanations given by the Commission with regard to the merits of the delegations on the other.

i. Commission Replies Regarding the Characteristics of Delegations

A number of Commission proposals sent to national parliaments concerned cases in which a pre-Lisbon implementing act demanded an alignment to the new division between delegated and implementing acts.[66] Thus, often when national parliaments maintained that a proposal empowered the Commission to regulate an essential element by means of delegated acts, the Commission simply stated that the proposal 'merely takes account of the fact that the new Articles 290 and 291 TFEU introduce a new system of conferral of powers to the Commission to replace the one provided by the TEC'.[67] In the view of the Commission, it did nothing more than introduce into the text of the existing regulation the required legal basis for these acts.[68] The Commission saw its role in this respect as only classifying the existing implementing acts under the respective Lisbon Treaty definitions of either delegated act or implementing act. As explained by the Commission, 'delegated acts have been provided in all cases of "quasi legislative acts" in the sense that they regulate non essential elements of the legislative act, are of general application and amend or complete the legislative act'.[69] Further, '[i]mplementing acts have been provided for all acts of an "executive" nature, in the sense that Member States are responsible for implementation, and there is a need for uniform application'.[70] The Commission argued that it adjusted the original legislative acts according to objective legal criteria of Articles 290 and 291 TFEU; thus these changes concern only non-essential elements of a legislative act.[71] Consequently, proposed regulations did not grant the Commission any new powers to adopt acts in areas not regulated at the EU level. The Commission has also countered the arguments that the criteria to distinguish between delegated and implemented acts were not clear by simply stating that they are included in Articles 290 and 291 TFEU and in the Commission Communication on the Implementation of Article 290 TFEU.[72] In consequence, the Commission did not see the need to 'repeat the criteria in each and every proposal that aligns an existing regulation to the Treaty of Lisbon'.[73]

66 See section II of this chapter.
67 Commission reply of 24.05.2011 to the Polish Sejm on COM(2010) 537.
68 ibid.
69 Commission reply of 04.05.2011 to the Polish Sejm on COM(2010) 539.
70 ibid.
71 Commission reply of 18.09.2012 to the Austrian Bundesrat on COM(2012) 150.
72 Commission reply of 24.05.2011 to the Polish Sejm on COM(2010) 537.
73 ibid.

The Commission disagreed also that a delegation by means of a delegated act should be replaced with an implementing act if the delegation concerned an essential element of the legislative proposal. In its reply to the Lithuanian Seimas, the Commission rightly underlined that the Treaty does not allow for the conferral of powers to the Commission to adopt essential elements of a legislative act by means of implementing acts either; essential elements are 'the reserved domain of the legislator'.[74]

Moreover, in order to assuage parliaments the Commission stressed the guarantees for the EP and the Council, both of which retain control of the delegated power through the possibility of opposing a delegated act adopted by the Commission or even revoking the delegation of powers to the Commission.[75] The Commission committed itself in its communication on Article 290 TFEU[76] to a 'systematic consultation' of the national experts in the preparatory phase.[77]

With regard to the new legislative proposals, such as the Tobacco Products Directive, the Commission replied to the concerns of national parliaments in a very succinct way, rebutting all their arguments against the delegation of powers with regard to essential elements of the proposal. The Commission maintained that the delegations of power provide for 'clear and concise criteria, giving limited discretion to the Commission'.[78]

Furthermore, countering the recurring accusation of a high number of delegations within one proposal, the Commission argued that the TFEU does not set a formal limit on the number of delegated or implementing powers that may be conferred on the Commission.[79] With regard to the duration of the delegations, the Commission argued that the Common Understanding on Delegated Acts of 2011 allowed empowerments for both determined and undetermined periods of time.[80] The Commission underlined its preference for lack of constraints such as a time-limited delegation because such constraints limit its ability to respond to developments.[81] The Commission further argued that the EP and the Council could always revoke the delegation.[82] However, there was at least one case in which the Commission agreed with the Italian Senato della Repubblica and accepted a five-year limit to a delegation.[83]

ii. Commission Replies Regarding the Merits of Delegations

With regard to the merits of specific delegations, especially in cases in which national parliaments underlined delegation of essential powers, the Commission mainly focused

[74] Commission reply of 08.04.2011 to the Lithuanian Seimas on COM(2010) 537.

[75] Commission reply of 18.09.2012 to the Austrian Bundesrat on COM(2012) 150. See also Commission reply to the Luxembourg Chambre des Députés of 12.09.2011 on COM (2010) 799 and of 15.06.2011 on COM(2010) 738.

[76] COM(2009) 673.

[77] Commission reply of 18.09.2012 to the Austrian Bundesrat on COM(2012) 150.

[78] Commission reply to the Italian Senato (25.06.2013), the Hellenic Vouli ton Ellinon (25.06.2013) and the Bulgarian Narodno Sabranie (18.07.2013) on COM(2012) 788. See also Commission reply of 13.03.2013 to the Opinion of the Italian Senato della Repubblica on COM(2012) 150.

[79] Commission reply of 22.10.2013 to the Austrian Bundesrat on COM(2013) 267; Commission reply of 30.10.2013 to the Austrian Bundesrat on COM(2013) 260.

[80] Commission reply of 18.09.2012 to the Austrian Bundesrat on COM(2012) 150.

[81] Commission reply of 22.05.2012 to the French Sénat on COM(2011) 452.

[82] Commission reply of 11.12.2012 to the opinion of the Italian Senato della Repubblica on COM(2012) 238 issued within political dialogue.

[83] Commission reply of 06.04.2011 to the opinion of the Italian Senato della Repubblica on COM(2010) 393 issued within political dialogue.

on clarifying the wrong understanding of the delegation by a national parliament. In other cases, still sustaining its position, the Commission justified the delegations by a need for innovation and future technological development, efficiency or taking away from the Member States the disproportionate burden of regulation in all technical topics.

First, in a number of cases the Commission clarified a wrong interpretation of delegations by the national chambers.[84] The Commission proposal amending the Council Regulation on Support for Rural Development by the European Agricultural Fund for Rural Development (EAFRD) offers an illustration of such a situation. This regulation provided the Commission with the possibility to issue delegated acts to 'adopt specific conditions for the co-financing of interest rate subsidies and of other financial engineering instruments in order to ensure the efficient use and coherent implementation of the EAFRD'.[85] In this regard, the Polish Senat claimed that the proposal delegates to the Commission the power to regulate issues concerning levels of co-financing of support instruments that constituted a 'vital aspect' of the regulation.[86] The Commission replied that the provision criticised by the chamber did not concern the level of the co-financing of support, but allowed for 'adoption of specific conditions for the use and operation of interest rate subsidies and other financial engineering instruments'.[87]

Another example in which the Commission was obliged to clarify the use of delegated acts concerned the proposal amending an existing regulation establishing common rules for support schemes for farmers.[88] One of its provisions empowered the Commission to adopt 'rules on the definition in the national legislation for "inheritance" and "anticipated inheritance"' by means of delegated acts.[89] This provision aimed to 'clarify specific situations that may occur in the application of the single payment scheme'.[90] In their reasoned opinions, the Polish Sejm and the Senat, the Luxemburgish Chambre des Députés, and the Lithuanian Seimas opined that such a delegation interfered with substantive inheritance law, an area not covered by EU competence.[91] The Commission, replying to the chambers, emphasised that it did not aim to define the notions of 'inheritance' and 'anticipated inheritance', but only to provide a legal basis for the existing provision, which asserted that the definition in the national legislation for 'inheritance' and 'anticipated inheritance' should be applied.[92]

Beyond the cases in which the Commission explained to national parliaments the specifics of delegated powers, a wide range of replies used the argument of innovation and

[84] See Commission reply of 13.05.2011 to the Luxembourg Chambre des Députés on COM(2010) 537 regarding Art 36 bis of the proposal; Commission reply of 24.05.2011 to the Polish Sejm on COM(2010) 537 regarding Art 74(4) and Art 86 of the proposal; Commission reply of 25.03.2014 to the German Bundesrat on COM(2013) 721.

[85] Art 71(5) of proposal COM(2010) 537.

[86] Polish Senat, Reasoned opinion of 25.11.2010 on COM(2010) 537.

[87] Commission reply of 15.04.2011 to the Polish Senat on COM(2010) 537.

[88] 'Proposal for a Regulation of the European Parliament and the Council amending Council Regulation (EC) No 73/2009 establishing common rules for direct support schemes for farmers under the common agricultural policy and establishing certain support schemes for farmers' COM(2010) 539 final.

[89] Art 45a(3)a of the proposal.

[90] ibid.

[91] Polish Sejm, Reasoned opinion of 25.11.2010; Polish Senat, Reasoned opinion of 25.11.2010; Luxembourg Chambre des Députés, Reasoned opinion of 30.11.2010; Lithuanian Seimas, Reasoned opinion of 17.11.2010, all on COM(2010) 539.

[92] Commission reply of 20.04.2011 to the Lithuanian Seimas; of 15.06.2011 to the Luxembourg Chambre des Députés; of 04.05.2011 to the Polish Sejm; and of 13.04.2011 to the Polish Senat, all on COM(2010) 539.

future technological development to defend the conferral of power on the Commission. For example, the Italian Camera dei Deputati assessed that the proposal for the General Data Protection Regulation offered the Commission 'extremely broad-ranging powers to adopt delegated acts relating to almost every one of the most important elements of the proposal'.[93] In its reply, the Commission asserted that the regulation was 'deliberately drafted as a technologically neutral legal instrument' used 'to anticipate all technological developments of the next twenty years' so that the regulation can be supplemented without every case leading to a revision of the regulation itself.[94] Moreover, as the Commission maintained in its reply to the German Bundesrat on the same legislative proposal, more detailed rules 'would result in an inflexible and unwieldy legal text which would not be open to innovation and new technologies'.[95] The Commission referred to innovation and technical development in a number of replies to national parliaments.[96]

The third approach in the Commission replies was to underline the efficiency of delegations. For example, the UK House of Commons in its reasoned opinion on the proposal for a regulation on prudential requirements for credit institutions and investment firms[97] was hesitant with regard to Article 443 of the proposal.[98] This provision allowed the Commission to adopt delegated acts to introduce stricter prudential requirements for a limited period of time. The delegation of power was applicable in situations of changes in the intensity of micro-prudential and macro-prudential risks that arise from market developments, in particular on the recommendation or opinion of the European Systemic Risk Board (ESRB). The UK House of Commons found this delegation of power to be in breach of Article 290 TFEU. In the view of the chamber, prudential requirements were an essential element of the regulation.[99] Yet, the Commission in its reply argued that the recommendations or opinions of the ESRB will help to ensure 'the efficient and effective' use of the delegated powers.[100]

The final argument recurring in Commission replies concerned lifting the burden of regulation from the Member States. The Commission argued that leaving the regulation of technical topics to the Member States would be 'disproportionate and administratively burdensome'.[101] In contrast, the Commission perceived the regulation by means of delegated acts as a flexible and proportionate approach.

[93] Italian Camera dei Deputati, Reasoned opinion of 04.04.2013 on COM(2012) 11.

[94] Commission reply of 21.02.2013 to the Italian Camera dei Deputati on COM(2012) 11.

[95] Commission reply of 10.01.2013 to German Bundesrat on COM(2012) 11.

[96] See Commission reply of 22.06.2011 to the Luxembourg Chambre des Députés on COM(2011) 530 and of 17.09.2014 on COM(2014) 180; Commission reply of 13.02.2014 to the Austrian Bundesrat on COM(2013) 620.

[97] 'Proposal for a Regulation of the European Parliament and the Council on prudential requirements for credit institutions and investment firms (Text with EEA relevance)' COM(2011) 452 final.

[98] UK House of Commons, Reasoned opinion of 12.10.2011 on COM(2011) 452.

[99] ibid.

[100] Commission reply of 10.07.2012 to the UK House of Commons on COM(2011) 452. The Commission offered a similar justification for the delegation of power in Commission reply of 08.06.2016 to the Austrian Bundesrat on COM(2015) 595.

[101] Commission reply of 22.10.2013 to the Austrian Bundesrat on COM(2013) 267. See also Commission replies of 30.10.2013 and 23.10.2013 to the Austrian Bundesrat concerning COM(2013) 260 and COM(2013) 262, respectively.

D. Evaluation of the Exchange Between National Parliaments and the Commission

To assess the role of national parliaments as a new interlocutor in delegated rule-making vis-a-vis the Commission, the issue of the quality of the Commission's replies and the Commission's willingness to take the comments of national parliaments on board demand further attention.

First, the quality of Commission replies to national parliaments, especially immediately after the entry into force of the Lisbon Treaty, was not satisfactory. The reasoned opinion of the Polish Senat on the Single CMO Regulation proposal illustrates this point well. In this case, the Polish Senat lamented the excessively far-reaching powers to adopt delegated acts and questioned a long list of delegations, in fact, drafting its opinion exclusively on that point.[102] The Commission addressed these claims in a general formula on aligning the CMO Regulation to the post-Lisbon division into delegated and implementing acts without devoting any effort to assessing each provision mentioned by the Polish Senat.[103] Moreover, on another occasion, the Commission did not reply to the concerns of the Luxembourgish Chambre des Députés with regard to the executive acts.[104]

Second, the effectiveness of the reasoned opinions with respect to the ability to shape the delegation is questionable. The examination of the parliamentary opinions and the Commission's replies show that the Commission has not acknowledged the correctness of any of the points of the parliaments or, consequently, amended any of its proposals. This is compatible with the Commission's practice regarding adjusting or discussing further the proposals critically opined by national parliaments.[105] Only in one case did the Commission reply to the national parliament that the Council's general approach had implemented some changes in line with the expectations of that chamber.[106]

E. The Court's Assessment of the New Tobacco Products Directive

The Court has also been involved in the assessment of the Tobacco Products Directive, but the reasoned opinions did not play any major role in the proceedings. Specifically, three cases—two requests for a preliminary ruling and an action for annulment—were brought to the CJEU, unsuccessfully challenging the Tobacco Products Directive after its adoption.[107] In the case *Pillbox 38 (UK) Ltd v The Secretary of State for Health*, the referring UK court questioned the validity of the directive in light of the subsidiarity principle, invoking in this context the reasoned opinions issued under the political mechanism established by Protocol No 2.[108] The CJEU, however, highlighted that the reasoned opinions were issued under

[102] Polish Senat, Reasoned opinion of 03.03.2011 on COM(2010) 799.

[103] Commission reply of 20.09.2011 to the Polish Senat on COM(2010) 799.

[104] Luxembourg Chambre des Députés, Reasoned opinion of 16.11.2010 on COM(2010) 475 and Commission reply of 13.04.2011. Yet, as the chamber criticised the delegated acts only in the preliminary remarks, the Commission might have distinguished it from the subsidiarity violations arguments.

[105] Commission Reports COM(2011) 344, 6–11 and COM(2012) 373, 8–9.

[106] Commission reply of 12.06.2012 to the French Sénat on COM(2011) 650.

[107] See further ch 1.

[108] Case C-477/14 *Pillbox 38*, ECLI:EU:C:2016:324, para 143.

the initial political monitoring of the subsidiarity principle established by Protocol No 2.[109] In contrast, it was the obligation of the Court to conduct a substantive assessment of whether the directive is compatible with the principle of subsidiarity and to conduct a procedural assessment of whether the procedural safeguards provided by Protocol No 2 were complied with.[110] Since the Court did not receive any request to review the compliance of the directive with the procedural safeguards of Protocol No 2, it proceeded to the substantive assessment of the directive, concluding that no subsidiarity violation was at stake.[111] The reasoned opinions of national parliaments issued against the Commission proposal did not play any role.

In the other request for a preliminary ruling, the CJEU was asked specifically about whether a number of empowerments to the Commission to adopt delegated and implementing acts infringed Articles 290 and 291 TFEU.[112] However, the Court found those questions inadmissible since they were not related to the purpose of the main proceedings, namely, the implementation of the directive by the UK.[113]

Ultimately, so far no case against the new Tobacco Products Directive has managed to invalidate it. Nonetheless, the Court made a clear distinction between the political character of the reasoned opinions and the judicial review of the principle of subsidiarity. Clearly, the Court will not base its judgment on the views of national parliaments.

IV. ASSESSMENT

This chapter has analysed examples of the arguments raised by national parliaments under Protocol No 2 with regard to delegations encompassed in a draft legislative act. How can this activity of national parliaments be assessed?

Within the political safeguards surrounding delegations established by the Lisbon Treaty, one can distinguish between those that aim to protect federalism and those that aim to protect democracy.[114] Accordingly, Article 290 TFEU provides a political safeguard of democracy around delegated acts by granting to the EP the power to revoke delegations or to place an objection with regard to delegated acts.[115] Indirectly, the Council's competence to revoke the delegation or express an objection to a delegated act also protects the federal values, since the Council is controlled by the Member States.[116] Article 291 TFEU foresees a political safeguard of federalism, introduced in the form of Regulation 182/2011, around the adoption of implementing acts in the form of committees staffed with national experts. In consequence, this committee system allows the Member States to control the exercise of implementing powers. The constitutional logic here is one of 'vertical separation of power' between the EU and the Member States.[117] In turn, the delegated acts depict the 'horizontal separation of powers' between the Commission and the EU legislator.[118]

[109] ibid, para 145.
[110] ibid, para 146.
[111] ibid, paras 147–51. See also Case C-547/14 *Philip Morris Brands and Others*, ECLI:EU:C:2016:325, paras 216–28.
[112] C-547/14 *Philip Morris Brands and Others*, para 28.
[113] ibid, paras 42–46.
[114] Schütze (n 20) 663.
[115] ibid 691.
[116] ibid.
[117] ibid 690.
[118] ibid.

Besides the political limits, the Court offers a judicial safeguard in the form of the non-delegation doctrine.[119] Under this doctrine, the determination that elements are essential to a given act is not for the EU legislator alone to decide, but, rather, 'must be based on objective factors amenable to judicial review'.[120] The Court exercises a broad review of issues such as whether a secondary act failed to observe one of the essential elements of the matter expressly laid down by the basic act[121] or whether a secondary act contains an essential element of the basic act.[122] However, the division between delegated and implementing acts remains under limited judicial review of manifest errors of assessment.[123] With regard to implementing acts, a judicial safeguard arguably is needed less, as Article 291 TFEU refers to 'mechanisms for control by *Member States*'.[124]

Against this background of political and judicial safeguards of delegated rule-making, the national parliaments' practice of assessing the delegations of power to the Commission to adopt a delegated or implementing act does not appear to offer much added value. The fact that essential elements of an area are reserved for the legislative act and thus cannot be the subject of a delegation of power represents a horizontal separation of powers, aiming to protect EU democracy. The reasoned opinions assessing such delegations, focusing instead on protecting national democracy, do not contribute to maintaining horizontal separation of power in the EU.

In the case of delegations of power to adopt an implementing act, the control of implementing acts is already accomplished by the Member States themselves through the committee system established under Regulation 182/2011. This allows the Member States to take part directly in the decision-making process surrounding implementing acts. The added value of national parliaments' exercise of control over the delegations to adopt an implementing act seems, therefore, questionable.

In light of this, the political dialogue presents an avenue that national parliaments may use to raise criticism with regard to delegations to adopt delegated and implementing acts. Political dialogue, an informal avenue of communication between the national parliaments and the Commission, may concern any aspect of a Commission proposal, not only its subsidiarity as the EWS.[125] Indeed, some of the opinions issued within the political dialogue so far concern the delegation of essential elements of the act,[126] the number of delegations,[127] the duration of the delegation[128]—especially its undetermined period[129]—or the distinction

[119] ibid 692.

[120] Case C-355/10 *Parliament v Council*, ECLI:EU:C:2012:516, para 67.

[121] Case C-303/94 *Parliament v Council*, ECLI:EU:C:1996:238, para 31.

[122] C-355/10 *Parliament v Council*, para 79.

[123] Case C-427/12 *Commission v Parliament and Council* (*Biocides*), ECLI:EU:C:2014:170, para 40.

[124] Schütze (n 20) 693.

[125] See ch 2.

[126] See, eg, Polish Senat, opinion of 13.03.2013 on COM(2013) 18; German Bundesrat, opinion of 02.03.2012 on COM(2011) 866; Italian Senato della Repubblica, opinion of 01.08.2012 on COM(2012) 150; of 01.08.2012 on COM(2012) 136; of 07.11.2012 on COM(2012) 548; Romanian Senat, opinions of 24.11.2010 on COM(2010) 537 and 539; Czech Senát, opinion of 20.05.2010 on COM(2010) 119.

[127] See, eg, Austrian Nationalrat, opinion of 04.09.2012 on COM(2012) 238; Italian Senato della Repubblica, opinion of 13.06.2012 on COM(2012) 11; Romanian Camera Deputaților, opinion of 27.04.2011 on COM(2011) 615; German Bundesrat, opinion of 16.12.2011 on COM(2011) 615.

[128] See, eg, Italian Senato della Repubblica, opinion of 21.11.2012 on COM(2012) 350 and COM(2012) 360.

[129] See, eg, Italian Senato della Repubblica, opinion of 01.08.2012 on COM(2012) 238; Romanian Senat, opinion of 30.11.2011 on COM(2011) 615; German Bundesrat, opinion of 16.12.2011 on COM(2011) 615.

between delegated and implementing acts.[130] To a lesser extent, the opinions criticised the delegations to adopt the implementing acts.[131] Interestingly, the Italian parliament, which was very active in the political dialogue, often highlighted the argument that Commission proposals encompassing a delegation comply with subsidiarity, as only the EU can amend European legislation and update it to the new procedures of delegated acts and implementing acts introduced by the Lisbon Treaty.[132] Moreover, some of the opinions were positive, pointing to the conformity of delegations with Article 290 TFEU.[133]

Finally, it is worth noting that the discussion on the role of national parliaments in the area of delegated and implementing acts has been evolving.[134] For example, the Italian Senato della Repubblica demanded that draft delegated acts are submitted directly to national parliaments for assessment.[135] The Danish Folketing boldly proposed that national parliaments should be permitted to initiate the mechanism of revocation of the delegation by the EP and the Council.[136] Those voices show that national parliaments are willing to move beyond the scrutiny of the delegations within the Commission proposals and conduct a more active scrutiny in the area of delegated rule-making.

V. CONCLUSION

The purpose of this chapter was to demonstrate the increasing role that national parliaments have adopted with regard to the new rules of delegation under the Lisbon Treaty. The case study of the Commission proposal on the Tobacco Products Directive offered an apt overview of the prevailing concerns of national parliaments with regard to delegation by means of delegated acts. Specifically, the issues at stake are the delegation of powers beyond the regulation of non-essential elements of a proposal, along with the duration of delegation, and the excessive number of delegations. Further, with regard to the delegations to adopt implementing acts, the major problems highlighted by national parliaments concern the subject matters that implementing acts may regulate and the use of delegated acts instead of implementing ones. The problems identified by the national parliaments are consistent with those signalled in the process of study of the new system of delegation of powers.[137]

[130] German Bundesrat, opinion of 26.11.2010 on COM(2010) 539 and 537.

[131] See, eg, Czech Senát, opinion of 08.02.2012 on COM(2011) 880.

[132] See, eg, Italian Senato della Repubblica, opinion of 28.11.2012 on COM(2012) 403.

[133] See, eg, Italian Senato della Repubblica, opinion of 18.12.2012 on COM (2012) 584; of 21.11.2012 on COM(2012) 530; of 29.11.2011 on COM(2011) 555.

[134] For an early assessment of the role of national parliaments in this area see COSAC, 16th Bi-annual Report on EU Practices and Procedures (2011) 55–61.

[135] Italian Senato della Repubblica, Resolution of the 14th Permanent Committee, Doc XVIII N 102, (25.11.2015) 10.

[136] *Twenty-Three Recommendations to strengthen the role of national parliaments in a changing European governance* (Danish Folketing European Affairs Committtee, 2014) 5. In contrast to that, the UK government took a more reserved position, arguing that granting such a power to the Parliament might overburden it and that the existing parliamentary scrutiny of delegated acts should be improved. See *Review of the Balance of Competences between the United Kingdom and the European Union Subsidiarity and Proportionality* (UK Government, 2014) 61.

[137] CF Bergström and D Ritleng, 'Patterns and Findings: Five Central Themes' in CF Bergström and D Ritleng (eds), *Rulemaking by the Euroepan Commission: The New System for Delegation of Powers* (Oxford, Oxford University Press, 2016) 263.

Against this background, the Commission pre-eminently argued that delegations to adopt delegated and implementing acts were a necessary adjustment to the distinctions introduced by the Lisbon Treaty and did not create any new competence for the EU. Moreover, on the merits of specific delegations, especially in cases in which national parliaments underlined the delegation of essential elements, the Commission made the case for an erroneous interpretation by national parliaments. In other instances, the Commission promoted the need for openness to technical innovation and efficiency in defending its position. Overall, the Commission did not oblige itself to change any of its proposals.

While attempting to show how national parliaments use the EWS to extend their scrutiny into areas in which they did not gain any control competence under the Lisbon Treaty, such as the adoption of delegated and implementing acts, this chapter has questioned the added value of national parliaments' reasoned opinions. As has been argued with regard to delegations by means of delegated acts, not only is it a question of 'horizontal division of power', but it is also that the EP and the Council were granted a competence to revoke or object to the power of the Commission, offering a political safeguard of democracy in this area. Concerning the delegations to adopt implementing acts, the control of the implementing powers is already in the hands of the Member States, either through adoption of national laws implementing EU acts or through national experts in the committees. Therefore, the Lisbon Treaty seems to offer a sufficient political safeguard of federalism in this case, also. Against this background, the scrutiny of delegations by national parliaments under the EWS does not appear to provide any added value in making the decisions taken as closely as possible to the citizen.

8

Subsidiarity and Fundamental Rights Legislation

I. INTRODUCTION

THE 'FUNCTIONAL LEGAL order' of the Community aimed at economic integration of national economies and was 'not meant to *protect*, but rather to *change* [democratic societies]'.[1] Step by step, human rights started restricting the discretion of the supranational institutions.[2] The ambition became, however to make 'human rights … *determine* rather than simply *limit* the European legal system and would move to the forefront of its institutions' activity', placing them at the core of the Community order.[3] Yet, before the EU Charter of Fundamental Rights (the Charter) was proclaimed, it was first the jurisprudence of the Court of Justice of the European Union (the Court/CJEU) and the provisions of the Treaty itself, for example, Article 141 EC (now Article 157 of the Treaty on the Functioning of the European Union (TFEU)), that enhanced the position of human rights in the Community.[4] The subsequent amendments, especially the Amsterdam Treaty and the introduction of Article 6 of the Treaty on the European Union (TEU), further strengthened fundamental rights in the EU.[5] In the Lisbon Treaty, each paragraph of the redrafted Article 6 TEU refers to a different fundamental rights source, depicting three 'Bills of Rights': the EU Fundamental Rights Charter (the Charter), the European Convention on Human Rights (ECHR), and fundamental rights as general principles of EU law resulting from the constitutional traditions common to the Member States.[6]

Little research has been conducted on the growing EU legislation with consequences for the protection of EU fundamental rights. This chapter, therefore, investigates the relationship between the subsidiarity principle and fundamental rights protection. Specifically, under the Early Warning System (EWS), national parliaments often review EU draft legislative acts, the objective of which is fundamental rights protection, for their consistency with the subsidiarity principle. How do the subsidiarity principle and safeguarding fundamental rights work together? Under which circumstances is one level more apt to protect fundamental rights than the other? These questions are asked with the view that the EU is founded on values common to the Member States such as 'respect for human dignity,

[1] A von Bogdandy, 'The European Union as a Human Rights Organization? Human Rights and the Core of the European Union' (2000) 37 *Common Market Law Review* 1307, 1308.

[2] ibid.

[3] ibid.

[4] P Craig, *The Lisbon Treaty: Law, Politics, and Treaty Reform* (Oxford, Oxford University Press, 2010) 193–95.

[5] ibid 195.

[6] R Schütze, 'Three "Bills of Rights" for the European Union' (2011) 30 *Yearbook of European Law* 131.

freedom, democracy, equality, the rule of law and respect for human rights, including rights of persons belonging to minorities'.[7]

This chapter is structured as follows. Section II offers a short review of the fundamental rights standards of the EU with an insight into the guidelines established by the Commission for legislative drafts in this regard. Section III discusses three possible configurations in which the reasoned opinions address fundamental rights depending on whether a Commission proposal pursues an aim of fundamental rights protection or not. Therefore, this section focuses on the reasoned opinions on Commission proposals for which fundamental rights protection is not the objective of the act at stake and, next, on the reasoned opinions concerning proposals for which fundamental rights protection is one of the objectives of a Commission proposal. Section IV explores the setting in which fundamental rights protection is the main objective of a draft legislative act. To this end, this chapter takes the Commission proposal 'Women on Boards' as a case study of subsidiarity scrutiny in the field of fundamental rights.[8] The assessment of the applicability of the subsidiarity mechanism in the field of fundamental rights protection follows in section V.

II. FUNDAMENTAL RIGHTS IN THE EU DRAFT LEGISLATIVE ACTS

Since the Charter gained a legally binding character with the entry into force of the Lisbon Treaty, the Commission has prepared a strategy paper for its departments with a set of guidelines 'to make the fundamental rights provided for in the Charter as effective as possible'.[9] Accordingly, the Commission departments should highlight the fundamental rights aspects in preparatory consultations (eg, Green Papers), in impact assessments and in the drafting of legislative proposals (in recitals of the preamble and the explanatory memorandum to the proposals). Similarly, throughout the legislative process, the Commission signalled its readiness to help the EU legislator in reviewing whether its amendments to the proposals comply with the Charter.[10] The operational guidance of 2011 focuses, in turn, on the fundamental rights justification in impact assessments.[11] The operational guidance gives examples for the drafters of impact assessments that illustrate how to approach fundamental rights at different stages, while consulting interested parties or examining the impact on fundamental rights of the different policy options. Finally, the Interinstitutional Agreement of 2016 underlines again that the Commission should explain in explanatory memoranda and impact assessments how EU proposals comply with fundamental rights.[12]

[7] Art 2 TEU.

[8] 'Proposal for a directive of the European Parliament and of the Council on improving the gender balance among non-executive directors of companies listed on stock exchanges and related measures' COM(2012) 614 final.

[9] 'Communication from the Commission, Strategy for the Implementation of the Charter of Fundamental Rights by the European Union' COM(2010) 573 final. On the Commission's implementation of this strategy see A Williams, 'Human Rights in the EU' in A Arnull and D Chalmers (eds), *The Oxford Handbook of European Union Law* (Oxford, Oxford University Press, 2015).

[10] COM(2010) 573, point 1.2.

[11] Commission Staff Working Paper, 'Operational Guidance on taking account of Fundamental Rights in Commission Impact Assessments' SEC(2011) 567 final, 5, available at: ec.europa.eu/governance/impact/key_docs/docs/sec_2011_0567_en.pdf.

[12] Interinstitutional Agreement between the European Parliament, the Council of the European Union and the European Commission on Better Law-Making [2016] OJ L/123/1, points 12 and 25 (Interinstitutional Agreement of 2016).

Accordingly, Commission proposals follow the established recommendations to different degrees. The explanatory memorandum of the Commission proposal on 'Women on Boards' targeting gender inequality on corporate boards, discussed in detail in this chapter, contains a section on consistency of the proposal with EU fundamental rights policy and the Charter. The explanatory memorandum went especially into the principle of positive action of Article 157(4) TFEU and the Court's criteria on when positive action is compatible with the principle of equal treatment. Although the explanatory memorandum lists these criteria, the explanatory memorandum makes only a broad reference to one of the proposal's provisions. The impact assessment, however, offers a more profound analysis of the compliance of the proposal with the relevant Charter rights. In this sense, the impact assessment does not come across as 'superficial', a regular flaw of impact assessments.[13] Similarly, the impact assessment for the Commission proposal strengthening the presumption of innocence offers a relatively comprehensive fundamental rights assessment.[14] In contrast, the explanatory memorandum of the proposal on the European Public Prosecutor's Office (EPPO), discussed in chapter three, does not contain a separate section on fundamental rights and is almost silent in this respect. The impact assessment of the EPPO proposal similarly does not offer a detailed analysis on the compliance of the proposal with the fundamental rights at stake.[15] Instead, it explores the impact on fundamental rights by each of the policy options. This approach can be explained by the fact that fundamental rights protection as such is not the main focus of the EPPO proposal.

In theory, a limited usefulness of impact assessments for fundamental rights proposals might be connected with the nature of fundamental rights. This is because of the qualitative rather than quantitative assessment involved, a factor which this chapter elaborates upon in section V, below. Before that, however, this chapter will explore how national parliaments assess fundamental rights aspects of Commission proposals.

III. FUNDAMENTAL RIGHTS IN THE REASONED OPINIONS

This chapter divides the Commission draft legislative acts to which national parliaments issued their reasoned opinions depending on whether the objective of such a legislative proposal is the protection of fundamental rights.[16] The reason for this division is that the subsidiarity principle considers the question of which level of government is more apt to achieve the objectives of the proposed action.

[13] I de Jesús Butler, 'Ensuring Compliance with the Charter of Fundamental Rights in Legislative Drafting: The Practice of the European Commission' (2012) 37 *European Law Review* 397, 417.

[14] Commission Staff Working Document, 'Impact Assessment Accompanying the document Proposal for measures on the strengthening of certain aspects of the presumption of innocence and of the right to be present at trial in criminal proceedings' SWD(2013) 478 final.

[15] Commission Staff Working Document, 'Impact Assessment accompanying the document Proposal for a Council Regulation on the establishment of the European Public Prosecutor's Office' SWD(2013) 274 final.

[16] This partially builds upon Muir's division of EU fundamental rights legislation into two groups: first, setting fundamental rights standards, and second, concerning fundamental rights protection on a specific subject matter. See E Muir, 'The Fundamental Rights Implications of EU Legislation: Some Constitutional Challenges' (2014) 51 *Common Market Law Review* 219, 221.

A. Commission Proposals Without a Fundamental Rights Objective

This section gives an overview of reasoned opinions in which national parliaments assess fundamental rights issues in legislative proposals that have no fundamental rights objective. Despite this, national parliaments argue that the level of protection proposed by the Commission is not satisfactory. Specifically, in the view of national parliaments, a draft legislative act may violate fundamental rights provided for in the EU Charter or the ECHR, as well as in a Member State's constitution, and hence lead to a violation of the subsidiarity principle and, in consequence, to the issuing of a reasoned opinion. The Commission proposal establishing the EPPO exemplifies the type of EU draft legislative act without a fundamental rights objective. Specifically, the objective of this proposal was the effective fight against offences affecting the EU budget.[17]

In what turned out to be the second 'yellow card' ever triggered, a number of national parliaments found that the Commission proposal on the establishment of the EPPO infringed a number of fundamental rights. The UK House of Commons argued that the Commission's proposal does not provide for a high enough level of protection of suspects' rights: for example, 'the lack of detail on arrangements for judicial review undermines the proposal's compliance with the Rule of Law'.[18] In the same vein, the Cypriot Vouli ton Antiprosopon found that the rights of suspects are insufficiently protected under the proposal, as it includes investigative measures that are not allowed 'under the national law of all Member States'.[19] Similarly, the Czech Senát highlighted a possible violation of a number of fundamental rights. The first infringement concerned the right to a lawful judge, 'due to [the] broad discretion' of the EPPO in the choice of the competent national court.[20] The second violation referred to the right to a fair trial, because of the single-instance decision-making of the EPPO, the absence of appellate procedures, and the absence of a procedure for adjudication on the objection of prejudice of the EPPO.[21] The Czech Senát found these aspects to be compromising the fundamental rights protection under the national constitution and the EU Charter.[22]

In its replies to national parliaments, the Commission included the opinions regarding fundamental rights into the group of arguments 'other than subsidiarity violations' and hence declared their falling outside the scope of the EWS. Nonetheless, the Commission promised that these concerns would be 'duly taken into account in the process of negotiating the Proposal and will be addressed in the political dialogue, and namely in the individual replies to be sent to the relevant national Parliaments'.[23] Acting through the political

[17] See Explanatory Memorandum, point 3.3.

[18] UK House of Commons, Reasoned opinion of 23.10.2013, point 17.

[19] Cypriot Vouli ton Antiprosopon, Reasoned opinion of 18.10.2013 on COM(2013) 534, 4.

[20] Czech Senát, Reasoned opinion of 09.10.2012 on COM(2013) 534, point II 6.

[21] ibid.

[22] See similar issues raised by the EU Fundamental Rights Agency: Opinion of the European Union Agency for Fundamental Rights on a proposal to establish a European Public Prosecutor's Office, FRA Opinion 1/2014, (04.02.2014).

[23] 'Communication from the Commission to the European Parliament, the Council and the National Parliaments on the review of the proposal for a Council Regulation on the establishment of the European Public Prosecutor's Office with regard to the principle of subsidiarity, in accordance with Protocol No 2' COM(2013) 851 final, point 2.1.

dialogue, the Commission pointed out that Article 11(1) of the proposal containing the basic principles of the EPPO's activity ensures that the actions of the EPPO respect the rights enshrined in the Charter. Specifically, with regard to the Cypriot Vouli ton Antiprosopon's concern on investigative measures, the Commission underlined that the proposal enshrines a catalogue of instruments available to the EPPO and applicable in all Member States, instruments which safeguard legal certainty, and coherence in investigation and will stop the fragmented use of investigative measures in crimes with an EU dimension.[24] In addition, the most intrusive investigative measures will demand the authorisation of a national court. With regard to the reasoned opinion of the Czech Senát, the Commission underlined that the right to a lawful judge is not compromised because the EPPO is a national authority for the purposes of judicial review.[25] The CJEU can interpret the regulation and ensure uniform application via the preliminary reference procedure. Judicial review also applies to the choice of jurisdiction. With regard to the right to a fair trial, the Commission explained that Article 27 of the proposal concerning prosecution before national courts provides clear, strict and objective criteria, leaving the EPPO limited discretion within the trial. The cases of conflict of interest can be brought before the European Public Prosecutor (EPP), and the case might then be reassigned. Moreover, the European delegated prosecutors (EDPs), the EPP, or his deputies might be dismissed.

While the reasoned opinions in the EPPO case addressed fundamental rights constraints as a subsidiarity violation, the reasoned opinion of the Swedish Riksdag on the Commission proposal for a regulation on measures to reduce the cost of deploying high-speed electronic communications networks provides a contrasting example.[26] This proposal aimed to enable the establishment of high-speed electronic communications networks and was based on Article 114 TFEU.[27] The Swedish Riksdag assessed the proposal negatively, pointing out that 'certain parts of the proposal are wide-ranging and intrusive, mainly regarding the right of landowners and the protection of ownership rights'.[28] Nevertheless, the Riksdag agreed with the Commission's assessment that the subsidiarity principle had not been violated, because only the EU level may improve the conditions for the implementation and functioning of the internal market in that area.[29] The Swedish example seems, however, to be an isolated case. In the EPPO case, the fundamental rights arguments are some of many raised in the reasoned opinions that tip the balance towards a subsidiarity violation, while in the Riksdag's reasoned opinion, a clear line between a subsidiarity violation and fundamental rights is drawn.

In sum, these examples show that reasoned opinions often include general comments on the consequences of Commission proposals for fundamental rights. However, the points raised by national parliaments do not concern the question of which level, the EU or Member States, is more apt to achieve the objective of the Treaties, such as the fight against

[24] Commission reply of 13.03.2014 to the reasoned opinion of the Cypriot Vouli ton Antiprosopon on COM(2013) 534.

[25] Commission reply of 13.03.2014 to the reasoned opinion of the Czech Senát on COM(2013) 534.

[26] 'Proposal for a Regulation of the European Parliament and the Council on measures to reduce the cost of deploying high-speed electronic communications networks' COM(2013) 147 final.

[27] See Art 1 of the proposal.

[28] Swedish Riksdag, Reasoned opinion of 30.05.2013 on COM(2013) 534.

[29] It could however be questioned whether the opinion of the Swedish Riksdag can be perceived as a reasoned opinion when no subsidiarity violation has been argued.

EU fraud or deploying high-speed electronic communications infrastructure to improve the conditions for the establishment and functioning of the internal market. In consequence, those matters concern the substance of the proposal, and it is debatable whether they should be addressed in the reasoned opinions.[30]

B. Commission Proposals with Fundamental Rights Protection as One of the Objectives

The second type of configuration of the relationship between the national standards of fundamental rights protection and those offered by a Commission proposal concerns situations in which the EU draft legislative act in question aims to achieve a number of objectives, only one of them being fundamental rights protection. The Commission proposals on 'General Data Protection Regulation' and third-country seasonal workers illustrate this setting.[31]

The objective of the General Data Protection Regulation was twofold: first, to provide rules relating to the protection of individuals with regard to the processing of personal data, and second, to offer rules relating to the free movement of personal data.[32] When assessing this proposal, the members of the Bundesrat contended that the Commission proposal lags behind German regulation in this area. Specifically, German law already offers 'nuanced data protection guarantees, which are more readily enforceable and offer a higher degree of legal security than the highly abstract individual provisions of the draft Regulation'.[33] The Belgian Chambre des représentants raised an identical argument on the higher level of data protection in Belgium, including in the public sector.[34] In the view of the Belgian Chambre des représentants, the directive should 'clearly demonstrate that it sets only a minimum standard while allowing national legislators to provide a higher level of protection, particularly in the areas of government, social security and health'. Finally, the French Sénat maintained, in general terms that 'in the area affecting the rights of citizens, the proposed regulation should not prevent Member States of the possibility to temporarily maintain more protective national provisions so that EU-wide harmonization will not lead to a decreased protection'.[35]

The second example discusses the directive on third-country seasonal workers. This directive attempted to manage migration flows by setting transparent rules for the admission and stay in order to protect them from social dumping. First, some national parliaments

[30] See ch 3.

[31] 'Proposal for a Regulation of the European Parliament and the Council on the protection of individuals with regard to the processing of personal data and on the free movement of such data (General Data Protection Regulation)' COM(2012) 11 final, and 'Proposal for a Directive of the European Parliament and of the Council on the conditions of entry and residence of third-country nationals for the purposes of seasonal employment' COM(2010) 379 final.

[32] Art 1(1) of the proposal.

[33] German Bundesrat, Reasoned opinion of 30.03.2012 on COM(2012) 11. See also Bundesrat Stenografischer Bericht of 30.03.2012, 180.

[34] Belgian Chambre des représentants, Reasoned opinion of 06.04.2012 on COM(2012) 11, par 2 in Rapport fait au nom de la Commission de la Justice, DOC 53 2145/001, 13.

[35] French Sénat, Reasoned opinion of 04.03.2012 on COM(2012) 11 (own translation).

condemned the proposal as granting rights to third-country nationals that are too weak to diminish the possibility of wage and social dumping.[36] For example, in comparison to the directive, Austria has granted seasonal workers the same rights as their own nationals in order to prevent their abuse. Further, the Dutch Eerste and Tweede Kamer expressed a differentiated view with regard to the directive. On the one hand, the Houses of the Dutch Parliament declared that third-country seasonal workers should stopped being exploited.[37] On the other hand, the Parliament maintained that European and global (International Labour Organization) agreements sufficiently protect the socio-economic rights of seasonal workers. To contest the proposal, the Czech Senát went even further. The Czech Senát focused specifically on the equal treatment with nationals of the hosting Member States with regard to such issues as freedom of association and affiliation and membership of an organisation representing workers, social security and the benefits defined in Article 3 of Regulation (EC) No 883/04 on the coordination of social security systems; the payment of statutory pensions based on the worker's previous employment; access to goods and services; and the supply of goods and services made available to the public.[38] The Parliament disagreed with a possible situation wherein the social rights of third-country seasonal workers will be more protected than those of the EU citizens from newer Member States that faced restrictions on the free movement of workers for a transitional period after they joined the EU.[39] In the same vein, the Polish Senat argued that the obligation on the employers of seasonal workers to provide evidence that a seasonal worker will have accommodation ensuring an adequate standard of living is more far-reaching compared with conditions applicable to local and other Member States' workers.[40]

These two examples of responses of national parliaments to Commission proposals allow two conclusions. First, when national parliaments question the protection of fundamental rights in Commission proposals with mixed objectives, the reasoned opinions point out both that a proposed EU standard might be too high or too low. For example, in the case of the proposed Data Protection Regulation, only the national parliaments in the Member States with standards that are supposedly higher than EU standards pointed to the fundamental rights issue in their reasoned opinions. However, in the case of the proposal on third-country seasonal workers, one which touches on socio-economic rights, both the parliaments of Member States that are destinations for cheap labour (eg, the Netherlands) and of those that provide this labour (ie, Poland, the Czech Republic) highlighted problems with the Commission proposal.

Second, the 'non-economic common objectives', such as fundamental rights protection, may coexist in Commission proposals next to other objectives such as 'market objectives' on the elimination of obstacles to trade or distortions of competition or, as in the examples above, the free movement of data or the management of migratory flows, are often not easy

[36] Austrian Bundesrat, Reasoned opinion of 05.10.2010 and Austrian Nationalrat, Reasoned opinion of 14.09.2010 on COM(2010) 379.

[37] Dutch Eerste and Tweede Kamer, Reasoned opinion of 14.10.2010 on COM(2010) 379.

[38] Art 16(2) of the proposal.

[39] Czech Senát, Reasoned opinion of 22.06.2010 on COM(2010) 379.

[40] Polish Senat, Reasoned opinion of 21.10.2010 on COM(2010) 379.

to distinguish from each other.[41] National parliaments should thus raise concerns about the fundamental rights in their reasoned opinions, as long as these are within the subsidiarity assessment. However, the next section will show the challenges of the subsidiarity assessment of 'genuine' fundamental rights proposals connected to the value choices enshrined in this reasoning.

IV. CASE STUDY OF A 'GENUINE' FUNDAMENTAL RIGHTS PROPOSAL

The case study of the 'Women on Boards' proposal exemplifies the third type of relationship between the subsidiarity principle and fundamental rights. The proposal represents a type of draft legislation wherein fundamental rights protection is the main objective. The fundamental right at stake in this case study is gender equality on public company boards. At first glance, gender equality has more of an economic justification than a social or moral one.[42] Nonetheless, the adoption of directives on equality and the Court's jurisprudence has given the principle of equality the status of a fundamental right, with dual economic and social roles.[43]

A. Divergent Standards at National Level

The financial crisis triggered the review of corporate governance codes; diversity in corporate boards became a new issue, indeed, '[t]he policy focus in Europe is almost entirely on gender diversity'.[44] Member States have taken divergent approaches to the position of women on boards: some introduced binding legislation, others non-binding corporate governance codes, while still others remained inactive.

Following Norway, a pioneering non-EU Member State at the time of the introduction of the 'Women on Boards' proposal, Belgium, France, Italy, the Netherlands and Spain had in place binding quota legislation for listed companies.[45] Belgium approved a law in 2011 aimed at achieving a share of women of one-third by 2017 for executive and non-executive boards in state-owned and listed companies or in 2019 for small and medium listed enterprises.[46]

[41] B de Witte, 'A competence to protect. The pursuit of non-market aims through internal market legislation' in P Syrpis (ed), *The Judiciary, the Legislature and the EU Internal Market* (Cambridge, Cambridge University Press, 2012) 26.

[42] C Barnard, 'Gender Equality in the EU: A Balance Sheet' in P Alston (ed), *The EU and Human Rights* (Oxford, Oxford University Press, 1999) 217.

[43] ibid.

[44] PL Davies and KJ Hopt, 'Corporate Boards in Europe—Accountability and Convergence' (2013) 61 *American Journal of Comparative Law* 301, 326.

[45] Commission Staff Working Document, 'Impact Assessment on Costs and Benefits of Improving the Gender Balance in the Boards of Companies Listed on Stock Exchanges, Accompanying the document Proposal for a Directive of the European Parliament and of the Council on improving the gender balance among non-executive directors of companies listed on stock exchanges and related measures' SWD(2012) 348 final, 49–52.

[46] Loi modifiant la loi du 21 mars 1991 portant réforme de certaines entreprises publiques économiques, le Code des sociétés et la loi du 19 avril 2002 relative à la rationalisation du fonctionnement et la gestion de la Loterie Nationale afin de garantir la présence des femmes dans le conseil d'administration des entreprises publiques autonomes, des sociétés cotées et de la Loterie Nationale, Moniteur Belge, 14.09.2011, Ed 2. See new Art 518 bis of the Code des sociétés.

If the number of board directors of a different sex does not reach the quota, any next appointment made in breach of that rule will be invalid and the benefits for board members suspended. France adopted a binding quota in 2011, set to 40 per cent by 2017, with an intermediate target of 20 per cent by 2014, and it applies to all listed companies and large unlisted companies.[47] Any appointment made in contravention of the provision on gender quotas which does not have the effect of remedying the unbalanced board composition is null.[48] However, decisions taken by board members appointed in violation of the quota would remain valid. Also in 2011, Italy approved a quota of one-third for female members of boards in all stock exchange listed companies and state companies by 2015.[49] The new law sanctions non-compliant companies with a warning and a four-month deadline to comply. If the company does not change its rules, it is to receive a fine of €20,000 and a second warning. If, within a further three months, no changes are introduced, the illegally appointed board members lose their positions. In the Netherlands, the Civil Code amended in 2011 proscribes that if the 30 per cent quota is not reached by the larger private and public limited companies, the mechanism of 'comply or explain' does not offer any sanction, but demands an explanation in the annual report and an action plan to improve the situation.[50] There are no sanctions for not reaching the 30 per cent quota.[51] In Spain, since 2007 state-owned companies should observe a 'balanced presence' of both genders of between 40 and 60 per cent, yet the law foresees no sanctions.[52]

Beyond the legislative quota, in some Member States, corporate governance codes recommend a target. For example, in the UK, the Lord Davies review (a government-endorsed commission) recommended a voluntary 25 per cent quota by 2015 to be reached by FTSE-100 companies. In Poland, the corporate code recommends that public companies ensure a balanced gender proportion on the management and supervisory boards.[53] Companies should report on the gender balance on their websites.

Other Member States are lagging behind.[54] Although Austria has introduced non-binding targets of 25 per cent and 35 per cent by 2013 and 2018, respectively, they concern only supervisory boards of state-owned companies.[55] Similarly, a 33 per cent quota was introduced in Greece in 2000, but, again, it concerns only fully or partially owned state companies.[56]

[47] Loi 2011-103 du 27 janvier 2011 relative à la représentation équilibrée des femmes et des hommes au sein des conseils d'administration et de surveillance et à l'égalité professionnelle, JORF no 0023 du 28 janvier 2011, 1680 and its reinforcement LOI no 2014-873 du 4 août 2014 pour l'égalité réelle entre les femmes et les hommes.

[48] Art 1 Loi 2011-103.

[49] Art 1 Legge 12 luglio 2011, n 120, Modifiche al testo unico delle disposizioni in materia di intermediazione finanziaria, di cui al decreto legislativo 24 febbraio 1998, n. 58, concernenti la parità di accesso agli organi di amministrazione e di controllo delle società quotate in mercati regolamentati, GU n 174 del 28-7-2011.

[50] Wet van 6 juni 2011 tot wijziging van boek 2 van het Burgerlijk Wetboek in verband met de aanpassing van regels over bestuur en toezicht in naamloze en besloten vennootschappen, Staatsblad 2011, 275. See also European Parliament, Legal Instruments for Gender Quotas in Mangement Boards, PE 474.413, 10.

[51] SWD(2012) 348 final, 51.

[52] Disposición adicional primera, Ley Orgánica 3/2007, de 22 de marzo, para la Igualdad Efectiva de Mujeres y Hombres.

[53] Dobre praktyki spółek notowanych na GPW. Dokument uchwalony w lipcu 2007 r, z późniejszymi zmianami i uzupełnieniami dokonanymi w latach 2010 i 2011, 12, available at: www.gpw.pl/pub/files/PDF/foldery/dobre_praktyki_GPW.pdf.

[54] See further Table 1.

[55] SWD(2012) 348 final, 54.

[56] ibid. See that the Commission's impact assessment qualified those measures as 'no action', probably because of their limited effect and focus on state companies.

B. The Commission Proposal

In 2011, the Commission took the first steps to increase gender equality in companies. Specifically, the Commission encouraged publicly listed companies in the EU to sign a 'Women on the Board Pledge for Europe', to commit to an increase in the number of women on their boards by self-regulatory measures, and by making commitments, to achieve a proportion of women on boards of 30 per cent by 2015 and 40 per cent by 2020.[57]

However, only 24 companies signed the pledge proposed by the Commission.[58] Lack of visible engagement by companies in improving the situation triggered the now famous statement by Commissioner Reding: 'I don't like quotas, but I like what quotas do'.[59] In November 2012, the Commission put forward a proposal for a directive 'on improving the gender balance among non-executive directors of companies listed on stock exchanges and related measures'.[60]

The aim of the Commission proposal is 'a floor of 40% presence of the under-represented sex among the non-executive directors of companies listed on stock exchanges'.[61] The idea behind the proposal is to 'promote gender equality in economic decision-making' and, in consequence, to achieve the Europe 2020 objectives.[62]

Specifically with regard to fundamental rights, the Commission stated, following Articles 2 and 3(3) TEU, that equality between women and men is one of the EU's founding values and core aims. Moreover, Article 8 TFEU provides that 'in all its activities, the Union shall aim to eliminate inequalities, and to promote equality, between men and women'. The Commission also argued that the proposal promotes the EU Charter rights, such as equality between women and men (Article 23) and the freedom to choose one's occupation (Article 15). Article 21, which encapsulates the anti-discrimination principle in the Charter, read together with the exception allowing measures on specific advantages in favour of the under-represented sex spoke also in support of the conformity of the proposal with the Charter. Finally, because the focal point of the proposal was on non-executive board members only, the interference with the right to run a business (Article 16) and right to property (Article 17) was, in the view of the Commission, proportional.

The legal basis of the proposal is Article 157(3) TFEU, which comprises the EU competence to adopt measures ensuring 'the application of the principle of equal opportunities and equal treatment of men and women in matters of employment and occupation, including the principle of equal pay for equal work or work of equal value'.[63] On proportionality, the Commission stressed that the proposal provides only for a minimum harmonisation and does not regulate small and medium-sized enterprises, for which following the quota requirement might have been overly burdensome.

[57] European Commission, MEMO/11/124 (01.03.2011).

[58] European Commission, Press release of 14.11.2012 'Women on Boards: Commission proposes 40% objective'.

[59] 'Waving a big stick, Quotas for women on boards in the European Union are moving a little closer' *The Economist* (10 March 2012).

[60] COM(2012) 614 final.

[61] Explanatory Memorandum, 5.

[62] ibid.

[63] See further 'Detailed explanation of the choice of the legal basis for the Commission's proposal for a Directive on improving the gender balance among non-executive directors of companies listed on stock exchanges and related measures' SWD(2013) 278 final.

Concerning the subsidiarity principle, the proposal went on to explain the differences between the less and more supportive national provisions on gender balance in companies. Compared with other EU draft legislative acts, the Commission provided a subsidiarity assessment more elaborate than usual. The legal diversity resulted in a range from 3 per cent to 27 per cent of women on the boards.[64] Relying on its impact assessment, the Commission emphasised that female representation on boards will not reach 40 per cent by 2020 without further measures. Additionally, some Member States held back from regulating this area for fear of becoming less competitive. Finally, the legal diversity was apt to produce problems in the functioning of the internal market, such as exclusion from public procurement because of a lack of compliance with national binding quotas in another Member State. In sum, because only an EU-level action could effectively achieve a 40 per cent female quota and diminish the internal-market-related problems, the proposal was in conformity with the subsidiarity principle.

Whereas the directive applies the notion of 'under-represented sex', the preamble shows quite clearly that it aims to enhance the presence of women on company boards.[65] The central provision of the proposed directive is Article 4, which sets a target for listed companies to achieve that women hold 40 per cent of the director positions on non-executive boards by 2020, or by 2018 in the case of listed companies that are public undertakings.[66] The non-executive boards are those that are 'not engaged in the daily management of the company and any member of a supervisory board in a dual board system'.[67] This distinction from executive members is important, as the proposal foresees that the directive's objective is met in cases in which the female members hold at least one-third of all director positions, both executive and non-executive.[68] Member States may exclude from the application of a 40 per cent quota listed companies for which the members of the under-represented sex represent less than 10 per cent of the workforce.[69] With regard to the executive boards, the proposal obliges the listed companies to make individual commitments on gender balance.[70] This obligation has a 'comply or explain' sanction.[71]

The Commission also explained the reason why only non-executive board members fall within the scope of the directive. Namely, the limitation is necessary in order to diminish the impact on the day-to-day management of companies. Also, the directive covers only publicly listed companies for a number of reasons: first, these companies are economically important and have higher visibility; second, they set standards for the private sector as a whole; and third, they have larger boards and a similar legal status across the EU, a situation which allows for more comparability.[72]

The appointments should be carried out 'on the basis of a comparative analysis of the qualifications of each candidate, by applying pre-established, clear, neutrally formulated and

64 Explanatory Memorandum, 9.
65 See recital 16 of the preamble.
66 As provided for in Art 10(2) of the proposal, the directive will expire in 2028.
67 Art 2(4) of the proposal.
68 ibid, Art 4(7).
69 ibid, Art 4(6).
70 ibid, Art 5(1) of the proposal.
71 ibid, Art 5(2) and (3).
72 Explanatory Memorandum, 5.

unambiguous criteria'.[73] However, the proposal does not oblige the companies to appoint women so that their membership will be 50 per cent or more of the non-executive members of the board, so that no 'excessive constraints' are put on companies.[74] In the selection procedure, Article 4(3) specifies that female candidates should be chosen if they are

> equally qualified as a candidate of the other sex in terms of suitability, competence and professional performance, unless an objective assessment taking account of all criteria specific to the individual candidates tilts the balance in favour of the candidate of the other sex.

The 'objective assessment' is a 'savings clause', which avoids granting absolute and unconditional priority to female candidates.[75] Member States will be obliged to secure that listed companies reveal the qualification criteria for the selection if requested by an unsuccessful candidate. National judicial systems must shift the burden to the listed companies to prove that the rules of the choice of female candidates were not breached.

The improvement of the gender balance is also directed at the situation of executive boards. The directive proscribes that listed companies should commit to improve the representation of both sexes among executive directors by 2020, or by 2018 in the case of listed companies that are public undertakings.[76] This is the so-called 'flexi quota' requiring companies to set their own individual targets for female members on executive boards.[77] The listed companies should report on the improvements in gender equality on executive and non-executive boards.[78]

Finally, the Commission proposal foresees that Member States introduce sanctions for infringements of national provisions implementing the directive. Article 7(2) of the proposal, following the general formula in equality legislation on 'effective, proportionate and dissuasive' sanctions, demonstrates that they may take the form of administrative fines or a court's annulment of an appointment contrary to the directive's rules.

The Commission proposal is 'relatively modest'—full gender parity has not been foreseen, and with a 'quite soft' quota, because at an advanced stage in a career, it is hard to define 'equality of qualification'.[79] Yet, taking into account the persistent problem of low rates of female representation, the proposal seems 'suited and necessary' to address this problem and should be complemented in the future by educational measures and parental leave and childcare policies, which are at the origin of the need for gender quotas.[80]

C. Reasoned Opinions of National Parliaments

Eight national parliaments issued reasoned opinions on this proposal: the Danish Folketing, the Czech Poslanecká sněmovna, the UK House of Commons and House of Lords, the

[73] Art 4(1) of the proposal.

[74] Explanatory Memorandum, 12.

[75] A Peters, *Women on Board: The EU Commission's Proposal for a Directive on Improving the Gender Balance among Non-Executive Directors of Companies Listed on Stock Exchanges and Related Measures* (2012).

[76] Art 5(1) of the proposal.

[77] SWD(2012) 348 final, 52.

[78] Art 5(2) of the proposal.

[79] Peters (n 75).

[80] ibid.

Dutch Eerste and Tweede Kamer, the Polish Sejm, and the Swedish Riksdag. The threshold for the 'yellow card' was not met, yet the arguments against the proposal require attention from the perspective of this chapter.[81]

The Czech Poslanecká sněmovna argued that the Commission violated the subsidiarity principle in that 'the adoption of affirmative measures in accordance with Article 157, paragraph 4 TFEU should be taken as closely as possible to the citizens, in this case, at the level of the Member States'.[82] In the same vein, the Danish Folketing maintained that national initiatives can attain a more balanced gender participation on boards and hence the proposal does not comply with the subsidiarity principle.[83]

Parliaments stated that the evidence on which the Commission relies is not sufficient for the proposal of EU measures. For example, the Polish Sejm underlined the problems with the Commission's evidence on the cause of gender under-representation, whereas the UK House of Commons argued that the Commission did not submit evidence confirming problems encountered within the internal market.[84]

Moreover, the UK House of Commons and the Dutch Eerste and Tweede Kamer argued that the reforms in many Member States began only recently and that there is not yet sufficient evidence for the need of the EU to act.[85] For example, in Sweden, the companies listed on stock exchanges have taken steps by self-regulation aiming to achieve an equal gender distribution, whereas in the Netherlands, the upcoming reform sets the female equality target at 30 per cent.[86] As the Polish Senat summarised it, 'the proposal is in effect aimed at substituting for legislation of those Member States, which do not decide to adopt positive legal measures to promote the under-represented sex'.[87] Following that approach, the UK House of Lords proposed that the Commission should issue non-binding recommendations to Member States to introduce some policy changes.[88]

The Polish Sejm posited that the proposal is contrary to the subsidiarity principle, because the 40 per cent target only for non-executive directors reinforces gender stereotypes.[89] In particular, the non-executive positions require less specialist knowledge and experience. An additional argument raised in the political dialogue by the Czech Senát was that the applicability of the directive to the non-executive boards only limits the real impact on gender equality.[90]

[81] The Czech Senát (22.03.2013.), Romanian Camera Deputatilor (16.04.2013) and the Portuguese Assembleia da República (08.01.2013) have issued opinions within the 'Barroso dialogue'. The Portuguese Parliament's opinion was supportive towards the proposal, no subsidiarity violation has been stated. The Romanian Parliament took in general a positive stance on the proposal with some reservations. The Czech Parliament was against the proposal, arguing that the Commission should first focus on the issues such as 'discrimination in maternity and paternity leave, gender pay gap and overcoming of gender stereotypes'.

[82] Czech Poslanecká sněmovna, Reasoned opinion of 06.12.2012 on COM(2012) 614.

[83] Danish Folketing, Reasoned opinion of 14.12.2012 on COM(2012) 614.

[84] Polish Sejm, Reasoned opinion of 04.01.2013 on COM(2012) 614.

[85] UK House of Commons, Reasoned opinion of 18.12.2012 on COM(2012) 614; Dutch Tweede and Eerste Kamer, Reasoned opinion of 18.12.2012 on COM(2012) 614.

[86] The reform entered into force in 2013. See Deloitte, 'Women in the boardroom. A global perspective', 5th edn (Global Center for Corporate Governance, 2017) 61.

[87] Polish Senat, Reasoned opinion of 09.01.2013 on COM(2012) 614.

[88] UK House of Lords, Reasoned opinion of 17.12.2012 on COM(2012) 614.

[89] Polish Sejm, Reasoned opinion of 04.01.2013 on COM(2012) 614.

[90] Czech Senát, Reasoned opinion of 22.03.2013 on COM(2012) 614, point II 6.

Another argument against the directive raised by national parliaments was that the distinction between executive and non-executive directors envisaged in the proposal demands changes in national legislation.[91] In fact, both the Polish Sejm and Swedish Riksdag underlined that the position of board members is not identical to that of a worker.[92] Board membership is often based on trust, and the direction and remuneration components might be missing.

Finally, some of the national parliaments issued an opinion within the political dialogue. Although some of the opinions were critical towards the Commission proposal, none of them established a subsidiarity violation, and the French Assemblée nationale even endorsed the EU target.[93]

In sum, the core of national parliaments' argument was that Member States have already introduced some measures and that they are better placed to improve the position of women on boards. In their view, the Commission had advanced insufficient evidence to the contrary.

Table 1: Policies on Gender Equality across the Member States

Member State	Share of women among members on boards %	National approach at the time of the scrutiny of Commission proposal COM(2012) 614	Reasoned opinion/political dialogue
Finland	27	Corporate Governance Code	
Latvia	26	No action	
Sweden	25	Corporate Governance Code	RO
France	22	Legislative Quota	PD
The Netherlands	19	Legislative Quota	RO
Denmark	16	Corporate Governance Code	RO
Germany	16	Corporate Governance Code	
United Kingdom	16	Corporate Governance Code	RO
Bulgaria	16	No action	
The Czech Republic	15	No action	RO/PD
Lithuania	15	No action	
Slovenia	15	No action	
Slovakia	13	No action	
Poland	12	Corporate Governance Code	RO

(continued)

[91] UK House of Lords, Reasoned opinion of 17.12.2012 on COM(2012) 614.

[92] Polish Sejm, Reasoned opinion of 04.01.2013 on COM(2012) 614 and of the Swedish Riksdag of 20.12.2012 on COM(2012) 614.

[93] Czech Senát, Opinion of 22.03.2013; French Assemblée nationale, Opinion of 22.11.2012; French Sénat, Opinion of 05.03.2013; Romanian Camera Deputatilor, Opinion of 16.04.2013; Estonian Riigikogu, Opinion of 19.12.2012; Portuguese Assembleia da República, Opinion of 08.01.2013, all on COM(2012) 614.

Table 1: ***(Continued)***

Member State	Share of women among members on boards %	National approach at the time of the scrutiny of Commission proposal COM(2012) 614	Reasoned opinion/political dialogue
Belgium	11	Legislative Quota	
Spain	11	Legislative Quota	
Austria	11	No action	
Romania	10	No action	PD
Ireland	9	No action	
Luxembourg	6	Corporate Governance Code	
Italy	6	Legislative Quota	
Estonia	6	No action	PD
Greece	6	No action	
Portugal	6	No action	PD
Hungary	5	No action	
Cyprus	4	No action	
Malta	3	No action	

Source: Prepared from data on female presence on corporate boards between 2004 and January 2012 in Commission Staff Working Document, Impact Assessment on Costs and Benefits of Improving the Gender Balance in the Boards of Companies Listed on Stock Exchanges, SWD(2012) 348 final, 58 and information on reasoned opinions and opinions under the 'political dialogue' according to IPEX.

Table 1 illustrates the percentage of women on boards, the national approach to the problem (legislation, corporate governance code), and whether the given Member State submitted a reasoned opinion or an opinion under the political dialogue on the proposal. The Table shows that reasoned opinions tended to be issued by parliaments in those Member States that had no existing legal quota and relatively high shares of women on boards. In these Member States, corporate governance codes or companies themselves set the targets (Sweden, Denmark, the UK, Poland, the Czech Republic). National parliaments with relatively low shares of female participation on boards tended not to submit a reasoned opinion.

D. The Commission's Reply

In its reply to the national parliaments, the Commission welcomed the legislative initiatives taken at the national level to improve the situation of women on boards in the Netherlands, Denmark and the UK.[94] Nonetheless, the Commission rejected self-regulation as an effective means to achieve gender equality. The Commission remained firm on its position,

[94] Commission reply of 17.07.2013 to the reasoned opinion of the Dutch Eerste and Tweede Kamer; of 17.07.2013 to the Danish Folketing; of 19.06.2013 to the UK House of Commons on COM(2012) 614.

arguing that the majority of Member States are not committing to increasing gender equality in big companies, and an action at the EU level is indispensable in this regard. However, Member States may follow their national approaches as long as they can show that their existing national measures are 'of equivalent effectiveness of reaching the target of a 40% representation of both sexes on company boards by 2020'. The Commission also explained that 'the method of achieving 40% would be binding (obligation of means), but not the 40% target itself (which is a target to attain)'.[95] This approach, in the view of the Commission, strengthens the compliance of the proposal with the principles of subsidiarity and proportionality.[96]

Replying to the argument raised by the Swedish Riksdag regarding the hampering of shareholders' rights in appointment decisions, the Commission underlined that the proposed directive does not force the shareholders to take any specific appointment decisions.[97] The directive, in view of the Commission, aims only to make the appointment procedures more transparent, but the qualification criteria remain set by the companies themselves, applying the rules of the directive on the preference for equally qualified candidates of the under-represented sex.

In relation to the gender stereotypes argument raised by the Polish Sejm, the Commission stressed that the directive also covers executive directors to the extent that listed companies should make their own commitments also in relation to executive directors.[98] Additionally, as listed companies can show that members of the under-represented sex hold at least one-third of all board positions, including executive directors, there is therefore no danger of prejudice.

E. Current Proceedings at the EU Level

The directive has not been adopted yet (August 2017). In the EP, the draft report submitted for the first reading introduced some changes such as extending the scope of the directive to non-listed public undertakings that do not fall under the definition of SME and to non-listed large undertakings.[99] The report also proposes the tightening of sanctions. Listed companies that 'do not establish, apply or respect the foreseen procedures for the appointment or the election of non-executive directors shall be subject to effective, proportionate and dissuasive sanctions'. Specifically, these companies should be excluded from public calls for tender and partially excluded from the award of funding from the European structural funds.

In the EP plenary debate on 19 November 2013, Commissioner Reding welcomed the amendments proposed in the report, but she was more reluctant with regard to the

[95] Commission reply of 17.07.2013 to the Danish Folketing on COM(2012) 614.

[96] Commission reply of 17.07.2013 to the Polish Senat on COM(2012) 614.

[97] Commission reply of 07.06.2013 to the Swedish Riksdag on COM(2012) 614.

[98] Commission reply of 17.07.2013 to the Polish Sejm on COM(2012) 614.

[99] European Parliament, Report on the proposal for a directive of the European Parliament and of the Council on improving the gender balance among non-executive directors of companies listed on stock exchanges and related measures, A7-0340/2013 (25.10.2013).

strengthening of sanctions, an action which may transpire to be disproportionate.[100] Subsequently, on 20 November 2013, the EP approved the Commission proposal. The legislative resolution provided the additional sanctions applicable to infringements of the national provisions adopted pursuant to the directive: an exclusion from public calls for tenders and a partial exclusion from the award of funding from the European structural funds.[101]

The proposal is currently awaiting the Council's first reading. Thus far, the Council is in deadlock and was unable to reach a general approach. The Council presidency proposed compromise solutions such as a flexibility clause that enables Member States to choose the means by which to achieve the EU target and suspends the procedural rules on the appointment process if a national measure already in place is equally effective or if the share of women is close to the 40 per cent gender quota.[102] The deadline for achieving the quota was extended in that proposal until the end of 2020. The Maltese presidency in the Council has then again attempted to reach an agreement on the proposal by extending the deadlines at stake by two years.[103] In sum, the Council amendments offer more flexibility to the Member States for the achievement of the EU target without compromising on that target.

In the meantime, facing the delays in the Council, the EP urged the Council to adopt the directive swiftly.[104] The EP sees the proposal as an important step for equal representation in the public and private sectors. Moreover, the EP concludes that progress in this respect has been made in Member States that adopted binding legislation on gender quotas.

F. Assessment

There exist a number of arguments favouring gender equality on corporate boards. These arguments give expression to the principle of equality, the principle of a social market economy, and the principle of democracy.[105] First, establishment of the gender quotas articulates the principle of equality between men and women, one of the foundational values of the EU, as expressed in Article 2 TEU. Moreover, one of the aims of the EU is to promote gender equality, as provided for in Article 3(3) TEU and Article 8 TFEU. There is no doubt that the proposed directive contributes to this aim of the EU Treaties. Second, the EU's objective to support a social market economy[106] demands the comprehensive participation

[100] ibid 14. Gender balance among non-executive directors of companies listed on stock exchanges (debate), 19.11.2013, PV 19/11/2013–14.

[101] European Parliament, 'Legislative Resolution of 20 November 2013 on the proposal for a directive of the European Parliament and of the Council on improving the gender balance among non-executive directors of companies listed on stock exchanges and related measures' P7-TA(2013)0488. For an overview of the amendments proposed by the EP see also Council, 'Outcome of the European Parliament's first reading' No 16284/13 (18.12.2013).

[102] Council document 14343/15 (30.11.2015).

[103] Council document 9496/17 (31.05.2017).

[104] European Parliament, 'Resolution of 14.03.2017 on equality between women and men in the European Union in 2014-2015', point 29.

[105] JC Suk, 'Gender Parity and State Legitimacy: From Public Office to Corporate Boards' (2012) 10 *International Journal of Constitutional Law* 449, 452; and M Szydło, 'Gender Equality on the Boards of EU Companies: Between Economic Efficiency, Fundamental Rights and Democratic Legitimisation of Economic Governance' (2015) 21 *European Law Journal* 97.

[106] Art 3(3) TEU.

of companies and other actors such as trade unions and NGOs in the establishment of legal provisions that will bind them.[107] Gender equality is hence necessary to give legitimacy to industrial democracy and economic and social governance.[108] Third, the principle of democracy speaks in favour of the directive. The example of Scandinavian and French corporatism shows that formal cooperation between the state and corporations demands that representative corporations legitimise state action.[109] In consequence, '[t]he state's legitimacy is compromised when the largest corporations fail to represent half of humanity if these corporations are recognized as exercising state power'.[110]

Even if the individual equality, social market economy, and democracy arguments speak in favour of the Commission's proposal, the question remains whether the proposal is compatible with the principle of subsidiarity. The proposal has been perceived to be in violation of the subsidiarity principle because it is too early to establish the ineffectiveness of national measures.[111] Instead of imposing reforms, then, the EU should, following Article 4(2) TEU on the EU's respect of national identities, support and respect the actions of the Member States.[112]

However, one should consider the existing female participation on corporate boards and the existing regulatory instruments across the different Member States in this respect. Table 1 indicates that, at the time when the Commission presented its proposal, the existing share of female board members, even in those Member States with the relatively highest numbers, was well below the proposed EU quota. The percentage of women on corporate boards in Finland, Latvia, Sweden, or France was between 22 and 27 per cent. Therefore, even those Member States that can boast the highest share of women within the EU fall well short of the 40 per cent quota, and even further short of equal representation. Nonetheless, the legal instruments in place in those Member States varied widely: there were recommendations for corporations in Finland and Sweden, no national legal measures in Latvia, and France had adopted a quota. This divergence in the approach among Member States with a high share of women indicates that a quota is not necessarily essential to reach a higher percentage of women on boards. Still, the outcomes in these countries are far from balanced board membership. Finally, the fact that a relatively high participation rates was achieved in Latvia with no formal instrument does not imply that other Member States would succeed without a legally binding quota.

All reasoned opinions on the 'Women on Boards' proposal arrived from Member States with a relatively high share of women, while none was issued by a parliament of a Member State with less than 10 per cent share of women. The national parliaments that did submit a reasoned opinion may argue that they are relatively far on the path towards equal rights as compared with those with low numbers, and thus they could achieve the EU target on their own. However, it is again worth pointing out that those Member States fall short of the proposed EU target and of equal gender representation more generally. More importantly from the subsidiarity perspective, there are also several Member States with very low shares

[107] Szydło, 'Gender Equality on the Boards of EU Companies' (n 105) 11.

[108] M Szydło, 'Constitutional Values Underlying Gender Equality on the Boards of Companies: How Should the EU Put These Values Into Practice?' (2014) 63 *International & Comparative Law Quarterly* 167, 183.

[109] Suk (n 105) 463.

[110] ibid 459.

[111] Szydło, 'Gender Equality on the Boards of EU Companies' (n 105) 16.

[112] ibid.

of women on boards and currently no action in place to rectify this situation. Therefore, those Member States appear to be unable to achieve the objective of gender balance, and their inability thus justifies the need for the EU to act.[113]

V. SCRUTINY OF FUNDAMENTAL RIGHTS PROPOSALS WITHIN THE EWS

The central question of this chapter is how subsidiarity relates to fundamental rights protection. In other words, under which circumstances is one level of government more apt to protect fundamental rights than the other level?

The application of the subsidiarity principle to EU legislative proposals on fundamental rights is conditioned on two premises: first, the EU does not have an exclusive competence in fundamental rights protection; and second, the EU competence is subsidiary to the protection offered in this regard at the national level.[114] Following the principle of subsidiarity, the level at which the protection of fundamental rights can be better achieved should prevail over that in which it cannot be sufficiently safeguarded. Yet, in those instances in which the EU should act, a 'forceful and comprehensive human rights policy' might violate the subsidiarity principle.[115]

The subsidiarity test as such has been criticised as inadequate to guide the setting of fundamental rights standards because of the function of the subsidiarity principle and the nature of fundamental rights.[116] First, while the subsidiarity principle concerns the choice of the right level for the exercise of competences in a transnational context, some pieces of EU legislation express a fundamental right '*within* States'.[117] In consequence, there is a 'mismatch' between the function of the EU subsidiarity principle and the function of EU fundamental rights standard-setting.[118] Second, the nature of fundamental rights is that they express values; this is in contrast to the subsidiarity test based on effectiveness. In consequence, a comparative efficiency test cannot be applied to conflicting fundamental rights standards that concern prioritising and balancing values.[119]

Moreover, the 'Women on Boards' proposal only marginally concerns truly transnational situations with substantive cross-border effects. Such a case would exist, for example, if a female member of a non-executive board would like to take advantage of the freedom of movement in the internal market and apply for a similar position in another Member State.[120] The case study proves that this piece of genuine fundamental rights legislation demanded from the national parliaments a value assessment: whether this right should be protected to a greater extent despite the lack of a clear cross-border situation. Nonetheless, fundamental rights clearly can concern transnational situations. Examples include the

[113] See ch 2.

[114] LFM Besselink, 'Entrapped by the Maximum Standard: On Fundamental Rights, Pluralism and Subsidiarity in the European Union' (1998) 35 *Common Market Law Review* 629, 677.

[115] von Bogdandy (n 1) 1317.

[116] Muir (n 16) 239.

[117] ibid 240.

[118] ibid 241.

[119] ibid.

[120] COM(2012) 614, Explanatory Memorandum, 3; recital 13 of the proposal's preamble.

Commission proposal on the right to strike or the draft directive strengthening certain aspects of the presumption of innocence and of the right to be present at trial in criminal proceedings that concerned judicial cooperation in criminal matters with a cross-border dimension.[121]

The question of effectiveness inherent in the subsidiarity test may, however, also apply to fundamental rights when applied to the practicalities of ensuring the protection of a fundamental right, for example, by indicating in the impact assessment how a binding quota will improve women's position in companies. To some extent, such thinking might seem to reduce the right to a specific numerical measure. In contrast, gender equality and its protection obviously go beyond the numerical share of women on a limited set of corporate boards.

One can also think about the protection of fundamental rights and subsidiarity looking at the issues of 'process', 'outcome' (capacity of the levels of authority to deal with certain issues), and 'willingness' rather than subsidiarity as an efficiency measure, which is a more open-ended approach to the allocation of the exercise of fundamental rights competences.[122] With regard to the decision-making process and willingness, Grainne de Búrca argued that, on the one hand, fundamental rights matters are best decided at the national level because that level has 'the information, the capacity and the political legitimacy to intervene'.[123] On the other hand, the balance can be tipped in favour of the EU or international level, which is 'less mired in the immediacy of a local political situation [and] is the more appropriate actor in certain human rights matters, since it is more likely to have the will, the independence, the wider experience and the normative authority to act'.[124] From the perspective of outcome, de Búrca argued that the national level might be more appropriate with regard to issues such as expressing the constitutional values and establishing the institutions for protection in a particular community, while an international institution might be more appropriate at monitoring and censuring how the community protects certain minimum guarantees or fulfils its other obligations. On the contrary, the international level can be better placed to establish shared international values and standards of protection in human rights, while the national, regional, or local level is better placed to govern the observance and implementation of those values and standards. The consequence is an 'inevitable interaction between those different levels and actors in adopting and carrying through a particular policy in a given sphere'.[125]

Looking at the proposal on 'Women on Boards' in light of de Búrca's views, acting at the EU level could increase the level of protection significantly in those Member States that at this point have very low shares of women on boards, such as Malta (3 per cent), Hungary (5 per cent) and Greece (6 per cent). This could help these Member States overcome national-level constraints such as, for example, the position of national parties concerning women in society. For example, the vote of the Polish Sejm on the reasoned opinion on the 'Women

[121] COM(2012) 130 and 'Proposal for a Directive of the European Parliament and of the Council on the strengthening of certain aspects of the presumption of innocence and of the right to be present at trial in criminal proceedings' COM(2013) 821 final.

[122] G de Búrca, 'Re-appraising Subsidiarity's Significance after Amsterdam' (2009) Harvard Jean Monnet Working Paper Series 7/99, 2–3.

[123] ibid 4.

[124] ibid.

[125] ibid.

on Boards' proposal clearly indicated the political cleavages on this issue.[126] Similarly, the left-wing government in Sweden, dissatisfied with the slow progress attempted to introduce legislation that would fine listed companies that do not have a 40 per cent share of women on their boards.[127] The government was opposed by the centre-right and a far-right party, holding together the parliamentary majority.[128] It is exactly this type of political constraint at the national level that proves the need for an EU-level proposal to increase protection of fundamental rights. The EU proposal on gender quotas thus seems to be a more apt measure to tackle gender equality on companies' boards than leaving the issue to be regulated at the national level. While Germany has adopted the Law for Equal Participation of Men and Women in Positions of Leadership (FüPoG), in force only since 1 May 2015, it has included a 30 per cent quota since the beginning of 2016.[129] The quota concerns under-represented gender on non-executive boards of all publicly listed German companies with employee representation on their boards, a group that includes around 100 of the largest German companies. Whenever a seat on a board becomes available it has to be filled with a woman or remain empty until the 30 per cent quota is met. Since the law has come into effect, the share of women on non-executive boards increased from 21.7 per cent in 2015 to 28.1 per cent in 2017.[130] Again, although improving the situation on German company boards, the quota and the share of women on boards in Germany falls short of gender equality.

VI. CONCLUSION

This chapter studied the interaction of the EWS and the EU's role as a 'community of values' with a complex system of fundamental rights protection, showing that not only the judicial process but also national parliaments act as 'watchdogs' of fundamental rights.[131] In this light, the involvement of national parliaments adds—next to the EP and the Council—to the politicisation of fundamental rights in the EU through the review of the subsidiarity principle.

In particular, this chapter presented how national parliaments deal with fundamental rights questions in their reasoned opinions. To this end, this chapter analysed three types of Commission proposal depending on whether and to what extent their objective is fundamental rights protection. With regard to the EU draft proposals without such a fundamental rights objective, for example, the EPPO Regulation, this chapter argued that concerns of national parliaments regarding fundamental rights protection deal with the substance of the proposal falling out of the scope of the EWS. Next, the analysis of reasoned opinions on Commission proposals with mixed objectives, which partially pursue fundamental rights protection, revealed that national parliaments argue that standards proposed by the EU are too low or too high. Finally, this chapter used the 'genuine' fundamental rights proposal

[126] Sejm, Sprawozdanie Stenograficzne z 31. Posiedzenia Sejmu Rzeczypospolitej Polskiej, 04.01.2013, 133. See ch 5.

[127] See Deloitte (n 86) 69.

[128] See 'Sweden rejects quotas for women on boards of listed companies' *The Guardian* (12 January 2017).

[129] Gesetz für die gleichberechtigte Teilhabe von Frauen und Männern an Führungspositionen in der Privatwirtschaft und im öffentlichen Dienst vom 24 April 2015 (BGBl I S 642).

[130] See: www.bmfsfj.de/quote/daten.html.

[131] On the EP and the Council role, see Muir (n 16) 221.

'Women on Boards' as a basis to discuss whether the subsidiarity review, which is based on assessing effectiveness of an action at different levels, is apt to deal with the value balancing inherent in fundamental rights protection.

In particular, this chapter pondered the fact that fundamental rights might in some circumstances have a rather limited cross-border dimension. While the 'Women on Boards' proposal, when reduced to quantitative values such as quotas, can undergo national insufficiency and comparative efficiency tests, it is also true that, as a value, gender equality reaches beyond the purely numerical share of women on boards in public companies. Assuming, however, that subsidiarity is applicable to choosing the more apt level of protection of fundamental rights, at times the local political constraints may tip the balance in favour of the more willing, independent and experienced action of the EU legislator, while at other times, national political legitimacy concerns may tilt the balance towards the national legislator, leaving only the monitoring function to the EU level. Yet, the universality of fundamental rights speaks in favour of legislative initiatives at EU level.

In sum, the question of whether the EWS can apply to scrutiny of Commission proposals with fundamental rights objectives should be answered positively. In their reasoned opinions assessing the subsidiarity principle, a national insufficiency and comparative efficiency test should take into account issues such as the local boundaries of the political process, political legitimacy, and the willingness to act and the value of universality of fundamental rights.

Conclusion

THIS BOOK SET out to explore the EU principle of subsidiarity, as viewed through the lens of the experience with the Early Warning System (EWS). This new mechanism, introduced by the Lisbon Treaty in Protocol No 2, allowed national parliaments to review whether EU draft legislative acts are compatible with the subsidiarity principle via a reasoned opinion. This process expresses the idea that the EU level should act only when the objectives of the proposed policy cannot be sufficiently achieved at the national level and, by reason of its scale or effects, the EU can better pursue that action.

Section I of this concluding chapter first summarises the findings of the book. Section II assesses how the current practice of the EWS relates to the two principal reasons behind endowing national parliaments with the policing of the subsidiarity principle, which were to increase the EU's democratic legitimacy and to diminish its 'competence creep'. Section III considers other reforms enhancing the role of national parliaments in the EU legislative process.

I. FINDINGS OF THE BOOK

The purpose of this book was to examine the EU principle of subsidiarity in light of the functioning of the EWS. On the basis of the Lisbon Treaty, national parliaments have been granted a new function, namely to scrutinise the EU's compliance with the subsidiarity principle. However, the consequences of the introduction of Protocol No 2 for the principle itself have been largely unexplored; in particular the content of the reasoned opinions has not undergone a detailed analysis.

Chapter one studied the origin, the development and the character of the subsidiarity principle in the EU context. Subsidiarity was already present in the papal encyclical of 1931 and existed in German constitutional law before it was established in the Union, first in the Maastricht Treaty and then in the Lisbon Treaty, as a principle to organise the exercise of shared competences. As such, it deals with the question central to the organisation of any federal system, even though the degree to which other countries rely on the subsidiarity principle formally varies significantly. Chapter one highlighted two possible approaches taken in Switzerland and the US, respectively. The chapter then reviewed the guidelines on the application of the EU subsidiarity principle established in the 'Overall Approach' and in the Amsterdam Protocol. It then discussed the links between the principles of Article 5(3) of the Treaty on the European Union (TEU)—namely conferral, subsidiarity and proportionality—that have an impact on the scope of national parliaments' review under the EWS. The Court of Justice of the European Union's (the Court) reading of the subsidiarity principle has not substantially changed since the entry into force of the Lisbon Treaty and the subsidiarity action available under Protocol No 2 has not yet been employed. The chapter then turned to discuss the decision to involve national parliaments in the policing of the subsidiarity principle as a remedy to the EU's perceived democratic deficit and 'competence creep'.

Having set the stage, the subsequent chapters then considered the principle of subsidiarity and the EWS from the perspective of national parliaments. Chapter two examined the gradually increased presence of national parliaments in the EU Treaties, culminating in the new powers granted under the Lisbon Treaty. The EWS to date has offered national parliaments the strongest competence in the EU legislative process. The chapter explored the details of the EWS, the competences of national parliaments and the EU institutions, as well as its practice in the context of interparliamentary cooperation. The product of the first six years under the EWS—a significant number of reasoned opinions, including three 'yellow cards'—offered the basis for a study that shed light on how national parliaments understand their role under the EWS. To this end, the analytical framework presented in chapter three provided textual, structural and functional arguments supporting a narrow understanding of the subsidiarity principle for the purpose of the EWS. The analysis of the first three yellow cards triggered by national parliaments indicated a general trend that national parliaments understand their role under the EWS in broad terms, while a closer examination of the proposals at stake did not seem to raise subsidiarity concerns. A careful study of the content of the reasoned opinions showed that national parliaments often marry subsidiarity and the proportionality principle and scrutinise the legal basis of Commission proposals, indicating that they understand subsidiarity in terms of a policy question.

The book also examined how national parliaments organise their subsidiarity review under the EWS. To this end, chapter four outlined different review systems including a centralised, mixed and decentralised procedure, depending on the involvement of the relevant parliamentary committees. While it was hypothesised that the mixed system would produce the largest number of reasoned opinions, a direct impact could not be established. Chapter five studied the content of debates and votes on issuing a reasoned opinion in four Member States (the UK, Germany, Poland and Belgium). National parliaments in those Member Statas appear to have gained some independence from their governments when issuing a reasoned opinion. Moreover, a significant convergence of views between the governing majority and the opposition in parliament was observed under the EWS. Nonetheless, certain differences along the traditional Left–Right axis and socio-economic cleavages remained visible in the admittedly rather rare cases of disagreement. The chapter also argued that the EWS permitted the expression of the concerns of the regional parliaments. Finally, the analysis of the parliamentary debates in the four Member States also made the case that defending idiosyncratic national interests and fighting against the redistributive character of EU policies, rather than concerns about subsidiarity per se, represent some of the key motivations behind issuing a reasoned opinion.

Chapters six, seven and eight provided three cases studies highlighting different aspects of the subsidiarity principle and its enforcement under the EWS. The study of the complete set of 379 reasoned opinions,[1] indicated that many of them confronted the Commission proposals because of a putative violation of the principle of conferral (chapter six). Much more unexpectedly, reasoned opinions addressed the delegations in the Commission proposals to regulate by means of delegated and implementing acts, an area where political safeguards of federalism are already in place (chapter seven). In both cases, the

[1] Based on Commission reports on subsidiarity and proportionality for years 2009–16. Additionally this number included 29 reasoned opinions that were issued in 2017 on Commission proposals with document number COM(2016).

Lisbon Treaty did not grant national parliaments a competence to conduct a review in these fields. This leads to the conclusion that the national parliaments used their participation in the EWS and their broad approach to increase their prerogatives in the EU legislative process. Chapter six, however, suggested that the reasoned opinions are often misguided when assessing the compliance of Commission proposals with the principle of conferral, in some cases simply misunderstanding the limits of EU competence. Similarly, when national parliaments assessed Commission proposals with delegations by means of delegated acts, they in fact delved into a question of 'horizontal division of power'. This appears to be redundant because the Lisbon Treaty has provided a political safeguard in the area of delegated acts, as the European Parliament (EP) and the Council can revoke the delegation of power to the Commission or express an objection to the delegated act within a certain period, thereby stopping it from entering into force. Further, with regard to the delegations to adopt implementing acts, the Lisbon Treaty offered sufficient safeguards: Member States control the implementing powers, either through the adoption of national laws implementing EU acts or through national experts in committees.

Finally, chapter eight, with a focus on EU fundamental rights, established that the subsidiarity test of proposals with fundamental rights objectives is not easily conducted in the usual efficiency terms or as a cross-border test, since the review in question focuses largely on values and not externalities of Member State actions. In those cases, when scrutinising the subsidiarity principle in their reasoned opinions, national parliaments should take into account the local boundaries of the political process, political legitimacy and the willingness of each level to provide protection to fundamental rights.

II. THE EWS AS AN ANSWER TO THE 'DEMOCRATIC DEFICIT' AND 'COMPETENCE CREEP'?

Upon its introduction, the EWS was perceived as a tool that would combine the fight against 'competence creep' with one that would bring more democratic legitimacy to the EU. This section addresses the question as to whether it has achieved these objectives.

A. 'Democratic Deficit'

In her post-Lisbon assessment of the state of EU democracy Gráinne de Búrca underlined that despite

> numerous efforts [having] been put over the decades, particularly in the last decade and a half to strengthen its democratic quality, we still see intractable democratic difficulties in the EU: popular alienation, distance between the ordinary citizen, the voter and the EU as a governing entity. The essence of democracy … —responsiveness to a real person—remains elusive in the EU context despite the work that has been done to build democratic institutions, despite parliamentary elections, a powerful European Parliament, the democratically elected members of the Council of Ministers, enshrined principles of transparency, a strong EU court, layers of constitutional rights protection.[2]

[2] G de Búrca, ICON·S 2014 Inaugural Conference Speech (June 2014).

This rather pessimistic account of the EU's democratic legitimacy does not refer directly to the EWS. Nonetheless, the Lisbon Treaty clearly provided an opportunity to enhance the EU's representative democracy by involving directly elected national parliaments.[3] Thus we can ask whether the EWS in fact improved the EU's democratic credentials. This question is addressed first from the perspective of the impact of reasoned opinions on the legislative process. Second, this section critically assesses the claim that by conducting a broad scrutiny of Commission proposals, national parliaments enhance the democratic legitimacy of the EU. Third, this section discusses whether the EWS somewhat strengthens the position of those national parliaments that are otherwise weakest in the scrutiny of EU affairs overall.

First, one way to measure the influence of the EWS on the EU's democratic legitimacy is to examine whether the reasoned opinions have any real impact on the legislative process. Legally, changes in response to reasoned opinions are generally not required. Article 7 of Protocol No 2 only provides that the institution from which a draft legislative act originates shall take account of the reasoned opinions issued by national parliaments. Therefore, except where an 'orange card' is triggered, there is no necessary direct link between national parliaments' submissions and the decisions of the EP or the Council concerning the content of the draft legislative act.

Even if no changes are required legally, the European institutions may still respond to the criticism of national parliaments. For example, in the case of the 'Women on Boards' proposal, discussed in chapter eight, the position of the EP shows support for the Commission proposal and even argues for strengthening it, while the negotiations in the Council have not yet been concluded as of September 2017. The tabled amendments in the negotiations point towards offering more flexibility to the Member States on the achievement of gender equality on corporate boards. Similarly, the adopted Tobacco Products Directive studied in detail in chapter seven indicates that some aspects of the reasoned opinions with regard to delegations of power to the Commission have been taken on board by the EU legislator.[4] Nonetheless, one cannot empirically ascertain the influence of national parliaments in these changes, as neither the Council nor the EP referred directly to the reasoned opinions as the reason for amending the proposal.

The EWS is not the only avenue for national parliaments to influence the EU legislative process. The 'Barroso initiative' presents a valuable alternative for addressing non-subsidiarity related issues relating to Commission proposals. The changes reported by the Commission, as well as discussed in the literature,[5] show that the Barroso initiative has indeed had an impact on the EU law-making process.

Second, it is often claimed that, by conducting a broad scrutiny of Commission proposals, national parliaments enhance the democratic legitimacy of the EU. Specifically, national parliaments are seen as 'completely political, and therefore "multifunctional", and thus should be free to interpret the meaning and the function of their interventions in the EU

[3] R Bellamy and S Kröger, 'Domesticating the Democratic Deficit? The Role of National Parliaments and Parties in the EU's System of Governance' (2014) 67 *Parliamentary Affairs* 437.

[4] See A Héritier, C Moury and K Granat, 'The Contest for Power in Delegated Legislation' in CF Bergström and D Ritleng (eds), *Rulemaking by the European Commission: The New System for Delegation of Powers* (Oxford, Oxford University Press, 2016) 120–26.

[5] D Jančić, 'The Barroso Initiative: Window Dressing or Democracy Boost?' (2012) 8 *Utrecht Law Review* 78, 85.

decision-making process differently, according to the context and to the case in question'.[6] An approach that is too formal and legalistic can 'condemn the new procedures as ill-targeted'.[7] Giving national parliaments more leeway with regard to competence and proportionality control is capable of enriching the debate about the quality of EU law, especially as no 'red card' veto is foreseen.[8]

This book argues that broadening the scope of national parliaments' involvement may be counterproductive. When the national parliaments triggered their first yellow card against the draft proposal on the right to strike on the basis of broad scrutiny under the EWS, the Commission decided to withdraw its proposal. Although the Commission justified the withdrawal on the basis of the possible lack of necessary support in the Council and the EP in the future, national parliaments claimed that their reasoned opinions were the reason for the Commission's action. Their 'yellow card' thus was perceived to carry the force of a 'red card'. However, an implicit veto from a broad application of subsidiarity review by national parliaments would be significant and may negatively affect the delicate balance of powers between the Member States and the EU.[9] Indeed, the Commission's refusal to withdraw the proposals targeted with the two subsequent yellow cards can be seen in part as a move on the part of the Commission to push back against this implicit red card.[10]

Moreover, a broad approach under the EWS would mean replicating the role already played by the Barroso initiative. By the end of 2016, the number of opinions sent within the political dialogue (3,473) outnumbered those within the EWS. This implies that allowing broadly drafted reasoned opinions would also have probably increased the total number of reasoned opinions received by the Commission. For the Commission to address these formally as required under the EWS would likely have involved concessions on the speed and efficiency of the legislative procedure, and would probably not satisfy national parliaments.

Third, the EWS can contribute to diminishing the 'democratic deficit' by strengthening the position of national parliaments that are otherwise weak in their scrutiny of EU affairs. Nonetheless, the degree of involvement by national parliaments in the EWS shows little relationship with their strength in EU affairs more generally. Using one of the latest rankings on the strength of national parliaments in EU affairs,[11] and comparing it with the Commission's annual reports on EWS participation, we find that, among the national parliaments that are the most active in the EWS, some are ranked as very strong (eg, Sweden and Poland), while some are ranked as particularly weak (eg, France and Luxembourg) with regard to their strength in terms of scrutiny of EU affairs. Likewise, among those least active

[6] N Lupo, 'National parliaments in the European integration process: re-aligning politics and policies' in M Cartabia, N Lupo and A Simoncini (eds), *Democracy and Subsidiarity in the EU* (Bologna, Il Mulino, 2013) 127. See also Marija Bartl, who makes the point that an important component of democratic deficit is the absence of expressly political actors that could be brought in through subsidiarity review. See M Bartl, 'The Way We Do Europe: Subsidiarity and the Substantive Democratic Deficit' (2015) 21 *European Law Journal* 23.

[7] S Weatherill, 'Competence Creep and Competence Control' (2004) 23 *Yearbook of European Law* 1, 45.

[8] ibid 46.

[9] See ch 3.

[10] There might have also been other reasons why the Commission maintained its proposals. See ch 3.

[11] J Karlas, 'National Parliamentary Control of EU Affairs: Institutional Design after Enlargement' (2012) 35 *West European Politics* 1095, 1102. This ranking is based on such indicators as the scope of parliamentary scrutiny of EU affairs; involvement of parliamentary committees in the scrutiny; mechanisms of influence such as mandating; the binding character of the scrutiny; and the role of the upper chamber. It also takes into account new Member States.

under the EWS, the national parliamentary control in Finland and Slovenia is classified as strong, while that in Belgium and the Czech Republic is classified as weak. It thus seems that the EWS does not generally empower weak parliaments with a new avenue of impact on EU affairs, but that some parliaments rely on the EWS to have more say on Commission proposals.[12]

In sum, this section assessed the experience with the EWS against the objective of improving the EU's democratic legitimacy. First, in the absence of explicit evidence, it is impossible to trace the causal impact that the reasoned opinions had within the legislative procedure, but there are some signs that reasoned opinions and yellow cards do have consequences for Commission proposals. Second, the argument that granting national parliaments broad scrutiny powers under the EWS would be required to truly imbue the process with democratic legitimacy must be rejected as it would endanger the EU's institutional balance established by the Treaties.[13] Third, while EWS participation cannot be directly linked to the empowerment of weak parliaments in their scrutiny of EU affairs more generally, it does present an opportunity for national parliaments to actively scrutinise Commission proposals disregarding their relative strength elsewhere. I thus conclude that the EWS provides an effective but limited avenue for national parliaments to influence EU legislation. However, on balance it is unlikely to fully address the concerns behind the EU's democratic deficit.

B. 'Competence Creep'

The question of 'competence creep' not only deals with the issue of whether the EU has a competence or whether a legal basis has been chosen correctly. It also asks whether the shared competence can be executed at national level, instead of being assimilated into the EU's competences. It thus at least partly directly overlaps with the objective of the subsidiarity principle, but is broader in scope, and includes the question as to whether the EU has a competence to act in the first place. Chapter six illustrated the frequent concerns of national parliaments regarding the lack of competence and the choice of legal basis of Commission proposals. It was pointed out that, in some cases, the reasoned opinions are misguided in their analysis of the provisions enabling EU action. Moreover, the comparative institutional analysis presented in chapter three indicated that the Court is better suited to conduct this type of scrutiny.

By contrast, 'competence creep' understood as a condition in which a shared competence that can be executed at national level is instead exercised at the EU level directly concerns the subsidiarity principle. Both the Netherlands and the UK made enquiries into the EU's creeping competence from this perspective.[14] In June 2014, after a review of EU legislation conducted by each of the Dutch ministries in its area of specialisation, a list of

[12] However, it has been shown elsewhere that the EWS might have a larger than expected impact on national parliaments' scrutiny of EU affairs, at least for those parliaments that had previously been rather inactive pre-Lisbon, even if that greater degree of activity is not reflected in the number of reasoned opinions issued. See E Miklin, 'Beyond subsidiarity: the indirect effect of the Early Warning System on national parliamentary scutiny in European Union affairs' (2017) 24 *Journal of European Public Policy* 366, 381.

[13] J-P Jacqué, 'The Principle of Institutional Balance' (2004) 41 *Common Market Law Review* 383.

[14] Editors, 'Review of the Balance of Competences' (2014) 41 *Legal Issues of Economic Integration* 127.

'54 points of action' was drawn up, aiming to initiate a process towards 'European where necessary, national where possible'.[15] The Dutch proposal listed a number of recommendations including, for example, that the legal basis of EU proposals should be clearly stated. Where the EU has no competence, it should also refrain from making recommendations. EU proposals should concentrate on the main lines of policy and their goals, and avoid detailed regulation. Finally, impact assessments should be used more often so that the proportionality principle is safeguarded.[16] The 'points of action' provided a list of areas which the Dutch government perceived as better left to Member States, yet without introducing any treaty change. Some 'points of action' highlight that the issue at stake 'can best take place at national level' or that the issue does not have a 'transnational character'.[17] Yet, clearly not all these problems directly concern subsidiarity. In some cases, the Dutch government argued that no legislation was necessary,[18] and (only) in one case the legal basis was found to be problematic.[19] Other points concerned different aspects of proportionality,[20] and the substance of proposals.[21] This review of EU competences offered by the Dutch government shows a trend similar to that envisaged in this book.

In December 2014, the UK government concluded its own two-year 'Review of the balance of competences'.[22] The aim was to analyse the meaning of EU membership for the UK national interest. The first report in the series enquired into the balance of competences between the UK and the EU in the Single Market.[23] It resolved that there is an overall benefit to the UK from participation in the internal market, confirmed by the evidence submitted, increasing both the EU's and UK's GDP relative to what it would otherwise have been, underlining however that 'much depends on the future direction of the Single Market'.[24] Furthermore, in the area of health, the balance of competence was likewise assessed as 'broadly appropriate'.[25] Moreover, it is 'generally strongly in the UK's interests to work through the EU in foreign policy', and that Member States should remain in charge of the Interparliamentary Conference for the Common Foreign and Security Policy and the Common Security and Defence Policy, while some comparative disadvantages were also indicated.[26] With regard to the EU's supporting competences in culture, tourism and sport, they were seen as 'on balance either beneficial to the future development of these sectors and UK national interest or had the potential to be so'.[27] Some reports were more ambivalent.

[15] Ministerie van Buitenlandse Zaken, Testing European legislation for subsidiarity and proportionality—Dutch list of points for action. See also M Emerson, 'The Dutch wish-list for a lighter regulatory touch from the EU' *CEPS Commentary* (1 July 2013).

[16] Ministerie van Buitenlandse Zaken, Testing European legislation for subsidiarity and proportionality—Dutch list of points for action, 1–3.

[17] ibid, see points 11, 23, 25, 31 and 36.

[18] ibid, see points 26 and 41.

[19] ibid, see point 54.

[20] ibid, see points 1, 30, 39.

[21] ibid, see point 47.

[22] UK government, 'Review of the Balance of Competences between the United Kingdom and the European Union'. All reports are available at: www.gov.uk/review-of-the-balance-of-competences.

[23] Report on the Single Market, July 2013.

[24] ibid, point 3.45.

[25] Report on Health, July 2013, point 5.1.1.

[26] Report on Foreign Policy, July 2013, points 6.2, 6.3 and 6.4.

[27] Report on Culture, Tourism and Sport, February 2014, point 3.1.

For example, the report on the free movement of persons was seen both as positive for the UK economy, but also framed in negative terms as creating competition on the job market and problems connected with public services and housing.[28] Nonetheless, even in this case, the problem does not seem to be 'competence creep': the EU was not encroaching on a competence of a Member State; it was rather the effect of a certain policy. The final report that focused on the subsidiarity and proportionality principles indicated some proposals to improve respect for the subsidiarity principle and the role of national parliaments within it.[29] Overall, the UK competence review fell short of establishing 'competence creep' in the EU.[30]

In sum, as the Dutch and British reports show, 'competence creep' does not represent the main problem faced by the EU, as is sometimes argued. Thus, the fact that there have been only three yellow cards so far should not be interpreted as an argument that the EWS represents an ineffective mechanism for decreasing the EU's 'competence creep'. Instead, it may be fully consistent with the paucity of cases where the EU exceeds its competences.

III. OUTLOOK: REFORM PROPOSALS

This section focuses on the possibilities for strengthening the role of national parliaments—both within the EWS and beyond—that have been debated by parliaments and scholars alike. The national parliament most prominently involved in the reform discussions, the UK House of Lords, proposed, inter alia, to include the proportionality principle within the scope of the subsidiarity review and argued that the 'yellow card' should lead the Commission to drop a proposal or to amend it.[31] More generally, national parliaments have been making a case with regard to two recurring issues: to be accorded more time for their scrutiny, by extending the deadline for submission of reasoned opinions; and to improve the quality of Commission replies to the reasoned opinions.[32] Other reform proposals argue for broadening the scope of the EWS: some signal the need for merging the Barroso initiative and the EWS; others the need to bring the principle of conferral and the substance of proposals under the EWS.[33] However, such reforms would require treaty amendment.

Additionally, the reform proposals have moved beyond improvements within the existing yellow card procedure. In particular, proposals that would allow national parliaments to block the legislative procedure ('red card') have been discussed. The possibility for national

[28] Report on the Single Market: Free Movement of Persons, summer 2014.

[29] Report on Subsidiarity and Proportionality, December 2014.

[30] Indeed, the UK House of Lords European Union Committee has criticised the government for failing to provide a final summarising report and to publicly promote the outcomes. In fact, the UK government was accused of 'burying' the report as it did not prove that EU action was excessively affecting the UK. See House of Lords, European Union Committee, *12th Report of Session 2014–15*; 'Lords accuse Tories of "burying" review that cleared EU of interference' *The Guardian* (25 March 2015).

[31] House of Lords, European Union Committee, *12th Report of Session 2014–15*, paras 79 and 95.

[32] COSAC, 19th Bi-annual Report, 27.09.2012, 28; COSAC, 24th Bi-annual Report, 04.11.2015, 17–23; COSAC, 26th Bi-annual Report, 18.10.2016, 23–25.

[33] S Garben, 'Confronting the Competence Conundrum: Democratising the European Union through an Expansion of its Legislative Powers' (2015) 35 *Oxford Journal of Legal Studies* 55, 87; D Jančić, 'The Game of Cards: National Parliaments in the EU and the Future of the Early Warning Mechanism and the Political Dialogue' (2015) 52 *Common Market Law Review* 939, 942. See on this issue, ch 3.

parliaments to put forward EU legislative proposals or to seek amendments to the existing legislation ('green card') has been already operating as an informal initiative of the national parliaments. The 'red card light', a proposal made by Donald Tusk shortly before the UK referendum on Brexit, was the only initiative emanating from the EU, rather than national parliaments, or academia, representing the only instance where the EU seemed to make a concession towards national parliaments. A selection of the most prominent proposals is discussed and assessed in the following section.

A. 'Green Card'

Over the six years since the entry into force of the Lisbon Treaty national parliaments successfully managed to organise themselves and launch a 'green card' procedure. This procedure, known also as a 'test of democratic responsiveness'[34] or 'enhanced political dialogue,'[35] was officially suggested by the Conference of European Affairs Committees (COSAC) in 2013[36] and was further elaborated with the input of some of the national parliaments.[37] The core idea of the green card is to allow a number of national parliaments to work together to suggest new or amend existing EU legislation.[38] National parliaments have discussed within COSAC the particularities of the green card, for example: its scope; the relevant threshold to trigger the card; the deadline to join the initiative; and the involvement of the EP.[39] Although national parliaments have not adopted any formal rules of procedure on the green card, the green card has been operating informally and has so far been triggered three times: in two cases a new initiative was proposed, while in one case the proposal aimed at revising the Audiovisual Services Directive.[40]

The first and most successful green card, inviting the Commission 'to adopt a strategic approach to the reduction of food waste within the EU', was launched by the UK House of Lords in July 2015 gathering 16 signatories (out of 41 national parliaments and their chambers).[41] The Commission replied that it will be attentive to the suggestions of national parliaments when working on the Circular Economy package.[42] The proposed package

[34] D Chalmers, 'Democratic Self-Government in Europe: Domestic Solutions to the EU Legitimacy Crisis' (2013) 15 *Policy Network Paper* 9.

[35] COSAC, 24th Bi-annual Report (n 32) 10.

[36] Contribution of the XLIX COSAC Dublin, 23–25 June 2013, point 31.

[37] See House of Lords, European Union Committee, *9th Report of Session 2013–14*, para 58; Danish Folketing European Affairs Committee, 'Twenty-Three Recommendations to strengthen the role of national parliaments in a changing European governance' (January 2014) 2; Tweede Kamer, 'Ahead in Europe. On the role of the Dutch House of Representatives and national parliaments in the European Union' (09.05.2014) 14.

[38] On different understandings of what 'green card' procedure can mean see C Fasone and D Fromage, 'From Veto Players to Agenda-Setters? National Parliaments and Their "Green Card" to the European Commission' (2016) 23 *Maastricht Journal of European and Comparative Law* 294, 312. See also K Borońska-Hryniewiecka, 'From the Early Warning System to a "Green Card" for National Parliaments: Hindering or Accelerating EU Law-making?' in D Jančić (ed), *National Parliaments after the Lisbon Treaty and the Euro Crisis* (Oxford, Oxford University Press, 2017); M Serowaniec, 'Towards the "green card"—strengthening the role of national parliaments in EU affairs?' [2015] *Toruńskie Studia Polsko-Włoskie* 29.

[39] See COSAC, 23rd Report, 06.05.2015, 31–39; COSAC 24th Biannual Report (n 32) 10–17.

[40] Luxembourg Chambre des Députés, Conference of Speakers of the EU Parliaments, 22–24 May 2016, Background note, Session III, 2.

[41] Letter of 22.07.2015 from Lord Boswell of Aynho to the European Commission.

[42] Commission reply of 17.11.2015, C(2015) 7982 final.

arguably addressed the majority of national parliaments' considerations which coincided with other initiatives in that policy area at the time, yet the Commission did not introduce a separate legislative proposal on food waste.[43] The green card initiated in July 2016 by the French Assemblée nationale and supported by seven other signatories calling on the Commission to introduce a proposal on the strengthening of corporate social responsibility had a similar result.[44] However, the Commission replied that it will not propose further legislation, instead citing a number of policy actions undertaken or in progress in the area.[45]

The process of establishing the 'green card', as compared with the 'yellow card' provided by Protocol No 2, was therefore truly bottom-up in nature. To the extent that the green card functions only as a suggestion, rather than an obligation, for the Commission to propose a draft legislative act, the procedure does not violate the right to initiative vested in the Commission in Article 17(2) TEU. Placing the Commission under an obligation to propose a corresponding piece of legislation could have a negative impact on the EU's balance of powers, which is an 'essential constitutional value'.[46] It can compromise the role of the Commission as an initiator of EU legislation. Moreover, the operation of a modest green card (without obligation for the Commission) might run in parallel with the already existing possibility of an invitation from the Council for the Commission to present a proposal.[47] National parliaments can always convince their governments to back their proposal through this forum.[48]

B. 'Red Card'

In contrast to the 'green card', the 'red card' proposals have a negative or destructive potential for the EU's functioning. The red card proposals draw from the original red card procedure discussed and ultimately rejected by the European Convention.[49] That original red card procedure conditioned rejection of a Commission proposal on the basis of two-thirds of parliaments submitting a reasoned opinion.[50]

The red card proposals have taken various forms over the years after the entry into force of the Lisbon Treaty. These proposals concern either triggering the card during the ongoing EU legislative procedure, particularly in its final phase ('late card');[51] or only after the EU

[43] Borońska-Hryniewiecka (n 38) 252. See European Parliament, The Role of National Parliaments in the EU after Lisbon: Potentialities and Challenges (2017) 37.

[44] French Assemblée nationale, Corporate social accountability: proposal for an initiative by the European Commission, available at: ec.europa.eu/dgs/secretariat_general/relations/relations_other/npo/docs/france/own_initiative/oi_green_card_corporate_social_responsibility/oi_green_card_corporate_social_responsibility_assemblee_opinion_en.pdf.

[45] Commission reply of 15.12.2016, C(2016) 8579 final.

[46] B de Witte, 'Community Law and National Constitutional Values' (1991) 18 *Legal Issues of Economic Integration* 1, 7.

[47] Art 241 TFEU.

[48] See the evidence given by Commissioner Šefčovič to the House of Lords, Select Committee on the European Union Inquiry on the Role of National Parliaments in the European Union, Evidence Session No 6 Heard in Public, Question 94 (07.01.2014).

[49] See ch 3.

[50] See Contribution by Gisela Stuart, member of the Convention 'The Early Warning Mechanism—putting it into practice' CONV 540/03 (06.02.2003) 3.

[51] See Dutch Tweede Kamer, 'Ahead in Europe' (n 37) 43.

act has been adopted. Another distinction in the proposals is between granting parliaments individual or collective rights under the red card.

Accordingly, one of the red card proposals vests a group of national parliaments with a red card power during the EU legislative process. Such a red card could be triggered by either at least 40 per cent of votes of national parliaments stating that the proposal is not compatible with the subsidiarity and/or proportionality principles; or by at least 25 per cent of votes, if these votes represent at least 33 per cent of the EU's population; or in case of EU acts demanding unanimity, by one-eighth of votes.[52] Another proposal labelled 'a test of relative democratic authority' conditions the success of an EU draft legislative act on active support of two-thirds of national parliaments.[53] Lack of such a support would force the Commission to cast aside the proposal, in consequence allowing national parliaments to block the EU legislative procedure. Another version of the red card is the suggested 'Final Check System', allowing those national parliaments that have submitted a reasoned opinion to check the act agreed by the EU legislator.[54] Such an act would not be finally adopted, if a certain threshold of national parliaments' votes finds the act to be 'fundamentally changed' as compared with the initial proposal, with the Court as the final arbiter in those cases.[55] In the same vein, yet focusing on competences of individual parliaments, the UK House of Commons advanced the idea of a mechanism, according to which the Parliament can decide prior to the adoption of a particular EU legislative proposal that it should not apply to the UK.[56] Its consequence would be that the government opposes the proposal, including voting against it. A final type of red card concerns already adopted EU acts: an individual national parliament could introduce laws disapplying EU law in cases where an independent study shows that an EU act produces costs that outweigh the benefits for the Member State.[57] The idea of disapplication of EU law found support in the UK House of Commons which suggested a possibility for the chamber to disapply parts of the existing acquis.[58]

Not all the national parliaments support introduction of a red card. For example, the Dutch Tweede Kamer negatively assessed the late card allowing the majority of national parliaments to reject the decision of the EU legislator.[59] The Dutch Tweede Kamer argued the act adopted by the EU legislator is legitimate and national parliaments should instead focus on the process of drafting of EU acts.

Granting national parliaments a red card power that could halt the EU legislative procedure has been perceived as 'an enormous concession to the supposed wisdom of national Parliaments at the expense of efficient problem-solving initiated by the Commission and carried forward by the Council and the European Parliament'.[60] A veto power for national

[52] D Wyatt, *Response to Call for Evidence questions on Subsidiarity, Proportionality, and Article 352 TFEU* (2014) 2 available at: www.gov.uk/government/consultations/subsidiarity-and-proportionality-review-of-the-balance-of-competences.

[53] Chalmers (n 34) 9.

[54] Garben (n 33) 88.

[55] ibid.

[56] House of Commons, European Scrutiny Committee, *Reforming the European Scrutiny System in the House of Commons, Twenty-fourth Report of Session 2013–14*, para 170.

[57] Chalmers (n 34) 10.

[58] House of Commons, European Scrutiny Committee, *Reforming the European Scrutiny System* (n 56) para 171.

[59] See Tweede Kamer, 'Ahead in Europe' (n 37) 30.

[60] Weatherill, 'Competence Creep and Competence Control' (n 7) 44.

parliaments would negatively affect the distribution of power in the EU which has proved to be successful without granting too much control to the Member States.[61] Therefore, it would likely be disruptive and have a negative impact on the functioning of the EU, if national parliaments could intervene to stop the EU legislator—a power which was explicitly denied them at the European Convention. Finally, the possibility to disapply EU law by national parliaments, even if only in limited cases, could disintegrate the EU system and break the EU principle of loyalty enshrined in Article 4(3) TEU. This principle commands Member States to take measures 'to ensure fulfilment of the obligations arising out of the Treaties or resulting from the acts of the institutions of the Union'.

C. Institutional Reforms

In June 2014, the chairpersons of a majority of the EU affairs committees of national parliaments addressed a letter to Jean-Claude Juncker, the presidential nominee of the Commission. They called for a working group, which would include members of national parliaments and representatives of EU institutions, with the aim of drafting 'an action plan on ways to strengthen the role of national parliaments in the European Union'.[62] The letter underlined that the participation of national parliaments must move beyond the subsidiarity review and the oversight of their respective governments' actions in the Council. In this regard, the letter explained that three national parliaments (the Dutch Tweede Kamer, the UK House of Lords and the Danish Folketing) had advanced some proposals, which focus on the following questions. The first question concerned designing a democratic framework that would take into account the enhanced role of the EU in economic governance, while at the same time respecting the prerogatives of national parliaments. The second and third questions enquired more generally about possible ways national parliaments can contribute to the good functioning of the EU, and to ensuring that EU citizens are not 'alienated' from the EU decision-making process.

Such a working group has not been created. Instead, in February 2016 a draft declaration 'on a subsidiarity implementation mechanism and a burden reduction implementation mechanism' suggested another mechanism.[63] It obliged the Commission to create a mechanism for the review of existing EU legislation for its compatibility with the subsidiarity and proportionality principles with the aim of providing 'full implementation' of subsidiarity. The task force about to be introduced seems to go in this direction: Jean-Claude Juncker, the President of the European Commission, in his 2017 State of the Union speech has signalled an immediate launch of a Subsidiarity and Proportionality Task Force headed by the Commission's First Vice President, to ensure that the EU acts only where it can add value. The task force will include MEPs and members of national parliaments.[64] This institutional

[61] S Weatherill, 'Using National Parliaments to Improve Scrutiny of the Limits of EU Action' (2003) 28 *European Law Review* 909, 912.

[62] Joint Letter to Jean-Claude Juncker, 'on the establishment of a Commission working group on the role of national parliaments in the EU' (30.06.2014).

[63] European Council, Draft declaration of the European Commission on subsidiarity implementation mechanism and burden reduction implementation mechanism, 02.02.2016, EUCO 7/16.

[64] European Commission, President Jean-Claude Juncker's State of the Union Address 2017, Press release, (13.09.2017).

development can be positively assessed, since it focuses on subsidiarity and proportionality, rather than suggesting an open-ended role for the task force, thereby coupling it with the existing forms of interparliamentary cooperation in the EU.[65] Nonetheless, a lack of details on the operation of the task force precludes drawing conclusions on its value for the enforcement of the subsidiarity principle.

D. 'Red Card Light'

Thus far, the furthest the EU has gone to offer concessions toward a deeper involvement of national parliaments at the EU level is the proposal that relies on the already existing mechanism for national parliaments to control EU affairs, namely through influence on their representatives in the Council. The proposal provides a procedure that could be branded a 'red card light' and was introduced as a means of helping to keep the UK in the EU by offering a way to enhance the role of national parliaments.[66] The proposal of Donald Tusk, President of the European Council, envisioned that if the reasoned opinions, submitted within 12 weeks of the publication of an EU draft, represent more than 55 per cent of votes allocated to national parliaments (at least 31 of the 56 available votes) they will be 'comprehensively discussed' in the Council.[67] If the EU draft legislative act is not changed in a manner reflecting the concerns of national parliaments in their reasoned opinions, the Council will discontinue the consideration of that draft.

This proposal differed from Lisbon's 'yellow' and 'orange' card schemes in a number of ways. In particular, the changes concerned the time frame, applicable thresholds and the effects of the procedures. First, the extended submission deadline would have probably satisfied national parliaments, yet it was unclear whether the extension to 12 weeks under Tusk's proposal would also have been applied to the existing yellow and orange card procedures.[68] Second, although the mechanism of assignment of votes to national parliaments did not change, Tusk's proposal offered a new threshold of votes to be met by national parliaments, which differed from the threshold under Protocol No 2. To activate the procedure proposed by Tusk, the necessary threshold was 55 per cent of the votes allocated to national parliaments. Therefore, out of 56 votes of national parliaments, 31 would have been needed to meet the 'more than 55 per cent' threshold in Tusk's proposal, compared with 19 for a yellow card, and 29 for an orange card. The new procedure thus required only slightly more votes than the existing orange card which, thus far, has never been successfully triggered. Third, the most substantial change concerned the consequences of activating the new procedure. Tusk's proposal seemed to omit the phase in which the Commission can respond to national parliaments. Instead, Tusk's proposal moved directly to the Council discussion, at which point Member States' representatives were to 'discontinue' the consideration of the EU draft act, if that draft was not amended to accommodate the 'concerns' expressed by national parliaments.

[65] N Lupo and C Fasone, *Interparliamentary Cooperation in the Composite European Constitution* (Oxford, Hart Publishing, 2016).
[66] Draft Decision of the Heads of State or Government, 'A New Settlement for the United Kingdom within the European Union' (02.02.2016).
[67] Section C, pts 2–3.
[68] COSAC, 24th Bi-annual Report (n 32) 22.

In sum, Tusk's proposal made it a condition of stopping the legislative procedure dependent on whether the requests of national parliaments were met. In comparison, the orange card provided for discontinuation only if the Council finds a breach of the subsidiarity principle. It is worth noting that important details of the procedure were left unspecified by Tusk, such as who is responsible for amending the proposal and more importantly for verifying whether the concerns of national parliaments were addressed. This seemed problematic, as in its interaction with the national parliaments, the Commission has often expressed itself satisfied that the concerns of the parliaments expressed in the reasoned opinions have been addressed by the original proposal.[69] Nevertheless, Tusk's proposal demanded a more active response from EU institutions than the orange card.

Moreover, one should note that Tusk's proposal did not grant national parliaments a veto power over any aspect of a Commission proposal. Tusk's proposal mentioned that the discontinuance of the legislative procedure was conditional on the non-accommodation of the 'concerns' expressed in the reasoned opinions, with the ultimate decision taken by the Council, away from the national parliaments.

Furthermore, Tusk's proposal referred throughout to reasoned opinions on the non-compliance of proposals with the subsidiarity principle, although, as this book has demonstrated, national parliaments adopt a broad approach to such a subsidiarity review. It was unclear whether under Tusk's proposal, such a broad interpretation of the subsidiarity principle would also have been adopted in the Council. If so, this might have caused difficulties in amending a proposal in a way that properly takes account of all the different aspects raised by national parliaments and in consequence also made it easier to halt the legislative procedure because of the lack of accommodation of the demands of the parliaments.

A broad reading of Tusk's proposal would have therefore probably been more in line with David Cameron's wish of strengthening national parliaments by allowing a threshold of national parliaments 'to stop unwanted legislative proposals'.[70] The 'red card light'—which would have still demanded a treaty amendment—by focusing on the Council negotiations, seemed to offer a compromise solution without threatening to disrupt the EU legislative procedure. Yet, in the referendum of 23 June 2016, the UK decided to leave the EU and Tusk's proposal has not been discussed since.

E. Using the Existing Tools of Scrutiny

Nevertheless, the proposal tabled by Tusk, although unsuccessful, highlighted the role of the Council in any scrutiny of EU legislation by national parliaments. Depending on the relationship between parliaments and their governments represented in the Council, the ministers might have shown more or less flexibility with the 'concerns' of their national parliaments and with whether a consensus on stopping or continuing with the legislative procedure could have been achieved. This leads to what is arguably the best way forward to enhance the outcome of reasoned opinions under the current EWS model.

[69] See House of Lords, European Union Committee, *9th Report of Session 2013–14*, para 87.
[70] Letter from David Cameron to Donald Tusk of 10.11.2015, 4.

The introduction of the EWS seems to have diverted attention in academia away from other means of parliamentary control such as scrutiny of national representatives' action in the Council. In fact, the EWS is only one of the many ways in which national parliaments participate in the EU legislative process.[71] Their main function in EU affairs is to control the ministers representing the Member States in the Council.[72] Through their national representatives in the Council, national parliaments can still make their concerns on Commission proposals heard at the EU level.[73] Yet, only a very few national parliaments play the dual role of both 'government watchdog' and 'policy shaper', combining exercising control over the government with influencing its policy.[74] Moreover, some national parliaments do not fully exercise the control powers that have already been made available to them.[75] Although the Council acts by qualified majority voting, unless provided otherwise in the Treaties,[76] consensus is still usually sought in the Council.[77] By pursuing greater control over their own national governments, national parliaments can thus significantly contribute to the shape of EU legislation.

It remains to be seen whether and how the EWS can be upgraded in the future. However, any meaningful reform would demand a treaty amendment. Until then, the control of national governments in EU affairs remains a readily available, viable and effective tool, to be employed by national parliaments, in addition to the EWS.

[71] K Auel and C Neuhold, 'Multi-arena players in the making? Conceptualizing the role of national parliaments since the Lisbon Treaty' (2017) 24 *Journal of European Public Policy* 1547.

[72] Weatherill, 'Using National Parliaments to improve scrutiny of the limits of EU action' (n 61) 912.

[73] On the relationship between national parliaments and their government see especially COSAC, 27th Bi-annual Report, 03.05.2017, 11–12.

[74] C Neuhold and J Smith, 'Conclusion: From "Latecomers" to "Policy Shapers"?—The Role of National Parliaments in the "Post-Lisbon" Union' in C Hefftler et al (eds), *The Palgrave Handbook of National Parliaments and the European Union* (Basingstoke, Palgrave Macmillan, 2015) 675.

[75] See D Fromage, 'Executive Accountability to National Parliaments in Post-crisis EU Affairs: The Persistent Shortcomings in the Council and European Council Oversight' in D Jančić (ed), *National Parliaments after the Lisbon Treaty and the Euro Crisis: Resilience or Resignation?* (Oxford, Oxford University Press, 2017).

[76] Art 16(3) TEU.

[77] See FM Häge, 'Coalition Building and Consensus in the Council of the European Union' (2013) 43 *British Journal of Political Science* 481.

Bibliography

Auel, K, 'Democratic Accountability and National Parliaments: Redefining the Impact of Parliamentary Scrutiny in EU Affairs' (2007) 13 *European Law Journal* 487.

Auel, K and Benz, A, 'The politics of adaptation: The Europeanisation of national parliamentary systems' (2005) 11 *The Journal of Legislative Studies* 372.

Auel, K and Neuhold, C, 'Multi-arena players in the making? Conceptualizing the role of national parliaments since the Lisbon Treaty' (2017) 24 *Journal of European Public Policy* 1547.

Auel, K and Raunio, T, 'Debating the State of the Union? Comparing Parliamentary Debates on EU Issues in Finland, France, Germany and the United Kingdom' (2014) 20 *The Journal of Legislative Studies* 13.

Azoulai, L, 'Introduction' in L Azoulai (ed), *The Question of Competence in the European Union* (Oxford, Oxford University Press, 2014).

Bagehot, W, *The English Constitution*, 2nd edn (Boston, MA, Little, Brown and Company, 1873).

Baker, LA, 'Putting the Safeguards Back into the Political Safeguards of Federalism' (2001) 46 *Villanova Law Review* 951.

Barber, NW, 'Subsidiarity in the Draft Constitution' (2002) 11 *European Public Law* 197.

—— 'The Limited Modesty of Subsidiarity' (2005) 11 *European Law Journal* 308.

Barnard, C, 'Gender Equality in the EU: A Balance Sheet' in P Alston (ed), *The EU and Human Rights* (Oxford, Oxford University Press, 1999).

Barrett, G, '"The King is Dead, Long Live the King": The Recasting by the Treaty of Lisbon of the Provisions of the Constitutional Treaty Concerning National Parliaments' (2008) 33 *European Law Review* 66.

—— 'Monti II. The Subsidiarity Review Process Comes of Age … Or Then Again Maybe It Doesn't' (2012) 19 *Maastricht Journal of European and Comparative Law* 595.

—— 'Long Train Running: The Slowly Developed (and Slowly Developing) Role of Ireland's Oireachtas in EU Affairs' in C Hefftler et al (eds), *The Palgrave Handbook of National Parliaments and the European Union* (Basingstoke, Palgrave Macmillan, 2015).

Bartl, M, 'The Way We Do Europe: Subsidiarity and the Substantive Democratic Deficit' (2015) 21 *European Law Journal* 23.

Bednar, J, *The Robust Federation: Principles of Design* (New York, Cambridge University Press, 2009).

Bellamy, R and Kröger, S, 'Domesticating the Democratic Deficit? The Role of National Parliaments and Parties in the EU's System of Governance' (2014) 67 *Parliamentary Affairs* 437.

Bergström, CF and Ritleng, D, 'Patterns and Findings: Five Central Themes' in CF Bergström and D Ritleng (eds), *Rulemaking by the European Commission: The New System for Delegation of Powers* (Oxford, Oxford University Press, 2016).

Bermann, GA, 'Taking Subsidiarity Seriously: Federalism in the European Community and the United States' (1994) 94 *Columbia Law Review* 331.

Besselink, LF, 'Entrapped by the Maximum Standard: On Fundamental Rights, Pluralism and Subsidiarity in the European Union' (1998) 35 *Common Market Law Review* 629.

—— 'National Parliaments in the EU's Composite Constitution: A Plea for a Shift in Paradigm' in P Kiiver (ed), *National and Regional Parliaments in the European Constitutional Order* (Groningen, Europa Law Publishing, 2006).

Bickenbach, C, 'Das Subsidiaritätsprinzip in Art 5 EUV und seine Kontrolle' [2013] *Zeitschrift Europarecht* 523.

Biondi, A, 'Subsidiarity in the Courtroom' in A Biondi, P Eeckhout and S Ripley (eds), *EU Law After Lisbon* (Oxford, Oxford University Press, 2012).

Birkinshaw, P, 'A Constitution for the European Union? A Letter from Home' (2004) 10 *European Public Law* 57.

Blanke, T, 'The Principle of Subsidiarity in the Lisbon Treaty' in N Bruun, K Lörcher and I Schömann (eds), *The Lisbon Treaty and Social Europe* (Oxford, Hart Publishing, 2012).

Borońska-Hryniewiecka, K, 'Regions and subsidiarity after the Treaty of Lisbon: overcoming the "regional blindness"' in M Cartabia, N Lupo and A Simoncini (eds), *Democracy and Subsidiarity in the EU* (Bologna, Il Mulino, 2013).

—— 'From the Early Warning System to a "Green Card" for National Parliaments: Hindering or Accelerating EU Lawmaking?' in D Jančić (ed), *National Parliaments after the Lisbon Treaty and the Euro Crisis* (Oxford, Oxford University Press, 2017).

—— 'Regional parliamentary empowerment in EU affairs. Building an analytical framework' (2017) 23 *The Journal of Legislative Studies* 144.

Brouillet, E, 'Canadian Federalism and the Principle of Subsidiarity: Should We Open Pandora's Box?' (2011) 54 *The Supreme Court Law Review: Osgoode's Annual Constitutional Cases Conference* 601.

Brouillet, E and Ryder, B, 'Key Doctrines in Canadian Legal Federalism' in P Oliver, P Macklem and N Des Rosiers (eds), *The Oxford Handbook of the Canadian Constitution* (Oxford, Oxford University Press, 2017).

Buzogány, A, 'Learning from the Best? Interparliamentary Networks and the Parliamentary Scrutiny of EU Decision-Making' in B Crum and JE Fossum (eds), *Practices of Interparliamentary Coordination in International Politics* (Colchester, ECPR Press, 2013).

Calabresi, SG and Bickford, LD, 'Federalism and Subsidiarity: Perspectives from US Constitutional Law' (2014) 55 *Nomos LV* 123.

Calliess, C, *Subsidiaritäts-und Solidaritätsprinzip in der Europäischen Union* (Baden-Baden, Nomos, 1996).

—— 'Subsidiaritätskontrolle durch Bundestag, Bundesrat und Landesparlamente, § 23' in W Kluth and G Krings (eds), *Gesetzgebung—Rechtsetzung durch Parlamente und Verwaltungen sowie ihre gerichtliche Kontrolle* (Heidelberg, CF Müller, 2013).

Calliess, C and Beichelt, T, 'The Europeanization of the Bundestag: From Observer to Player?' [2013] *Bertelsmann Stiftung* 31.

Carter, CA, 'Rethinking UK Parliamentary Adaptation in EU Affairs: Devolution and Europeanisation' (2013) 19 *The Journal of Legislative Studies* 392.

Cass, DZ, 'The Word that Saves Maastricht? The Principle of Subsidiarity and the Division of Powers within the European Community' (1992) 29 *Common Market Law Review* 1107.

Cavatorto, S, 'Italy: Still Looking for a New Era in the Making of EU Policy' in C Hefftler et al (eds), *The Palgrave Handbook of National Parliaments and the European Union* (Basingstoke, Palgrave Macmillan, 2015).

Chalmers, D, 'Democratic Self-Government in Europe: Domestic Solutions to the EU Legitimacy Crisis' (2013) 15 *Policy Network Paper*.

Chalmers, D, Davies, G and Monti, G, *European Union Law: Cases and Materials* (Cambridge, Cambridge University Press, 2014).

Christiansen, T, Högenauer, A-L and Neuhold, C, 'National Parliaments in the post-Lisbon European Union: Bureaucratization rather than Democratization?' (2014) 12 *Comparative European Politics* 121.

Cieślik, Z and Pawłowski, B, 'Zmiana roli parlamentów narodowych w Unii Europejskiej (według Traktatu reformującego Unię Europejską, przyjętego w Lizbonie, w dniach 17–18 października 2007 r), Mozliwosc badania zasady pomocniczosci w polskim parlamencie' (2007) 16 *Zeszyty Prawnicze* 37.

Constantinesco, V, 'Les compétences et le principe de subsidiarité' (2005) 2 *Revue trimestrielle de droit européen* 305.

Cooper, I, 'The Watchdogs of Subsidiarity: National Parliaments and the Logic of Arguing in the EU' (2006) 44 *Journal of Common Market Studies* 281.
—— 'A "Virtual Third Chamber" for the European Union? National Parliaments after the Treaty of Lisbon' (2012) 35 *West European Politics* 441.
—— 'A yellow card for the striker: national parliaments and the defeat of EU legislation on the right to strike' (2015) 22 *Journal of European Public Policy* 1406.
—— 'The politicization of interparliamentary relations in the EU: Constructing and contesting the "Article 13 Conference" on economic governance' (2016) 14 *Comparative European Politics* 196.
Craig, P, *The Lisbon Treaty: Law, Politics, and Treaty Reform* (Oxford, Oxford University Press, 2010).
—— 'Delegated Acts, Implementing Acts and the New Comitology Regulation' (2011) 36 *European Law Review* 671.
—— 'The European Union Act 2011: Locks, limits and legality' (2011) 48 *Common Market Law Review* 1881.
—— *EU Administrative Law* (Oxford, Oxford University Press, 2012).
—— 'Subsidiarity: A Political and Legal Analysis' (2012) 50 *Journal of Common Market Studies* 72.
Crum, B and Fossum, JE, 'Practices of Interparliamentary Coordination in International Politics: the European Union and Beyond' in B Crum and JE Fossum (eds), *Practices of Interparliamentary Coordination in International Politics* (Colchester, ECPR Press, 2013).
Cygan, A, *National Parliaments in an Integrated Europe: An Anglo-German Perspective* (The Hague, Kluwer Law International, 2001).
—— *Accountability, Parliamentarism and Transparency in the EU* (Cheltenham, Edward Elgar Publishing, 2013).
—— 'Regional Governance, Subsidiarity and Accountability within the EU's Multi-Level Polity' (2013) 19 *European Public Law* 161.
—— 'COSAC: Birth, Evolution, Failures and Perspectives' in N Lupo and C Fasone (eds), *Interparliamentary Cooperation in the Composite European Constitution* (Oxford, Hart Publishing, 2016).
Dann, P, 'Looking through the federal lens: The semi-parliamentary democracy of the EU' (2002) Jean Monnet Working Paper 5/02.
Davies, G, 'The Post-Laeken Division of Competences' (2003) 28 *European Law Review* 686.
Davies, PL and Hopt, KJ, 'Corporate Boards in Europe Accountability and Convergence' (2013) 61 *American Journal of Comparative Law* 301.
de Búrca, G, 'The Principle of Subsidiarity and the Court of Justice as an Institutional Actor' (1998) 36 *Journal of Common Market Studies* 217.
—— 'Re-appraising Subsidiarity's Significance after Amsterdam' (2009) Harvard Jean Monnet Working Paper Series 7/99.
—— ICON·S 2014 *Inaugural Conference Speech 26.06.2014* (2014).
de Búrca G, and de Witte, B, 'The Delimitation of Powers Between the EU and its Member States' in A Arnull and D Wincott (eds), *Accountability and Legitimacy in the European Union* (Oxford, Oxford University Press, 2002).
de Jesús Butler, I, 'Ensuring Compliance with the Charter of Fundamental Rights in Legislative Drafting: The Practice of the European Commission' (2012) 37 *European Law Review* 397.
de Wilde P, 'Why the Early Warning Mechanism does not Alleviate the Democratic Deficit' (2012) OPAL Online Paper Series 6/2012.
de Witte, B, 'Community Law and National Constitutional Values' (1991) 18 *Legal Issues of European Integration* 1.
—— 'A competence to protect. The pursuit of non-market aims through internal market legislation' in P Syrpis (ed), *The Judiciary, the Legislature and the EU Internal Market* (Cambridge, Cambridge University Press, 2012).

Delgado del Saz, S, 'Die Rolle der nationalen Parlamente nach dem Vertrag von Lissabon—ein Vergleich zwischen spanischem und deutschem Recht' (2011) 67 *Berliner Online-Beiträge zum Europarecht* 30.

Delreux, T and Randour, F, 'Belgium: Institutional and Administrative Adaptation but Limited Political Interest' in C Hefftler et al (eds), *The Palgrave Handbook of National Parliaments and the European Union* (Basingstoke, Palgrave Macmillan, 2015).

Devuyst, Y, 'The European Union's Institutional Balance after the Treaty of Lisbon: Community Method and Democratic Deficit Reassessed' (2007) 39 *Georgetown Journal of International Law* 247.

Dias Pinheiro, B, 'The Role of COSAC in the Changing Environment of National Parliaments in the EU: An Identity Crisis?' in N Lupo and C Fasone (eds), *Interparliamentary Cooperation in the Composite European Constitution* (Oxford, Hart Publishing, 2016).

Driessen, B, 'Delegated legislation after the Treaty of Lisbon: An analysis of Article 290 TFEU' (2010) 35 *European Law Review* 837.

Editors, 'Review of the Balance of Competences' (2014) 41 *Legal Issues of Economic Integration* 127.

Edward, D, 'Subsidiarity as a Legal Concept' in P Cardonnel, A Rosas and N Wahl (eds), *Constitutionalising the EU Judicial System: Essays in Honour of Pernilla Lindh* (Oxford, Hart Publishing, 2012).

Elsmore, MJ and Obolevich V, 'Thank You for Not Smoking: The Commission's Proposal for a New Tobacco Products Directive—Legally Sound, but Does it Hit the Spot?' (2013) 38 *European Law Review* 552.

Emerson, M, 'The Dutch wish-list for a lighter regulatory touch from the EU' *CEPS Commentary* (1 July 2013).

Emilianides A, Christou, O and Ioannou, C, 'The Cypriot Parliament and EU Affairs' in C Hefftler et al (eds), *The Palgrave Handbook of National Parliaments and the European Union* (Basingstoke, Palgrave Macmillan, 2015).

Emiliou, N, 'Subsidiarity: An Effective Barrier Against "the Enterprises of Ambition"?' (1992) 17 *European Law Review* 383.

Estella de Noriega, A, *The EU Principle of Subsidiarity and its Critique* (Oxford, Oxford University Press, 2002).

Evans, M and Zimmermann, A, *Global Perspectives on Subsidiarity*, vol 37(Dordrecht, Springer, 2014).

Fabbrini, F, 'Europe in Need of a New Deal: On Federalism, Free market, and the Right to Strike' (2012) 43 *Georgetown Journal of International Law* 1175.

Fabbrini, F and Granat, K, 'Yellow card, but no foul: The role of the national parliaments under the subsidiarity protocol and the Commission proposal for an EU regulation on the right to strike' (2013) 50 *Common Market Law Review* 115.

Farrand, M (ed), *The Records of the Federal Convention of 1787* (New Haven, CT, Yale University Press, 1911).

Fasone, C, 'Parliamenti nazionali e controllo di sussidiarietà: il secondo "cartellino giallo" sull'istituzione della Procura europea' (2014) 33 *Quaderni Constituzionali* 165.

—— 'Ruling the (Dis-)Order of Interparliamentary Cooperation? The EU Speakers' Conference' in N Lupo and C Fasone (eds), *Interparliamentary Cooperation in the Composite European Constitution* (Oxford, Hart Publishing, 2016).

—— 'Italian Regional Councils and the Positive Externalities of the Early Warning Mechanism for National Constitutional Law' in A Jonsson Cornell and M Goldoni (eds), *National and Regional Parliaments in the EU-Legislative Procedure Post-Lisbon* (Oxford, Hart Publishing, 2017).

Fasone, C and Fromage, D, 'From Veto Players to Agenda-Setters? National Parliaments and Their "Green Card" to the European Commission' (2016) 23 *Maastricht Journal of European and Comparative Law* 294.

Fasone, C and Lupo, N, 'Transparency vs Informality in Legislative Committees: Comparing the US House of Representatives, the Italian Chamber of Deputies and the European Parliament' (2015) 21 *The Journal of Legislative Studies* 342.

Figulová, A, 'The Slovak Parliament and EU Affairs: In Need of a Wake-Up Call' in C Hefftler et al (eds), *The Palgrave Handbook of National Parliaments and the European Union* (Basingstoke, Palgrave Macmillan, 2015).

Finke, D and Dannwolf, T, 'Domestic scrutiny of European Union politics: Between whistle blowing and opposition control' (2013) 52 *European Journal of Political Research* 715.

Follesdal, A and Hix, S, 'Why there is a Democratic Deficit in the EU: A Response to Majone and Moravcsik' (2006) 44 *Journal of Common Market Studies* 533.

Follesdal, A and Muñiz Fraticelli, V, 'The Principle of Subsidiarity as a Constitutional Principle in the EU and Canada' (2015) 10 *Les ateliers de l'éthique/The Ethics Forum* 89.

Fromage D, *Les parlements dans l'Union Européenne après le Traité de Lisbonne: la participation des parlements allemands, britanniques, espagnols, français et italiens* (Paris, L'Harmattan, 2015).

—— 'Increasing Inter-Parliamentary Cooperation in the European Union: Current Trends and Challenges' (2016) 22 *European Public Law* 749.

—— 'The Second Yellow Card on the EPPO Proposal: An Encouraging Development for Member State Parliaments?' (2016) 35 *Yearbook of European Law* 5.

—— 'Executive Accountability to National Parliaments in Post-crisis EU Affairs: The Persistent Shortcomings in the Council and European Council Oversight' in D Jančić (ed), *National Parliaments after the Lisbon Treaty and the Euro Crisis: Resilience or Resignation?* (Oxford, Oxford University Press, 2017).

—— 'Regional Parliaments and the Early Warning System: An Assessment and Some Suggestions for Reform' in A Jonsson Cornell and M Goldoni (eds), *National and Regional Parliaments in the EU-Legislative Procedure Post-Lisbon: The Impact of the Early Warning Mechanism* (Oxford, Hart Publishing, 2017).

Fromage, D and Kreilinger, V, 'National Parliaments' Third Yellow Card and the Struggle over the Revision of the Posted Workers Directive' (2017) 10 *European Journal of Legal Studies* 125.

Fryda, C, 'The Role of the COSAC Secretariat within the Evolving Landscape of Interparliamentary Cooperation: Challenges for the Future' in N Lupo and C Fasone (eds), *Interparliamentary Cooperation in the Composite European Constitution* (Oxford, Hart Publishing, 2016).

Fuksiewicz, A, 'Sejm i Senat rok po wejściu w życie Traktatu Lizbońskiego-dostosowanie do reformy instytucjonalnej' [2011] *Instytut Spraw Publicznych* 1.

Gagatek, W, 'Polityczne i prawne znaczenie zasady pomocniczości w UE (po 20 latach od wejścia w życie Traktatu z Maastricht)' [2013] *Europejski Przegląd Sądowy* 31.

Garben, S, 'Confronting the Competence Conundrum: Democratising the European Union through an Expansion of its Legislative Powers' (2015) 35 *Oxford Journal of Legal Studies* 55.

Garlicki, L, *Polskie Prawo Konstytucyjne: Zarys Wykadu* (Warsaw, Liber, 2006).

Gattermann, K and Hefftler, C, 'Beyond Institutional Capacity: Political Motivation and Parliamentary Behaviour in the Early Warning System' (2015) 38 *West European Politics* 305.

Gluck, AR, 'Federalism from Federal Statutes: Health Reform, Medicaid, and the Old-Fashioned Federalists' Gamble' (2013) 81 *Fordham Law Review* 1749.

Goldoni, M, 'The Early Warning System and the Monti II Regulation: The Case for a Political Interpretation' (2014) 10 *European Constitutional Law Review* 90.

Granat, K, 'Institutional design of the Member States for the ex post subisidiarity scrutiny' in M Cartabia, N Lupo and A Simoncini (eds), *Democracy and Subsidiarity in the EU: National Parliaments, Regions and Civil Society in the Decision-Making Process* (Bologna, Il Mulino, 2013).

—— 'Interparliamentary Cooperation and the Simplified Revision Procedures' in N Lupo and C Fasone (eds), *Interparliamentary Cooperation in the Composite European Constitution* (Oxford, Hart Publishing, 2016).

—— 'Like Two Peas in a Pod? The Functioning of the Early Warning Mechanism in the Czech Republic and Poland' in A Jonsson Cornell and M Goldoni (eds), *National and Regional Parliaments in the EU-Legislative Procedure Post-Lisbon* (Oxford, Hart Publishing, 2017).

—— 'National Parliaments as Political Safeguards of Federalism: Interparliamentary Cooperation in the EU, US and Switzerland' in D Jančić (ed), *National Parliaments after the Lisbon Treaty and the Euro Crisis Resilience or Resignation?* (Oxford, Oxford University Press, 2017).

Groen, A and Christiansen, T, 'National Parliaments in the European Union: Conceptual Choices in the European Union's Constitutional Debate' in C Hefftler et al (eds), *The Palgrave Handbook of National Parliaments and the European Union* (Basingstoke, Palgrave Macmillan, 2015).

Groussot, X and Bogojević, S, 'Subsidiarity as a Procedural Safeguard of Federalism' in L Azoulai (ed), *The Question of Competence in the European Union* (Oxford, Oxford University Press, 2014).

Grzelak, A and Łacny, J, 'Kontrola przestrzegania unijnej zasady pomocniczości przez parlamenty narodowe–pierwsze doświadczenia' (2011) 32 *Zeszyty Prawnicze* 11.

Guilloud-Colliat, L, *L'action normative de l'Union européenne* (Bruxelles, Brulyant, 2014).

Häge, FM, 'Coalition Building and Consensus in the Council of the European Union' (2013) 43 *British Journal of Political Science* 481.

Halberstam, D, 'Federalism: Theory, Policy, Law' in M Rosenfeld and A Sajó (eds), *The Oxford Handbook of Comparative Constitutional Law* (Oxford, Oxford University Press, 2012).

Hazell, R, 'Westminster as a Three-in-One Legislature for the United Kingdom and its Devolved Territories' (2007) 13 *The Journal of Legislative Studies* 254.

Hefftler, C et al (eds), *The Palgrave Handbook of National Parliaments and the European Union* (Basingstoke, Palgrave Macmillan, 2015).

Heilbronner, M, 'Die Justiziabilität des Subsidiaritätsprinzips im Lichte der Subsidiaritätsprotokolle' in I Pernice (ed), *Der Vertrag von Lissabon: Reform der EU ohne Verfassung?; Kolloquium zum 10 Geburtstag des WHI* (Baden-Baden, Nomos, 2008).

Héritier, A, 'Institutional Change in Europe: Co-decision and Comitology Transformed' (2012) 50 *Journal of Common Market Studies* 38.

Héritier, A et al, *Changing Rules of Delegation: A Contest for Power in Comitology* (Oxford, Oxford University Press, 2013).

Héritier, A, Moury, C and Granat K, 'The Contest for Power in Delegated Legislation' in CF Bergström and D Ritleng (eds), *Rulemaking by the European Commission: The New System for Delegation of Powers* (Oxford, Oxford University Press, 2016).

Herranz-Surrallés, A, 'The EU's Multilevel Parliamentary (Battle)Field: Inter-Parliamentary Cooperation and Conflict in Foreign and Security Policy' (2014) 37 *West European Politics* 957.

Heun, W, *The Constitution of Germany: A Contextual Analysis* (Oxford, Hart Publishing, 2011).

Högenauer, A-L, 'The Dutch Parliament and EU Affairs: Decentralizing Scrutiny' in C Hefftler et al (eds), *The Palgrave Handbook of National Parliaments and the European Union* (Basingstoke, Palgrave Macmillan, 2015).

Högenauer, A-L and Neuhold, C, 'National Parliaments after Lisbon: Administrations on the Rise?' (2015) 38 *West European Politics* 335.

Holzhacker, R, 'The power of opposition parliamentary party groups in European scrutiny' (2005) 11 *The Journal of Legislative Studies* 428.

Horsley, T, 'Subsidiarity and the European Court of Justice: Missing Pieces in the Subsidiarity Jigsaw?' (2012) 50 *Journal of Common Market Studies* 267.

Huff, A and Smith, J, 'Westminster and the European Union: Ever-Increasing Scepticism?' in C Hefftler et al (eds), *The Palgrave Handbook of National Parliaments and the European Union* (Basingstoke, Palgrave Macmillan, 2015).

Isensee, J, *Subsidiaritätsprinzip und Verfassungsrecht: eine Studie über das Regulativ des Verhältnisses von Staat und Gesellschaft* (Berlin, Duncker & Humblot, 2001).

Jachtenfuchs, M and Krisch, N, 'Subsidiarity in Global Governance' (2016) 79 *Law and Contemporary Problems* 1.

Jackson, VC, 'Subsidiarity, the Judicial Role, and the Warren Court's Contribution to the Revival of State Government' (2014) 55 *Nomos LV* 190.

Jacobs, A, 'Towards Community Action on Strike Law?' (1978) 15 *Common Market Law Review* 129.
Jacqué, J-P, 'The Principle of Institutional Balance' (2004) 41 *Common Market Law Review* 383.
Jančić, D, 'The Barroso Initiative: Window Dressing or Democracy Boost?' (2012) 8 *Utrecht Law Review* 78.
—— 'Representative Democracy Across Levels? National Parliaments and EU Constitutionalism' (2012) 8 *Croatian Yearbook of European Law and Policy* 227.
—— 'The Game of Cards: National Parliaments in the EU and the Future of the Early Warning Mechanism and the Political Dialogue' (2015) 52 *Common Market Law Review* 939.
—— 'EU Law's Grand Scheme on National Parliaments: Perpetual Missing Link or a Solution for Democratic Legitimacy?' in D Jančić (ed), *National Parliaments after the Lisbon Treaty and the Euro Crisis: Resilience or Resignation?* (Oxford, Oxford University Press, 2017).
Jenkins, S and Roscoe, DD, 'Parties as the Political Safeguards of Federalism: The Impact of Local Political Party Activity on National Elections' (2014) *44 Publius: The Journal of Federalism* 519.
Jonsson Cornell, A, 'The Swedish Riksdag as Scrutiniser of the Principle of Subsidiarity' (2016) 12 *European Constitutional Law Review* 294.
Jonsson Cornell, A and Goldoni, M, *National and Regional Parliaments in the EU-Legislative Procedure Post-Lisbon: The Impact of the Early Warning Mechanism* (Oxford, Hart Publishing, 2017).
Karlas, J, 'National Parliamentary Control of EU Affairs: Institutional Design after Enlargement' (2012) *35 West European Politics* 1095.
Kiiver, P (ed), *National and Regional Parliaments in the European Constitutional Order* (Groningen, Europa Law Publishing 2006).
—— *The National Parliaments in the European Union: A Critical View on EU Constitution-Building*, vol 50 (The Hague, Kluwer Law International, 2006).
—— 'European Treaty Reform and the National Parliaments: Towards a New Assessment of Parliament-Friendly Treaty Provisions' in J Wouters, L Verhey and P Kiiver (eds), *European Constitutionalism Beyond Lisbon* (Antwerp, Intersentia, 2009).
—— *The Early Warning System for the Principle of Subsidiarity: Constitutional Theory and Empirical Reality* (London, Routledge, 2012).
Kilpatrick, C, 'Internal market architecture and the accommodation of labour rights: As good as it gets?' (2011) 4 EUI Working Papers, Department of Law.
Knutelská, V, 'Cooperation among National Parliaments: An Effective Contribution to EU Legitimation?' in B Crum and JE Fossum (eds), *Practices of Interparliamentary Coordination in International Politics* (Colchester, ECPR Press, 2013).
Komesar, NK, *Imperfect Alternatives: Choosing Institutions in Law, Economics, and Public Policy* (Chicago, IL, University of Chicago Press, 1994).
Kramer, LD, 'Putting the Politics Back into the Political Safeguards of Federalism' (2000) 100 *Columbia Law Review* 215.
Kreilinger, V, 'A Watchdog over Europe's Policemen: The New Joint Interparliamentary Scrutiny Group for Europol' (2017) Jacques Delors Institute Working Paper 197.
Kumm, M, 'Constitutionalising Subsidiarity in Integrated Markets: The Case of Tobacco Regulation in the European Union' (2006) 12 *European Law Journal* 503.
Ladner, A, 'Switzerland: Subsidiarity, Power-Sharing, and Direct Democracy' in F Hendriks, A Lidström and J Loughlin (eds), *The Oxford Handbook of Local and Regional Democracy in Europe* (Oxford, Oxford University Press, 2011).
Łazowski, A, 'The Polish parliament and EU affairs: An effective actor or an accidental hero?' in J O'Brennan and T Raunio (eds), *National Parliaments within the Enlarged European Union: from 'victims' of integration to competitive actors?* (London, Routledge, 2007).
Lecours, A, 'Belgium' in A Griffiths (ed), *Handbook of Federal Countries* (Montreal & Kingston, McGill-Queen's University Press, 2005).

Lenaerts, K, 'The Principle of Subsidiarity and the Environment in the European Union: Keeping the Balance of Federalism' (1993) 17 *Fordham International Law Journal* 846.

—— 'Subsidiarity and Community Competence in the Field of Education' (1994) 1 *Columbia Journal of European Law* 1.

Lenaerts, K and Van Nuffel, P, *Constitutional Law of the European Union* (London, Sweet & Maxwell, 2011).

Leyland, P, *The Constitution of the United Kingdom: A Contextual Analysis (Constitutional Systems of the World)* (Oxford, Hart Publishing, 2012).

Lijphart, A, *Patterns of Democracy: Government Forms and Performance in Thirty-Six Countries* (New Haven, CT, Yale University Press, 2012).

Linder, W and Steffen, I, 'Swiss Confederation' in K Le Roy and C Saunders (eds), *Legislative, Executive, and Judicial Governance in Federal Countries* (Montreal, McGill-Queen's University Press, 2006).

Lindseth, PL, 'Delegation is Dead, Long Live Delegation: Managing the Democratic Disconnect in the European Market-Polity' in C Joerges and R Dehousse (eds), *Good Governance in Europe's Integrated Market* (Oxford, Oxford University Press, 2002).

—— *Power and Legitimacy: Reconciling Europe and the Nation-State* (Oxford, Oxford University Press, 2010).

Louis, J-V, 'The Lisbon Treaty: The Irish "No": National Parliaments and the Principle of Subsidiarity– Legal Options and Practical Limits' (2008) 4 *European Constitutional Law Review* 429.

—— 'Quelques remarques sur l'avenir du contrôle du principe de subsidiarité' in A De Walsche and L Levi (eds), *Mélanges en hommage à Georges Vandersanden: promenades au sein du droit européen* (Bruxelles, Bruylant, 2008).

Lupo, N, 'National parliaments in the European integration process: re-aligning politics and policies' in M Cartabia, N Lupo and A Simoncini (eds), *Democracy and Subsidiarity in the EU* (Bologna, Il Mulino, 2013).

—— 'Il terzo "cartellino giallo" e i multiformi usi dell'early warning system' [2016] *Quaderni Constituzionali* 571.

—— 'The Scrutiny of the Principle of Subsidiarity in the Procedures and Reasoned Opinions of the Italian Chamber and Senate' in A Jonsson Cornell and M Goldoni (eds), *National and Regional Parliaments in the EU-Legislative Procedure Post-Lisbon: The Impact of the Early Warning Mechanism* (Oxford, Hart Publishing, 2017).

Lupo, N and Fasone, C, *Interparliamentary Cooperation in the Composite European Constitution* (Oxford, Hart Publishing, 2016).

Martinico, G, 'Dating Cinderella: On subsidiarity as a political safeguard of federalism in the European Union' (2011) 17 *European Public Law* 649.

Maurer, A, 'National Parliaments in the European Architecture: From Latecomers' Adaptation Towards Permanent Institutional Change?' in A Maurer and W Wessels (eds), *National Parliaments on their Ways to Europe: Losers or Latecomers?* (Baden-Baden, Nomos, 2001).

Maurer, A and Wessels, W, 'Major Findings' in A Maurer and W Wessels (eds), *National Parliaments on their Ways to Europe: Losers or Latecomers?* (Baden-Baden, Nomos, 2001).

—— 'National Parliaments after Amsterdam: From Slow Adapters to National Players?' in A Maurer and W Wessels (eds), *National Parliaments on their Ways to Europe: Losers or Latecomers?* (Baden-Baden, Nomos, 2001).

Mayer, F, 'Competences—Reloaded? The vertical division of powers in the EU and the new European constitution' (2005) 3 *International Journal of Constitutional Law* 493.

—— *Stellungnahme zum öffentlichen Expertengespräch Prüfung des unionsrechtlichen Subsidiaritätsprinzips im Unterausschuss Europarecht des Rechtsausschusses des Deutschen Bundestages am 16. Juni 2010* (2010).

Mellein, C, 'Die Rolle von Bundestag und Bundesrat in der Europäischen Union' [2011] *Zeitschrift Europarecht-Beiheft* 13.

Miklin, E, 'Inter-Parliamentary Cooperation in EU Affairs and the Austrian Parliament: Empowering the Opposition?' (2013) 19 *The Journal of Legislative Studies* 22.

—— 'The Austrian Parliament and EU Affairs: Gradually Living Up to Its Legal Potential' in C Hefftler et al (eds), *The Palgrave Handbook of National Parliaments and the European Union* (Basingstoke, Palgrave Macmillan, 2015).

—— 'Beyond subsidiarity: the indirect effect of the Early Warning System on national parliamentary scutiny in European Union affairs' (2017) 24 *Journal of European Public Policy* 366.

Muir, E, 'The Fundamental Rights Implications of EU Legislation: Some Constitutional Challenges' (2014) 51 *Common Market Law Review* 219.

Nettesheim, M, 'Die Integrationsverantwortung-Vorgaben des BVerfG und gesetzgeberische Umsetzung' (2010) 63 *Neue Juristische Wochenschrift* 177.

Neuhold, C and Smith, J, 'Conclusion: From "Latecomers" to "Policy Shapers"?—The Role of National Parliaments in the "Post-Lisbon" Union' in C Hefftler et al (eds), *The Palgrave Handbook of National Parliaments and the European Union* (Basingstoke, Palgrave Macmillan, 2015).

Norton, P (ed), *National Parliaments and the European Union* (London, Frank Cass, 1996).

—— 'Introduction: Adapting to European Integration' in P Norton (ed), *National Parliaments and the European Union* (London, Frank Cass, 1996).

—— 'Cohesion without discipline: Party voting in the House of Lords' (2003) 9 *The Journal of Legislative Studies* 57.

Nugent, JD, 'The Informal Political Safeguards of Federalism' (Midwest Political Science Association, Chicago, 27–30 April 2000).

—— *Safeguarding Federalism: How States Protect their Interests in National Policymaking* (Norman, OK, University of Oklahoma Press, 2012).

O'Brennan, J and Raunio, T, 'Introduction: deparliamentarization and European integration' in J O'Brennan and T Raunio (eds), *National Parliaments within the Enlarged European Union: from 'victims' of integration to competitive actors?* (London, Routledge, 2007).

Öberg, J, 'Subsidiarity as a Limit to the Exercise of EU Competences' [2016] *Yearbook of European Law* 1.

Oliver, D, 'Reforming the United Kingdom Parliament' in J Jowell and D Oliver (eds), *The Changing Constitution*, 7th edn (Oxford, Oxford University Press, 2011).

Pace, R, 'The Maltese Parliament and EU Affairs: A Slow Awakening to Its Responsibilities' in C Hefftler et als (eds), *The Palgrave Handbook of National Parliaments and the European Union* (Basingstoke, Palgrave Macmillan, 2015).

Pernice, I, 'Framework Revisited: Constitutional, Federal and Subsidiarity Issues' (1995) 2 *Columbia Journal of European Law* 403.

Pescatore, P, 'Mit der Subsidiarität leben' in O Duc, M Lutter and J Schwarze (eds), *Festschrift für Ulrich Everling* (Baden-Baden, Nomos, 1995).

Peters, A, *Women on Board: The EU Commission's Proposal for a Directive on Improving the Gender Balance among Non-Executive Directors of Companies Listed on Stock Exchanges and Related Measures* (2012).

Peters, J, 'National Parliaments and Subsidiarity: Think Twice' (2005) 1 *European Constitutional Law Review* 68.

Piedrafita, S, 'The Spanish Parliament and EU Affairs in the Post Lisbon Treaty Era: All Change?' (2014) 20 *Journal of Legislative Studies* 1.

Poiares Maduro, M, 'Europe and the constitution: what if this is as good as it gets?' in JHH Weiler and M Wind (eds), *European Constitutionalism Beyond the State* (Cambridge, Cambridge University Press, 2003).

—— *A New Governance for the European Union and the Euro: Democracy and Justice* (Florence, European University Institute, 2012).
Poiares Maduro, M and Azoulai, L, 'Introduction' in M Poiares Maduro and L Azoulai (eds), *The Past and Future of EU Law: The Classics of EU Law Revisited on the 50th Anniversary of the Treaty of Rome* (Oxford, Hart Publishing, 2010).
Pollack, MA, 'The End of Creeping Competence? EU Policy-Making Since Maastricht' (2000) 38 *Journal of Common Market Studies* 519.
Popelier, P and Lemmens, K, *The Constitution of Belgium. A Contextual Analysis* (Oxford, Hart Publishing, 2015).
Rau, M, 'Subsidiarity and Judicial Review in German Federalism: The Decision of the Federal Constitutional Court in the *Geriatric Nursing Act* Case' (2003) 4 *German Law Journal* 223.
Raunio, T, 'The Finnish Eduskunta and the European Union: The Strengths and Weaknesses of a Mandating System' in C Hefftler et al (eds), *The Palgrave Handbook of National Parliaments and the European Union* (Basingstoke, Palgrave Macmillan, 2015).
Reif, K and Schmitt, H, 'Nine Second-order National Elections—a Conceptual Framework for the Analysis of European Election Results' (1980) 8 *European Journal of Political Research* 3.
Reuter, K, *Praxishandbuch Bundesrat: Verfassungsrechtliche Grundlagen, Kommentar zur Geschäftsordnung, Praxis des Bundesrates* (Heidelberg, CF Müller, 2007).
Ritleng, D, 'The dividing line between delegated and implementing acts: the Court of Justice sidesteps the difficulty in *Commission v Parliament and Council (biocides)*' 52 *Common Market Law Review* 243.
Ritzer, C, Ruttloff, M and Linhart, K, 'How to Sharpen a Dull Sword—The Principle of Subsidiarity and its Control' (2006) 7 *German Law Journal* 733.
Romaniello, M, 'Beyond the Constitutional "Bicameral Blueprint": Europeanisation and National Identities in Belgium' in M Cartabia, N Lupo and A Simoncini (eds), *Democracy and Subsidiarity in the EU* (Bologna, Il Mulino, 2013).
Rosas, A and Armati, L, *EU Constitutional Law: An Introduction* (Oxford, Hart Publishing, 2010).
Rozenberg, O and Hefftler, C, 'Introduction' in C Hefftler et al (eds), *The Palgrave Handbook of National Parliaments and the European Union* (Basingstoke, Palgrave Macmillan, 2015).
Russell, M, 'The Territorial Role of Second Chambers' (2001) 7 *The Journal of Legislative Studies* 105.
—— *The Contemporary House of Lords: Westminster Bicameralism Revived* (Oxford, Oxford University Press, 2013).
Scharpf, FW, *Governing in Europe: Effective and Democratic?* (Oxford, Oxford University Press, 1999).
Schilling, T, 'A New Dimension of Subsidiarity: Subsidiarity as a Rule and a Principle' (1995) 14 *Yearbook of European Law* 203.
Schima, B, 'Die Subsidiaritatskontrolle durch die nationalen Parlamente nach dem vertrag von Lissabon' (2013) 68 *Zeitschrift für öffentliches Recht* 373.
Schorkopf, F, 'The European Union as an Association of Sovereign States: Karlsruhe's Ruling on the Treaty of Lisbon' (2009) 10 *German Law Journal* 1219.
Schütze, R, 'Lisbon and the federal order of competences: A prospective analysis' (2008) 33 *European Law Review* 709.
—— *From Dual to Cooperative Federalism: The Changing Structure of European Law* (Oxford, Oxford University Press, 2009).
—— '"Delegated" Legislation in the (new) European Union: A Constitutional Analysis' (2011) 74 *Modern Law Review* 661.
—— 'Three "Bills of Rights" for the European Union' (2011) 30 *Yearbook of European Law* 131.
—— *From Dual to Cooperative Federalism: The Changing Structure of European Law* (Oxford, Oxford University Press, 2013).
Serowaniec, M, 'Towards the "green card"—strengthening the role of national parliaments in EU affairs?' [2015] *Toruńskie Studia Polsko-Włoskie* 29.

Steffani, W, 'Amerikanischer Kongreß und Deutscher Bundestag' in W Steffani (ed), *Parlamentarische und präsidentielle Demokratie* (Opladen, Westdt Verlag, 1979).

Stone Sweet, A and Mathews, J, 'Proportionality Balancing and Global Constitutionalism' (2008) 47 *Columbia Journal of Transnational Law* 72.

Suk, JC, 'Gender Parity and State Legitimacy: From Public Office to Corporate Boards' (2012) 10 *International Journal of Constitutional Law* 449.

Szydło, M, 'Constitutional Values Underlying Gender Equality on the Boards of Companies: How Should the EU Put These Values into Practice?' (2014) 63 *International & Comparative Law Quarterly* 167.

—— 'Gender Equality on the Boards of EU Companies: Between Economic Efficiency, Fundamental Rights and Democratic Legitimisation of Economic Governance' (2015) 21 *European Law Journal* 97.

Tans, O, 'Conclusion: National Parliaments and the European Union: Coping with the Limits of Democracy' in O Tans, CM Zoethout and J Peters (eds), *National Parliaments and European Democracy: A Bottom-up Approach to European Constitutionalism* (Groningen, Europa Law Publishing, 2007).

—— 'Introduction: National Parliaments and the European Union: In Search of Common Ground' in O Tans, CM Zoethout and J Peters (eds), *National Parliaments and European Democracy: A Bottom-up Approach to European Constitutionalism* (Groningen, Europa Law Publishing, 2007).

Taylor, G, 'Germany: The subsidiarity principle' (2006) 4 *International Journal of Constitutional Law* 115.

—— 'Germany: A slow death for subsidiarity?' (2009) 7 *International Journal of Constitutional Law* 139.

Timmermans, C, 'Subsidiarity and Transparency' (1999) 22 *Fordham International Law Journal* 106.

Toth, AG, 'The Principle of Subsidiarity in the Maastricht Treaty' (1992) 29 *Common Market Law Review* 1079.

—— 'Is Subsidiarity Justiciable?' (1994) 19 *European Law Review* 268.

Tridimas, T, 'The Rule of Reason and its Relation to Proportionality and Subsidiarity' in A Schrauwen (ed), *Rule of Reason: Rethinking Another Classic of European Legal Doctrine* (Groningen, Europa Law Publishing, 2005).

Uerpmann-Wittzack, R and Edenharter, A, 'Subsidiaritätsklage als parlamentarisches Minderheitsrecht?' (2009) 44 *Europarecht* 313.

Vandamme, TA, 'From Federated Federalism to Harmonized Federalism? The Case of EU Subsidiarity Scrutiny in Spain and Belgium' (2011) Amsterdam Law School Research Paper 2011/05.

Vandenbruwaene, W, 'The Judicial Enforcement of Subsidiarity. The comparative quest for an appropriate standard' in P Popelier, A Mazmanyan and W Vandenbruwaene (eds), *The Role of Constitutional Courts in Multilevel Governance* (Antwerp, Intersentia, 2013).

Vandenbruwaene, W and Popelier, P, 'Belgian Parliaments and the Early Warning System' in A Jonsson Cornell and M Goldoni (eds), *National and Regional Parliaments in the EU-Legislative Procedure Post-Lisbon* (Oxford, Hart Publishing, 2017).

Vara Arribas, G and Bourdin, D, *The Role of Regional Parliaments in the Process of Subsidiarity Analysis within the Early Warning System of the Lisbon Treaty* (EIPA and ECER, 2011).

Vara Arribas, G and Högenauer, A-L, 'Legislative Regions after Lisbon: A New Role for Regional Assemblies?' in C Hefftler et al (eds), *The Palgrave Handbook of National Parliaments and the European Union* (Basingstoke, Palgrave Macmillan, 2015).

von Bogdandy, A, 'The European Union as a Human Rights Organization? Human Rights and the Core of the European Union' (2000) 37 *Common Market Law Review* 1307.

von Bogdandy A and Bast J, 'The European Union's Vertical Order of Competences: The Current Law and Proposals for its Reform' (2002) 39 *Common Market Law Review* 227.

—— 'The Federal Order of Competences' in A von Bogdandy and J Bast (eds), *Principles of European Constitutional Law* (Oxford, Hart Publishing, 2010).

von Danwitz, T, 'Subsidiaritätskontrolle in der Europäischen Union' in K Hansmann, K-P Dolde, S Paetow and E Schmidt-Assmann (eds), *Verfassung-Umwelt-Wirtschaft Festschrift für Dieter Sellner zum 75 Geburtstag* (München, CH Beck, 2010).

Watts RL, *Comparing Federal Systems* (Montreal & Kingston, McGill-Queen's University Press, 2008).

Weatherill, S, 'Using National Parliaments to Improve Scrutiny of the Limits of EU Action' (2003) 28 *European Law Review* 909.

—— 'Competence Creep and Competence Control' (2004) 23 *Yearbook of European Law* 1.

—— 'Better Competence Monitoring' (2005) 30 *European Law Review* 23.

—— 'Finding a Role for the Regions in Checking the EU's Competence' in S Weatherill and U Bernitz (eds), *The Role of Regions and Sub-National Actors in Europe* (Oxford, Hart Publishing, 2005).

—— 'The Limits of Legislative Harmonization Ten Years after Tobacco Advertising: How the Court's Case Law has Become a Drafting Guide' (2011) 12 *German Law Journal* 827.

—— *The Internal Market as a Legal Concept* (Oxford, Oxford University Press, 2017).

Weber, M, *Weber: Political Writings* (Cambridge, Cambridge University Press, 2003).

Wechsler, H, 'The Political Safeguards of Federalism: The Role of the States in the Composition and Selection of the National Government' (1954) 54 *Columbia Law Review* 543.

Weiler, JHH, 'The Transformation of Europe' (1991) 100 *Yale Law Journal* 2403.

—— 'The Reformation of European Constitutionalism' (1997) 35 *Journal of Common Market Studies* 97.

—— 'In the Face of Crisis: Input Legitimacy, Output Legitimacy and the Political Messianism of European Integration' (2012) 34 *Journal of European Integration* 825.

—— 'Fateful Elections? Investing in the Future of Europe' (2014) 12 *International Journal of Constitutional Law* 273.

Weiler, JHH, Haltern, UR and Mayer, FC, 'European Democracy and its Critique' (1995) 18 *West European Politics* 4.

Wieczorek, I, 'The EPPO Draft Regulation Passes the First Subsidiarity Test: An Analysis and Interpretation of the European Commission's Hasty Approach to National Parliaments' Subsidiarity Arguments' (2015) 16 *German Law Journal* 1247.

Williams, A, 'Human Rights in the EU' in A Arnull and D Chalmers (eds), *The Oxford Handbook of European Union Law* (Oxford, Oxford University Press, 2015).

Winzen, T, 'European integration and national parliamentary oversight institutions' (2013) 14 *European Union Politics* 297.

Wouters, J and Raube, K, 'The Interparliamentary Conference on Common Foreign and Security Policy: A Quest for Democratic Accountability in EU Security Governance' in N Lupo and C Fasone (eds), *Interparliamentary Cooperation in the Composite European Constitution* (Oxford, Hart Publishing, 2016).

Wyatt, D, 'Is the European Union an Organisation of Limited Powers?' in A Arnull et al (eds), *A Constitutional Order of States? Essays in EU Law in Honour of Alan Dashwood* (Oxford, Hart Publishing, 2011).

Zahn, R, 'Revision of the Posted Workers Directive: A Europeanisation Perspective' (2017) 19 *Cambridge Yearbook of European Legal Studies* 1.

Ziller, J, 'French Reactions to the Treaty Establishing a Constitution for Europe: from Constitutional Welcome to Popular Rejection' in A Albi and J Ziller (eds), *European Constitution and National Constitutions: Ratification and Beyond* (The Hague, Kluwer Law International. 2007).

—— 'Le principe de subsidiarité' in J-B Auby and J Dutheil de la Rochèr (eds), *Traité de droit administratif européen* (Bruxelles, Bruylant, 2014).

Index

NB–Page numbers in **bold** refer to information in tables

www.ingramcontent.com/pod-product-compliance
Lightning Source LLC
Chambersburg PA
CBHW081415220926
51613CB00010B/200
9781509908677